ADVANCES IN PRESENCING

ADVANCES IN PRESENCING

Volume 3

Edited by
Olen Gunnlaugson, Ph.D.
William Brendel, Ed.D.

TRIFOSS BUSINESS PRESS

*Dedicated to the emergence of presencing as a
viable field of research and practice*

About the Editors

Olen Gunnlaugson, Ph.D. is an Associate Professor in Leadership and Organizational Development at Université Laval (Canada) where he teaches MBA courses in leadership, management skills and group communications to managers, leaders and executives. With a research background in Leadership Development, Group Communication and Leadership Coaching, he received his Ph.D. at the University of British Columbia and did his Post-Doctorate at Simon Fraser University, Vancouver.

To date, his work has been published in 13 books as well as 35 articles and chapters in leading academic journals and books. He has presented and keynoted at numerous international conferences, received five faculty level awards for teaching from universities in Canada and the USA and taught several thousand emerging leaders and executives at leading schools in Canada, USA, Austria, Sweden and South Korea. Over the past several years, he has been researching and developing Dynamic Presencing, with a book recently released in 2020. Dynamic Presencing is a five journey method for developing our existing presencing practice into an orienting way of being, leading and living.

William Brendel, Ph.D. is an Assistant Professor of Organization Development and Change at Penn State University and is the CEO of the Transformative Learning Institute. William has over 20 years of experience as an organization development consultant, researcher, author and trainer. His publications on mindful leadership and organizational change span academic journals and popular press. His consultation and workshops have led to measurable transformations in organizational culture and performance across the U.S., China, India and Africa. William has previously held academic positions at Texas A&M, Temple University, and the University of St Thomas, where he has taught graduate courses in Organization Development, Leadership Development, Change Management, Talent Management, Group Dynamics, and Transformative Learning. William received his Doctorate in Adult Learning and Leadership, and Master's degree in Organizational Psychology at Columbia University in New York.

Table of Contents

CHAPTER 1

Reflections on Advances in Presencing - Volume III

Olen Gunnlaugson and William Brendel

It is with great pleasure that we introduce the book series: *Advances in Presencing*. Over the past fifteen years Otto Scharmer and colleagues work with Theory U has played a vitalizing role in bringing together an international community of practice comprised of progressively minded organizations, communities and leaders who are committed to stewarding a more promising future for humanity. Since the last scholar-practitioner book on Theory U was released in 2013, there has been a growing collective interest in deepening and broadening the conversation with Theory U.

This three volume Series invites contributing voices from the Presencing Institute, independent researchers, scholar practitioners, consultants and many others into the conversation. Where the last research volume *Perspectives on Theory U: Insights from the Field* (Gunnlaugson et. al, 2013) focused more on the voices of academics and management scholar-practitioners, given how the Theory U community has grown over the past five years, we felt it was important to offer an updated practitioner focus on Theory U as a whole, with an interest in how this work, including the practice of presencing is being applied both individually and collectively.

As editors, we faced a number of thought-provoking challenges while developing this series. The first is that presencing presents a paradox. While it values a form of knowing beyond conventional thinking or downloading, in order to be considered a full-fledged paradigm of knowledge creation there needs to be some bracketing of its own conceptual real estate. In reading through the chapters in this book one will quickly discover that presencing as a practice, is in a phase of exploration, with no finite horizon or boundary informing its development. Intentional or not, presencing concepts and practices include and subsume neighboring practices and paradigms, most notably those of Buddhist, Existentialist and the consciousness-based wisdom traditions.

For instance, Vipassana or insight meditation tradition, which predates presencing by 2,600 years, is itself a methodology of letting go of the ego in order to let new insight into the nature of the self present itself freshly each moment. Not surprisingly, presencing resembles separate, modern Buddhist applications such as mindful leadership, which positions meditation as a secular inlet for organizational influence and creativity. Similarly, Theory U, for which presencing plays a central role, incorporates concepts from design thinking such as the use of empathy and rapid-prototyping.

Theory U practitioners also refer to presencing as a social field, which is very similar to the Buddhist concept of codependent origination, and what existentialists like Heidegger refer to as a field of care. Following from these observations, the question then becomes going forward, what essential differences distinguish presencing from its counterpart orientations and practices? What does presencing actualize and bring into being that these similar approaches do not? Given its growing significance in personal change, shared learning and social transformation projects across a wide cross section of fields, as academic practitioners continue to explore and develop upon their own sense and application of presencing, how might presencing begin to emerge as a field of research and praxis in the coming years and decades ahead?

One of the current values of presencing is how the aforementioned and other perspectives and practices are being woven together and updated in our current global context, an effort that is echoed through each of the three volumes of this book series. This has the effect of bringing these respective approaches to life in an experimental fashion, aligned with a growing collective human effort for a hopeful future versus a profitable quarter or immediate sense of stress reduction. How does presencing accomplish this? For one, scholars and practitioners have been compelled to upcycle English verb tenses and adjectives in order to describe particular nuances of learning in new ways with particular points of emphasis.

Those who are new to the concept of presencing often report a sensitivity to this shift in "languaging", and the same will be true for those who read this series; each chapter pushes the limits and limiting nature of the English language. This is necessary to the extent that presencing introduces concepts that the English language fails to describe. For instance, in drawing from Scharmer's distinctions in Theory U, presencing practitioners often talk about the connection of the head, heart, and hands as a more holistic framework for moving from a space of understanding to a space of knowing. In contrast, Sanskrit does not treat these concepts as separate and distinct, but rather, through the term "Citta" refers to a single heart-mind integration.

At some point readers may find themselves asking, is presencing a process that makes all other learning paradigms and activities more creative and useful, or is it the other way around? To navigate these conceptual challenges, this book series includes a tapestry of applications from a variety of contexts across the globe, spanning multiple languages, and accomplishing a variety of aims. It also honors ancient wisdom traditions from which presencing borrows and benefits, while at the same time cultivating emerging lineages and practices such as Dynamic Presencing.

To accomplish these eclectic aims, this three volume book series incorporates insight from both presencing scholars and practitioners, ensuring a balance of critical and creative perspectives that have been peer-reviewed, offering current perspectives on how Theory U is being adapted across a broad range of organizations, companies and contexts that are united in the deeper impulse of learning to shape and build a life-affirming emerging future for all stakeholders. By weaving these and other perspectives into the larger conversation of Theory U, we are of the mindset that these and other updates will ensure that the Series reaches a wider scope of reading audience and catalyzes interest across both the Academic and Practitioner world. Finally, we are at point in history where these two cultures intersect and it is our interest to shine the light on this intersection in a way that inspires a myriad of applications in the world with real projects and research efforts that are not only informed by this framework and but also practitioners capable of co-facilitating and co-leading and embodying these initiatives.

A guiding intention of this Series since its inception has been to raise further awareness of the applicability of critical and creative applications of Theory U to our colleagues, students, ULAB hubs, international communities of practice and beyond, further conveying how this body of work is informing, enriching, and sustaining new developments across a wide variety of disciplines. In effect, this Series will give a current pulse on the current scholar practitioner voices and perspectives on Theory U and presencing through featured writings on the experiences, challenges, and promise of this emerging field. It is our estimation that this work as a whole has the real promise to open up a new space of possibility for engaging a more coherent and resonant future for all concerned, which we know is not only possible but essential for humanity to shift its current course of risks that threaten our shared future in the twenty first century.

Inspired by the Theory U projects of Otto Scharmer and colleagues of the Presencing Institute, Theory U and presencing are approaching a tipping point as a viable, comprehensive praxis for stewarding change and global transformation. To illustrate and support this development, *Advances in Presencing* includes perspectives and applications by academics, researchers, teachers, change makers, consultants, community activists and thought leaders.

Overview of Chapters

In chapter 2, "Social Presencing Theater", Arawana Hayashi offers a description of Social Presencing Theater by describing a few of the practices and some of the premises on which the work is based. Social Presencing Theater is a method created by the Presencing Institute that brings heartfelt awareness into Theory U-based change efforts. It supports individuals, teams, and larger systems in the process of self-awareness—revealing both blind spots and creative potential. The chapter outlines a practitioner's perspective. It begins by emphasizing the important of a grounded embodied presence and offers the 20 Minute Dance as a practice for cultivating the connection between our individual body and the Earth body. It then describes how this sense of presence enables our awareness to expand to include our social bodies, the groups that we inhabit, and the social field, the invisible but sensed field of interdependent relationships. It then describes how to apply these practices to concrete situations using Stuck and 4-D Mapping practices. Social Presencing Theater encourages us to suspend the proliferation of judgments and opinions and to trust unfolding experience and "body knowing." It supports the uncovering of insights, wisdom, and creative direction as they engage in awareness based systems change.

In chapter 3, "Moving towards Collective Presencing on a National Scale through u.lab Scotland" Keira Oliver, Anne Winther and Kirsty Deacon share that since 2015, over 1,800 people in Scotland have participated in a global, massive online open course (MOOC) called "*u.lab*". This growing community of practitioners form u.lab Scotland and together, through a number of different expressions, constitutes a move towards Collective Presencing. Over the last three years, the Scottish Government has commissioned research studies to understand the impact of participation on u.lab participants. In this chapter they describe the course, its infrastructure and the research findings suggesting how u.lab Scotland may be acting as a "greenhouse for social innovations of the future" (Scharmer, 2009, p. 337). An evolving theory of change is explored which proposes ulabscot participants are: gaining greater understanding and ability to change themselves; interacting more authentically and purposefully with others; working with others more intentionally, creating supportive structures which are evolving and becoming better connected over time; and changing the system through iterative action.

In chapter 4, "Italian u.lab Hubs" Rachel Hentsch shares how the globally-resonating principles of Theory U have evolved locally through the u.lab community in the city of Rome, Italy. The chapter examines the hosting prototypes and models created and adapted by the Rome hosting team between August 2016 and October 2018, and the results obtained, including some comparisons with other hubs from different cities across Italy. The various elements that typically make up a u.lab hub are mapped to understand how they each contribute to shaping the vitality and longevity of a given hub. This study aims to capture and reflect upon a fragment of the journey that Theory U and its ramifications can imprint in terms of awakening collective potential, and a more carefully stewarded future for humankind and the planet. This chapter also identifies factors that can contribute to the success of hub hosting so that similar efforts may better meet the needs of their audiences.

In chapter 5, "Tending the Social Field in Higher Education" Eva Pomeroy and Nicolo Francesco Bernardi follow Scharmer in pointing out that from a 4.0 perspective on education, learning is sourced through the social field. This means, then, that the primary role of the educator is to tend to that field by *holding space* for transformative learning and change. In this chapter, they explore what it means to hold space for transformative learning within the context of higher education by inquiring into our experience as Hub Hosts of the Concordia U.lab Social Innovation Hub between 2016 and 2019. They highlight key aspects of concern that surfaced for us as 'holders of space', such as holding discomfort, working with flexible structures, providing sufficient stability and the quality of our attention, and explore the extent to which these reflect the properties of 4.0 Education. They end with a reflection on the role of intentional inquiry (structured weekly debriefs) in supporting our effort to cultivate a generative social field for transformative learning.

In chapter 6, "Embedding Theory U and Awareness-based

Practices within Higher Education: From Developing a Team to Building a Prototype" Vivianna Rodriguez Carreon and Beatriz Carrillo outline the development of a pilot project at the University of Sydney that aimed to foster self-awareness and perspective transformation in students, while building their leadership capacities towards pro-social behavior. The chapter maps the evolution – from idea to prototype – of the project, focusing on the nature and qualities of the collaboration between the two researchers. The framework underpinning both the research collaboration and the pilot project with students was the methodology, principles and tools of Theory U and the u.lab MOOC. Theory U provides a systems framework that builds on phenomenology, embodied cognition, systems thinking, and collective leadership theories to help foster personal, institutional and societal change. Further, the researchers' experiences engaging with the global u.lab community became part of the phenomenological human experience reflected in the writing process. Cultivating the interior condition of the team members and the first two principles for prototyping - "Intention" and "Core team" - were identified as integral to the ontological engagement of the researchers. The chapter concludes with a discussion of three crucial principles for cultivating the interior condition of team members, and which also aided the collective intelligence of the social field to emerge.

In chapter 7, "Social Fields as an Awareness-Based Approach to Reconnect Self, Other, and Whole" Ursula and Luca Versteegen address the puzzle of having knowledge and how this often fails to translate into collective action. Taking a social field approach, they argue that a social field's configuration determines individual and collective self-awareness and, in turn, an action's quality. To motivate this idea, they first discuss three cases exemplifying how the reconfiguration of a social field alters awareness and action. Drawing from Gestalt psychology and social field literature, they then suggest understanding social fields as a Gestalt evolving from one's experience of social time and social space. Specifically, they conceive social fields as a tool describing the conditions facilitating particular qualities of behavior. Understanding Theory U as a method to alternate a social field's configuration, they share an example showing how awareness and action can be integrated in practice and close the chapter by providing avenues for future research.

In chapter 8, "The Four Fields of Dynamic Presencing" Olen Gunnlaugson introduces the fourth journey of primary communicating in his work on Dynamic Presencing, which builds from the Theory U rendering of presencing as a single social field to include four distinct yet interconnected presencing field locations. Each presencing field-space represents a phenomenological location that helps practitioners engage the field dynamics of presencing at the subtle felt-sensemaking level of their experience. Within this new presencing field geography, there is the individual field location or i-space and three new collective field locations of presencing: you-space, we-space and all-space. The chapter explores how with a grasp and understanding of how to work with these four new locations in the presencing field, practitioners can engage a more situational-precise mode of presencing in their day to day work and lives. This gives rise to more differentiated presencing field dynamics and a new presencing field awareness that can be explored in different ways and contexts where presencing is being applied. As practitioners learn to engage presencing in unique and varied ways across each field horizon, this increases their overall field-awareness and capacity for a fluid engagement of presencing inside and across various workplace and life situations. Overall, this chapter makes a case for the four fields to help Theory U practitioners foster greater awareness of how our emerging presencing self interfaces through the particular presencing field one is engaging.

In chapter 9, "Contemplative Being, Becoming, and Knowing: The "Work" at the Bottom of the U in a Graduate Program in Contemplative Inquiry" Charles Scott makes a case for the work at the core of our being represents the vital contemplative work done at the bottom of the U. The process of drawing from Source involves the contemplative work to which both Jaworski and Gunnlaugson refer. In the chapter, he outlines a graduate program in contemplative inquiry that represents an institutionalized commitment to the creation of space and time in which individuals are exploring this emerging contemplative territory—in effect, engaging in the work at the bottom of the U. This is the subjective and intersubjective work (co-presencing) of Dynamic Presencing that brings us in contact with these possibilities, potentials, and the unmanifest. In the chapter, Charles draws from his experience of contemplative practice and show how aspects of this Dynamic Presencing and Theory U work are being enacted in a university graduate studies program in contemplative inquiry. Data gathered from students and faculty demonstrate that we have been creating a collective container of consciousness that nurtures and advances participants, that the program addresses the challenges we face in both the present and future with an increasingly complex, connected, changing, and sometimes chaotic world. They have found that this contemplative work not only allows them to access their deepest Self but also to engage more fully and wisely with the communities that require this emergent wisdom and the actions that arise from it.

In chapter 10, "Ready for U: A facilitator's reflective offerings" Amy Barnes shares some practices intending to help practitioners facilitate U-type processes, where enablers for desired breakthroughs and deep shifts can only be found in spaces of expanded awareness. These core practices have evolved over time by integrating and adapting approaches from the fields of Gestalt psychotherapy, bodywork, embodied practices and art-making. In the process of reflecting on past experiences, the author noticed that in the majority of cases, her interventions followed a typical flow containing broad stages of acknowledging what is present, dealing with the past, presencing what needs to unfold, and taking action to move forward. In movement terms, these typical interventions flowed in ways akin to the left-to-right movement of the 'U' in Theory U. However, she also noticed that in a few cases, significant breakthroughs came about in a different way. They occurred when energy and attention were primarily placed on presencing what was the 'next now' and in so doing, relevant aspects of past experiences took care of themselves. This counter-movement is a right-to-left 'pull' rather than the more usual left-to-right flow. It is potentially an exciting and different orientation to facilitating change and transformation, and presents new possibilities for practitioners.

In chapter 11, "The Long Arc of the Universe" Chris Taylor

and colleagues share a collection of stories, poems and first-hand accounts from the frontline of global change, curated to provide a felt-sense of how presencing lives in the places where the future is starting to breakthrough. Not so much an academic account or even a comprehensive review, more a sensing into new and emerging trends and forces. And an invitation to notice where presencing might already be happening around you. An invitation to step into the space of liminality and see how the future wants to shape your life.

In chapter 12, "The dance between structure and skill: Experiences from the LiFT project's experiments with the Collaboratory, an agile tool for applying Theory U in diverse contexts" Elke Fein points out that Theory U based methods have proven extremely effective in bringing together diverse groups of stakeholders to develop joint actionable visions and to translate these into project prototypes that can make a difference for society and the environment. Among the pioneers of applying Theory U to complex societal challenges is the 50+20 working group of the World Council of Business Schools for Sustainable Business who gave birth to the method of the "Collaboratory", based on the insights of Scharmer's theory. The Collaboratory is a compact, consolidated and at the same time very flexible and agile format, which helps to frame and scaffold stakeholder involvement processes in a way that optimally supports diverse groups of stakeholders to address problems of common concern in an outcome-oriented way. So, while theory U is a *theory*, the Collaboratory can be considered a *meta-method* that offers tools for implementing the core insights of theory U. The international EU funded strategic partnership "Leadership for Transition (LiFT)" has been experimenting with this format for over four years. Among the learnings gained while hosting about a dozen Collaboratories in six European countries and accompanying them by action research are substantial qualitative insights, which can deepen and differentiate our understanding of Theory U in action.

In chapter 13, "Social Presencing Theater: Practical Application in Organizations" Michelle Moore provides an overview of Social Presencing Theater with examples of application in organizations. The first half of the chapter provides a definition of SPT, examples of why organizations might apply SPT, and describes the core principles which are the foundation for SPT. This is followed by descriptions of exercises, with the first four being primarily preparatory, and generally practiced without specific organizational input. These include 20 Minute Dance, Duet, Village and Field Dance. The last four SPT exercises are applied and are framed within the individual or organizational context and can be used to guide decisions and actions. Applied exercises include Stuck, 4D Mapping, Case Clinic and Seed Dance. The second half of the chapter describes actual cases of SPT applied in ten organizations in several countries along with a conclusion on the evolution of SPT.

In chapter 14, "Applying Theory U through SHAPE to Develop Student's Individual Entrepreneurial Orientation in a University Eco-System" Thea Van der Westhuizen looks at the way Theory U has served as theoretical underpinning in the SHAPE training program for young entrepreneurs in South Africa (Shifting Hope, Activating Potential Entrepreneurship). An illustrative account is given of a single representative event in the program calendar – "Meet Your Business Friend Day" – where student trainees were provided with a carefully structured opportunity to begin partnering and interacting with experienced business practitioners and other entrepreneurial mentors. Details are given in the chapter of the sequence of events for the day, in the course of which the experiences of both trainees and mentors can be seen as reflecting particular phases in the Theory U Curve. In the SHAPE social technology (which at the same time as training entrepreneurs is also an on-going systemic action learning and action research project) a particular concern has been the need, in the South African context, to cultivate an entrepreneurial mindset among youthful participants who for the most part come from a community culture that tends to give very little encouragement for the entrepreneurial endeavor. Discussed in detail in the chapter are key individual entrepreneurial orientation propensities that SHAPE seeks to cultivate and that relate closely to key elements in Theory U. The Theory U concept of *co-initiating* illuminates issues in risk-taking propensity. The Theory U concept of *co-inspiring* is closely involved in entrepreneurial innovation, in mentorship for innovation, and in the particular issue for the SHAPE students of being receptive to inspiration. The SHAPE program, particularly in its mentorship and partnering focus, is very explicitly concerned with developing and encouraging proactiveness, as illuminated by the Theory U concepts of *co-creating* and *co-evolving*. Issues of *Open Mind*, *Open Heart* and *Open Will* are likewise acutely relevant to the young aspirants enrolled in SHAPE and are expanded on in the chapter.

In the final chapter 15, "Using Theory U tools and principles to plan, organize and manage a Sporting Event in a Sustainable Way" Cristiana Buscarini, Sara Franzini Gabrielli and Fabio Cerroni's explore the application of the culture of sustainability in the organization of sporting events following the ISO 20121 guidelines, through the tools proposed by the Theory U. Until today few events have been organized following these guidelines. This reason inspired them to start an investigation into the application of ISO 20121 in several activities during sporting events. To do this, they applied three tools of Theory U: sensing journey, stakeholder interview and shadowing in some sporting events, both at national and international levels, confirming that these approaches foster internal cohesion and strengthen relationships within an organization and across different stakeholders. Additionally, in their chapter, they identify "listening" as the single most valuable asset and tool in this process.

Closing Remarks

In closing, a guiding intention of this Series is to raise further awareness of the applicability of Theory U and presencing to our colleagues, students, ULAB hubs, international communities of practice and beyond, further conveying how this growing body of work is informing, enriching, and sustaining new developments across a wide variety of disciplines globally. In effect, by showcasing current voices and perspectives on Theory U and presencing, this Series also seeds the participation of future critical and appreciative streams of research on the different methods of presencing, their respective communities of practice and the value derived from such scholarly-practitioner undertakings. In this sense, Advances in Presencing offers important guidance and inspiration to colleagues currently involved in this work. By encouraging not only further elaboration and refinement of the Theory U framework and presencing approaches that are currently being explored and applied globally, this Series is also encouraging paradigmatic breakthroughs that may also provide new updates and prototypes to be followed and possibly further developed elsewhere. As a whole, Advances in Presencing affirms our convictions, and those of many of the invited authors, that this new, exciting, and extraordinarily important emerging field is one that has the promise to be of great service to humanity in the years and decades ahead.

CHAPTER 2

Social Presencing Theater (SPT)

How do we listen to our body-knowing to access the wisdom that lives in us?[1]

Arawana Hayashi

Introduction

I invite you to consider a possibility ... that wisdom lives in each of us. And, perhaps that wisdom also lives in all of us collectively. By *wisdom*, I mean a knowing that is not defined or fettered by, not filtered through, the conceptual frameworks of this small, separate unit that we call "me." This wisdom is a fresh way of looking, a big perspective, an awareness that comes from openness, from spaciousness, from non-concept, from direct experience. It is a "knowing"—knowing how to care for this planet and all the beings living here. And this knowing is desperately needed now.

Human beings are not short on wisdom. However, we are short on how to awaken this sleeping wisdom within us, individually and collectively. This wisdom is in each of our body-mind systems. And throughout time, women and men have been able to access this knowing—this wisdom that is inherent in being human. Social Presencing Theater (SPT) has its roots in mindfulness-awareness, in embodiment, in the performing arts, and in a conviction that the nonverbal experience of "feeling" can be a gateway to accessing wisdom. This simple and organic sense of feeling can be the basis for cultivating a good human society.

My journey of interest in this body-oriented knowing began many years ago. I was trained in dance from childhood and have spent my entire career as a dancer, dance teacher, improviser, and choreographer. For thirty years I studied with a Japanese master of *Bugaku*, an ancient Japanese court dance. I also worked with professional performers, and with people who don't call themselves dancers, and also with children—in the theater, in workshops, in communities, and in schools.

For decades I have also studied the teachings of Chögyam Trungpa, Rinpoche, a Tibetan Buddhist master, teacher, and artist. He taught Dharma art, or the art of non-aggression. He taught on perception, on something coming from nothing, on art in everyday life as a way to create an enlightened society.

In 2003, I met Otto Scharmer. He invited me to bring my work to the network of change makers at Presencing Institute. With Theory U, he articulates an approach to social change that includes the body's intelligence as well as practices to cultivate open-mindedness and open-heartedness. Within the Presencing Institute I have collaborated with him and other colleagues to create the series of practices called Social Presencing Theater. These practices are designed to make "social presencing," or social awareness, visible to us. The root of the word *theater* comes from the Latin root, *theatrum*, which means, "a place for viewing, for seeing." With SPT we are invited to see and sense the inherent healthiness and sanity in a team, or an organization, or a social system.

Embodiment: Feeling the Body

Practicing SPT brings us into the body. Through the practice we are able to connect with our body and our senses—and not feel constantly pulled into thinking, conceptualizing, and projecting. The language of the body is feeling. By that, I do not mean emotions, but instead, sensation—a feeling sense, a tuning-in to the body: its posture, its qualities, its sense of being. The feeling of the body is present in our experience. We know how it feels to live in the body, connected to and grounded on this planet, this good earth.

We often experience a kind of war between the body and the mind. The mind wants the body to be, to look, to feel different from how it actually does. The mind's voice is louder than the body's voice. Many of us need practices that allow our thinking mind to "step back" and our body's feeling to come forward. We need to feel our body to maintain physical and mental health and to experience coherence and wellbeing.

To support this sense of presence in SPT, we encourage practitioners to do a "20-Minute Dance" each day. It may sound complicated, but it could not be simpler. The instructions:

- Lie down on the floor.
- Take 20 minutes to alternate between moving and stillness, doing whatever thebody feels like doing, for example, moving from stretching the body along thefloor, to rising into a sitting position, to standing, while paying attention to thefeeling of the body when it is resting and when it is moving.
- Apply mindfulness by resting your attention on the feeling in your shoulder or the feeling in your lower back, or the feeling in your hand ... wherever there issensation in the body. Let go of thoughts. No agenda, no judgment.

From a sense of unconditional appreciation, we notice that our body/mind system naturally moves toward synchronization or coherence. We feel the balance between the groundedness of the earth and the openness of the sky. We feel a sense of basic healthiness, even if our life has stress and difficulty. We have a sense of who we are, and we have a deep sense of knowing that who we are is basically healthy and good.

When the body and mind are synchronized, our system feels basic wellbeing, even a sense of unconditional confidence. We do not have to worry and self-centralize. Instead, we naturally tend to extend outward—to feel curious and connected to others and to our surroundings. We feel more available to others. We experience a "social field." The social field is the interior condition or quality of relationships in a social system, the felt quality of the organization, the environment, the quality of the culture and the people. There is a saying attributed to the thirteenth-century Zen Buddhist master Dogen Zen-ji, "to know oneself is to forget oneself. And to forget oneself is to become enlightened by all things."

One way of knowing oneself is to develop the habit of feeling present, living in this human body without complaint or judgment, and being always curious about this body-mind system. An accessible sense of what we mean by "enlightened by all things" could be that our awareness extends out to all aspects of our everyday life—that all people, things, and circumstances are speaking to us, teaching us what it is to be a human being with others on this planet. At this particular time, we need to uncover this wisdom in ourselves and we need to see it and acknowledge it in others. Relying solely on conceptual thought uses only a part of our natural intelligence.

The Earth Body

These days, many of us are caught up in speed, demands, and goal-orientation, which seem pervasive in our society. We are seduced by the speed and convenience that technological advancements now allow. We sit at desks. We look at screens. We forget about our lower body, about our organic connection to Mother Earth. We forget the feeling of grass under our bare feet. We forget the smell of the forest and the sound of waves on the beach. Many children and adults in cities never have the opportunity to be immersed in a natural environment, to plant seeds, to walk in fields. This is why in SPT we always spend some time each day lying on the floor.

We stretch out on the floor and let our thoughts sink down into the body, and we let our body sink into the floor, and we let our connection with the floor sink into the bigger body of planet Earth. We feel the resources, the wealth, and the reliability of the

Earth. We feel how the Earth body is holding us close, otherwise we would float off into space. We feel how this Earth body is our support and our ground. We feel our place in this very moment on the planet. Each of us, right now, has a place on the planet. We can feel in that place a deep sense of belonging on Earth.

Social Body and Social Field

We are always a part of a social body. The family or household is a primary social body. Teams at work are social bodies. A school, company, organization, or community—each is a social body within the larger social body of humanity. Do we feel this? When you are on an airplane, do you feel this as the flight #277 social body? In the subway car, do you feel that for this short ride uptown, this is one of your social bodies? We share the same space. We co-create an environment. Do we feel ourselves as an interdependent part of all the social bodies we live in? Do we experience the social fabric that we co-create moment by moment with others?

In SPT we have several practices for sensing the social body. The primary one is called the Village, in which everyone in the group engages in simple everyday movements and practices for sensing the whole. As we engage with others, we notice under what conditions we feel more open or more closed. "Open" and "closed" are not moral judgments. They are experiences that we all have from moment to moment. Each moment we have louder or quieter experiences of opening up or of closing down; of letting go of hesitations and judgments, or of hanging on to our familiar stories and opinions.

We can open to both what we feel and what is happening around us. That might be pleasant or unpleasant, but we can be curious, we can wonder. We move forward, we take a chance. Closing has a different feeling. We notice our edges turning in, our walls going up, our judgments, opinions, beliefs, and assumptions arising with their accompanying feelings of wanting to hide, push away, run from, strike out against, complain about, seduce, or ignore. The feelings themselves are quite innocent. They arise from habit. However, if we solidify them, defend them, out of a lack of awareness, then they become experiences that we call "absencing," the opposite of "presencing."

Presencing in the language of Theory U is a combination of two words: *presence* and *sensing*. In the Theory U process, we engage our sense perceptions, sensing "out" into our world or context, and sensing "in" to our own experience. I have heard Otto Scharmer describe this as, "our attention is 100% out and 100% in." We practice paying attention to our own attending, to what in Theory U is called the "Four Fields of Attention." We can attend by filtering our experience through our own conceptual frameworks, our own psychological habits. We can pay attention to facts; we can pay attention in an empathic way. And we can also attend from a larger sense of the whole open awareness. The term *presencing* describes this open awareness and open-hearted-ness that is the basis for creativity and compassionate action in the world. Social presencing describes collective awareness.

Social Presencing Theater makes social systems visible, tangible. Because we are engaged physically, the choices we make—where we go, what we do—and the resulting patterns we create, are visible to everyone. We can clearly see and experience the moment-to-moment co-creation of a social reality, the making of social fabric and connectivity.

The invitation is to notice both personally and on a collective level the elements of society building. We notice feelings of connection and disconnection, inclusion and exclusion, initiating activity and following, supporting or building on others' offerings, joining, contrasting. We notice center, and periphery; power building and dissolving. We notice activity and rest; coherence and chaos. We are co-creating social reality in a self-organizing system. Are we creating the society that we want to live in? Is wisdom creating this Village? Are presence, curiosity, and compassion creating this Village? It is our capacity to feel our humanness that knows how to create social reality.

"Village practice" began for me in about 1975, when I was teaching movement improvisation at the School of the Museum of Fine Arts in Boston. I had no idea what I was doing, so the class consisted of a room full of students making up movements and trying to connect with others' movements in a freeform and random way.

Perhaps because of the absence of direction or instruction, the students seemed to exhibit qualities such as connectedness and inventiveness, but without coherence or structure. For the most part, the dancers enjoyed the freedom of the experience, but despite that I had a longing for spatial clarity and some sense of spontaneous composition in time—some clear shaping of time and space. I was interested in improvisation as performance, and also in performance that did not depend on the dance technique, or on the personality or attractiveness of the dancer. My experience as a participant, a viewer, and as the instructor, was that the work was too rambling and self-indulgent, and it lacked the power of underlying coherence and beauty that one experiences, for example, in great jazz, another improvised art form. I began to notice that the quality of the experience—the depth of it— depended largely on how I and the others paid attention to the moment-by-moment unfolding of our collective experience.

A friend suggested that I find a structure in which to investigate the essential elements of the process. This made sense to me, so I began with paring down the dancers' "movement vocabulary" to simple, ordinary, everyday movements such as standing, sitting, lying down, walking, turning, and bowing without arm or hand gestures. The attention was placed on doing simple things as fully and as well as possible, and on paying attention to the whole of the space. Rather than getting caught in an activity with one other person or a small group, we were allowing our attention to include the whole of the space or the village. I was influenced by a phrase that was popular in the 1970s: "In Bali we have no art. We do everything as well as possible."

The initial Village instruction remains the same today: everyday movements, mindfulness of body, extending out awareness antennae to include a sense of others in the space as being participants with oneself in one social body. Participants learn how they co-create with others in groups. They do the Village practice, then they are invited into a conversation about what they noticed, what they created together, and how they participated. They notice their own patterns and habits, as well as those of others.

31

They can reflect on how, in their daily life, they are engaging in their teams, organizations, and families. A few themes we notice are Inside-Outside, Projection, Same-Different.

Inside-Outside and Group Skin

To begin the practice, I ask people to gather in groups of five. After doing so, groups immediately form a group skin. They start off immediately with a sense of what "inside" means to them and what is outside their group boundary. Some groups have a more tightly woven "sense of skin" than others. For example, in some groups, if one person moves too far from what others perceive as "the group," then someone might worry that they are no longer with the group. Or if a person faces out from what others perceive as "inside," this can also trigger a sense of alarm for some.

Meanwhile, other individuals or groups doing the same practice may have no such sense of threat or problem with group members moving out or turning away from the group. Folks might even wander off (even join other groups!) and the skin stretches to include them. There is no right or wrong. This is another way that SPT reflects the patterns that we collectively enact as we create the social fabric of our teams and organizations. Each practice is followed by a dialog conversation. One topic that tends to arise in these dialogs is that of inclusion and exclusion.

Projection and Sense-Making

The Village provides a window for noticing how much we tend to project our own interpretations on to others and on to situations. Each person in the group speaks from the "I" voice only. We can easily observe that it is difficult to describe a moment of non-verbal experience in words. We tend to immediately jump to interpret our experience rather than stay with the fresh sensing-feeling. We tend to quickly try to put our experience into a category, into a box that might contain the voice of judgment or a psychological explanation. And, we tend to think that others are interpreting their experience in the same way that we are interpreting ours.

For instance, say one person in the group sits with her head down. Another thinks, "oh, that person is not connecting. I need to go near so I can support her." This could be a kind thought and gesture, or it might be a limiting habit. The sitter might describe how lovely it felt to be sitting alone, and how she felt the other person as an intrusion into her space. We invite everyone to suspend sense-making in order to stay with the actual feeling quality of each moment of experience. In this way, we can relax our ideas and let choices arise from the whole.

Same-Different

Another theme that arises in Village practice is our preference for sameness or contrast. It might be revealed in the process that the whole group—or some members in the group—values harmony, balance, closeness, and connection. They might choose movements or positions in the space that express this value. They might choose a level (sitting or standing) or movement that is the same as others. Groups often form into a circle, sitting relatively close together, all facing inward. This inward-focused circle is almost an archetypal pattern that expresses balance and belonging for some—and claustrophobia and over-control for others.

Other groups or individuals might value freedom, a sense of space, or individual autonomy. Their Village might look completely disconnected to an outside observer, but the members might feel happy to have wide awareness and a looser sense of being tuned in to the group. They might value difference, contrast, and innovation. Again, this could be another kind of archetype. And, of course, there are many variations and manifestations of patterns between these two. SPT provides a way of engaging in physically creating something with others that allows the body-knowing to come into the reflection on social fields. A social field might be described as the "interiority," the feeling quality, of a social system. In the SPT work, we are not looking for a specific goal or optimal "solution." There is not a "right" way as opposed to a "wrong" way. Instead, we are using SPT as a way to have a shared, embodied experience that leads to a collective reflection. SPT is a way of getting a deeper sense of how we co-create our social situations together.

Turning Toward Stuck

The work of Social Presencing Theater at the Presencing Institute has focused on applying embodied presence and social body awareness to societal acupuncture points—leverage points for change. Two primary practices are the Stuck exercise and 4-D Mapping. We bring the body-knowing from the 20-Minute Dance, and the awareness of the social space from the Village experience, and we apply the resulting insight and awareness to specific issues—stuck areas that can be personal, organizational, or societal.

We invite participants to bring an issue that feels stuck for them. This is not psychotherapy or psychodrama. It is a work-related issue. For example, someone is trying to create or innovate but their effort is not going forward. This could be due to external obstacles (conflict with a coworker or lack of funding) or inner obstacles (lack of confidence). Our experience with Social Presencing Theater tells us that being "stuck" is a gold mine.

Embedded in "stuck" are insight, clarity, and wisdom. We turn toward the "stuck" to listen and to feel. We learn nothing if we push it away. We ask people to embody their feeling of "stuck" in a body shape or sculpture. We call that "sculpture 1," an aspect of our current reality. There is an obstacle to what we are trying to create or accomplish. Then through a Theory U process, we sense into the body sculpture and let the body move in whatever way it feels like moving, until it stops in a second shape or posture. We call this "sculpture 2." We say one sentence from our sculpture 2. Then we reflect on the difference between the first sculpture and the second one. What was the journey from sculpture 1 to sculpture 2? What was the initial impetus for changing? What was the difference between the two postures? How and when did the feeling quality shift? What surprised you? And how could this inform the particular situation you are experiencing in your life or work?

This is not a problem-solution method. It is an opportunity to invite the body's wisdom into the reflection to gain a deeper understanding and insight into how to engage and move forward in a fresh and invigorated way.

It may seem counter-intuitive, but we are suggesting that people move into a body shape that engages, clarifies, and enhances a feeling of discomfort. There is some aspect of the current reality that holds some discomfort that can be labeled as "a place where I feel stuck." That feeling could be called uncertainty, irritation, boredom, confusion—it makes no difference what it is because the method is always the same. What is important is developing the capacity to feel whatever we feel, without labeling it good or bad, without immediately categorizing it in terms of past experience, be it psychological or historical, and without immediately trying to get rid of the experience.

This can be done individually or in teams, where each person embodies a "force" that is keeping the person "stuck." "Stucks" are body shapes that might feel weighed down or curled inward, or when arms and legs are stretched in different directions. There are many possibilities that might reveal archetypal patterns of stuckness. The "stuck" person builds a social sculpture with a few others who help the person feel the forces that are preventing her from moving. It becomes clear that nobody is stuck alone, but that each of us is embedded into personal, organizational, and societal systems that need to move and change.

The four people in the social sculpture form a social being that wants to move. One of our SPT practitioners used the "Stuck" exercise with two organizations that were having difficulties working with each other. Each of the organizations performed a "Stuck" that embodied their experience. Each organization's team witnessed the other's "Stuck." They were able to identify with each other, to see familiar patterns and to better understand both their differences and their common ground. Because this experience was co-created and felt in the body, they had greater collective understanding than would have been possible with only talking about the issues.

Another recent example was a "Stuck" in which the stuck person felt that he was pulled in two directions. His body was twisted. His legs and feet were pointing in one direction, and his head and eyes were oriented in the opposite direction.

He began the process by asking one person in the group to sit in the place his feet were pointing toward, to face him, and to pull gently on his vest. He then asked the second person to stand with her arms extending toward him, in the place toward which his eyes and arms were oriented. He then asked the third person to put her hands in front of his heart.

So, Person One pulled him down in the direction that his feet were pointing. Person Two met his gaze and extended her hands toward him. Person Three sat in front of his chest with her hand on his heart. This was sculpture 1, an embodiment of how the stuck person was experiencing his current situation.

After the people in the sculpture had remained still for quite a long time to clarify and sense in to the sculpture they had made, the movement began. They let go of any ideas about what "should" happen, and they followed their physical sensations and their respective senses of where and how the social sculpture wanted to move. That movement continued until the stuck person's entire body came out of its twisted shape and oriented itself to face the direction that his eyes were looking toward.

Person One, who had been pulling down on his vest, came to stand beside him. Person Two remained steady in her position and joined hands with the stuck person. Person Three moved closer and knelt down to add support. This was sculpture 2. From their places in sculpture 2, each person shared on sentence that described their journey from sculpture 1 to sculpture 2.

In the practice, the stuck person does not tell the others about their situation before they begin the process of moving from sculpture 1 to sculpture 2. The less they know, the fresher and less contrived their movements can be.

So, in this case, there was no discussion about the situation the stuck person wanted to explore before the practice began. After the team had completed the process, there was a team reflection. In the reflection, the stuck person revealed that the direction of his feet felt like the weight of his current obligations. The direction of his gaze and head orientation was indicating his wish to go in a new direction with his work.

An insight that arose from this particular "Stuck" was that the forces keeping the stuck person feeling stuck, also had the potential to be supportive. The team reflected on how this might inform the stuck person about his real-life situation.

Reflection on the process revealed that a conversation could be possible between Person One (pulling him down) and Person Two, who was reaching out to him. They both become supportive in sculpture 2. Maybe they share a common goal, despite seeming to go in different directions? They felt potential there. The stuck person shared that he experienced a surprising sense of warmth in the physical connection with the third person. He described the feeling in his body as a reminder that warmth could be the ground for taking the next steps. The team then had a few minutes to journal about their reflection.

One hypothesis in this work is that the body-mind system will naturally go toward health. It does not want to be sick or stuck. Perhaps the social body-mind system, whether a family, a team, or an organization, also wants to go toward health? Our work is to enable these systems to sense themselves, to bring awareness to the situation. Once we become aware of our stuck patterns by feeling them in our body, without judgment, we can tune in to the shift, or movement, that the system yearns for. We are not looking for a solution, *per se*. We are open to seeing and feeling what might come next if we suspend our ideas and judgments, and trust that our sense perception experiences will reveal insights and wisdom.

When we attend to the moment-to-moment unfolding of experience with tremendous awareness we can collectively move freely ahead toward creative outcomes.

4-D Systems Mapping

This approach to "leaning into" the current situation, sensing more deeply into it to experience what IT wants to do, where IT wants to move, is applied to systems change in 4-D Mapping. This allows complex stakeholder groups like those in education, health care, or banking, to see and sense themselves as a whole. Out of this deep "knowing oneself," there is a sense that the system can learn, the system can notice its own inherent wisdom and move toward this knowing.

SPT is a practice of seeing, sensing, and knowing oneself. That "oneself" can be a person, as in a spiritual practice, but it can also be a collective. In the 4-D Mapping practice, each of the stakeholders in a system is embodied. Someone in the group chooses to embody a particular stakeholder (if we are sensing into the school system, let's say it is a primary school teacher) by creating a body shape or posture that expresses the stakeholder. In SPT, these body shapes are full of communicative information. They contain keys to truth. The person enters the "playing space," creates their body shape, and offers a few words that arise spontaneously from the body shape. We are using the body shape to boycott the tendency to "think something up." We are encouraging the synchronization between the body and the mind.

One by one, participants enter the "playing space," by embodying other stakeholder roles (in an education setting this might be a student, a principal, a parent) and offering their words. They embody their experience of a current reality—how it feels to be part of this current system. In 4-D Mapping we always include three stakeholders whose voices are not often heard. The Earth is a stakeholder role. The Marginalized, those who suffer the most on this planet, is a stakeholder role, and the Highest Potential of the system is also always present as a stakeholder role in 4-D Mapping. Those who are marginalized and suffer most on the planet always have a place in the sculpture.

When all the stakeholders are settled into their "social sculpture," feeling the whole sculpture as a living being that might be called, for example, "the school system as we now experience it," they are ready for the next step. Next, they go through a process of attending, sensing, and letting go of ideas of what they "should" be doing. They begin to move, directed by their own body-knowing and their awareness of the whole. They do not think or plan or manipulate their experience. They rely on a simple moment-to-moment attending to what this being, this social body, wants to do and where it wants to go. They allow the singularity of their individual stakeholder roles to soften, so that they can feel the sense of the whole system. They shift from ego-system orientation to eco-system awareness—from silo-consciousness to presencing.

After a few minutes they settle into a second "social sculpture." From their positions in the new sculpture, they will again offer a sentence or phrase. This is followed by a dialog process that allows the group members to hear each others' experience. At this point, we begin to see deep patterns in the system that were not previously apparent: patterns that were keeping the system stuck, and also patterns that were generative and full of potential. We are surprised to see two unlikely stakeholders moving close to one another and notice that there might be a seed of possibility there. We see that we have made choices that exclude parts of the system. We notice that we have all gathered close together, leaving no breathing room. We share using simple words: "I saw," "I felt," "I did." We try not to interpret or project, but instead to evoke the direct experience.

We see how power works in that system and how those who are marginalized also play a role in that dynamic. Sometimes we see inversions. Those who are in the center move to the periphery. Those who are standing, sit down. We see how the system yearns to organize itself into coherence—sometimes successfully and sometimes not so. But the process is designed not to "get it right." The process is designed to make the system see and sense itself. The method is awareness—being aware of the whole and making choices from the open space. We bring this physical art-based method to serve in enabling generative social fields.

One of our observations is how frequently the second sculpture is more tangled and more estranged than the first sculpture. From a conventional point of view, there might be a tendency to feel that this was not a "good" outcome. Often, we want to see a quick fix, a positive shift immediately. But hidden in many systems is real stuckness, deep under the iceberg of symptoms. As the people in the group experience this, they also feel the sadness of being stuck. There is a gap between where we currently are and where we want to be. And the habits that got us to this current reality are not going to change overnight. In SPT we consider this sense of collective sadness to be a very positive step forward. We can know the facts, but until we feel the depth of our shared humanity and the deep longing to create a good society, we will continually be pulled to complacency because the challenges feel overwhelming. This shared grief that can arise from 4-D Mapping is a powerful motivating force for us to collectively commit to working together to find ways to move forward.

Closing Reflections

Circling back to the invitation I offered at the beginning of this chapter, please consider how wisdom lives in each of us both individually and collectively. In what ways do we have the capacity for "eco-system awareness," as Otto Scharmer describes it? Assuming we have the collective capacity to relax out of our "ego-system" tendency to think small, to think in silos, to make choices based on self-protection, how can we grow beyond these ingrained societal tendencies? What do we need to open up to a more tangible eco-system awareness that will bring us closer to our inherent wisdom and to knowing how to care for this planet and all beings who inhabit it?

Social Presencing Theater is an embodied practice. Practice is something we *do*, and do repeatedly. We engage over and over again to deepen our experience and our understanding. Being in our physical body, firmly planted on the Earth body and in our various social bodies is something we do day after day, year after year. Mindfulness of body, embodied presence, awareness of our social bodies and of the open space of creativity are all innate and we can cultivate these qualities and practices. SPT practices are a way of life—a way of integrating ourselves and our world. The practices reveal our limiting habitual patterns as well as our vast, open mind and heart. We need to practice because we tend to forget about our inherent wisdom. We forget who we are. We forget our interdependence with all living things. We forget that it is our job to help out this world. We practice to remember our true human nature.

We can celebrate the innate healthiness of our own body-mind system. We do not need to worry so much about ourselves. We can open up and feel our natural capacity to connect and communicate with others as social bodies. We can recognize patterns that lead to unwanted outcomes, and we can rejoice in our collective longing to make this world a better place. We know that *we* co-create social reality, social fabric, in every move we make. Every conversation, every e-mail, every action creates either a non-aggressive open possibility or a cut-off, disconnected experience. We know that we have incredible power to influence, shape, and benefit this society.

Social Presencing Theater is used for self-reflection, as an intervention method in social systems, and as an arts-based research methodology. It is held by the Presencing Institute and is an integral part of applying Theory U in organizations, communities, and large systems. All of the practice instructions are open-sourced, part of the collective commons. Trainings are offered in Europe, North and South America, Asia, and Australia. These practices arise from a deep conviction in our ability to listen to the body knowing, and an unwavering conviction in the basic goodness, wisdom, kindness, and courage of all beings and all collections of beings. It is available for everyone.

It gives us great joy to know that a high school student can facilitate these practices. Our work going forward is to both deepen our experience and also to make the work more accessible to everyone. We continue to deepen our capacity to pay attention to the moment-by-moment unfolding, or emerging, of experience, and to attend to this experience we call a social field shift. We continuously work to refine how we describe our basically non-verbal moments. And we aspire to make the work accessible and supportive of change agents. Our world needs all of us and needs this body-sensing-knowing intelligence in order to bring our world and all its beings back into balance.

CHAPTER 3

Moving towards Collective Presencing on a National Scale through u.lab Scotland

Keira Oliver, Anne Winther and Kirsty Deacon

In *"Theory U: Leading from the future as it emerges"* Scharmer uses the term "collective presencing" to describe the highest level of conversation, sensing and acting in the social field from the meso to mundo levels:

> Circle 4: Collective Presencing & Co-Creation: Such conversations convene emerging stakeholders in constellations that need one another in order to shape the future collectively. Together they sense and actualize emerging opportunities. Thus the inner circle [labelled Collective Presencing] functions rather like a greenhouse for social innovations of the future. It incubates ideas, intentions and experimental microcosms that will allow future possibilities to emerge, take shape and develop. Of the social conversation types displayed in figure 19.2, those in the inner circle are empirically the most rare and the most strategically important. (2009, p. 337)

While we are still some way off Collective Presencing at the mundo level, we have evidence of collective presencing happening at the meso levels under the "greenhouse" of u.lab Scotland. Over the last four years more than 1,800 people in Scotland have participated in a global, three-month, massive online open course (MOOC) called *"u.lab: Leading from the Emerging Future"*. It is developed and offered free of charge by the Massachusetts Institute of Technology (MIT) and the Presencing Institute each September. This growing community of practitioners form u.lab Scotland and together, through a number of different expressions, constitutes a move towards Collective Presencing; where the quality of listening and conversation shift towards a generative stage, or what Scharmer (2018) calls "a holding space for bringing something new into reality that wants to be born" (p. 27). Over the last three years, the Scottish Government has commissioned research studies to understand the impact of participation on u.lab participants. In this chapter we describe the course, its infrastructure and the research findings.

The course, theory and associated infrastructure and support

What is u.lab?

u.lab is based on the Theory U methodology or U process (Scharmer and Kaufer, 2013); a framework, an approach and set of tools which aim to draw "our attention to the *blind spot* in leadership today: the "interior conditions", the sources from which we operate both individually and collectively" (Scharmer, 2018, p. xi). By doing so, it helps participants become aware of, and shift, the paradigm of thought they are working from in order to enhance the impact of their existing work and bring new ideas into action in their personal lives, organisation or community. It supports participants to create a shift in acting from an egotistical perspective to one of the whole system, with the explicit intention to co-create a society for the benefit of us all.

u.lab provides a set of tools which can be used to enable a whole system to be observed, to allow time to sit with a problem or a challenge without the need to move immediately to a "fix" and to then begin to look for new ways of dealing with issues through co-creation and collaboration. As Oliver and Deacon (2017) found, "the U process draws on many diverse theoretical standpoints, bringing together elements, for example, of systems theory, design methods, co-production, asset-based approaches and improvement science. The tools focus on enhancing personal and collective leadership in times of great change and complexity by developing the capacity to listen deeply, discovering ways of having "different" conversations, bringing in voices from the margins and working collaboratively and creatively to enact personal, organisational or community change" (p. 4).

There are two dimensions to u.lab:

1. The content and individual practice (online and individual)
2. Collective sensing and practice (in person, in self-organising hubs and within teams)

While all the materials can be accessed online and worked through by individuals on their own, the emphasis in u.lab is on practicing the learning and making a change in the "real world". As such, u.lab encourages participants to enhance their individual impact by connecting with others and developing relationships and support locally and globally using social media and in-person "coaching circles" and "hubs" (local study and practice groups).

What is u.lab Scotland?

MIT and the Presencing Institute ran the first u.lab course in January 2015 as a prototype. A small group of participants from the public and voluntary/third sector in Scotland took part and thought it would be of interest to a wider audience. Supported by the Scottish Government, they convened a series of three national gatherings over the summer of 2015 to explore the potential for u.lab in Scotland before it ran again in Sept 2015. Around 800 people attended these events. These conversations were the beginnings of the u.lab Scotland community.

Scotland is the first country to develop a network of peer support for u.lab participants at a national level – called u.lab Scotland (or ulabscot). This collective sensing level comprises of an evolving and growing network of individuals, hubs and a u.lab Holding Team.

The u.lab Holding Team is a group of participants from the voluntary/third sector, National Health Service (NHS), academic institutions, Scottish Government and private individuals with a common intention to support the growth and sustainability of u.lab in Scotland. It does this by sensing into the needs of the ulabscot community by being rooted in that community themselves. The original ulabscot Holding Team formed after the prototype u.lab in January 2015.

u.lab Scotland comprises of additional ways for people to connect and share experiences and learning throughout the year, not just while the course is running. This includes the use of social media platforms such as a blog (www.ulabscot.com), Facebook group and Twitter and gathering at events convened either by u.lab participants themselves or by the u.lab Holding Team.

Scotland is also the first country to have had its own content included within the u.lab course. Participants from Scotland and the global u.lab community are invited to opt in to this additional content. Affectionately referred to as the "SMOOC" (Scottish Massive Open Online Course), the content of the SMOOC focuses on the ways in which the principles of Theory U are already present or influencing policy and approaches to how we work in Scotland.

From the SMOOC data, we know that since 2015:

- Over 1,800 people have taken part in u.lab in Scotland
- Approximately 100 self-organising hubs have formed across the country
- Each of these hubs had at least one volunteer host or co-hosting team
- People have taken part from national and local govern-

ments, the National Health Service, non-profits and charities, social enterprises and business.

Participants from Scotland in 2017 were:

- 65% female
- Ranged across age brackets from 18 to 24 years, to 65 to 74 years old
- The largest age group continues to be 45 to 54 years, making up just over a third of participants.

In early 2016, after u.lab 2015 had finished, a group of Scottish participants gathered to explore how to prepare for u.lab 2016. To encourage more community ownership, they invited all 2015 participants to consider holding u.lab "taster sessions" in their local areas; open to the public and for those with an interest to come along and experience what u.lab might be like for them. A taster session pack was also produced to support taster hosts. As a result, over twenty taster sessions were hosted by u.lab participants around Scotland, from Thurso to Glasgow, with many more hosted specifically for teams or organisations. Since then, many more taster sessions and events have been hosted.

As ulabscot grew, more coherence emerged around its activities. The course itself covers a few months, but preparing for and then acting on the learning grew into a yearly cycle:

Late spring/ summer	Preparations for u.lab e.g. intro and taster sessions, hubs forming
Sept to Dec	u.lab course is active: hubs and coaching circles meet, three to four live sessions take place throughout the course, culminating in a final live session in December

| January onwards | Continuing to implement learning into action; sharing of stories of impact, events held to support different parts of the process held by participants themselves or the ulabscot Holding Team. |

u.lab Scotland is not an organisation. It is a community of people with an open invitation to anyone practicing Theory U in Scotland. As it continued to grow, its global impact was realised in the hosting of the world's first "u.lab Hub Host Training Programme" in Edinburgh in June 2017. As a result, the programme hosting team from Scotland, the Netherlands and the Basque Country welcomed over fifty hub hosts from Scotland and around the world. It was a deep transformative experience for many of its participants. The programme was so successful in supporting participants to host hubs in their local communities and organisations, it was repeated again in Edinburgh in April 2018.

The ulabscot Holding Team

The ulabscot Holding Team has been an emergent group and after 18 months of meeting, the team recognised the need for its boundaries to be more permeable to invite more voices in and operate around more self-organising principles. In spring 2017, the u.lab Scotland Holding Team decided to broaden its reach by inviting anyone participating in u.lab to its six-weekly u.lab Scotland "sensing" meetings. This extended u.lab Scotland to be far more collective in its approach, as u.lab participants from across central Scotland "check-in", "share stories from the field", and intentionally attempt to reach more generative levels of dialogue and collective presencing in order to co-design the u.lab Scotland space for the future.

The team continued to extend its reach to remote areas and multiple sites by using on-line video conferencing platforms. In total, over 25 participants have been involved with the Holding Team to date. It continues to experiment with itself as a Collective Presencing entity. One such example was when the team gathered in March 2018 to sense into the changing role of one of its members and how this might influence the preparation from the forthcoming u.lab. Using a constellation approach to embody the situation, there was a tangible shift of energy in the room as the team explored the current and a potential future scenario. The team took on more of a sense of a collective in their endeavour and the individual experienced a shift in how she felt about herself in this work.

Why and how is the Scottish Government supporting u.lab?

The Scottish Government is supporting the growth of u.lab in Scotland to help support communities make the changes they want to see. It sees u.lab as a public participation platform for innovation and learning which:

1. Helps turn ideas into action, making real change in the real world.
2. Is explicitly focused on when you want qualitatively different results than you have realised in the past, in order to respond to changes happening around you
3. Addresses why change might not always happen as we would expect – by inviting participants to connect to what they feel is really important and use that as a source of motivation and energy to turn their ideas into action.

The Scottish Government also sees u.lab practices as an important element of Collective Leadership for Scotland's offer, which draws colleagues from across our public services to help collaborate on complex, systemic issues in service of wider public service transformation (Collective Leadership for Scotland, 2020).

The Scottish Government is not leading or directing u.lab in Scotland. It responds to the needs of U practitioners, taking direction from the ulabscot Holding Team, where it is best placed to do so. Over the years it has supported u.lab in Scotland by

convening the Holding Team meetings, accepting and supporting others to accept invitations to provide taster sessions and
share our learning, supporting a Hub Host Programme, and initiated the first ever systematic research into the impact of u.lab at
a country level in 2016 and continuing this research by commis-
sioning the Centre for Human Ecology to do a repeat study in
2017.

What impact is u.lab having so far?

u.lab Scotland is a movement of people across geographical
areas, sectors and issues, creating their own social changes. As
there are as many intentions and outcomes for u.lab as participants, impact has been assessed in terms of what it means for the
participants themselves. This can happen at the personal, interpersonal and organisational or system levels.

This chapter brings together the findings from research into
the impact of u.lab since 2015. Eighteen people were interviewed
in 2016 and 28 were interviewed in 2017 using semi-structured
interviews. Of those, 16 and 24 were analysed respectively (some
of the interview recordings were of a low quality and could not be
accurately transcribed and analysed). Some of the findings are
included here. More in-depth analysis of the 2016 cohort is available in Pomeroy & Oliver (2018, 2020).

Our research and the continual dialogue with the u.lab and
u.lab Scotland communities is helping to surface a greater understanding of what a theory of change might be. While it was not
focused on Collective Presencing per se, it does illustrate how
u.lab Scotland may be acting as a "greenhouse for social innovations of the future... [incubating] ideas, intentions and experimental microcosms that will allow future possibilities to emerge,
take shape and develop" (Scharmer, 2009, p. 337).

Below, you will find some overall themes that emerged from
listening to participants. Two inter-related and often conflated
areas were the practice of Theory U and the infrastructure and
support of u.lab; for example, a practitioner can often refer to
using a "u.lab" approach, when they mean using Theory U.

Themes from the research related to both of these: first, what impact Theory U had on the individual and their ability to act within their wider system and, secondly, the impact the u.lab infrastructure (hubs, coaching circles, u.lab Scotland and u.lab global connections and networks) had on the individual.

Personal to systemic impact

The data from 2016 suggested the tentative emergence of a theory of change of how Theory U may be helping participants create their own positive impacts (figure 1).

An Emerging Theory of Change?

u.lab facilitates the process of how a person can influence change in a system, through collective action, by enabling that person to:

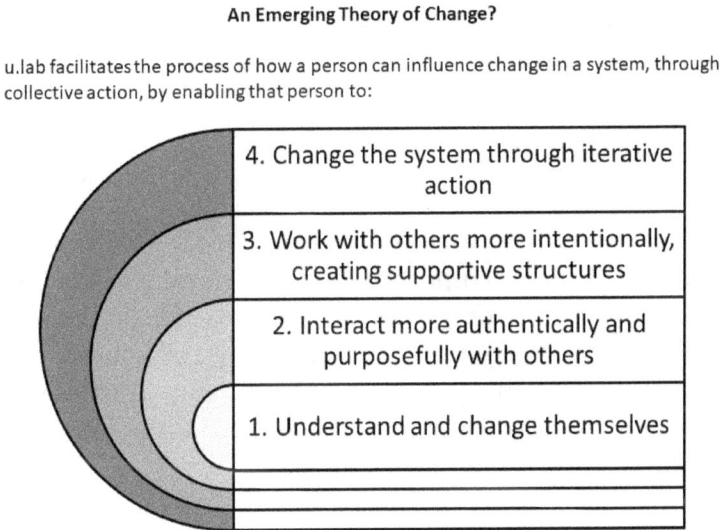

4. Change the system through iterative action

3. Work with others more intentionally, creating supportive structures

2. Interact more authentically and purposefully with others

1. Understand and change themselves

Figure 1. A potential theory of change (Oliver and Deacon, 2017)

u.lab and Theory U appeared to be giving practical and moral support in how to create the conditions to bring about the change participants wanted, in an expanding circle of influence; starting firstly with the participants themselves and increasing out towards impacting on a wider scale, helping participants to:

1. Understand and change themselves first – to connect with what work they are called to do and understand more deeply, what is required of them, including the internal

barriers that may be stopping them from acting.

2. Interact more authentically and purposefully with others, seeing different perspectives and the value of moving from a mental model of "me" to "we" when it comes to seeking understanding and solutions.

3. Work with others more intentionally, creating supportive infrastructure to create change more inclusively and coherently.

4. Change the system through putting deeply explored and co-created ideas into iterative action.

The findings from the 2017 research (Winther & Oliver, 2017) continue to suggest impact in these four areas and an evolution in the theory of change, as outlined below.

1) Greater understanding and ability to change themselves.

By far, the most distinct impact at this stage is the personal impact u.lab has had on participants. A central tenet of Theory U is that "the success of an intervention depends on the interior condition of the intervener" (O'Brian. as cited in Scharmer, 2003, p. 18). Therefore, much of the content and practice creates opportunities for participants to realise deep insights about themselves and improve the quality of their interior condition as it were.

u.lab enables participants to cultivate a personal change practice which many find empowering and energising. For example, it helps to clarify their intention, allowing them to slow down to understand what is important to them and what is really going on in the system they want to change, letting go of things that don't serve them any longer, and suspending judgement and fear long enough to listen well and put their ideas into action quickly.

"If I was to summarise it I would just say that I'm more present and focusing on the right things; that I'm taking the time to be more reflective; I'm testing my approaches to things; I'm taking risks about doing things differently and I'm making sure that I'm taking people on the journey with me. In fact, more importantly we're developing that journey together." Chief Executive, Charity Organisation

A common characteristic of participants who experience profound personal changes with u.lab is that they tend to be at a point of transition in their own lives. u.lab is most useful when going through a process of personal change because it is a catalyst to facilitate personal development and strengthens their ability to sit with uncertainty in a more generative way. For several interviewees this engagement with u.lab was "*serendipitous*". A significant number of participants have taken part multiple times to either deepen their experience or to focus on particular aspects or practices they found helpful in their lives and work.

However, it was recognised that personal transformation doesn't always feel comfortable. Slowing down before acting is counter-cultural and difficult in times of austerity and mounting systemic failures. u.lab also opened-up participants to notice dysfunction in a way they had not before; for some, it was difficult to realise that they may also play a part in it. Some had been cynical or jaded in their work where it felt like things never really changed and were looking for a constructive way to move forward. u.lab helped them recognise that instead of blaming the system, it was empowering to see that they are part of that system and how they can make a change, even if it is a small change at first. For a number of participants, their u.lab journey had helped them integrate their work and life more closely or to make changes in their life or career.

For one participant in the public sector, "*it took me from scunnered to hopeful*" (scunnered is a Scots word for feeling world-weary and down-trodden by something). This was supported by another participant:

"...this scunneredness is what brought us together and gives me hope that things can get done differently. We'll still get things wrong – and we're trying to do things differently – but if we're still applying open heart, open mind, open will and the courage and the compassion and the getting rid of the fear that we're invited to do – then we will be doing things differently." Practitioner, National Health Service

2) Interacting more authentically and purposefully with others.

A further strong impact for participants was the improved ability to have different kinds of conversations to produce improved outcomes. This was due to developing their capacity to connect with others as people first (particularly within their work settings), and to listen deeply without judgement. Many recognised the importance of noticing and acknowledging the emotional aspect of change to improve their relationships.

One of the most common changes cited by participants was to bring the tools and techniques they learned through u.lab into their workplace to help create a more supportive culture that is open and ready for change. Some changed how they structured and participated in meetings with their teams, partners and others in their system, to put more emphasis on learning and supporting each other and to move the ethos of relationships away from 'what I need' to 'what we need' and 'how I can help others'. Some participants also stated they are acting with a greater worldview and more holistically.

3) Working with others more intentionally, creating supportive structures.

u.lab is about accessing a wider array of knowledge, in order to create new insights and ideas and put them into action through prototyping. Many participants struggled with the term "prototype", misinterpreting it as a "thing" or fully workable solution to a pertinent issue rather than it being about a process of translating an idea or concept into experimental action. However, when probed a bit deeper, all participants were prototyping or experimenting with how to prepare and create conditions for change in their own lives and teams.

While the importance of preparing the conditions for change is recognised by many leaders and scholars, how to do this in day to day work situations seems to be more difficult to articulate and act on. Changing ourselves and improving relationships were recognised by participants as vital factors in this, as were the ability to build trust, be authentic and find meaning in the work that you do. These were all aspects that participants felt u.lab helped them with significantly.

Public and charity/not-for-profit sector workers reported that it has helped them reconfirm their commitment to public service and given them a sense of personal agency to make positive changes in their work and organisation. They have been using the approach as a different way of engaging and building trust within their own teams and stakeholders and increasingly with the wider public. The approach and tools have been used to reframe how conversations and engagement processes have been held.

One example of this is the Fire Starter Festival, a self-organised and cross-sector festival of collaborative learning events celebrating creativity and innovation in public services (https://firestarterfestival.com/). It illuminates creative, disruptive and innovative ways in which we can all transform ourselves, our organisations and the wider system. The idea was sparked by Karen Lawson of the Scottish Government through her participation in u.lab 2015. She prototyped the idea in January 2016 hosting a festival of 5 events with 100 people. The festival has grown both in size and geographic spread since then: 35 events with 1000 people in 2017, to 100 events involving over 3,500 people in 2020. The festival has now spread to Ireland and Wales and in 2018, was endorsed and launched by the First Minister of Scotland.

4) Changing the system through iterative action.

u.lab is still a relatively new intervention and for those who want to make change in their lives, within big systems such as the NHS or Education, or indeed even at an organisational level, there is a recognition of the need for perseverance and resilience. The ground is being prepared for change here through the actions being taken by hubs and individuals. However, even at this early stage, there are examples of ideas from u.lab already making an impact in discrete and systemic ways.

For example, as a result of her u.lab participation, Valerie

Jackman, then-Lecturer at Edinburgh College, prototyped a new type of further education course, co-designed by the students to improve their own lives:

"I'm passionate about young people and I'm passionate about education. In my experience I've come across lots of young people in education who really don't have a strong sense of self and who really don't know what they want to do next. So, from the second round of u.lab, I really had this seed of an idea that I wanted to develop a course for young people to help them get to know themselves better; get to know how they think; how they manage mental health; how they interact with others; where their strengths are... and then start to explore the things that they're really interested in that are meaningful and purposeful."

You can read more about Valerie's prototype in Winther, A. et al (2019).

A common theme from participants was the difficulty in securing support from line and senior managers in their organisations to participant in u.lab as part of their personal development or implementing the approach in their workplace. As a result of this, and in recognition that the u.lab course may be too time-intensive for senior leaders to commit to, the Scottish Government hosted a two-day *"Shaping Scotland"* learning event with 130 senior leaders from across all sectors and geographic areas in December 2016. The event created a space for them to collectively, and individually, generate new insights and new actions that would bring change in Scotland. The event aimed to explore the fact that a core part of how we lead during times of uncertainty will be addressing the role of ourselves and attending to the relational aspects of leadership. The event was inspired and co-created by u.lab participants and co-hosted with Otto Scharmer and created a crack in the system that allowed the possibility for a new form of leadership to find its way in.

Experiences of the u.lab learning and support infrastructure

While the content and practices within u.lab are creating powerful changes for participants, they also attributed much of this to the additional u.lab learning infrastructure (e.g. hubs, coaching circles, u.lab Scotland and u.lab global connections and networks).

There is no "set" way of participating in u.lab - it is experienced differently by all those taking part in it, particularly influenced by which parts of the learning and support infrastructure they choose to engage in. Some participants join local hubs, some coaching circles, some both and others complete only the online materials. Some participants, either individually or collectively, work their way through the course as it runs, some take more time to complete it or do it at other times of the year.

The purpose and value of hubs and coaching circles in changing ourselves.

Hubs, coaching circles and case clinics are a core part of the u.lab learning experience. A hub (gathering of participants) and coaching circle (practicing a u.lab tool called a case clinic with a group) are spaces for experiential learning with others. This is in contrast to the often more cerebral experience of the online course material. The value of the experiential learning by participants is high. Within coaching circles and hubs, lasting relationships have been formed at much deeper levels than the participants would have expected.

"I found it quite informing the more I did... the more I was connected to people that felt the same. I found it actually really inspiring. So, we weren't alone. I wasn't alone. I was sort of sitting on being on the outside thinking, is it just me that feels this way? There were lots of people in a similar space" Director, Business

An inspiring and unpredicted acupuncture point in the u.lab community has been the emergence of hub hosts. These are people who step up as community leaders, volunteering their time for the benefit of other participants and are instrumental to the success of the hub: bringing people together, organising the logistics of the meetings and, in many cases, facilitating the group.

u.lab & u.lab Scotland connections and networks.

As the previous section highlights, although u.lab is a MOOC, one of its most powerful impacts is through the creation of physical and virtual spaces for experiential and collaborative learning. u.lab provides, through the Presencing Institute website (https://presencing.org), the opportunity to make global connections by providing a virtual space for hubs and coaching circles and a channel to connect people with hubs in their local area. As a result of enabling these interpersonal connections, u.lab participants experience profound learning and opportunities to enhance their wellbeing. Participants have been happy to give up their time to offer mutual support and deepen the learning from the course in group settings. There is a spirit of altruism coming through.

u.lab Scotland (through the Holding Team) has been holding the space for building connections in Scotland since 2015 by promoting the u.lab courses and enabling participants to come together at live sessions and Scotland-wide gatherings (co-designed and delivered by the Holding team and supported with resources from the Scottish Government.) Participants have found that the u.lab Scotland network has been very helpful for making connections with others and "to find examples of how others are tackling similar problems".

Flexibility and depth of use of Theory U and its practices

The research has provided an opportunity to understand how the experiential learning from u.lab is being applied and of the flexibility and depth of use of Theory U practices. Analysis by Pomeroy & Oliver (2020, 2018) suggests that: participants in u.lab have learner readiness and value learning; participants were drawn to u.lab's theoretical/conceptual base which was new to many or put together in a novel way for others; it created significant changes in how participants saw themselves as being in the world, with intra-personal impact (knowing themselves better), relational impact (deep listening, greater empathising and understanding) and systemic impacts (new initiatives started, seeing and thinking about systems and issues). Although the themes from the 2016 cohort still apply to the 2017 cohort, they had matured in many ways: depth of personal journey; evolution of Theory U practice, challenges of applying Theory U.

Depth of personal journey

We found the depth of the personal journey varied in terms of the extent to which people actively applied the Theory. In other words, whether they simply utilise the tools and the framework; or whether they embrace and embark on a transformational personal journey. There are examples of participants using the u.lab tools without going deeply into the process, for example, without practicing mindfulness and embodiment or delving into the deep personal transformation. These participants are still able to create impact and transformational change, but it is unclear whether this is an indication of the flexibility of Theory U or a dilution or weak application of the approach. For some, the mindfulness and/or embodiment (which within u.lab is offered as the technique Social Presencing Theatre) are a step too far and conflict with their personal cultural and/or spiritual beliefs. Using co-sensing within organisations by taking the innovative tools (e.g. empathy and dialogue walks) is only as far as some are going. However, others have gone deeply into the U, immersing themselves in the theory and are taking the integrated package as a framework for their lives and their work.

The evolution of Theory U practice for repeated u.lab participants

When the main u.lab course finishes in December, u.lab participants continue to practice their learning from the course about Theory U and/or focus on their prototypes. Many then choose to re-join the following September to deepen their practice and learning. For those that have been u.lab alumni multiple times, the interviewees report that the experience of u.lab 2017 was different for them this time. For some, their intentions have been around deepening their learning. The alumni have been more specific with their intentions and are content to focus on specific areas of u.lab or Theory U without needing to revisit the whole course. In this way, alumni have been able to overcome the time commitment required to attend to the course in depth. Some of those that chose not participate the following year (mostly because of other commitments), took forward prototypes. Many have integrated Theory U with other approaches and practices.

Challenges to *"getting on wae"* applying Theory U

Pomeroy & Oliver (2020) identified that participating in u.lab gave people a degree of "action confidence"; in other words, they are more likely to take action than they were before. One participant describes it as helping him to *"get on wae it"* or to start putting what he'd learned into action more quickly. u.lab appears to help people overcome their perceived barriers (in particular, fear and cynicism) to taking action. However, it is important to note that the use of Theory U and application of its practices is not always readily accepted within organisations.

The language and culture associated with Theory U is problematic for some participants in a number of ways: they have found that some people do not want to engage with Theory U due to the language being quite academic and not easily aligning with local community dialect and culture. To create transformational change within organisations, participants have attempted to *"smuggle"* it into an organisation. For example, one participant explained the empathy walk to public health professionals (who needed to understand the reality of mental health and mobility issues for patients) as *"walking in other people's shoes"* while another participant called it *"shadowing."*

Evolving the emerging theory of change

As described in the section "Personal to Systemic", the 2016 data suggested an emerging theory of change. u.lab appeared to be giving practical and moral support in how to create the conditions for change, in an expanding circle of influence starting firstly with the participants themselves and increasing out towards impacting on a wider scale, as shown in figure 1.

The 2017 data supports these four concepts, but challenges the linearity of the emerging theory of change. There are a number of reasons for this:

First, although many participants say that they need to understand themselves first, before enacting change within communities or organisations, participants have described their learning journeys as iterative, suggesting a linear path of learning is unlikely. Even skilled practitioners need to continue their learning, to journal and adopt reflective practice. The personal journey is continual learning and self-enquiry.

Second, the experience of personal transformation and depth of immersion into Theory U appears to depend on an individual's willingness to engage. Also, many participants engage with u.lab when they encounter a time of change in their lives or at a time when they are ready to embrace the learning journey. More analysis needs to be done to investigate this, and especially the relationship of willingness to engage with tools that might be seen as more radical or personally challenging, such as Social Presencing Theatre, with the extent of personal transformation.

Third, the depth to which participants engage with the practice of Theory U is highly variable: for example, the depth of the presencing and co-sensing (i.e. self- and system-enquiry) and whether they embrace embodiment practices. Some participants chose to use just the practice tools (engaging much more through the "head"; having an open mind to new and often challenging data and information); whereas others have enacted a deeper journey, engaging through deep inner awareness (connecting with what is emerging through the "heart" – open to empathy - and "hand" – open to the will to take action).

Fourth, a good degree of existing self-awareness and experience of self-reflective practice also appears to make a difference in how deeply a participant goes using the Theory U approach and the resultant personal impact for them.

While all participants interviewed appear to have had some degree of transformation in their lives, the nature and depth of that change may be influenced in part to the points above. The personal journey is continual learning and self-enquiry with exploration of the inner self, even for skilled practitioners. The difficulty with any model such as this is that it is trying to depict something that is multi-faceted within two dimensions. There is no doubt people do move from their old self towards their highest future potential - the "Self" (Scharmer and Kaufer. 2013) with u.lab, implying directionality, but this does not necessarily imply linearity.

In figure 2 below, we have attempted to model an evolved theory of change. The circles reflect the areas of impact without implying linearity: greater understanding and ability to change self; more authentic, purposeful interactions with other; intentionally working with others to create supportive structures; and changing the system through iterative action.

The research has found that the emphasis on which circle(s) a participant experiences impact appears to be influenced by three contributing factors (although there are likely to be more):

- their entry point to u.lab – if they are at a transition point, are frustrated or there is a disruption in the current system
- their own "learner readiness" - some experience of self-reflective practice, willingness to learn, and
- the depth they take their practice to - applying just the tools (engaging the head) or integrating it to some level with their life, work and other existing practices (also engaging the heart and hand/will)

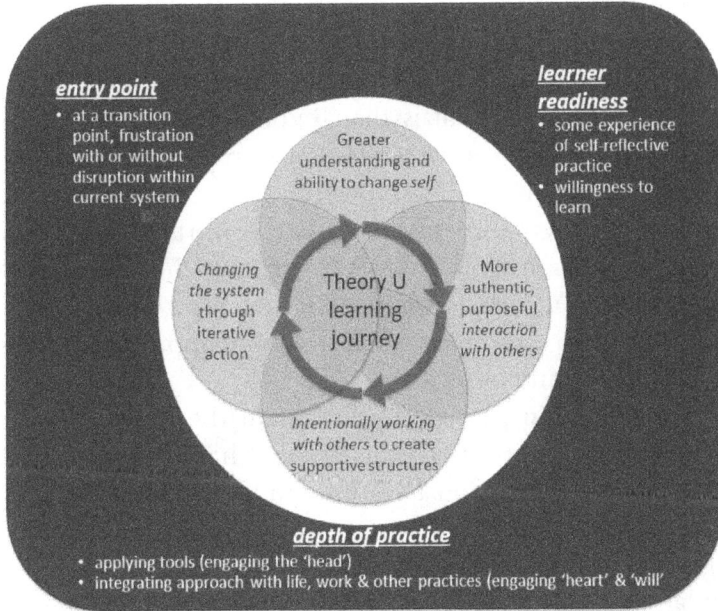

Figure 2. Updated theory of change model based on 2017 data (Winther and Oliver, 2018)

However, it is important to remember the purpose of the model at this stage: to aid in sense-making an individual's learning journey, rather than to categorise the journey. We find this interesting because we want to be able to demonstrate the change and also make sense of what has happened. An absolute and definitive model is not important, but as curious individuals we would like to be able to articulate and understand better what is going on.

The future of u.lab in Scotland

The impact of participating in the u.lab MOOC courses appears to be profound for many of the individuals involved. This positive impact enhances the participant's wellbeing, but also often affects positively the participant's lived experience and integrity, the quality of family and work life, their effectiveness as a change leader and their actions within their organisation or within society.

For those who are in a position of "learner readiness" for personal transformation, that is their experience of u.lab. Others, particularly experienced facilitators or change-makers, who may have participated in u.lab multiple times, talk about the impact of Theory U on their own practice. As an overarching theory of practice, or metatheory, Theory U becomes the *"mechanism"* to integrate other more specific theories or approaches into their lives or work, for example system thinking, appreciative inquiry, design thinking and others.

It has not been possible to document the many and varied innovations and innovative practices that have been initiated by u.lab Scotland participants as a result of their u.lab journeys (see Oliver and Deacon, 2017 for more) but we hope that this chapter has given a flavour of the creativity and impact they are having.

u.lab Scotland, as an overall convening space, may still operate largely as a collective sensing network. However, as stated in the introductory paragraphs, there is an argument to say that it is also acting as a "greenhouse for social innovations." It encompasses a mixture of meso collective presencing spaces such as the local hubs and coaching circles which are becoming better connected through things like the Hub Host Programme and Holding Team, each of which are also examples of collective presencing on a meso level.

The impact of u.lab in Scotland is still evolving as new participants join each year and alumni's experiences and learning permeate into their wider work. Currently, u.lab Scotland is a network supporting mainly personal transformation, but perhaps it could develop into a space where it facilitates collaborative prototyping and collective presencing on a national scale. Both of which may be especially important for helping participants to bring about system change, which is almost impossible to achieve as an individual.

To continue developing the greenhouse for collective presencing in Scotland, the following would be useful for u.lab Scotland:

- Continued development of strong local u.lab infrastructures and dedicated support for hub hosts in collaboration with the Presencing Institute's hub host support team impact.

- Greater emphasis on implementing the U process outwith u.lab - as u.lab practices embed, there is growing confidence in practitioners to implement the process in their work and organisations. There are already prototypes of varying scales being tested around the country.

- Continuing to prototype the ulabscot Holding Team - continue to learn and adapt the structure of the Holding Team particularly in line with the following point.

- Understand and promote coherence and alignment with other complementary approaches - u.lab incorporates and complements a lot of other change approaches, many of which have flourishing and embedded communities practicing in Scotland, such as Collective Leadership for Scotland, the Dialogue Community of Practice and improvement science. We hope to better understand and share the synergies of these practices.

As ulabscot continues to grow organically with increasing collective ownership and more coherence emerging around its activities, we will continue to explore and deepen our understanding of the impact of u.lab and of the conditions required to cultivate our ability for collective presencing on a national scale.

NB: The content of this chapter represent the authors' views alone and not that of the Scottish Government. The authors would like to thank Dr Svenja Meyerricks, in particular, from the Centre for Human Ecology for her support as a formal reviewer of this work.

References

Collective Leadership for Scotland (2020) *Who is Collective Leadership for Scotland?* Retrieved from: https://collectiveleadershipscotland.com/about-us/about-us/

Oliver, K. & Deacon, K. (2017) *u.lab Scotland: Sharing our Story 2015-2016*. Retrieved from: https://ulabscot.com/2017/06/29/from-scunnered-to-hopeful-ulabscot-impact-document/

Pomeroy, E. & Oliver. K. (2018) *Pushing the boundaries of self-directed learning: research findings from a study of u.lab participants in Scotland*, International Journal of Lifelong Education, 37:6, 719-733

Pomeroy, E. & Oliver. K. (2020) *Action Confidence as an Indicator of Transformative Change*
Forthcoming

Scharmer, O. (2003) *The Blindspot of Leadership*; Retrieved from: http://www.ottoscharmer.com/sites/default/files/2003_TheBlindSpot.pdf

Scharmer, O. (2009) *"Theory U: Leading from the future as it emerge"* San Francisco: Berrett-Koehler

Scharmer, O. & Kaufer, K. (2013) *"Leading from the Emerging Future"* Oakland, CA: Berrett-Koehler

Scharmer, C. O. (2018) *"Theory U: Core principles and applications."* Oakland, CA: Berrett-Koehler

Winther, A. & Oliver, K. (2018) *u.lab Scotland - Sharing our Story II.* (Unpublished manuscript) Workforce Scotland, Edinburgh

Winther, A., Jackman, V. & Oliver, K. (2019). *Massive Open Online Course u.lab: Creating Transformational Learning in Scotland.* In: Noble, M & Ross, C. Reclaiming the University for the Public Good. Cham: Palgrave Macmillan. 205-225.

CHAPTER 4

Italian u.lab Hubs:

A Study and Comparison of the Application and Adaptation of Theory U Principles and Practices to the Specificities of a Local Community of Learners in Rome and some other Italian Cities

Rachel Hentsch

Introduction

The following inquiry explores how the globally-resonating principles of Theory U have evolved locally through the u.lab community in Rome, Italy. It will examine the hosting prototypes and models created and adapted through hands-on experience by the Rome hosting team between August 2016 and October 2018, and the results obtained for each type of hosting experience. The Rome experience is compared with those of other Theory U-related hubs from different cities across Italy, in particular Brianza, Firenze, Livorno, Milano, and Trieste, and one virtual, online hub.

This inquiry is an attempt to map the various elements that

typically (or uniquely) make up a u.lab hub, and understand to what extent each of these elements-- the hosting team, the learner audience, the dynamics and relationships between team members, the programme structure, the location, the collective intention (or absence thereof) -- contribute to shaping and determining the vitality and longevity of a given hub.

We posit that prototyping is an ongoing and never-ending process. As both the workshops and hosting team configurations are in constant interactive evolution, this chapter does not expect nor attempt to reach any conclusions. It merely aims to capture and reflect upon a fragment of the journey that Theory U and its ramifications can imprint in terms of awakening a city's inhabitants to a new personal and collective potential, and a more carefully stewarded future for humankind and the planet.

This chapter also identifies factors that can contribute to the success of hub hosting so that similar efforts may better meet the needs of their audiences.

STORY: stages, iterations, and evolution of u.lab Hub Roma

Information around "u.lab Hub Roma" explored below includes materials from four founding members and data from digital social media spaces inhabited by the community. It also includes my personal experience as a u.lab Hub Roma participant in 2016, and my hub host experience with a team of seven other co-hosts from September 2017 until August 2018.

The Rome u.lab hub, as it existed until the time of writing (November 2018), has undergone five separate iterations since its inception in August 2016. Each subsequent new model has been based on experiences and conclusions drawn from the previous initiative, and has been adapted according to new externalities such as location constraints, member affluence, and team configuration.

Each model is examined according to the following points of comparison: hosting team configuration, team intention, team dynamics, learner audience, choice, and impact of venue and programme structure.

Hub Name and Period of Existence	Number of hub hosts in team	Enrolled	Hub participants at start	Hub participants at end	Location for hub activities	Paced alongside the u.lab 1x
u.lab Hub Roma 2016 2016 Sep-Dec	4	62	34	24 (-30%)	CFMT/Manageritalia	yes
u.lab Hub Roma Italiano 2017 Feb-Jun	4	78	53	19 (-64%)	CFMT/Manageritalia	no
u.lab Hub Roma 2017 2017 Sep-Dec	8	58	30	5 (-83%)	BIC Lazio	yes
UPractice Nov'17-Feb'18	5	10	7	4 (-43%)	Segni di Ripartenza	no
u.lab Hub Roma 2018 2018 Sep-Dec	4	11	8	n.a.	Manageritalia	yes

Table 1 – The chronological sequence of iterations and main characteristics of each phase of the Rome u.lab Hub

2016 SEP-DEC: u.lab Hub Roma 2016

A Hub Alongside the MOOC

The local u.lab Rome Hub was birthed in late summer 2016 with a bang, by four founding hub hosts with managerial, consultancy and coaching backgrounds, who came together and very quickly pulled together an action plan within a period of less than a month. The enormous global outreach, gratuitousness of the offering, and the unquestionable aspirational pull of the MIT brand were harnessed through the Rome hosting team's excellent ability to:

- Effectively communicate the Theory U vision through plugging into existing robust hub host networks, via mailing lists and social media channels;
- Provide well-located, spacious, and reputable venues for meetings. These included precincts of CFMT (Centro di Formazione Management del Terziario) near Termini sta-

tion, and Coaching Circles at Manageritalia Roma head-quarters, in the central area of Prati, and very near to public transport nodes.

This set of elements dovetailed right into a pre-existing local thirst for learning and innovation and generated considerable initial interest. In the context of a large city riddled with stuck energies and crippled by chronic logistical paralysis, the contamination potential was momentous and promising. Initial enrolments rolled in, and a good number of participants showed up at the beginning of the learning journey. The hosting team was fresh, motivated, and on its very own learning journey alongside the learner community. Subsequently, the global resonance of Theory U teachings and practices collided with the limitations of language, culture, and social background, with an overall decrease of about 30% in attendance between the launch of the learning journey and its closure (ref. Table 1). An attempt to create a solution that would better meet the unfulfilled needs of its members led to the second Rome Hub iteration, more closely tailored to the specificities of the local audience in terms of schedule, language, content delivery, and coaching.

2017 FEB-JUN: u.lab Hub Roma Italiano

u.lab Revisited - A Complete Customisation of the Learning Journey

At this point of its learning and facilitation journey, the hosting team was highly conscious of the inherent obstacles present in the plug-and-play format of the u.lab MOOC. They were also highly motivated to amplify their hosting capacity to share the Theory U learnings through a custom adaptation of the various programme elements, in response to the needs that had emerged from listening to their local audience. Thus was born the u.lab Hub Roma 2017 "Italian edition" with the same team of four hosting members, the same venue, and with the following new elements:

- A new evening schedule, outside of office hours, to better accommodate the constraints of those who were keen to participate but had not been able to do so during the MOOC live sessions; the latter, scheduled for 10 am Boston time, translated into 4 pm local Rome time;
- A set of videos subtitled in Italian: all relevant learning videos from the u.lab 1x online course underwent translation (the result of a goodwill effort on the part of the Italian u.lab community). A Youtube channel[2] held this collection of resources;
- translation from English to Italian of the digital tools and documents[3] provided by the Presencing Institute, including a customised version of the listening assessment tool.

Despite the effort to tailor the hub's offering to the necessities of its members, the pace of the learning journey still required a degree of commitment and continuity that was beyond what participants were able to sustain. This is reflected in the steep drop in participation, from 53 members at the beginning of the course, to 19 when the course ended, a decrease of well over half of the members (ref. Table 1). At this point the hosting group also began to run into some amount of internal friction, due to the toll the programme took on their time and energy, the load of running two u.lab cycles almost back-to-back, and the emergence of differing intentions around the hub vision and mission.

On the flip side, out of the course emerged a handful of passionate community members who were inspired enough to want to join forces with the hosting team and breathe life into the next iteration of the hub hosting journey.

2017 SEP-DEC: u.lab Hub Roma 2017

New Team, New Venue

The new team constellation of eight members comprised three veterans (the "old guard" from the previous two hub hosting experiences), and five new entries, of which I was one. We

71

convened over the summer of 2017 to discuss the future of the Rome hub, agree on a shared vision, and prepare for the session to be launched in mid-September, concurrently with the beginning of the 2017 edition of the u.lab online course on edX. The plan was that the hub would explore and develop three areas:

- capacity building (based on the MOOC programme in terms of content and pace),
- project consultancy (based on the members' range of personal expertise in various fields, ranging from coaching to teaching to management and entrepreneurship expertise), and
- research and development (experimental new methods and tools to be evolved).

Possible partnerships were explored and a sensing journey was undertaken by part of the hub team to establish a suitable location for the u.lab and coaching circle meetings. The aim was to possibly extend the u.lab reach to new audience segments and create consulting opportunities where Theory U might be applied. An agreement was struck with BIC Lazio (Business Innovation Centre), an organisation established by the Lazio Region for managing the regional network of incubators and promoting business development, for hosting the u.lab live sessions and coaching circles.

The u.lab cycle thus created was able to attract both new and old participants. Despite a promising start with 58 people enrolled, and the formation of three coaching circles, attendance soon dropped again as the programme unfolded. The usual barriers of time zones, language, pacing, and urban congestion took their toll on the community, with very few members reaching the finish line at the fourth and last live session. The location made it quite challenging to reach via public transport. Desired synergies with the BIC Lazio system did not occur: the latter acted merely as physical container space, and there was no cross-pollination despite the joint communication efforts.

The hosting team, however, was still enthusiastic, despite losing two of its eight members to other professional incumbencies (two of the novice hosts had underestimated the impact that hosting would entail).

A bespoke u.lab Hub Roma website and supporting online magazine series were created to facilitate the sharing of relevant information in a form that was as user-friendly as possible for an Italian public, which often found itself struggling with the structure and language of the contents on the official Presencing Institute website.

u.lab Hub Roma website and online magazine

As the MOOC cycle drew to a close, the remaining team of five hosts explored possibilities and ideas, including the project of creating a learning journey using elements of the u.lab course and reassembling them differently. This project included placing more emphasis on the tools and practices and looking for new ways to adapt the offering to the community. At this point, another (veteran) host stepped out of the team, due to accumulated hosting fatigue.

NOV 2017-FEB 2018: U.PRACTICE

A Practice-Based Independent Workshop Initiative

With the u.lab 2017 online course having reached its end, and therefore also the agreed collaboration time with BIC Lazio- - it was necessary to find a new hosting space. One of the team members from the remaining five was able, through professional connections, to secure a venue within a consulting firm, but this came at a cost-- albeit minimal. It meant that the project now needed to factor in some form of budgetary system and account- ing. Inevitably the topic of financial sustainability was raised, and became one of the ongoing topics within the hub hosting team. This led to more general debate about costs and returns, not only economically, but also in terms of time and personal commitment.

This fourth iteration of the Rome Hub started small-- with ten enrolments, seven initial participants-- and remained small, with four people showing up on the fifth and last session of a series of seminars that we named "UPractice" (ref. Table 1). Some of these were participants from previous u.lab cycles who wished to further their understanding and practice and stay connected with the local community of practitioners. The programme was designed around single Theory U practices, including stakehold- er interviews, coaching circles, prototyping-- with two-hour eve- ning sessions, minimal theoretical fundamentals, and maximum hands-on practice time. Members were asked to contribute a symbolic participation fee to help cover the hosting costs.

During this time, the hosting team convened twice, in-be- tween workshop sessions, to make space and apply Theory U practices -- presencing and 3-D sculpture -- to their journey as a team (ref. Fig.A). Team dynamics surfaced and were investigated. The ensuing feeling of cohesion was powerful. The overall picture and perception we all carried home from the half-day of presenc- ing spent together was one of great diversity and strong aspira- tions, but also of fragile equilibrium. The 3-D sculpture, created collectively with recycled materials, embodied joyous chaos and eclecticism, and a variety of rotating focal points that well represented the multi-faceted nature of our team and complex interstitial dynamics that held everything together as a whole.

Over time, one of the chronic and recurring weaknesses of the Rome Hub hosting team, as I have experienced it, has been an incapacity to create and maintain regular alignment meetings, necessary to fuel team spirit and energy, and dispel nascent tensions.

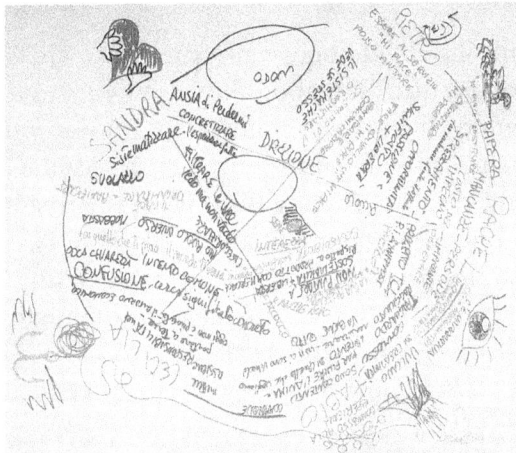

TEAM PRESENCING: HEART TALK

3-D SCULPTURE 1

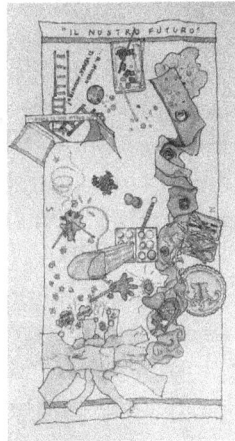

3-D SCULPTURE 2

Fig. A - Team Presencing Visuals

2018 SEP-DEC: u.lab Hub Roma 2018

A Return to the MOOC Format

When the u.lab 1x 2018 edition launched on 13th September 2018, the Rome Hub had, in the meantime, become fragmented, misaligned, and unprepared. Each host had gone off in their direction, the necessary team realignment had not taken place, and there was no longer a clear mission statement to unify team intention.

The mounting divide between some hosts who wished for a business-oriented direction and others who viewed the u.lab hub initiative as goodwill-based, resulted in an impromptu configuration: four members decided to return to the MOOC format and pace, and moved forward along the lines of the first hub iteration with a tiny audience of 8 participants (ref. Table 1).

I suppose the two big questions we were sitting with at that point were: "Where do we see ourselves in the next few years in terms of hosting? And: "Will we be able to bring new energies into the hub, to carry forward the work that needs to be done?"

METHOD: procedure and points of comparison

Case studies underpinned the research around hub hosting in other Italian cities. For the purpose of comparison, dialogues and a survey[4] were conducted with eleven different hub hosts from five different cities in Italy: Brianza, Firenze, Livorno, Milano, and Trieste-- plus one virtual, online hub. All hub hosts have been referring to the online Hub Host Guide[5] in varying degrees as a reference source for shaping and implementing their respective local initiatives. Many have been connecting online via remote weekly Hub Host Support video meetings on Zoom for dialoguing around specific hosting topics, best practices, and challenges[6].

Points of comparison, which helped to map analogies and divergences between the various hubs, included the following:

STATISTICAL DATA

- Year of hub foundation
- Number of hosts in the hub hosting team
- Number of participants in the hub during and after the online u.lab course cycle
- Hub programme (aligned with, or asynchronous to, MOOC yearly autumnal pace)
- Balance between theory and practice
- Average duration of hub meetings
- Participation rate over time and respective host hypotheses and interpretations of the variations
- Appreciation and impact of each type of Theory U tool or practice[7]
- Channels of communication used between hub hosts and participants
- Degree and type of use of social media in hub host communications
- Job opportunities directly or indirectly derived from hub hosting activities
- Overall degree of participation from members of the hub community
- Presence or absence of rules within the hub
- Management of levels of interest and commitment of hub participants
- Methods for collecting participant feedback

INTERPRETATIVE DATA

- Motivations, aspirations, and expectations of hub hosts
- Evolution of hub host roles over time
- Degree of enjoyment around the role of hosting a hub
- Future projections and intentions of hub hosts
- Perception of the degree of importance, in the success of a hub, of each of the following factors: location, hosting team, programme, participants, collective intention of hosting team, collective intention of participants

- Reflection on what could be done differently
- Reflection on the life-cycle of a hub

One point of comparison that was not taken into account during the period of research, but which has strongly emerged since completing the survey (and seems to greatly impact on the vitality of a hub), regards the internal cohesion of the hub hosting team. This includes the capacity for successfully harnessing or defusing conflicting internal energies.

RESULTS: comparing nine Italian hubs

Out of the nine different Italian hubs taken into consideration for the comparative study, the majority were founded in 2016, which was also the year in which u.lab Hub Roma was founded, and the u.lab MOOC saw its greatest global expansion. This included over 100,000 enrolled online learners from 185 countries around the world. Of these nine Italian hubs, one was no longer active, and two were only still partly active (at the time of writing). Hub sustenance over time appears to require more than merely aligning with the offerings of a freely accessible online programme. Yet, at the same time, the MOOC seems to be the minimum common denominator for a hub to assemble into a community.

The hosting teams typically count between two and five members, with teams of four being the most recurring formation[8]. This composition leads to a reflection on the balance between team diversity, agility, and cohesion. It is also interesting to note that four is the number of hub hosts that the Rome Hub started with, and has since returned to.

The number of participants in the hubs observed varies from six to over twenty, depending on the team's hosting capacity, venue, and communications management. Participation usually drops over time: over half of the hubs have witnessed a substantial decrease in attendance, in four of them participation appears to fluctuate, and only in one of the hubs has participation been sustainable.

Hub hosts report that some of the main factors that seem to cause a decrease in participation include: the absence of a regular meeting space, a regular schedule, tangible projects to work on, group stability, a reliable core team, host motivation, and connecting hub activities to people's professional sphere. Additional factors include: confusion generated by online programmes running in parallel (u.lab 1x and Transforming Capitalism Lab), lack of inter-hub collaboration within the same city, too many events, language barriers, challenges of the online format (enabling learner disconnect from the physical group), scheduling conflicts, and the fear on the part of learners of falling behind the overall learning pace, leading to abandonment.

Curiosity and interest levels amongst hub participants are always reportedly high but need to be maintained over time given numerous externalities and constraints of work and daily routine. It could also be framed better so that participants are made aware that Theory U teachings require a high degree of time, intellectual and emotional commitment.

Most hubs appear to have placed equal emphasis on the theory and practice of Theory U, with a clear understanding of the importance of applied, hands-on practice as being key to the effectiveness and impact of capacity building for learners.

Different hubs have adopted differing approaches to structuring and governing their communities, with some establishing and applying clear conduct and participation rules, while others go by an implicitly shared set of principles and intentions. Yet, others have left this aspect unaddressed.

The most appreciated and effective practices from Theory U are reportedly, and in decreasing order of preference: the Case Clinics, Social Presencing Theatre 4-D Mapping, Journaling and Stakeholder Interviews[9]. The u.lab MOOC creates a rhythm for the hubs to follow, although each hub then tailors its offerings to the specific requirements of its local community.

One promising observation is that despite an overall decrease in direct participation over time, hub members seem to tend to return in the long term to their hubs, or gravitate towards related initiatives within the hub's sphere of connections[10].

Five of the eleven hub hosts interviewed reported that their activity as hub hosts had created direct and indirect new work opportunities, both paid and voluntary. These include seminar speaking opportunities, training course offerings, communal initiatives, social community projects, socio-cultural immigration integration workshops, and private consultancy projects.

When asked about what motivated them to create a hub, hub hosts listed the following reasons: a desire to share and spread Theory U, the joy of shared and participative learning, the possibility of building together, the desire to impact the community, the aspiration to bring small or large changes to one's own city. Were these aspirations met? The results and feelings are definitely mixed. Some hub hosts report a sense of joy and gratification, while many voices have expressed frustration, fatigue, and disappointing outcomes concerning their initial expectations.

Language used to describe the aspects of hub hosting that have brought hub hosts most joy and satisfaction include: human connection, discovery, projects, feeling of being in a space of trust, unlocking potential, experiencing presencing, like sowing seeds, usefulness, learning, diversity, dialogue, contributing, growth, relationships, and evolution.

The role of each hub host has evolved, with varying phases and degrees of involvement, according to inner motivations, external constraints, and overall team and community dynamics. In their approach to their future roles as hosts, about one-quarter of those I have spoken to do not see themselves continuing as hub hosts at all.

CONCLUSIONS: the vitality and longevity of a hub

When I began my investigation, one of my objectives was to comprehend better why some hubs have tended to grow more than others, and which factors might influence this evolution the most. To do so, I set out to compare the composition and development of different hubs across Italy, to evaluate common traits and divergences in terms of their approach to theoretical learning and practical application, to see whether there is a correlation between this distribution, and participant engagement levels.

In hindsight, I might reframe the question slightly different-ly: "are hubs subject to a natural lifespan or physiological cycle of "x" years, whereby they will naturally die unless they absorb new elements and morph into a different system?" There seems to be an evident correlation between time elapsed, hosting fatigue, a decrease in member participation, and overall loss of momen-tum. All the data that has been gathered points in that direction. This leads me to wonder whether the energy for a host comes mostly from a place of learning, rather than teaching? Perhaps hosts are at their highest point of energy when they immerse themselves as part of the journey of discovery? So the question then becomes: how can we facilitate a community, and sustain a space, of joyful learning and growth?

Also, what emerged strongly from the conversations enter-tained with other hub hosts was the importance of setting the right expectations around the hub hosting role, right from the beginning. There is something to be said about the disappoint-ment that comes with being attached to outcomes, which is the opposite of the joy experienced by letting oneself be surprised. This was suddenly brought home to me when a few hosts shared with me their bitterness at having created a communications campaign with an estimated reach of some two thousand, yet had actually succeeded in convening only a dozen participants. Numerically speaking, that is a disappointing 6% "conversion rate." So what is it that we are really aiming for? More partici-pants? Or is it perhaps more about the quality of the holding space and interaction that we are able to foster and nurture?

Hub hosting must be approached with an open mind, heart, and will-- towards what is wanting to emerge, and not necessarily to what we, as hub hosts, believe we want to see.

This, in turn brings me to a final reflection about the impor-tance of not losing sight of the U journey as hub hosts. We too must "bend back the beam of observation"[11] onto ourselves and our team system, in a sort of meta U-process. To better serve the mission of creating more wellbeing for all, we must first remem-ber to look at ourselves and our impact in terms of how we are listening, observing, and what we are thereby generating. It is all too easy to forget ourselves in the busy-ness of doing, to lose the very awareness and wonderment that struck us when we first encountered Theory U.

RESOURCESBelow are a couple of resources-- a pre-hub-hosting checklist and a satisfaction survey template-- that I hope might provide some useful tools for currently active or future hub hosts.

PRE-HUB HOSTING CHECKLIST

Here is a checklist with some key points you might want to consider when preparing to host a hub:

- Hosting Team
  - o Roles
  - o Aspirations
  - o Background in Theory U
  - o Networks

- Learner audience
  - o Background
  - o Culture
  - o Language
  - o Schedule / time availability

- Location / venue:
  - o Accessibility?
  - o Capacity?
  - o Sustainability?

- Team curation: regular checking in and alignment

- Designing the journey – programme structure and timing:
  - o alongside the MOOC or
  - o self-paced cohort?

- Participant motivation: designing for endurance with interventions to help sustain participation numbers

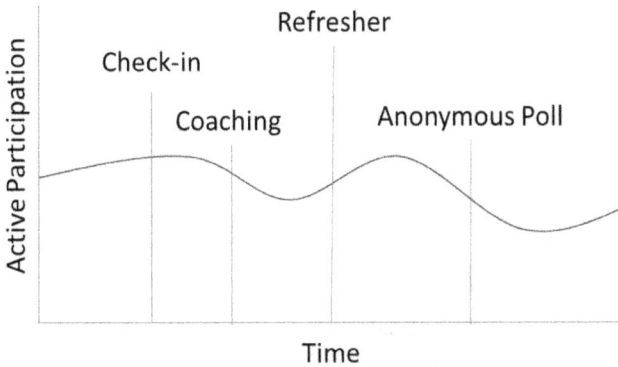

- Team motivation: make sure to include presencing practices (case clinics, 3-D sculpting)
- Connecting with other hub hosts: sharing difficulties and best practices

SATISFACTION SURVEY

It is good practice for hub hosts to conduct a satisfaction survey in order to improve their approach for the next time. Some questions you might want to ask your learners could be:

- Was the location used practical? Pleasant?
- Was the learning journey too slow? Too fast?
- Was it useful to be part of a cohort?
- Did you find the communications to be clear and helpful?
- Which of the Theory U practices was for you the most impactful?
- Was there a good balance between theory and practice?
- Would you like to stay connected with the learning community?
- Were you able to apply the learnings to your work? To

your life?

- Would you consider taking u.lab again?
- Would you be interested in helping to host a hub, or create a new one?
- Would you recommend u.lab to your family, your friends, your colleagues?
- What worked/didn't work/could be improved?

References

Arts, J. & Fransen, S. (2017). *Hub Host Guide*. Retrieved from https://juliearts.gitbooks.io/hubhostguide/content/welcome.html

Hentsch, R. (2018). Survey of Italian Hub Hosts from Brianza, Firenze, Livorno, Milano,

Trieste, Rome and virtual. Retrieved from https://drive.google.com/file/d/1fo0zsyrWqUh2osc1I4UKMn9poEw_SxP0/view?usp=sharing

Presencing Institute website, Resources. Retrieved from https://www.presencing.org/#/resource/tools

Scharmer, C.O. (2018). *The Essentials of Theory U - Core Principles and Applications*.

Oakland: Berrett:Koehler Publishers, Inc.

u.lab Hub Roma & u.lab Hubs Italy. (2017) Youtube channel. Retrieved from https://www.youtube.com/channel/UCbvJpH-TC-YMG36pmiX5EUw/videos

Mentions

- Sincere thanks to my hub co-hosts for the experience of co-sensing and co-creating together: Daria Marani Toro, Paolo Fedi, Pietro Bonato, Fabio Cortese, Cecilia Toni Saracini and Sandra Vaudagna
- Deep appreciation for their kind collaboration in sharing their thoughts and insights as hub hosts for the purposes of my research: Paolo Fedi, Daria Marani Toro, Elena Cobez, Marina Seghetti, Susan George, Enrico Maria Milič, Sandra Ermacora, Alessandra Zagli, Adriana Dell'Arte, Barbara Principi and Daniela Veneri
- Special thanks to my Eva Pomeroy, Presencing Institute colleague and friend, for the comments and suggestions contributed on my first draft

CHAPTER 5

Tending the Social Field in Higher Education

Eva Pomeroy and Nicolo Francesco Bernardi

Introduction

Scharmer (2017) describes the future of education – *4.0 Education* - as co-creative and innovation-centric, with a distinct new role for the learner and educator (see the Matrix of Educational Evolution below). A key feature of education 4.0 is that learning does not come from a designated teacher. Instead, learning is sourced *from the entire social field* (Scharmer, 2017). If the source of learning is the social field, then the central question of concern for the educator is how to cultivate the kind of social field that gives rise to meaningful learning.

Stage	Learner	Educator	Relationship	Organization	Governance
1.0: Input & Authority-Centric	Passive Recipient	Authoritarian	Downloading (Teacher Centric)	Centralized, Closed	Machine Bureaucracy: No Feedback Loop
2.0: Output & Efficiency-Centric	Memorizing Input	Expert	Testing (Input-Output)	De-centralized, Less Closed	Professional Bureaucracy: Slow Feedback Loop
3.0: Outcome & User-Centric	Explore New Questions	Facilitator	Dialogic	Networked, Opening	Learning System: Institutionalized Feedback Loop
4.0: Co-creative & Eco-System-Centric	Co-sense and Shape The Future	Midwife: Generative Coaching	Co-creative	Eco-system, Breathing In, Breathing Out	Innovation Eco-System: Shared Awareness of the Whole

Figure 1.0. Matrix of Educational Evolution (Scharmer, 2017)

The emergence of u.lab – the online-to-offline MOOC offering based on Theory U (Scharmer 2016, 2018; Scharmer & Kaufer, 2013) – offers the opportunity to 'explore through doing' the principles and properties of 4.0 Education. In this paper we share such an exploration in the context of higher education by reporting and reflecting on our experiences hosting the Concordia U.lab Social Innovation Hub from 2016 to 2019.

The original vision for the Concordia U.lab Social Innovation Hub was to create a learning space where the university community and the local community could come together to engage collectively in a mindfulness-based process of change and social innovation. More explicitly, we used the u.lab process and the Hub format to:

- bring together undergraduate and graduate students, faculty, staff and members of the local community as co-learners.
- embody Sharmer's conceptualization of education as a process of learning in direct contact with the community ("breathing in") to then go into the world and be in ser-

vice of such community ("breathing out"; Scharmer, 2019)

- support a deep cycle of learning that connects personal transformation to systems change.
- create a collectively-sourced learning community where members contribute to the process in a variety of ways, including in the design, facilitation and evaluation of the experience.

The core principle guiding the design of the Hub was to find the minimal structure that allows people to self-organize in meaningful ways. Thus, our intention in hosting the Hub was to design and hold a process that supports people's natural capacity for self-directed learning, within an emergent transformative learning context.

U.lab in the Context of Higher Education

u.lab exists at the convergence of two streams of innovation in higher education. The first is the move, over the past several decades, away from didactic models of teaching and learning toward those that a) recognize learner agency and b) view transformative learning as the pedagogical aim of adult education. Writing at the end of the last century, learning theorist John Heron commented on the "radical change" in higher and adult education taking place on both a theoretical and practical level. He commented, "[T]he basic and very simple premise of this change is that student learning is necessarily self-directed: it rests on the autonomous exercise of intelligence, choice, and interest" (Heron, 1989, p. 12). Twenty years later, we see abundant evidence of this radical change, one that shifts us from a consumption model, where knowledge is ingested for the purpose of reproduction, to one that is more holistic and instead focuses on empowering individuals to "become capable and honorable scholars, citizens and human beings" (Berger, Woodfin and Vilen, 2016, p. 5). The new emphasis reflects growth in and the emergence of domains of study and practice including community-engaged learning, transformative learning, self-directed learning,

action learning, design-based learning, and cooperative education, amongst others (Bache, 2008; Berger, Woodfin & Vilen,
2016; Burgess, 2012; Hart, 2004; Illeris, 2017; Merriam, 2001;
Merriam & Bierema, 2013; Mezirow, 2000; O'Sullivan & Taylor,
2004; Taylor & Cranton, 2012; Tennant, 2006).

The second, equally disruptive, innovation in education has
been brought on by technological advances: online learning.
Technology has enabled the creation and growth of e-learning,
blended learning, and flipped classrooms, for example. Perhaps
the most disruptive of the online learning spaces is the MOOC
(massive, open, online course), widely acknowledged in the literature as a disruptive force in higher education (Flynn, 2013; Robertson & de Aquino, 2015; Viehland, 2014; *see* Al-Imarah &
Shields, 2018 *for debate about the nature of this disruption*).

Pedagogically, u.lab aims to "put learners in the driver's seat
of learning" (Scharmer, 2015), reflecting the trend toward self-directed learning. Its intention has also been explicitly transformative, as implied in the course's original subtitle – Transforming
Business, Society, and Self. U.lab is also a MOOC, which means
that the learning process is radically accessible – essentially available to anyone with access to the internet. As such, u.lab leverages
new educational technology to amplify the pedagogical revolution in adult learning by making social technology for transformative learning available on a global scale. Thus far, over 160,000
people across 185 countries have participated in u.lab (www.pres-
encing.org).

Social fields, containers, and holding spaces

If the source of learning is the social field, we need to give
some consideration to the question: what is the social field? In
Theory U, the social field is a way of understanding collectives, or
social systems, that includes both their observable qualities, and
those that are less visible. By definition the unseen dimensions of
a collective are not possible to observe. Instead, they need to be
experienced. The social field, then, is a view of the social system
that takes into account both the outside view (the third-person)

and the experience within (the first- and second- person views). It places a particular emphasis on, "*the source conditions* that give rise to patterns of thinking, conversing, and organizing, which in turn produce practical results" (Scharmer, Pomeroy & Kaufer, 2021, p. 3). In other words, taking a social field perspective means paying attention to the quality of the collective space, the source of that quality, and its potential as a generative force.

This notion of the field in Theory U draws from Isaacs' earlier work. Isaacs (1999) describes the field as, "the quality of shared meaning and energy that can emerge among a group of people" (p. 242). He comments further,

> We cannot manufacture a "field". But we can create conditions under which a rich field for interaction is more likely to appear. These conditions make up what we have called the *container* for dialogue, in which deep and transformative listening becomes possible. You cannot work "on" a field. But you can create a "container".

Creating such containers is integral to the Theory U process. Scharmer (2018) states, "profound change happens in places, and this place needs to be intentionally created" (p. 102). He describes the container as, "the holding space that shapes and cultivates the web of relationships (Scharmer, 2018, p. 81-82). In 4.0 Education, the role of the educator is primarily about cultivating a holding space where transformative learning can take place.

The importance of the holding space in transformational work can be traced back to British psychoanalyst Donald Winnicott, who referred to "space" as a psycho-emotional construct where individuals and groups' development unfolds. Winnicott referred to "potential space" or "transitional space" as "the area that is allowed to the infant between primary creativity and objective perception based on reality-testing" (Winnicott, 1982, pp. 239-240). The potential space and the transitional objects that populate it provide a playground that exists between pure imagination and the objective world, where futures can be envisioned, possibilities entertained, past comforts recalled, and uncertainties managed. Winnicott also referred to "holding" as a key feature of a relationship that fosters an individual's positive exploration of such transitional space. "Holding" literally refers to a mother's holding her baby in her arms, and metaphorically to many other expressions of care offered by the parent. Although this notion of development and holding are based in childhood, Winnicott saw them as paradigmatic for later life. As the individual grows, the holding environment expands to include the father, the family, and all the various groups and experiences in which the person participates. The quality of such holding, or "the sense in which it engenders basic trust in one's surroundings, determines the extent to which the person can become a genuine, creative individual" (Van Buskirk & McGrath, 1999, p. 808).

The concept of holding space was adopted by psychoanalysis to refer to the therapist's attempt to create a safe emotional space in which the patient can experience and integrate a wide range of difficult emotions (Yogev, 2008). From psychoanalysis, the "holding" metaphor was adopted in new contexts such as education, particularly transformative and self-directed learning. Here, 'holding space' refers to features of the context that facilitate these types of learning, such as the presence of credible role models and the creation of a non-threatening learning environment, where participants feel free to experiment with what they are learning without feeling the threat of failure (Manz, 1991).

Scharmer (2016) provides some nuance to the dynamics of the relationship between transformation and holding space, "profound shifts in small groups tend to happen when the courage of risk-taking is supported by a holding space of deep listening with unconditional love" (Scharmer, 2016, p. 246). Bird (2018, p.37) also describes the connection between the quality of the holding space and the interactions that happen within it. She states,

> The weakness or strength of the container determines the likelihood of detrimental or successful conversation, for harmful or loving relations, for destructive or productive environments, for ill- or well-being.

Previous research into participants' experience of u.lab found that part of the effectiveness of the u.lab learning process is that it offers two levels of holding space – one global and one local (Pomeroy & Oliver, 2018). On the global level, the core u.lab team, comprised of Otto Scharmer and his direct collaborators, holds the process through the design and delivery of the content, as well as through online interaction. At the local level, participants are encouraged and supported to create their own learning spaces in the form of hubs, or "place-based local communities of change" (Presencing Institute, 2015). The Concordia U.lab Social Innovation Hub was one such place-based hub.

The Concordia U.lab Social Innovation Hub

The Concordia U.lab Social Innovation Hub was held annually in the autumn term each year from 2016 to 2019. The Hub was held by a hub host team made up of 3-4 people including a faculty member (first author) and graduate students (including second author). In two of the four years, the team included an undergraduate student and one year a member of the community joined the core holding team. Each week the Hub would come together to move through the u.lab process as a learning community. Initially the group met for nine weeks, eventually increasing to eleven.

The composition of the group varied from year to year, however approximately one-third of each cohort was made up of undergraduate students participating as part of the for-credit course *Leadership, Change and Social Innovation*. Another third came from other groups within the university – graduate students, staff and faculty. The final third were members of the local community, including people working at and leading community organizations, social entrepreneurs, coaches/consultants and other citizens.

In the months leading up the Hub, the host team engaged in outreach both in the university and in the local community, and held three two-hour "taster" sessions to introduce people to the u.lab process and the Hub.

Once u.lab began in mid-September, participants were asked to review the online material in their own time and at their own pace and the weekly in-person sessions were used for peer coaching, dialogue, and reflection exercises relevant to the course. One of the key practices in u.lab is the Coaching Circle. Small groups of 5-6 people met regularly during the hub to 'work' with the case of one group member. The group followed a structured process that allowed the case giver to share a current situation in which they are a key player and where gaining insight in the present moment would make a big difference moving forward (https://www.presencing.org/resource/tools/case-clinic-desc). The group members then act as coaches and provide feedback in non-traditional forms, such as metaphor, feeling, drawing and gesture.

Gatherings lasted 2 ½ to 3 hours. Although each session was different, the format below is representative of the process:

9:30-10:00	Session opening, including some form of check-in.
10:00-11:00	Large group exercise around a theme (such as co-initiating or prototyping), Open Space or small group dialogue
11:00-12:15	Coaching circles
12:15-12:30	Closing

Figure 2.0 Gathering Schedule

At four points during the course, the core u.lab team hosted a live session broadcast from MIT, which we would watch as a Hub, followed by dialogue groups around the themes raised in the live session. In those weeks, we did not hold coaching circles. We convened once again in mid-December each year to reconnect, watch the final live session and share progress on initiatives.

As a hub-team, we shared the responsibility for organizing, hosting, designing, and facilitating the Hub. Further, we invited and indeed requested that members contribute in any way that they were able, for example helping to set up and clear up the space, bringing snacks, contributing to the evaluation and design of the sessions, facilitate, and document the experience through photos, videos and blogs (*see* Figure 3).

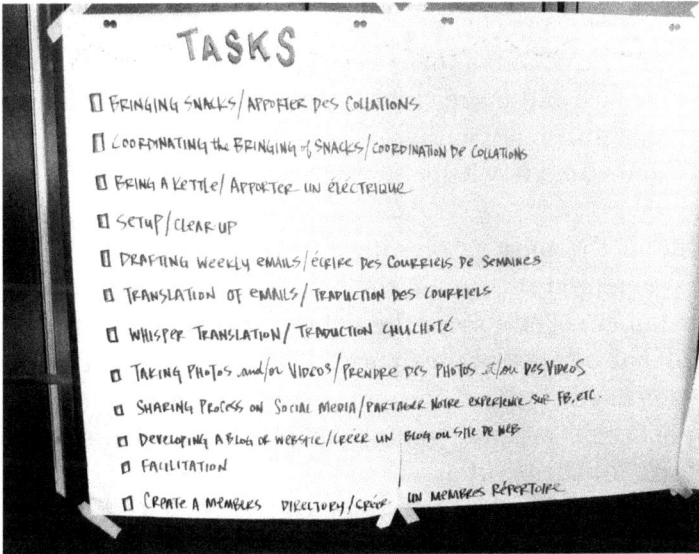

Figure 3.0 Task List

The size of the Hub varied from year to year, with some attrition during the process each year. In the initial two years, approximately 30-45 people came together each week, growing to 45-55 in the latter years.

Inquiry Framework

The Concordia U.lab Social Innovation Hub was a new endeavor and an entirely new kind of university classroom for us. In the first year of the hub, the host team met after each session to debrief and design the following week's session. At the end of the first year, we realized that our weekly debrief would benefit from more structure, so we designed an inquiry process that evolved over the subsequent three years. Our aim was to engage in a consistent, intentional inquiry into the experience that would:

- help us better understand participants' and our own personal experience of the learning space
- sense into the evolution of the learning community
- respond effectively as facilitators to the emerging needs and direction of the collective
- surface and make visible a new way of being and learning in a university setting
- generate knowledge that serves practice

One of the most interesting features of the weekly inquiry process emerged early on in the first year of the Hub. A community member asked to join the debrief session. His input was so helpful that we opened the debriefs to the whole Hub community and continued to do so from that point onward. On any given week, between two and ten Hub community members joined the host team for the debrief.

We selected six reflection questions to guide our debrief and asked these questions of ourselves consistently every week. When the session was over, the hub host team and any hub members interested in participating found a space in the gathering room and posted our inquiry questions on the wall. Some questions focused directly on evaluating the session that just took place, others focused on developing our understanding of the nature of the experience and what was emerging from it, and one focused explicitly on next-step action. Over the period 2017-2019, our intention for the hub clarified and this can be seen reflected in the evolution of our inquiry questions over time.

2017	2018	2019
• Where did we shine? • What was not in service? • What are we learning? • What is our sense of our collective place in the journey? • What questions are we asking? • What do we need to do next?	• What is being developed? i.e. What is the nature of the learning community being developed and what are its implications for higher education? • Where did we shine? • What was not in service? • What is our sense of our collective place in the journey? • What questions are we asking? • What do we need to do next?	• What is being developed and what is its implication for higher education? • Where did we shine? • What was not in service? • What is our sense of the collective and our place in the journey? • What questions are we asking?

Figure 4.0 Evolution of Inquiry

Just as our intention evolved, so did our inquiry process. In reflecting on our 2017 inquiry experience, we were drawn to developmental evaluation, with its emphasis on generating framing questions and its particular focus on the overarching question, *what is being developed?* (Patton, 2011, p. 229). Patton describes the appropriateness of this approach for complex situations. He states, "Developmental evaluation tracks and attempts to make sense of what emerges under conditions of complexity, documenting and interpreting the dynamics, interactions, and interdependencies that occur as innovations unfold" (Patton, 2011, p.7). We found developmental evaluation provides a framework that offers enough consistency for us to see developmental patterns over time, with enough flexibility to surface and respond to emergence in a new and innovative learning context. The question 'what is being developed' surfaces in 2018 and is refined the following year.

In addition, we added a new element to the inquiry process to help us meet our two primary tasks - to engage in generative reflection dialogue and to design the session for the following week - within the allocated time frame. When we gathered, we would first take 5 minutes to journal individually in response to the inquiry questions. This helped us to remain focused on our purpose and intention – to sense into the collective and the evolving learning journey. After that point, we would engage in open dialogue for half of our remaining time, ensuring we touched on all of the inquiry questions. The final segment of debrief focused on sketching a design for the next session based on our sensing into the needs, dynamic and evolution of the collective. The structured inquiry process supported the iterative cycle from action to reflection and back to action, generating greater consciousness and understanding of the Hub experience as it unfolded.

Holding Emergent Learning Spaces

To reflect on and share our learning about holding an emergent, transformative learning space, we draw on our weekly debrief records. The comments that serve as our data were generated in weekly debrief and design conversations between the hub hosts and participating hub members. Often those who chose to participate were members of the local community or graduate students. Occasionally, undergraduate students would also participate. We treat the data as a record of our collective reflection and, therefore, do not differentiate contributions of Hub members from contributions of Hub Hosts.

In our effort to cultivate a generative social field, three aspects of the experience held our attention:

- Course content
- Structure and session design
- The emotional-psychological space

The *content* shaping the learning process was largely provided by u.lab. It included both conceptual input and processes, and focused on skill or capacity-building. This kind of learning was highly valued by Hub members who commented on learning skills such as deep listening, collaboration, leadership and self-awareness, as well as learning tools and practices deemed useful to engage as agents of social change. Often these surfaced in response to the question: *what is being developed?*

Concrete tools, in this case body awareness and social presencing theatre (SPT), that draw upon competences and ways of being that are usually left out in higher education.
how and when to lead and when not.
People are not just learning about the world, about saying the right thing, but people are learning how to listen to another person.
soft skills, stillness, deep listening, self-awareness.
A new methodology of research, of individual search, a way of deciding, and to design projects; we are learning at the edge, we are learning and researching as we go, like in action research.

Working with already-established content allowed us to focus on the other two dimensions shaping the learning space: structure & session design and the emotional-psychological space. Although more attention has been paid to these dimensions in higher education in recent years, in many university classrooms they remain overshadowed by an emphasis on content delivery.

As mentioned, in thinking about the *structure and design* of each weekly session, our core design principle was to find the minimal structure that allows people to self-organize in meaningful ways. As such, we paid a great deal of attention to the structure and design of the weekly sessions and the extent to which they supported this kind of self-directed, transformative learning.

Integral to our consideration of structure was our concern for the *emotional-psychological space* of the Hub. This consideration was grounded in an understanding that transformational learning experiences are often characterized by a level of discomfort (Brendel & Cornett-Murtada, 2018; Conklin, Kyle & Robertson, 2012; Illeris, 2017; Mezirow, 2000). As psychologist Carl Rogers commented, "any significant learning involves a certain amount of pain" (in Illeris, 2017, p 43). Knowing we were working with a transformative learning process, we needed to be attuned and responsive to the emotional-psychological dimension of the learning experience.

Below we share our reflections on key aspects of holding the emergent learning space where the structural and emotional-psychological dimensions intersect: responsiveness, holding discomfort, flexible structures, sufficient stability and the quality of attention.

Responsiveness

A key aspect of supporting the holding space was to remain in contact with, and responsive to, the week-to-week experiences of the community. Each week we asked, "what is our sense of our collective place in the journey" and used this as a point of departure for planning the next session.

> right now we have a sense that the collective is not feeling like a collective yet, so we are going for this kind of soft closure that does not force an identity of the group.
>
> sense the energy shifted and there is a desire for speed; we need to seek ways to help people slow down.

When we were unable to connect with the collective experience, for example after a Social Presencing Theatre session held by an invited facilitator, it was a source of distress.

> What can we find out about how today went: Are people connecting the dots? Are they following the material on-line and putting it into context? We are doing a lot of stuff but is it making sense and is it perceived as coherent and relevant for people?

Connecting with our sense of the collective each week was the core practice that enabled us to hold the space for a generative social field to emerge. We will return to this point in our discussion.

Holding discomfort

The theme of discomfort did surface at times in the weekly debriefs. The source of this discomfort varied. In the early years, the structure of the classroom itself was unsettling for some learners. The discomfort associated with a new learning process and environment, especially for students enrolled in the course, surfaced through the theme of chaos – either real or perceived – and we saw ourselves as sitting on the edge of chaos and order.

> Our sense of the collective is that, on the one hand, we are forming, gelling, crystallizing and, on the other, we are in chaos.
>
> There is still a sense of chaos/uncertainty/feeling unsettled; we seem to be holding that space.

There was also some discomfort with the transformational nature of the learning process itself.

> I am stepping out of my comfort zone.
>
> The tricky thing here is that we are learning about this process at the same time as trying to apply it. This is not easy. I feel exhausted. It is a high demand. I need to know in which piece I am, am I in the learning, or in the doing.

Here for me it is more about learning, it is too much to have the doing happening at the same time.

The 'chaos' here seems to be more about the individuals in the hub feeling unsettled by the process rather than chaos due to context. Response to this seems to be simply holding or 'being with' the chaos, rather than acting on it.

Our sense holding this space was that the discomfort that could be experienced by Hub members has two aspects or sources. One was the discomfort or unsettledness inherent to transformative learning. In this case, it felt important to be aware of individuals' experiences and to continue to hold the process steadily, understanding that the experience of discomfort was integral to the learning. The other sense of discomfort, often connected to the word 'chaos' seems to imply that contextual factors may contribute unnecessarily to learners' discomfort, and that we needed to act on them. As a host team, we needed to discern the nature of the discomfort we sensed in order to respond effectively. We discuss this further below in our consideration of *sufficient stability*.

Flexible structures

As mentioned, we aimed to find the minimal structure that allowed people to self-organize in meaningful ways. Working with a minimal structure in a way that was responsive to learners' needs meant shifting along a spectrum from more structured design to less structured design in response to the hubs' development and the participants' needs. We often responded to these perceived needs through the session design. Consider the following from the launch day debrief.

Need to continue to have a very clear organization/structure to handle the large number of participants:

This occurred at a time when the group was at its largest and the collective could feel chaotic. The need for clarity of process seemed paramount. Later in the process, we were able to see how this need shifted.

One of the ways in which this structure changed as the needs of the community did was in developing structures that could flex to meet different and sometimes diverging needs. At times, this meant offering different options simultaneously, such as journaling, small group dialogue and larger group process. After one such session, Hub members commented:

> We are respecting each other deeply by diverging. It's counter-intuitive but diverging brings us more a sense of a collective.
>
> Having different options meant I could attend to my own needs but not disconnect; can be true to myself and still engage (like, not choosing to go off for a coffee even though that would have been an option).

One member described this kind of structure as offering the opportunity to be "alone together".

Closely related to the question of structure was the issue of framing. How much framing was needed before moving into process was a near-constant question in the debriefs. Sometimes the answer was unclear.

> Do people need more framing in terms of u.lab being a process that is all about *not jumping into action right away, but taking the time to observe and reflect?*
>
> How much framing do we need to give? I mean we could go in every single explanation and give tons of framing. We also need to let people have their experience, and learn at their pace and discover where they are as they go. What kind and quantity of framing is needed for what things?

Often, the feedback from Hub members was that new processes needed more framing rather than less and, over time, our approach to framing key processes evolved. The most concrete manifestation of this was the way in which we set up the Coaching

Circles. In the early years, we described the process briefly and provided a written handout for groups to follow. This evolved to a lengthier description with examples the following year. Most recently, we dedicated a significant part of the session where Coaching Circles were introduced to frame them and included a 'fishbowl' demonstration of the process which allowed the community to watch a condensed version of the process in action. We commented:

> After the Fishbowl, it felt smoother in circles. Great questions and comments came after it – they 'got it'.

Having found the demonstration of the Coaching Circles to be so effective, we repeated the process when preparing the group to move into another key exercise, 3D Mapping. We learned that when inviting people into learning modalities that differ significantly from traditional higher education settings, dedicating sufficient time to the framing of processes, including a demonstration, helped to foster greater capacity in the groups for engaging in those modalities. The result was that the groups were more autonomous and found the processes more effective and satisfying.

For processes that were less complex, we found they didn't need as much time for framing. However, the quality of the framing was brought to our attention. We began to sense that greater 'focus' was important and that this was particularly true when the structure of the process itself was quite open. This became clear to us early on when we experimented with 'seeding' an open space dialogue by asking Hub members to journal about the kind of conversation they would like to have before sharing these ideas in the group. After this experience we observed:

> Someone commented that the open space was focused, and that this was helpful. This highlights a nuance: tight focus helps to strengthen the container. That is different than tight structure.

Thus, a key aspect of holding emergent space is to be able to adapt the structure and framing of the learning experience along a spectrum from minimal to significant. Finding the right place on the spectrum is determined by a. the complexity of the learning process or exercise and b. the stage of development or the state of the learning community. As the learning community grows and matures, it is able to manage greater autonomy and needs less structure. Framing key processes well at the outset helps to foster this autonomy.

Sufficient Stability

In one year (2017), participants seemed to experience more significant discomfort than in the others. Not only did the faculty Hub Host need to step away from the process for several weeks, but the Hub did not have a permanent home. We used five different spaces over 10 weeks. While this could be an interesting feature of the experience, and was for some, for many the change of space was unsettling. This highlighted the impact of the physical space on the experience, perhaps particularly in an emergent learning environment.

> Role of physical space - noise, crowded, need chairs without arms
>
> Impressive the significance of the space. The kind of space. Today, in the Centre for Teaching and Learning, it was great.
>
> Changing spaces was not in service, took a lot of energy. Especially the fact that it was sometimes unexpected (final debrief) .

Working with different physical space became part of our work as hosts, and changes in space was something for which we felt we needed to compensate at times. What this surfaced was the need for stability felt amongst the group.

When the stability could not be provided through a consistent physical setting, we needed to counterbalance the disruption by consciously using the structure and design as an intervention.

Rhythm and ritual provided the counterbalance. Each session was held within a consistent framework that included a whole-community opening and some form of check in, a lengthier engagement including either coaching circles or a live session, and a whole-community closure. Having a consistent framework and sense of ritual for our sessions played an important role in holding the community.

> A strong container meets the stability need (place and/or process and/or holders of space); in our case, there seems to be an indication that consistent process holds the group. Although some coaching circles 'worked' and others didn't, and participation was variable, the hub "held"; as a Hub member commented, the need for consistency was met through consistent process. Despite all the other changes, it is arguable that the consistent overall process (circle, silence, some sort of check in, live session or coaching circles, closure) met people's stability needs.

Arguably, when the process is emergent and the nature of the learning itself (i.e. transformative) can be a source of discomfort, there needs to be enough consistency and stability for the discomfort not to become overwhelming. The term we chose to describe this – sufficient stability – evokes another term, one drawn from Winnicott's work described earlier. Winnicott (2012) introduced the idea of the "good enough" environment (also called the good enough mother) to describe a context that meets the necessary conditions for fostering growth. In educational spaces, the necessary stability conditions can be met through the ritual and rhythm of the learning process.

Quality of Attention

In the second year of the Hub, an interesting experience occurred about a third of the way the u.lab process that surfaced additional insight about structure. As mentioned above, one of the processes used in u.lab is the Coaching Circle, a structured group process that guides a group of 5-6 people through a careful consideration of the 'case' of one of its members. Each aspect of the process is allocated a certain amount of time, and one member is assigned to be the time-keeper and move the group through the process. Year after year, participants describe this as one of the most powerful aspects of their u.lab experience.

In one session early in our Hub hosting experience, we asked case-givers to share a comment about their experience in the coaching circles. Feedback was highly positive. One case-giver, in particular, stated that the way the process was held was something she experienced as extremely supportive and opened the space for her to engage in in-depth exploration of her challenge. Following the session, another case-giver approached us for a private conversation and shared that the way in which the time was kept in her group, and therefore the space was held, was experienced as disrupting the process and blocking the opportunity for generative dialogue. Group members left the session frustrated and needed to revisit the experience together before they could move on to another coaching circle the following week. The juxtaposition of these two experiences was particularly striking, given that each group was following an identical and highly structured process.

> We're seeing more and more how structure plays an important role, in containing and shaping the space and keeping the coaching circles in focus *only if there is a certain quality in the way the structure is upheld: with care and with the full intention to serve the person.*

This experience drew attention to the way in which structure holds the potential to create a sense of safety, but also to take that sense of safety away. Of equal importance to the structure itself is the way in which it is held. In the example above, this meant being attuned to the experience of the case-giver and moving through the process in a way that kept the individual and the case at the centre of the group's attention.

Another way that the quality of attention surfaced as significant was on the occasions when a hub member voiced a critique or questioning of some aspect of the process. While expressions of discord did not arise often, when they did they were highly visible. Flexible structures, such as open space, allowed the dissonance to be voiced and given a space to be explored with all who resonated.

> The space is open to testing, experimenting, questioning, people saying "I'm not feeling comfortable with this or that"
>
> Today gave students who wanted to "vent" a good working space.

Having structures built into the process that provided space for dissonance was important. In addition, the space needed to be held such that it was made clear dissonance was welcome. To the extent that we achieved this, it was by responding to questions and critiques by opening to them and making space for further inquiry and exploration, usually by suggesting or supporting small group dialogues for all those interested in the topic. Where it felt relevant (e.g. critiques about the hub itself), we would join those conversations as Hub Hosts.

Revisiting 4.0 Education

We began this article describing the Concordia U.lab Social Innovation Hub as an opportunity to 'explore through doing' the principles and properties of 4.0 Education. Scharmer (2017), in his Matrix of Educational Evolution, outlines five dimensions of education: learner, educator, relationship, organization and governance. Here, we use these dimensions to reflect on the nature of the space that we were holding and co-creating in community.

Once again, we draw from records of our weekly debriefs, particularly responses to the debrief question, "What is being developed?", in an effort to deepen our understanding of this emergent and emerging learning space.

Learners

"Holistic" is possibly the most common description people use when reflecting on the nature of learning in the hub and what it means to be a learner. As mentioned above, while many hub members express an appreciation for the conceptual frameworks, it is the learning that touches social, emotional and intuitive aspects of self that surfaces as most notable:

This is a proof of concept that it's possible to bring the whole self to an educational space. There is the idea that if people are allowed to bring their whole self it' s gonna derail into therapy, but here we see how bringing the whole self does not hamper the group.

A class where healing can happen.

A place where intuition and listening are allowed to be used

Our debrief was very emotional, and the fact we were there and holding was important, this is school but there is room for emotions, and for vulnerability.

Learning this way to me feels completely natural. Feels like what we are doing is really just learning like humans.

Having brought themselves as a whole to the learning experience, participants are now faced with two major learning tasks: one, they have to carve their own learning path, and two, they are asked to constantly reflect on what they are experiencing. The emphasis on discovering your own learning journey is highlighted in comments such as:

We got in groups to explore those themes because we were genuinely interested in those topics and in talking about it. We usually do that with friends. Here we are doing it with class.

It is about the process, not the grade, and therefore it becomes much more creative, there is no one direct place to go, the same words can resonate in different ways, and put together out in the world in different ways, when you are in regular learning settings it's more one way. But here people take it where they need to.

Some people adapted the empathy walk, owning the experience.

Reflection was seen as an integral part of the learning process:

A different way of asking questions, different kinds of questions can be asked, about: impact, change, process and self. You usually don't inquire about yourself.

A space to foster inquiry.

Thinking at a different level: what the learning I'm doing in this class means to me personally, and the implications it has for the world

The final comment, in particular, reflects Scharmer's (2017) matrix description of the learner as co-sensing and co-shaping the future.

Educator

All members of the community, including the Hub Hosts, entered into the process as learners. Hosts participated in Coaching Circles and other processes and committed to engaging in the work of deepening awareness of our own quality of attention. The resulting learner-educator relationship is profoundly different from a more traditional university learning experience and it enabled a much more distributed power structure. One outcome of the process is a more level relationship between 'students' and 'teacher'.

This is a place where students can give.

This is decentralized, people break up in their coaching groups, and then come back.

This is relational learning, here I can hug my professor! Yes, you can hug because here you are in a real relationship.

You can be more vulnerable, and open, and speak and it's okay not to have the answer, you are not given right/ wrong judgments, you are not quieted by the prof.

As implied in the previous section, the primary role of the 'educator' was to cultivate a generative social field that would then source the learning. Engaging in the dual role of guide and co-learner shifted the power dynamic from a more hierarchical model to a more collaborative one and enabled the formation of a learner-educator relationship that contributed to this cultivation.

Relationship

The primary aim in forming the Hub was to create a learning community in which we could move through the u.lab process together. The very nature of the learning described in the debrief reflections above is that the learning that takes place in a u.lab hub is relational learning. The capacities described cannot be learned in isolation; they must be learned in the context of the relationship. However, the importance of these relationships goes beyond that of a learning mechanism. The connections established through the Hub are in themselves a defining aspect of this experience and one of the ways it generates value for participants. As one student put it, "we are learning about community by being community."

The first feature that stands out in the Hub community is an organic quality of coming together. People seem to experience a certain freedom and spontaneity in how they decide to show up and how they relate to one another.

In our debriefing group there was time for everybody to speak, in a natural way. We were a group of 6, and we started by asking if we sensed that we are together... We sensed yes - it felt organic and meaningful, and we said yes.

> The informality, cozy, caring of the space is helpful.
> It felt natural.

A second feature is a feeling of intimacy or connectedness characterizing social exchanges in the hub. Rather than experiencing a formal or sterile learning environment, the debriefing comments describe interactions that are warm and personal:

> [There is] intimacy even if the group is very large.
> A strong sense of relational support and emotional coherence within the hub.
> [There is] something about the familiarity. There is something safe about being all together. Presencing is kind of fragile, and by being together there is a certain safety. Indeed, I was very grateful that I didn't have to do this alone.
> It's action oriented, puts more emphasis on the heart rather on the head, and it offers different measures of success, other than just hard cold measures, and it puts a lot of emphasis on collaboration.

A third feature that stands out, possibly connected to the sense of freedom just described, is a certain self-hosting capacity. On multiple occasions participants and hosts remark that the hub is organizing itself. Over time, there is a sense that the Hub, as a collective entity, is more autonomous and less in need of input from the hosts.

> Some people are naturally stepping up taking responsibility, for example [making sure] that everybody had a partner for the empathy walk.
> There is some great self-organizing. But that also meant that people went over time. The self-organizing overrides the time [keeping].
> Support and peer coaching group is something we came to value, so much so that at some point we did a coaching circle instead of a live session.

The Hub Host team continued to hold the space, organize, coordinate and facilitate throughout, and this was essential for maintaining a strong container. That said, Hub members increasingly took responsibility for their own well-being and learning path as well as the well-being of the community.

Organization

Scharmer describes the organizational principle around which 4.0 Education is built to be that of the ecosystem. The dynamic movement of the ecosystem is described as a process of breathing in and breathing out, "where action learners and action researchers move out into the real world and engage in the front-lines of societal change ("breathing out"); and change-makers from across sectors and systems regularly bring their experiences on campus in order to share, reflect, co-sense, and co-create new ways of operating ("breathing in")" (Scharmer, 2019). The learning process of u.lab guided learners to into their immediate contexts in between weekly gatherings to observe, listen, inquire, sense and act. Further, the inclusion of community members in a university-based hub meant that the breathing in process was constantly in play in the Hub. Community members brought into the room the current challenges we are facing in the local community, and in the world.

This repeatedly surfaced as a key aspect of the experience, often seen in the description of the learning in the Hub as "real".

It is a porous learning space, this is something that has implications for learning space. This space is multigenerational, open, anybody can come into it.

There is a feedback from the real world that is present through the co-presence of students and community, that creates a feedback mechanism that brings the real world into the room, without even having to go out there, the real world is right in here, we are part of it, the level of diversity in the room such that make the experience more relevant in terms of real world experience.

111

Learners expressed a sense of learning in service of something greater than themselves.

> [We are] tackling the real world. Higher education traditionally does not prepare us for the real world, the teacher is telling you their version of what the real world is and what to do with it. But here there is the flexibility to get in tune with the real thing, and discover what I want to do about it.
>
> We are thinking at a different level: what the learning I'm doing in this class means to me personally and the implications it has for the world.

Hub members brought an awareness of, and experience in, the local community ecosystem into the Hub learning space. Trhoughout the process, the question of action and impact in the community and in the world, including taking initial action steps to effect this action, was central to the process. These aspects of the Hub made manifest the 'breathing in and breathing out' quality that characterizes 4.0 Education.

Governance

Scharmer describes the governance structure of 4.0 Education as "innovation ecosystem: shared awareness of the whole". The Concordia U.lab Hub was set within the traditional governance structure of the university, with its tendency to operate on a more compartmentalized understanding of the system. That said, it is interesting to note that one prominent features in participants' description of the Hub experience is a sense of connectedness that goes beyond the immediate relationships and the Hub itself.

> I felt a sense of a bigger field. I felt the presence in the room more than I had before. The opening story about stakeholder interviews was powerful and generative. There were great feedback given - a good mix, students

and community members, people at different stages - it was great to get the feedback. And then, for the social field, the power of standing with that many people in the room, all standing. I was sensing emergence, the power of collective intention. There is a community across time, intertemporal, a community that is inter-cohort, in the sense that for some people it's the first time, for others the second, for others the third. There is a sense of continuity and stability. Something shareable. A generative social field gathering.

While people's actions remain local and often individual, they are set within an awareness of a broader context of which they are a part.

Cultivating a Social Field for 4.0 Education

In 4.0 Education, learning happens from the field. Operating from this perspective means that the social field is at the centre of the educational endeavour and the focal point of attention for those who hold and guide educational spaces. What happens in the field – or whole – matters. From a social field perspective, whole persons learn *in* action and *through* relationship in the context of a larger whole or community (see also *Recap of DoTS 2, 2019*).

The social field perspective pays particular attention to the source conditions that give rise to different qualities of relating which in turn give rise to practical results (Scharmer, 2016). The source conditions of these relationships are shaped in part by the inner place from which individuals in the system operate and in part by the quality of the container (Scharmer, Pomeroy & Kaufer, p.3). It is in attending to the quality of the container that a new role emerges for those who hold educational spaces.

The social field, once born, can be thought of as a living entity. To become a generative source of learning, it needs to be consciously attended to, held and nurtured. While our inquiry process revealed several aspects of holding space that helped us to create the conditions for a generative social field, one of the core operating principles embodied throughout this experience was never fully articulated until we began to engage in the reflection process for this article. This is the principle of remaining intentionally and consistently in contact with the evolving collective. Throughout the debrief process, our focus was on seeing and sensing what was happening in the collective and what needed to happen in response in order to support and deepen the learning process. In this sense, our focus of inquiry was at the level of the social field, as was the focus for intervention.

Our ability to remain connected and responsive to the social field was enhanced by integrating a formal process into the work for this purpose. This process was the post-session debrief and planning sessions. These sessions served to heighten our awareness of the evolving social field in two ways. First, the reflection question, "What is our sense of our collective place in this journey," brought our attention to the collective experience and did so in a space where there was time, a structure, and a shared intention to engage in reflection. Second, different members of the community joined the debriefs, providing a variety of voices from, and perspectives on, the collective experience so that we could see the whole from a microcosm of itself.

To help frame our understanding of the importance of remaining in contact with the whole while holding space for it, we find it useful to introduce a concept from Open Systems Theory (OST). A foundational concept in OST is that of directive correlation (Emery, 2000). Open Systems Theory views any given system as existing in a constant, bidirectional exchange with its environment. When a system acts on its environment, that action is called *planning*. The environment acts upon the system and becomes known to it through *learning* (Emery, 2000, p. 624). The relationship between the changing system and the changing environment can take different shapes depending on whether the two share their starting conditions and their direction of change. When a given system and its environment change in the same direction, driven by the same goal, it is more likely that an adaptive relationship develops between the two (*see Figure 5*).

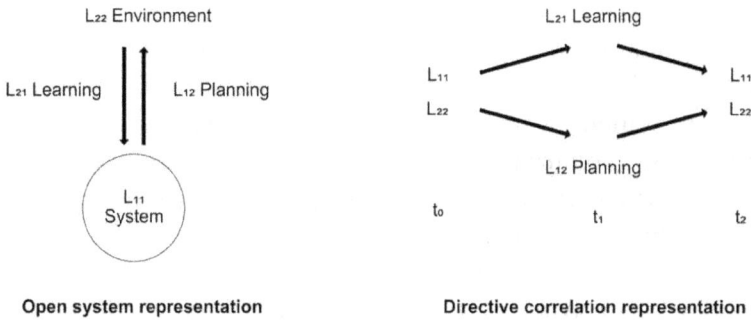

L_{22} Environment

L_{21} Learning $\quad$ L_{12} Planning

L_{11}
System

Open system representation

L_{21} Learning

L_{11} $\quad$ L_{11}
L_{22} $\quad$ L_{22}

L_{12} Planning

t_0 $\quad$ t_1 $\quad$ t_2

Directive correlation representation

Figure 5.0. Models of open system and directive correlation

To achieve such a relationship requires a conscious effort and structures to ensure that the system is in direct contact with its environment as each changes and evolves. For our purpose, the Hub-Host team can be thought of as a (design) system and the Hub the environment for which planning is undertaken. The Hub debrief process, and the fact that it included Hub members in addition to the hosting team, enabled this type of directive correlation.

An important aspect of the debrief process was that it included, but also moved beyond, evaluative reflection. What worked and what was not in service in a session were important factors to consider, but they were not sufficient for connecting with the social field in a way that enabled us to see and sense the field as it emerged and evolved. The questions, "What is our sense of our collective place in this journey" and "What questions are we holding?" helped us to move from seeing/evaluating to engaging on a felt level and accessing a deeper level of knowing and inquiry about the experience. Introducing journaling into the process supported the deepening of the inquiry. The question, "What is being developed here?" helped us to locate our immediate experience with our own emerging sense of a broader collective intention. Engaging in session design from a place of connection to the social field helped us to design our sessions in synchrony with the evolving whole.

Giesenbauer & Mueller-Christ (2020) describe education institutions in the 4.0 paradigm as being defined by "a focus on self-management, a strive for wholeness, as well as an awareness of their evolutionary purpose, taking responsibility and trying to actively participate in societal change" (p. 11). We see reflected in our weekly sensing debriefs several key aspects in this description. What is less reflected in the debriefing comments is the intention to contribute to the evolution of higher education in service of societal change. While that intention was held by the Hub Host Team, it may not have been foreground for all Hub members.

Conclusion

As a living entity, the social field needs to be nurtured and cultivated on an on-going basis. This is particularly true of a 4.0 Education experiment which considers the social field to be the primary source of learning. In our effort to cultivate a generative social field at the Concordia U.lab Social Innovation Hub we focused our attention on the quality of the holding space. Course content, session structure and the strong relational aspect of the learning all surfaced as significant factors shaping the quality of holding space and learner experience. As hub hosts, we found our 'holding' attention was often drawn to the design of sessions that were responsive to the evolution of the social field. To do this, we needed to be able to know the field as it evolved and to remain in close, conscious contact with its evolution.

One unexpected insight that surfaced in this regard was the significant role the weekly debriefs played in creating the conditions for a generative social field. We have come to realize that bringing a consistent, intentional inquiry process enhances our ability to attend to the whole and to design from a sense of connection to it. Initially, the decision to hold weekly debriefs was instinctual and unstructured. Over time, we became more con-

scious of the role of these debriefs in holding the space and cultivating the social field, and we became increasingly intentional in
our questioning and our process. The debriefs themselves became
our primary means for sensing into the whole. It was the structured interplay between sensing into the whole and then planning and embodying action from that place that became essential
in the holding of an emergent learning space. Somewhat paradoxically, it was the consistent and structured sensing and reflection process that allowed us to hold the space with fluidity and
responsiveness. As the social field evolved, we were able to design
and plan in direct correlation with it. This form of planning
helped us create a flexible container that mirrored and supported the learning and growth needs of the community as they came
into reality. In this way, the social field becomes the key source of
learning, rather than curriculum or content.

References

Al-Imarah, A. A., & Shields, R. (2019). MOOCs, disruptive innovation
and the future of higher education: A conceptual analysis.
Innovations in Education and Teaching International, 56(3), 258-269.

Bache, C. M. (2008). *The living classroom: Teaching and collective consciousness*. SUNY Press.

Berger, R., Woodfin, L., & Vilen, A. (2016). *Learning That Lasts, with
DVD: Challenging, Engaging, and Empowering Students with Deeper
Instruction*. John Wiley & Sons.

Bird, K. (2018). *Generative Scribing: A Social Art of the 21st Century*. PI
Press.

Brendel, W., & Cornett-Murtada, V. (2018). Professors Practicing
Mindfulness: An Action Research Study on Transformed Teaching,
Research, and Service. *Journal of Transformative Education, 7*(1),
4-23.

Burgess, D. (2012). *Teach like a pirate: Increase student engagement, boost
your creativity, and transform your life as an educator*. Dave Burgess
Consulting, Incorporated.

Bushe, G. R. (2010). Being the container in dialogic OD. *Practicing
Social Change, 1*(2), 10-15.

Conklin, J., Kyle, T., & Robertson, C. (2013). The essential transformation: How Masters students make sense and learn through

transformative change. *Management Learning*, *44*(2), 161-178.

Cranton, P. (1994). Self-directed and transformative instructional development. *The Journal of Higher Education*, *65*(6), 726-744.

Emery, M. (2000). The current version of Emery's open systems theory. *Systemic Practice and Action Research*, *13*(5), 623-643.

Flynn, J. T. (2013). MOOCS: Disruptive innovation and the future of higher education. *Christian Education Journal*, *10*(1), 149-162.

Giesenbauer, B., & Müller-Christ, G. (2020). University 4.0: Promoting the Transformation of Higher Education Institutions toward Sustainable Development. *Sustainability*, *12*(8), 3371

Hart, S. (2004). *Learning without limits*. McGraw-Hill Education (UK).

Heron, J. (1989). *The facilitators' handbook*. Nichols Publishing Company.

Illeris, K. (2017). *How we learn: Learning and non-learning in school and beyond* (2nd edition). London: Routledge.

Isaacs, W. (1999). *Dialogue and the art of thinking together: A pioneering approach to communicating in business and in life*. Broadway Business.

Manz, C. C., & Manz, K. P. (1991). Strategies for facilitating self-directed learning: A process for enhancing human resource development. *Human Resource Development Quarterly*, *2*(1), 3-12.

Merriam, S. B. (2001). Andragogy and self-directed learning: Pillars of adult learning theory. *New directions for adult and continuing education*, *2001*(89), 3.

Merriam, S. B., & Bierema, L. L. (2013). *Adult learning: Linking theory and practice*. John Wiley & Sons.

Mezirow, J. (2000). *Learning as Transformation: Critical Perspectives on a Theory in Progress. The Jossey-Bass Higher and Adult Education Series*. Jossey-Bass Publishers, 350 Sansome Way, San Francisco, CA 94104.

O'Sullivan, E., & Taylor, M. M. (Eds.). (2004). *Learning toward an ecological consciousness: Selected transformative practices*. New York: Palgrave Macmillan.

Owen, H. (2008). *Open space technology: A user's guide*. Oakland, CA: Berrett-Koehler Publishers.

Patton, M.Q. (2011). Developmental evaluation: Applying complexity concepts to enhance innovation and use. New York: Guilford Press.

Pomeroy, E., & Oliver, K. (2018). Pushing the boundaries of self-directed learning: research findings from a study of u. lab participants in Scotland. *International Journal of Lifelong Education*, *37*(6), 719-733.

Presencing Institute. (2015). *U.School Vision Paper*. Cambridge, MA. Retrieved from https://uschool.presencing.com/sites/default/files/u.school_Vision.pdf

Recap of DoTS 2 - Shifts in Education and Learning. (2019, May 14). Retrieved from https://www.presencing.org/news/news/recap-of-dots-2--reinventing-the-21st-century-university

Robertson, R. W., & de Aquino, C. T. E. (2015). Massive open on-line courses (MOOCs): global education paradigm shift?. *Revista Tecnología, Ciencia y Educación*, (1).

Scharmer, C. O. (2015, December 22). Education as activating social fields. *Huffington Post*. Retrieved from. https://www.huffpost.com/entry/mitx-ulab-education-as-ac_b_8863806

Scharmer, C. O. (2016). *Theory U: Learning from the future as it emerges*. 2nd ed. Oakland, CA: Berrett-Koehler Publishers.

Scharmer, C. O. (2017). *U.lab 2x : Education and Learning* [Video]. http://webcast.mit.edu/u.lab2x/live/6/

Scharmer, O. (2018). *The essentials of theory U: Core principles and applications*. Oakland, CA: Berrett-Koehler Publishers.

Scharmer, C. O. (2019, April 16). Vertical literacy: Reimagining the 21st Century university. *Field of the Future Blog – Medium*.

Scharmer, C. O., & Kaufer, K. (2013). *Leading from the emerging future: From ego-system to eco-system economies*. Oakland, CA: Berrett-Koehler Publishers.

Scharmer, C. O., Pomeroy, E. & Kaufer, K. (2021) *Awareness-Based Action Research: Making Systems Sense and See Themselves*. Burns, D., Howard, J. and Ospina, S. (Eds). The SAGE Handbook of Participatory Research. London: SAGE Publishing.

Taylor, E. W., & Cranton, P. (2012). *The handbook of transformative learning: Theory, research, and practice*. John Wiley & Sons.

Tennant, M. (2006). *Psychology and adult learning* (3rd edition). London: Routledge.

Van Buskirk, W., & McGrath, D. (1999). Organizational cultures as holding environments: A psychodynamic look at organizational symbolism. *Human Relations, 52*(6), 805-832.

Viehland, D. (2014). MOOCs as a disruptive force in online education. *Journal of Applied Computing and Information Technology, 18*(1), 2014.

Winnicott, D. W. (2012). Primary maternal preoccupation. In P. Mariotti (Ed.). *The maternal lineage: Identification, desire, and transgenerational issues* (pp. 59-66). Routledge.

Winnicott, D. W. (1982). *Playing and reality*. New York: Methuen.

Yogev, H. (2008). Holding in relational theory and group analysis. *Group Analysis, 41*(4), 373-390.

CHAPTER 6

Embedding Theory U and Awareness-based Practices within Higher Education: From Developing a Team to Building a Prototype

Vivianna Rodriguez Carreon and Beatriz Carrillo

Introduction: The *WHY*

The current context of rapid change, complexity, and uncertainty create high levels of anxiety among students. These have been further heightened during the COVID-19 pandemic, which has upended life as we know it. It has become evident that encouraging students' personal growth and resilience is as important as engaging them with abstract knowledge in their disciplines. In any learning and collaborative context, the inner condition from which we operate influences how we engage with others, as well as the knowledge, actions, and outcomes that emerge from that collaboration. In this chapter, we share our experiential journey introducing the principles and tools of Theory U to senior arts and social sciences university students enrolled in an interdisciplinary impact course. Within that course, we worked with a small group of students on the theme of personal transformation and collective leadership.

Empowered by Otto Scharmer's first two key principles for prototyping - "Intention" and "Core team"-, we reflected on Margaret Mead's statement: "Never doubt that a small group of thoughtful, committed citizens can change the world. Indeed, it is the only thing that ever has." (cited in Scharmer 2016: 193). As Scharmer asserts, once a core team of people aligns around an intention, that intention goes out into the world and creates a field of possibility around them that attracts other people and opportunities, makes helping hands show up, and doors open up that were closed before (Scharmer 2019). Between 2015 and 2019, we both undertook various iterations of u.lab 0x "Leading Change in Times of Disruption" and u.lab 1x "Leading From the Emerging Future", MOOCS offered by The Presencing Institute (PI) through MIT's edX. These online courses are underpinned by the conceptual framework of Theory U, which builds on phenomenology, embodied cognition, systems thinking, and collective leadership theories, with the aim of providing a platform for local and global processes fostering personal, organizational and societal change to emerge. Otto Scharmer identifies Theory U as "applied phenomenology - a mindful phenomenological practice for investigating the social field" (Scharmer 2016: 30). Key to the Theory U/u.lab framework is the recognition of the positive effects of awareness-based and contemplative practices on personal perspective transformation that can foster prosocial behavior. That transformation, in turn, allows for more productive and generative ways of connecting and collaborating with others, and for new knowledge and possibilities to emerge.

During the 2019 iteration of u.lab, through the PI's website, Beatriz located and contacted Vivianna, who was working at the same academic institution (University of Sydney, Australia). We discovered we worked within the same School and research networks, and that our offices were only a few doors away. Immediately after meeting in person we took action on our common interest to bring transformative learning experiences into the university. Our collaboration began with the intention to look for pathways and models to introduce Theory U and presencing principles and practices to transform learning at our university, as well as engagement and co-creation with the community. We argue that the work on personal transformation is necessary – and perhaps even a precondition – for transformative learning and innovative ideas to emerge in the context of higher education.

We observed that while universities are increasingly more open to introducing contemplative and awareness-based practices to deal with mental health issues among their students and staff (e.g. Galante 2018; Reavley 2018), using those practices as part of the formal learning process has not been widely considered or adopted (for two notable exceptions see: Iranzo Bennett et al. 2018; Brendel & Cornett-Murtada 2019). Reflecting on our own experiences engaging with u.lab, the related hubs and broader global u.lab community, as well as with Theory U and the related literature, we believe that the U journey proposed by Theory U offers a fruitful framework through which to deploy awareness-based and contemplative practices in the formal teaching and learning context. Further, being a framework that can be applied to any collaborative setting, it was also used to develop our relationship as educators and research collaborators, while students were also encouraged to do the same in their small teams.

After our first meeting, we continued to elaborate on the tools given by Theory U, and practicing Otto Scharmer's insight from his interview with Bill O'Brien, that "the success of an intervention depends on the interior condition of the intervenor." O'Brien identified that effective leadership did not depend so much on the *what* or the *how*, but on the "interior condition," the *inner place* from which leaders operate (Scharmer 2003: 2). We realized that the process of integrating the Theory U/u.lab framework, principles and tools within our university needed harvesting the space and the interior condition of our team. A phenomenological analysis in the way we experienced and developed our teamwork showed us the embedded principles that were not explicitly spoken about, although an implicit agreement based on respect and recognition had been established.

Cultivating our interior condition meant to have consistency in working and testing the different tools and finding those that resonated with us. Getting feedback on our day-to-day experience was supported by conversations with other colleagues and Theory U practitioners through virtual group meetings. In particular, we benefited greatly from our participation in the virtual meetings organized as part of the Societal Transformation Lab (u.lab-S). The Lab aims "to co-activate a worldwide movement for profound civilizational renewal" by bringing greater awareness into the three major divides of our time - the ecological divide, the social divide, and the spiritual divide (Presencing Institute 2019). Under its umbrella and lead by the PI team, the Lab holds a number of virtual meetings for the global u.lab community, including one focusing on education, which we also joined. Similarly, we identified and held meetings with Theory U practitioners within our university and in the broader Sydney area.

While we knew about various cases where academics and universities had put in place interventions that drew on Theory U principles and tools, there were no toolkits or guides to help us develop such an intervention at our institution. In December 2019, we thus decided to participate in the second part of the u.lab program for change-makers, the u.lab 2x "From Prototype to Ecosystem Impact." We put forward an initial proposal to the PI with the idea of finding leverage points within the university that would allow us to embed Theory U principles and tools in the curriculum. As already outlined, the Theory U framework also underpins our collaboration and intervention. Due to space issues, we have only briefly explained the key premises of Theory U, but a full development of the theory can be found in Scharmer (2016). Comprehensive information about the various u.lab courses can be found in The Presencing Institute's website. Our work is also informed by the various theories that have influenced Theory U, including in the areas of presencing and leadership (Senge et al. 2004; Scharmer 2003; Reams, Gunnlaugson & Reams 2014; Gunnlaugson & Brendel 2019); neuroscience (Bockler et al 2017; Singer, Ricard & Karius 2019); embodied cognition and living organisms (Varela, Thompson & Rosch 1993; Depraz, Varela & Vermersch 2000; Chemero 2009), systems thinking (Capra & Luisi 2014);

ecologies of knowing and learning (Barnett 2007; Barnett & Jackson 2020; Dieleman 2016); and, transformative learning (Mezirov 2000; Illeris 2014). We were also influenced by Krishnamurti's (1969) self-inquiry research and the sense of encounter in sensing systems by Harding (2009 and 2011). There is a wide literature on embodied learning and knowing, which we are unable to fully review in this chapter.

This paper maps the ongoing journey we embarked on to embed awareness-based practices that enable us and others to be more present within higher education and in interactions with the community. While originally envisioned as a face-to-face intervention, COVID-19 shifted both our communications and collaboration online. We were able to translate our experience learning and engaging with the virtual u.lab community into know-how for sharing Theory U practices online. The method is a phenomenological analysis on human experience, as action researchers we reflected on our work as digital participants. Mapping this project from the evolution of an idea and its development into a prototype, we framed the insights emerging from our collaboration. Drawing on awareness-based practices our responsibility to hold the space and enable difficult conversations during times of uncertainty was necessary. The COVID-19 pandemic brought vulnerabilities to the surface for both staff and students. In turn, it highlighted the importance of presencing to face uncertainty through sensing the digital space and enabling courage to emerge. While we built a resilient online collaboration we found three tacit understandings that gave us an insight into communication principles that we valued and will continue to use. This chapter concludes by introducing those three understandings, the 3Rs of resonate, respect and reanimate.

Starting a transformative education initiative within a university setting

For centuries, universities have been hierarchical institutions. Similarly, disciplines within universities have a curriculum hierarchy resulting in ranking and structured knowledge. Bleazby (2015: 677) states that "the more abstract, theoretical, cognitive, objective, universal and certain a subject's content appears, the higher is its status; while the lower end of the curriculum hierarchy has always been dominated by subjects associated with concreteness, practicality, corporeality, subjectiveness and, thus, contentiousness." She extends her argument drawing on Dewey's non-hierarchical notion of curriculum, where he conceives knowledge as dynamic. Dewey points out an inquiry as a tool for interaction and transformation, augmenting the possibility of "a curriculum grounded in authentic social problems that provoke students to integrate diverse disciplinary knowledge" (Dewey cited in Bleazby 2015: 672). Our aim for this case study was to draw on methods that enable a framework embracing embodied knowledge, and which could result in an effective non-hierarchical curriculum to enhance inclusivity through cross-disciplinary teamwork. At the same time, we acknowledged the challenges and constraints of navigating the administrative barriers for the effective delivery of such a framework.

An incremental social and technological disruption has been introduced in the educational environment to bring about innovation. However, to find the space for awareness-based enablers for integrating presencing, we needed to navigate the barriers of the complex system that is higher education. More traditional and hierarchical universities have struggled to lead those structural changes. Finding potential allies and collaborators to open a discussion is necessary. Underpinning a transition/transformation from ego to eco interactions – to uncover the blind spot in any change process – requires converging difficult conversations with deeper ways of sensing the field.

> "When we move further, from sensing to presencing, we become open to what might be possible, and we're inevitably led to the question "So what do we want to create?" But the "we" in this statement is a larger "we". The visions that arise out of genuine presencing come from "the field knowing itself," a spontaneous expression of discovering the power to shape our reality and our responsibility to an emerging future." (Senge et al. 2004: 132).

The larger "we" for us was the university. In 2016, Beatriz was introduced to u.lab by the founder of a Sydney-based NGO working with refugees settling in Australia. As an academic, Beatriz had always been interested in social justice issues, and as an educator, she also sought for ways to instill in her students a concern for social justice. She found u.lab provided a structured program, with principles and tools that could guide students to become more effective and compassionate leaders. In 2017, while teaching at Xi'an Jiaotong Liverpool University (XJTLU) in Suzhou, China, she introduced u.lab to students and staff. XJTLU is the largest Sino-foreign (P.R.C.-UK) joint venture university in China; its student body and particularly its staff are highly multicultural. With the support of a small university teaching grant, alongside u.lab 1x she hosted a Social Innovation Hub that met regularly throughout the duration of the online course. Upon her return to Australia in 2018, she wished to integrate u.lab and Theory U principles into her teaching at the University of Sydney. She also wanted to identify allies who might help transform how the university works, the way we teach, and the way we engage with the community.

My (Vivianna's) scholarly work focused on social issues, researching on the themes of empowerment, human agency, and resilience in the aftermath of war. In particular, I was collecting information on how people regain agency after trauma in the collective consciousness of post-war. My interest was to see what is the "vital core" under threat for the agent's survival. According to Sabina Alkire (2004) the vital core are "freedoms that are the essence of life". My case study from 2008 to 2013 was in rural Peru, where as in many other places men died in higher numbers during the armed conflict. Uncertainty gave rural women during the conflict the feeling of emptiness. Their cosmovision, the consciousness to their ways of knowing the world was under threat, and their vital core was compromised. I wanted to find the main tools for resilience, intrinsic motivations and the underlying factors that kept women's *anima* going, and how they found meaning amid adversity. I found that during the time I spent in the mountains of Peru, observing the locals, the everyday harvesting of food and grazing animals emitted a sense of encounter, or what Goethe called a stage of "sensorial perception" (Animate Earth, 2011). For Harding (2009), encounter is the act of intuitiveness, being attuned to observe without preconceptions. In an evolving manner, it is to sense the parts of the phenomenon. That intuition is a valid way of knowing (Animate Earth, 2011). The daily activity of surrendering into nature is living in presence. I sensed in my research journey there was unbroken wholeness between the people working in the land and the land. This daily practice of oneness unconsciously autoregulated the mind and body, creating a resilient agent.

In 2019, through social technology, a method which Scharmer (2002) claims to enable for people to be in *presence*, I joined the u.lab-S and hosted the hub Intercultural Cosmovisions Lab as part of my action research. During u.lab 1x in 2019 and u.lab 2x in 2020, I connected with sense makers to observe which enablers are critical for social connection. The weekly online interaction with various u.lab groups allowed for the practice of Theory U tools and underlined the importance of presencing in creating spaces for emerging conversations. Theory U shifted my perception in which I see a theory not only for the use of my research and practice, yet I aimed to embody the learning and experience in my own context (family, work and community). It was an invitation to become the observer and the observed on my interior condition from which I was operating. It is in this moment when I connected with Beatriz and started to shape the way I see my work's context, the education system.

The educational system works under unseen structural laws embedded over the decades—the abstract dynamics occurring on the everyday basis challenge new reforms. They are implicit, and it feels like an energy cloud in which it is hard to point out where the problem is. At the same time, it has paramount power over the dynamics existing within the system. Identifying the issue, the origin, the root, the causes, and the leverage points is the task. It is there, it is ungraspable, we can feel it, but we cannot see it. We, humans, focus on what we can see even though most of the changes in experience are not visible, or as Varela, Thompson and Rosch (1993) state, we conceptualize based on our perception, which is intentional. It is as if the collective unconscious has structured a social field that is filled with contradictions, and which can only be seen through a collective apperception. It seems that untangling this web collectively starts with identifying a social inquiry. How does the grass grow? That is, getting involved in an experiential knowing trial inspired by hermeneutics.

> Experiential knowing is the natural process we all go through...It is learning by doing, exploring, touching and moving things, taking them apart, twisting and bending them discovering that we sometimes can and sometimes cannot repair them. It is reflective in the sense that it is rooted in action while our actions inform us on the world around us, in a constant process of action-reflection-action. (Dieleman 2015: 78). Can we convert the previously presented ideas into concrete steps to teach and learn embodied and embedded transdisciplinary hermeneutical knowing? (Dieleman 2016: 274).

Universities have implemented a range of pedagogical strategies, including experiential and problem-based learning, collaborative and inclusive learning, student-led curriculum (Cook-Sather et al. 2014; Love et al. 2014). However, there are yet no clear pathways or models for how to foster students' personal transformation alongside their development as professionals within a particular discipline or field. How can educators promote more experiential ways of learning that integrate body, mind and environment (Dieleman 2016: 82), acknowledging the embodied nature of knowing and hence the importance of the inner condition (being) of the student? How do we teach students to access their senses and emotions to unlock new ways of knowing? What tools can be used to develop a transformative curriculum that addresses the big divides of our time – the ecological,social (unprecedented levels of inequality and fragmentation) and spiritual (increasing levels of burnout and depression resulting in a low of meaning and the loss of Self that embodies our highest future potential) divides? (Scharmer 2018: 4-5).

Facing these questions, we adopted the principles and methods of Theory U (Scharmer 2016; Scharmer and Kaufer 2013) as a framework for fostering self-awareness and perspective transformation in students, while building their leadership capacities towards prosocial behaviour. Ultimately, the goal of the university is to develop graduates that can lead positive change in and with their communities and organizations.

Identifying key issues and leverage points: working with the system rather than against itGenerating potential allies and collaborators was as crucial as finding the existing *possibilities* to integrating Theory U. Part of the challenge of integrating a phenomenological and systems approach is the *how*, the process, which is also part of the aim. Building on the already multidisciplinary field of leadership development, Theory U puts forward a framework that draws from systems thinking and presencing (Senge et al. 2004), embodied cognition, contemplative and awareness-based practices, and action research. Capra (1998) describes the criteria of systems thinking based on the observation of living organisms. We view relationships based on the systemic understanding of an interdependent ecosystem in which "all members of an ecological community are interconnected in a vast and intricate network of relationships, the web of life" (Capra & Luisi 2014: 353). The phenomenon of interacting with stakeholders is part of the "action"; the "doing" is intertwined with the framework. Discussing and planning among us was necessary to mature our intention, yet until we started to search for and reach out, we were not able to get feedback and iterate the intention of our pilot intervention. Do we let the possibilities be seen or do we search for them?

Action is an essential part of "where do we start?". The incubation process started even before we both connected, but fostering the process only started when we put out there what we wanted to generate. The vulnerability to connect is a courageous step to jumping into the unknown. This step permitted us to answer our inquiry about how we find people to connect with and start a conversation without a particular intention other than to 'see, sense and feel' – using Theory U terminology – what change might be possible. Emerging and evolving from self-inquiry (the "being"), fed into our inquiry regarding the potential related actions (the "doing").

Through courage, we either animate the capacity to learn

from experience provoking eagerness to see positive changes for connection, or we reproduce the same rhetorical tendency that leaves us in the habit of not acting. How do we create a dynamic towards action, one where we can engage through a dialogic process? How do we create the field that will help us identify potential allies that can assit us to harvest a dynamic network? How do we convey a tacit language in which the "hard to point" issues, known and unknown (blind-spots) are at the same time suspended, observed, and engaged, thus enabling us to start doing something about that?

Identifying the "sites" in the curriculum (i.e. a particular degree or course) and across the university (e.g. identifying u.lab practitioners in other parts of the University, including among non-academic staff) where our prototype may be able to trigger broader change (context: drive to improve the student experience; interest in interdisciplinary training and research; experiential and project-based learning; the university's evolving culture strategy) was the first step of our inquiry.

Our inquiries were as relevant as the potential solutions. We had ideas, and until we took the first steps towards putting them into practice, they did not become alive. Krishnamurti argues that we see ideas and action as disconnected, and because ideas are the past and action is the present, being in action is to be living the present (1969: 100). Our action intention was to pay attention to providing strong evidence to support the need for awareness-based practices, as critical tools for personal transformation, learning and leadership development. Beatriz identified a compulsory senior undergraduate course on Interdisciplinary Impact within the Faculty of Arts and Social Sciences, for which academics from across the Faculty were invited to contribute "case studies" that would provide an experiential learning component for students.

We submitted a case study proposal that put forward the idea of using the Theory U/u.lab framework to foster students' personal transformation and collective leadership capacities. The incorporation of case studies as the experiential leaning component in the course was in itself a pilot, providing both flexibility and constraints for the delivery of the case studies. Case study leads had freedom to choose content and activities. However, this also resulted in limited integration between the course syllabus and the content material in the case studies, which meant students found it hard to find synergies between the two. Another constraint was the formal study and consultation time allocated to the case studies. Throughout the thirteen weeks of the teaching semester, we were only able to meet with the students (via Zoom) on three separate one to two-hour sessions, which limited the amount of time we could spend clarifying the theory, and for students to experience first hand some of the awareness-based practices. Nonetheless, we provided students with a set of tools for them to research on Theory U and apply the experiential learning in their own projects. Being part of a course and - more importantly - part of a core component of the Bachelor of Arts, provided us with a platform to start embedding Theory U experiential learning into the curriculum and the university.

Building a conceptual framework for a transformative education: developing a prototypeIt was vital for us to develope a sound theoretical and methodological framework to underpin a prototype that aimed to foster personal transformation alongside curriculum, learning and organizational transformation. We titled our prototype case study: "Fostering students' personal transformation and leadership capacities for social change". Due to the limited amount of time we had to interact with the students, we decided to reflect, review, and refocus on what we would include in the case study. What would be the essential tools that could help unleash the student's self-awareness and collective leadership capacities in such a short amount of time?

Embodied cognition, neuroscience and leadership studies have documented the positive effects of awareness-based practices (e.g. mindfulness, self-reflection journaling, generative listening, etc.) on perspective transformation toward prosocial behaviour (Condon 2019; Dahl & Davidson 2019; Singer & Engert 2019). We argue that in the context of higher education, we need to not only engage students' intellects but also guide their personal growth, to foster in them collective leadership capacities for social change.

A core principle of the u.lab framework is the importance of experiential learning, which was pursued in all case studies part of the Interdisciplinary Impact course. A positive characteristic of the pilot was that the small teams included students from different disciplines, and the fact that the primary purpose of the case study was to deliver experiential learning. Theory U focuses on personal transformation and collective leadership, through a series of activities and exercises including practices such as an empathy walk; generative listening practices and reflective journaling; stakeholder interviews; 3D mapping and prototyping[12] We chose chose listening and mindfulness as the two main enablers of team building.

Listening is an underestimated skill that is nonetheless necessary for the resilience of our interior condition; to be open to our own human experience. Scharmer reflects on Edgar Schein's words when dealing with change: "Perhaps we have to go back to the data and start all over again" (2016, 31). Dieleman (2016) writes that one of the steps in transdisciplinary hermeneutics is training the body as an organ of perception. He argues that all educational programs should include teaching or training skills such as "listening to our body, breathing in conscious ways and being mindful in all our bodily processes" (Dieleman 2016: 85). Similarly, Bortoft describes the importance of slowing down to become aware of sensorial experiences (Bortoft cited in Senge et al. 2004: 46). We thus chose *mindfulness* as a key awareness-based practice, as a tool to "render the mind" present (Varela, Thompson & Rosch 1993: 24) and allows for "navigating in the world with open eyes and hearts" (Senge et al. 2004: 50). Mindfulness puts us in synchrony with the source of our feelings and perceptions (Van Der Kolk 2014: 208). The discovery that people have trouble being present is awareness as a result of the mindfulness practice and not a particular belief (Varela, Thompson & Rosch 1993). For transformation to occur, our emphasis is on creating habits that are cultivated.

Prototype: Personal and systems transformation - engaging students in the U journey

Through the concept of student engagement, universities are increasingly recognizing the importance of the ontological dimensions of learning. In understanding learning as an embodied experience, the task at hand is for universities to go beyond instruction of discipline-based knowledge and generic skills, to address the personal development and transformation of the "pedagogical being" – the student. Some of the qualities that the University of Sydney seeks to develop in its graduates include cultural competence; inventiveness; having an integrated professional, ethical and personal identity; and, influence. This implies the need for the student to develop throughout her studies a disposition for self-awareness and self-knowledge, perspective transformation, openness, generative listening and personal responsibility.

Most educators recognize that student engagement is mediated by the student's social world, sense of connection to others (peers and teachers) and sense of belonging (to the university community), as well as the fact that meaning-making and knowledge creation is a collective endeavour. Nonetheless, faced with an increasingly diverse student body, educators often have no frameworks to help support and foster authentic, collaborative learning and co-creation, let alone foster student personal growth. The dispositions and qualities related to "being" (sense of self) and "becoming" (personal transformation) (Barnett 2007: 102) – critical to collaborative and inclusive learning – are at best only indirectly cultivated in the learning experience. The challenge for universities and educators thus becomes one of moving from supporting educational development – primarily epistemological–, towards fostering an educational transformation that includes "open ontologies for an unknown world" (Barnett 2012: 72).

In his book, 21 Lessons for the 21st Century, historian Yuval Noah Harari (2018) argues that as the pace of change increases and technologies are developed that are likely to redefine the very meaning of "being human", the future has become more uncertain than ever before. To survive in such a world, he argues, one will need to learn resilience, have mental flexibility, and great reserves of emotional balance. To succeed in the face of uncertainty according to Harari (2018), one will need to work very hard on getting to know one's operating system, to know who one is and what one wants from life. For Harari, the most urgent and complicated question individuals now face is thus "Who am I?".

Higher education theorist Ronald Barnett (2012: 68) suggests that this uncertainty and "supercomplexity" of our time calls for the educational tasks for "learning for the unknown" to not only prepare students for a complex world (knowing in and for uncertainty), but also to engage in the ontological task of enabling individuals to prosper amid that supercomplexity. Heightened uncertainty has been linked to the rising incidence in mental health problems among young people (Willis 2019), for many of whom study problems are a key source of anxiety. However, it is essential for universities to not only address the mental health issues of their students as a psychological pathology, but also to tackle its underlying causes. Barnett proposes that universities address anxiety not only as a psychological disturbance affecting individuals, but as "a generalized understanding that the world is forever beyond any clear uncontestable understanding" (2012: 70), and – hence – that its underlying causes are systemic.

Reflection: The role of vulnerability in courage and teamwork leadership

While completing the writing of this chapter, the COVID-19 pandemic has spread throughout the world, including Australia, where we are both based. More than ever before, we feel that presencing is an essential tool enabling resilience. We sense the conditions created by this pandemic have made vulnerability and fear rise to the surface, but they have also allowed for compassion and other positive emotions to emerge.

Krishnamurti's self-inquiry on fear, invites us to reflect as to whether we are aware fear is in our conscious or subconscious (1969: 45). When vulnerability comes to the surface and we are conscious of it, as educators, we are called to take this into account and reflect on the framework we are working with. How do we use presencing to help us see vulnerability as a tool that can enable a courage that invites us to trust and act? Do we accept our vulnerability for what is emerging and connect with others' sense of being to courageously - as stated by Thomas Hübl (2020) - swim in the river that we were put in?

In light of the challenges and vulnerabilities created by the pandemic, we decided to refocus the aims of our project and put more emphasis into holding the space rather than to insist on a strict implementation of the u.lab/Theory U framework. Inducing reflection to enable a deeper conversation is valuable. However, consideration of how we hold the space where those conversations take place is equally vital to trusting the process and offering to witness the quest of the experience. Building such a container is thus as much about creating a safe space as it is about creating "energetic holding spaces for possibility" (Bird 2020). Theory U enables us to flexibly adapt the method to the context and re-invent the method for this "unprecedented" time we are experiencing.

Awareness-based knowledge implementation is abstract for many large organizations. COVID-19 has made many individuals and organizations open to vulnerability and has thus presented them with the possibility to open the heart and the will to enable integration. In this ongoing process, we believe that complex and hierarchical institutions face challenges to embedding holistic programs. In Vivianna's research, power is not "something" found in those who make the decisions, instead, power is the abstract energy sensed in the gap between the subjects and those representing its institutions (Rodriguez Carreon 2014). The nature of hierarchy is its fragmentation and the constructed levels of powers. Structures that are deeply rooted are not just a context, they form the field, the breathing space for social interactions. Nevertheless, they are also the space of possibility for new conversations to emerge and make the shift in perception of awareness-based practices in the public domain.

Going with the current programs within our institution rather than against them, we found to be beneficial. On our journey we started small (pilot within a larger faculty-wide course), we reflected on the actions taken, and we proposed a few questions that emerged from this case study. How did we form the core team? How did we prepare to deal with potential resistance to an awareness-based framework from fellow academics and from students? How do we find the time to implement a prototype for transformation alongside our regular work commitments and unexpected circumstances? How do we work with interdisciplinarity and a diverse student body (multicultural society, high numbers of international students, though most from high socio-economic status)? How do we challenge experiential learning methods prepared for the physical world and adapt them to the virtual world?

Nature of Collaboration: The 3 Rs in group work

How did we cultivate our interior condition as a leadership team? We believe this is the most important question because each of us is an individual expression, and the group needs principles for presencing to access collective intelligence. Below are the 3Rs cultivated in our teamwork:

Resonate

For the Self to be in resonance with the Other it is essential to have a sense of the meaning of encounter. Resonance is the *belief* in someone else's knowledge. In acoustics, resonating is to echo the music with words. Similarly, resonance with the other is the unconscious acknowledgement that a team member was believed. To feel believed activates the possibility for powerful healing to occur. In Unni Wikan's notes during her fieldwork at a Balinese community, she quotes a professor-poet who defined the concept of resonance as:

> It is what fosters empathy or compassion. Without resonance there can be no understanding, no appreciation. But resonance requires you...to apply feeling as well as thought. Indeed, feeling is the more essential, for without feeling we'll remain entangled in illusions (Wikan 1992: 463)

By resonating with the other we need a deeper recognition to the self-echoing the soul. Scharmer states that "a deeper recognition to unify with the inner life" is necessary to enable connection. By becoming aware within a group system, resonance will make possible staying attuned to one another. Further, Thomas Hübl (2020) explains that resonance is a function of responsiveness, which is to be in presence, different than being reactive. When we feel resonance among team members there is a synchrony with the other in leading a project and this also brings a sense of unity.

Respect

Respect is to let go of "wanting" to do or say something. It is to enable witnessing another person's "turn" to express what they know. Knowledge is to deeply sense the information from the other. When we say "I know" and feel with the heart, we embody what the other was offering, including information and emotion. It is to *respond with acknowledgment* to what the other person has to *give* without necessarily responding with a word but with a quality sense of listening, it is a tacit communication. Feeling respect for the other is to be free by its recognition of the will. In Peter Buber's words:

> The free man is he who wills without arbitrary self-will...He believes in destiny, and believes that it stands in need of him...yet does not know where it's to be found. But he knows that he must go out with his whole being. The matter will not turn out according to his decision; but what is to come will come only when he decides on what he is able to will. He must sacrifice his puny, unfree will, which is controlled by things and instincts, to his grand will, which quits defined for destined being (cited in Senge et al 2004: 143).

The container for *respect* is the trust on each other's embodied knowing. It is to feel believed, an inner action which enables confidence in ourselves to open will. In his "Ecology of Knowing" Dieleman (2016) emphasizes observation, listening, sensing and feeling. These facilitated the creation of a space that stimulated what needs to emerge. When respect is embedded, the group work is trusting the process, developing further the granularity of the emerging knowledge and will.

Reanimate

Reanimate is another pillar for teamwork. Check-in on the other member and re-animate and lift their spirit. Anima in many languages, translates as *soul*. To reanimate is to shine the soul of the team member. It is to meet the core of someone's feeling and effectively enable its liveness. For example: cheering somebody up can be seen as a form of support. It is an invitation to see the best in us and the best in others. To be able to do that, we have to be in an environment and mindset that echoes generative listening to enable reading between the spaces of talking. It is a permission to create joy through play in which sensing the body is an essential effect of the soul, and as Mathews points out on Aristotle's De Anima, it emanates from *imagination*.

> In most cases it seems that none of the affections, whether active or passive, can exist apart from the body. This applies to anger, courage, desire and sensation generally, though possibly thinking is an exception. But if this too is a kind of imagination, or at least is dependent upon imagination (Mathews 1977: 22).

These three base pillars were weaving while building the collaboration. The 3Rs became embedded and embodied principals for communication and collaboration toward forming and developing our vision and intention.

Conclusion

We agree with Senge et al's proposition that "Only when people begin to see from within the forces that shape their reality and to see their part in how those forces might evolve does vision become powerful" (2004: 132). It is necessary to harvest the team's interior condition and be able to sustain the space for profoundly sensing what is happening. Applications of presencing for transformative learning and community engagement in higher education require an ontological approach to *how* we hold a session and create a container for a collective learning experience.

References

Alkire, Sabina (2004) 'A Vital Core That Must Be Treated with the Same Gravitas as Traditional Security Threats.' *Security Dialogue* 35(3): 359-360.

Barnett, Ronald (2007) *A Will to Learn: Being a student in an age of uncertainty.* McGraw-Hill Education.

Barnett, Ronald (2012) 'Learning for an unknown future', *Higher Education Research & Development*, 31(1): 65-77.

Barnett, Ronald and Jackson, Norman (eds) (2020) *Ecologies for Learning and Practice: Emerging ideas, sightings and Possibilities*, Routledge.

Bird, Kelby (2020, March, 10) *Containers*. Medium, Presencing Institute. https://medium.com/presencing-institute-blog/containers-458a26083f00

Bleazby, J. (2015) 'Why some school subjects have a higher status than others: The epistemology of the traditional curriculum hierarch', *Oxford Review of Education*, 41(5): 671-689, DOI: 10.1080/03054985.2015.1090966

Bockler, Anne et al. (2017) 'Know Thyselves: Learning to understand oneself increases the ability to understand others', *Journal of Cognitive Enhancement*, 1:197-209.

Brendel, William and Cornett-Murtada, Vanessa (2019) 'Professors Practicing Mindfulness: An Action Research Study on Transformed Teaching, Research, and Service', *Journal of Trasnformative Education*, 17(1): 4-23.

Capra, Fritjof (2008) *The Web of Life: A New Synthesis of Mind and Matter*, Flamingo.

Capra, Fritjof and Luisi, Pier Luigi (2014) 'The ecological dimension of life' in *The Systems View of Life: A unifying vision*, Cambridge University Press.

Chemero, Anthony (2009) *Radical Embodied Cogintive Science*, Cambridge, MA: MIT Press.

Condon, Paul (2019) 'Meditation in context: factors that facilitate prosocial behavior', *Current Opinion in Psychology*, 28:15-19.

Cook-Sather, Alison et al. (2014) *Engaging Students as Partners in Learning and Teaching: A guide for faculty*, John Wiley & Sons.

Dahl, C. J. and Davidson, R. J. (2019) 'Mindfulness and the contemplative life: pathways to connection, insight, and purpose', *Current Opinion in Psychology*, 28: 60-64.

Depraz, Nathalie; Varela, Francisco J.; and Vermersch, Pierre (2000) *On Becoming Aware: A pragmatics of experience*, Amsterdam, Netherlands: John Benjamins Publishing.

Dieleman, Hans (2015) 'Transdisciplinary Hermeneutics; working from the inner self, creating ecologies of knowing', *Transdisciplinary Journal of Engineering & Science*. 6: 72-85.

Dieleman, Hans (2016) 'Steps to an Ecology of Knowing, and to Teaching Embodied Transdisciplinary Hermeneutics', *Autonomous University of Mexico City*. Available online: https://www.atlas-tjes.org/index.php/tjes/article/view/87

Galante, Julieta et al. (2018) 'A mindfulness-based intervention to increase resilience to stress in university students (the Mindful Student Study): A pragmatic randomised controlled trial,' *The Lancet Public Health*, 3(2): e72-281.

Gunnlaugson, Olen (2012) 'Fostering Conversational Leadership: A Response to Barnett's Call for an Ontological Turn', *International Journal of Progressive Education*, 8 (2): 49-59.

Gunnlaugson, Olen and Brendel, William (2019) *Advances in Presencing: Emerging Perspectives*. Trifoss Business Press. Vancouver.

Harding, Stephan (2009) *Animate Earth: Science, Intuition and Gaia*. Green Books.

Harding, Stephan (2011) *Animate Earth* Directed by Josh Good, Sally Angel, Clive Ardagh, Produced by Sally Angel, Josh Good, Angel TV, GKC Productions, stories4change. The Video Project

Harari, Yuval Noah (2018) *21 lessons for the 21st Century*. Penguin.

Hübl, Thomas (2020) *Honoring Our Fear, Finding Our Resilience in a Time of Crisis and Pandemic*. https://youtu.be/1SWiWqzCZt8

Illeris, Knud (2014) *Transformative Learning and Identity*, Routledge. Krishnamurti, J. (1969) *Freedom from the Known*, Harper One.

Iranzo Bennett, Rebecca et al. (2018) 'Mindfulness as an intervention for recalling information from a lecture as a measure of academic performance in higher education: a randomized experiement', *Higher Education for the Future*, 5(1): 75-88.

Krishnamurti, J. (1969) *Freedom from the Known*, Harper One.

Love, Anne G. et al. (2014) 'Integrating collaborative learning inside and outside the classroom,' *Journal on Excellence in College Teaching*, 25(3-4): 177-196.

Matthews, Gareth (1977) 'Consciousness and Life,' *Philosophy*, 52(199): 13-26.

Mezirow, Jack (2000) *Learning as Transformation: Critical perspectives on a theory in progress*, Jossey-Bass.

Presencing Institute (2019) *Societal Transformation Lab*. https://www. presencing.org/societal-transformation-lab.

Reams, Jonathan; Gunnlaugson, Olen; and Reams, Juliane (2014) 'Cultivating Leadership through Deep Presencing and Awareness Based Practices' in Kathryn Goldman Schuyler (ed) *Leading with Spirit, Presence and Authencity*, Jossey-Bass: 39-58.

Reavley, Nicola (2018) 'Mindfulness training in higher education students', *The Lancet Public Health*, 3(2): e55-e-56.

Rodriguez Carreon, Vivianna (2014) *Empowerment Formation: Women's Agency for Participation in Decision Making Within the Poverty and Conflict Context Case of Rural Peru*, unpublished PhD thesis, University of Sydney.

Scharmer, Otto (2002) 'Presencing – A Social Technology of Freedom', Interview with Dr. Claus Otto Scharmer. *Trigon Themen*, 2/2002. https://www.ottoscharmer.com/sites/default/files/2002_ ScharmerInterview_us.pdfScharmer, Otto (2003) *The Blind Spot of Leadership: Presencing as a Social Technology of Freedom*. Habilitation Thesis https://www.ottoscharmer.com/sites/default/files/2003_ TheBlindSpot.pdf

Scharmer, Otto (2016) *Theory U: leading from the future as it emerges*, the Social Technology of Presencing Second edition. Berrett-Koehler Publishers, Second Edition.

Scharmer, Otto and Kaufer, Katrin (2013) *Leading from the Emerging Future: From Ego-System to Eco-System Economies*. Berrett-Koehler Publishers.

Scharmer, Otto (2018) *The Essentials of Theory U: Core principles and Applications*, Berrett-Koehler Publishers.

Scharmer, Otto (2019) 'Module 4: Co-Creating, Prototyping Principles' in *u.lab: Leading From the Emerging Future*. MITx Edx

Senge, Peter; Scharmer, Otto; Jaworski, Joseph; and Flowers, Betty S. (2004) *Presence: Human Purpose and the Field of the Future*. Crown Business.

Singer, Tania and Engert, Veronika (2019) 'It matters what you practice: differential training effects on subjective experience, behavior, brain and body in the ReSource Project,' *Current Opinion in Psychology*, 28: 151-158.

Singer, Tania; Ricard, Matthiew; and Karius, Kate (eds) (2019) *Power and Care: Toward Balance for Our Common Future—Science, Society, and Spirituality*, MIT Press.

Van der Kolk, Bessel (2014) *Brain, Mind, And Body in the Healing of Trauma*, Viking.

Varela, Francisco J.; Thompson, Evan; and Rosch, Eleanor (1993) *The Embodied Mind: Cognitive science and human experience*, MIT Press.

Wikan, Unni (1992) 'Beyond the Words: The Power of Resonance,' *American Ethnologist* 19(3): 460-482.

CHAPTER 7

Social Fields As An Awareness-Based Approach To Reconnect Self, Other, and Whole

Ursula Versteegen and Luca Versteegen

Introduction

In spring 2020, the COVID-19 pandemic challenged the world. The experience of a shared threat provoked adaptations on different levels of society. On an individual level, the global community had to adapt to new forms of everyday life in schooling (Viner et al., 2020), work-life (Mækelæ et al., 2020), and family interactions (Alon, Doepke, Olmstead-Rumsey, & Tertilt, 2020; Thompson & Rasmussen, 2020) within weeks. As a society, federal governments freed unprecedented financial support for the economy (e.g., Partington, 2020; cf. Evans, Lawson, Fenton, & Donovan, for a review), new forms of collaboration evolved rapidly (e.g., Appuzzo & Kirkpatrick, 2020; Koelbl, Lüdke, Peters, Pitzke, & Stöhr, 2020), and citizens supported the needs of vulnerable subgroups and the greater good (Hirsch, 2020).

Whereas the obviousness of the challenge certainly required straightforward solutions, one might wonder if and how a new understanding of self, other, and whole might have facilitated these responses. More precisely, instead of a political debate that occurred far-off from its citizens, the COVID-19 pandemic posed a real challenge evolving rapidly in front of our eyes and required collective responses on a personal, community, national, and global level. These responses, in turn, emerged as moment-to-moment real-life experiences with practical consequences for all of us.

We interpret the COVID-19 pandemic as an example of how a directly shared experience alters the awareness of self, others, and whole. Taking a social field approach, we argue that the form of interbeing between individual, others, and whole within the salient landscape of social relationships informs the quality of resulting action. Whereas, as more fleshed out below, some configurations (i.e., the organization of interrelationships between self, other, and whole) create *stuckness* (Scharmer, 2016), we contend that an experience-elicited reconfiguration of the social field may enable collective action and system change by bridging the knowledge-action gap (Scharmer, 2019).

This chapter is divided into three parts. In part 1, we will briefly introduce social fields and argue for an integrated examination thereof from both social science and a phenomenological awareness-based social fields perspective. Based on that, we will explore three empirical cases in which particular shifts of awareness can be interpreted as reconfigurations of the social field. In the second part, we will suggest advancing the understanding of social fields in the context of phenomenology and Gestalt psychology. Applying a two-dimensional conceptualization of social fields (see Figure 1 (Matrix of awareness-based action; adapted with permission from Scharmer, 2016, p. 242; cf. Scharmer, 2017)), we discuss the configuration of self and other dependent on its absence and presence of source and self vs. other, as well as its effect on action. The final section describes a practical example of how U-practitioners can make the quality of each social field tangible, as well as propose questions for future research.

Presence of Source (Presencing)

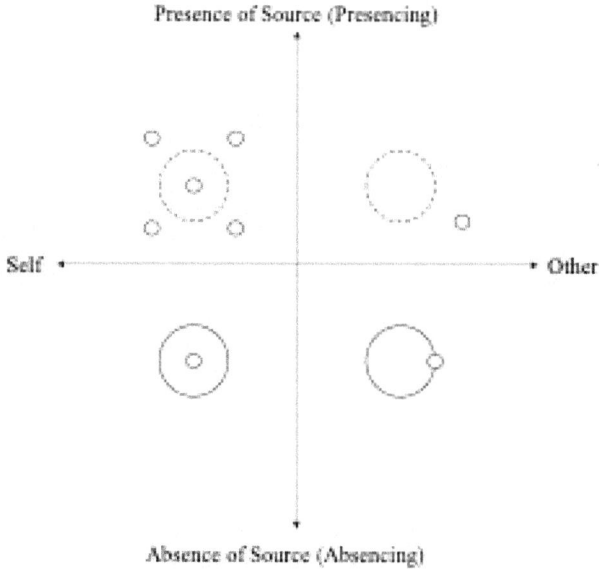

Self ← ———————————————————— → Other

Absence of Source (Absencing)

Figure 1.

Part I: Three Empirical Cases of Self, Other, and Whole

A Brief Introduction Into Social Fields

Scharmer (2016) describes social fields as social systems seen and experienced from within. In his framework, two axes compose four different configurations of social fields. First, the horizontal axis displays the extent to which one is aware of self vs. other. Second, the vertical axis describes the degree to which one is attentive to and operates from the source of a not-yet-embodied future that wants to emerge. The resulting quadrants compose four distinct patterns of awareness-based qualities of relationships between self, other, and whole. Starting from the lower left, one can understand these four fundamental patterns of action moving from *micro* (thinking/listening/individual), and, going counterclockwise, to *meso* (conversing/group), *macro* (structuring/institutions), and *mundo* (ecosystem coordinating/global

147

systems; cf. Scharmer, 2017, for a review). Put differently, the matrix of awareness-based action (Scharmer, 2016) thus spells out a landscape of four different qualities of action-awareness. In cell 1, thinking is restricted, individual, and potentially self-absorbed. In this mode, one operates from habitual awareness and the past, listens from a downloading perspective and habits of thoughts. In cell 4, in contrast, thinking is collective, visionary, and potentiality-driven, as it expresses the coordinating social body.

Again, our core argument for this chapter is that it is the way in which self, other, and whole are configured to each other that inform the way we behave. From cell 1 to cell 4, the change in configuration progressively enhances our ability to respond collectively. If one understands the ability for collective response as the necessary ingredient for response ability (Sacks, 2011), this implies that the likelihood for us to become collectively responsible increases the more the configuration of the social field shifts from cell 1 to cell 4.

If our argument finds support, this will help understanding why knowing often fails to translate into action (Scharmer, 2016). Put differently, finding the hidden factors driving from one configuration of social fields (i.e., cell 1) to another (i.e., cell 4) allows to move from the stuckness of numerous scattered individuals (i.e., cells 1 and 2) into a collective body acting out of an embodied shared knowing (i.e., cells 3 and 4). Next, we will briefly explain why a consideration of social scientific research is necessary before we discuss three cases in which a shift in the configuration of the social field seems to occur.

Integrating Awareness-Based Social Fields and Social Scientific Research

A central aim of this chapter is to explore the quality of the social field as the context of awareness from which any action is taken. Although a better understanding of the translation from awareness to action is vital for both researchers and practitioners, we contend that this connection still requires additional elaboration. With this chapter, we thus attempt to spark both awareness-based social fields researchers' and practitioners' interest in examining the underlying mechanisms through which different qualities of awareness predict corresponding types of action.

One approach to enable collective capacity for action following a change in self-perception is suggested by Theory U (Scharmer, 2009, 2016). Theory U-practice is focused on postures, processes, and tools that facilitate shifts in individual and collective self-perception towards a deepened and shared sense of reality as a condition for effective action. For more than 20 years, Theory U has been used to invent and prototype ways to deal with socio-ecological dysfunction and global disruption (see Scharmer, 2016, for examples).

However, opportunities to draw from various sources of social scientific theory and evidence have, to our knowledge, rarely been taken. A reason for this might be that, although these sources seem fruitful, their integration is challenging. On the one hand, an overemphasis of quantifiable third-person perspective research may deaden Theory U and other action-oriented approaches. On the other hand, the use of more rigorous scientific tools would allow underpinning action-oriented approaches and provide additional justification using them in the field more effectively. In short, it seems that an integration of these two approaches could provide scientifically proven but practically relevant results.

The purpose of this chapter is thus to take first steps into an exploration of how social fields and the reconfiguration thereof (i.e., the alternation of interbeing between self, other, and whole) based on altered individual and collective self-awareness determines the quality of an intended action and how it is being executed. This idea follows the awareness-based social fields research approach taken by the Presencing Institute (Scharmer, 2009, 2016), which claims that we first need to understand the role of awareness and collective consciousness change to fully embrace what social change entails and how it can be initiated. More precisely, this agenda follows three assumptions named by Scharmer, Pomeroy, and Kaufer (in prep.):

1. "You cannot understand a system unless you change it.
2. You cannot change a system unless you transform the consciousness of those enacting the system.
3. You cannot transform consciousness unless you make the system sense and see itself." (p. 2).

Hence, the first part of this chapter tries to prototypically explore three phenomena that substantiate shifts U-practitioners have been observing with current psychological research. To do so, we selected examples relating to some of the core movements in the U-process, which are seeing, sensing, and presencing. According to Theory U, the first step of transformational social change is about starting to see the challenge. The underlying assumption is that if different stakeholders (or, as social science would phrase it, belongingness to different in-groups; Turner & Oakes, 1986) can see a shared challenge, they will enhance their ability to act. The first empirical case thus describes how different forms of threat alter the experience of self and others and predicts different attitudes towards others.

Second, Theory U postulates that seeing is a different level of knowing than *sensing*. As a second empirical case, we will thus present a project that investigated the emotion of awe as a driver of an altered experience of the self, which then predicted a change in behavior towards more prosocial action.

Third, we will discuss research on the *overview effect* (Yaden et al., 2016) as an empirical case in which *presencing* becomes evident. This allows expanding our understanding of social fields from a third- and second-person perspective to a first-person perspective. As such, the overview effect is a first-person account illustrating the interplay of two interacting patterns of changing relationships; that is, a change in self-other and mind-body awareness, leading towards life-long behavior change in astronauts.

Empirical Case 1: Experiences of Self vs. Other Predicts Attitudes

Pyszczynski and colleagues (2012) examined how the experience of different types of threats impacts the perception of an outgroup. Across three studies, they found that while the perception of a local threat increased intergroup aggression, the "increased awareness of the shared threat of global climate change can, at least under some conditions, reduce support for war and promote efforts at peaceful coexistence and international cooperation." (p.363). Crucially, this finding suggests that although the perception of threat may increase aggression when experienced from a subordinate group perspective, "existential threat does not always increase intergroup conflict" (p.359). In contrast, when experienced from the stance of the superordinate group that is affected by the same shared threat, this threat may encourage people's support for peace-building and cooperation in the light of an experienced "common humanity" (p. 354).

Together, these findings suggest that the experience of a shared catastrophe may even have a unifying effect on conflicting parties. This is in line with the COVID-19 example given in the outset of this chapter, in which various regions and countries experienced a shared threat (i.e., the virus), consequences (i.e., curfews, quarantine, social distancing, etc.), and resulting societal debates (i.e., discussions on democracy and basic fundamental rights). Interestingly, a key explanation for why the pandemic produced both a trend toward subgroup salience (i.e., the national rivalry for medical supplies; Blasberg, Fahrion, Sarovic, & Schaap, 2020) and a trend for more subgroup support (i.e., cooperation in patient treatment; e.g., Hallam, 2020) may be found in consideration of whether the parties experienced the threat as shared. Based on Pyszczynski and colleagues (2012), one would argue that the pandemic created egocentric behavior and conflict when it was perceived as local, but initiated cooperation when it was seen as shared. From a social field's perspective, one might argue that perception of the threat as local and fear-driven produced the rivaling, aggressive trend (cell 2), while it facilitated cooperation and shared action when it was experienced as a common and whole-directed menace targeting shared humanity (cell 4).

In sum, as social fields are argued to be predictive for the quality of action, this empirical case is informative for understanding the attitude that underlies such behavior. The shift taken in this case is probably from cell 2 to cell 3, such that two opposing subgroups merged from a conflict configuration towards an integrated superordinate group bearing collective suffering. However, this case is limited in two aspects. First, even if an altered experience of oneself moved subgroup individuals to be members of a superordinate group, the experience still was an individual one, such that the response remained threat-based rather than driven by empathy. Second, although attitudes are an important predictor of behavior, an attitude does not always translate into respective behavior (Reeve, 2008). It is thus fruitful to look into another example, in which actual behavioral consequences of a changed self-experience have been assessed.

Empirical Case 2: The Impact of Self-Experience on Behavior

Piff, Dietze, Feinberg, Stancato, and Keltner (2015) investigated the effect of awe on prosocial behavior. While we may feel awe when listening to certain music, while being in nature, or during spiritual experiences, psychological research defines it as "an emotional response to perceptually vast stimuli that defy one's accustomed frame of reference in some domain" (Piff et al., 2015, p. 883; cf. Shiota, Keltner, & Mossman, 2007). Experiences of awe provoke this frame of reference to shift internally (Keltner & Haidt, 2003), and thus provides the inner capacity to fully relate to a situation or stimulus. Based on Piff and colleagues' (2015) understanding that awe elicits a "feeling of being diminished in the presence of something greater than the self, and the motivation to be good to others" (p. 883), one's position on the scale describing the relationship of self and whole in Scharmer's (2016) matrix of awareness-based action seems to move.

Interestingly, Piff and colleagues (2015) do not only find that people experiencing awe tended to be, compared to participants in various control conditions, more prosocial, and make more ethically correct decisions. Moreover, trying to understand why this particular emotion led to increased prosociality, the authors claimed a change in self-perception to be the underlying mechanism. Across five studies, they found that awe would trigger a "relative diminishment of the individual self and its interests vis-à-vis something perceived to be more vast and powerful than oneself" (p. 895), which, in turn, increased the likelihood for behaving prosocially. In short, the experience of awe as a response to something more meaningful than oneself indeed creates a feeling of relative insignificance, which then increases the inclination to contribute to the greater good. Building upon the first empirical case, this project does not only suggest that the experience of the self is important for attitudes but indeed directly informs the way we behave. Still, the shift in the social field configuration maintains a cell 3-quality as the action is, although prosocial and based on an empathetic emotion, an individual one. We will thus consider a third case that examined the impact of a change in self-perception on behavior in cell 4.

Empirical Case 3: A View From Above Changes Social and Earth Connectedness

The term *overview effect* has been coined by space philosopher Frank White (1987) in his research on the intense feelings that astronauts reported when seeing earth from space. It refers to a "cognitive shift in awareness" linked to "the experience of seeing firsthand the reality that the earth is in space" (Ferreira, 2016, p.1.). It brings together three types of relational shifts as experienced from various first-person and second-person accounts. First, these accounts describe a profound experience of awe reframing who one is and what one needs to do. Second, they describe the shift of awareness from a conceptual understanding of earth to connecting to a living being. Third, they describe a shift of identity from professional astronauts to experiencing themselves as the extended sensing organ of the human-earth body.

Edgar Mitchell, an Apollo 14 astronaut, described this experience as the development of "an instant global consciousness" (Yaden et al., 2016, p. 5). While experiencing earth from space seems to be more than a feeling, the earth seems to be perceived as more than just being an object. The experience engages the viewer-astronaut in a profound relationship with a living being that is coming into being. Indeed, astronaut James Irwin experienced a "beautiful, warm living object [that] looked so fragile, so delicate, that if you touched it with a finger, it would crumble and fall apart" (Irwin, 1973; as cited in Ferreira, 2016, p. 1), and astronaut Sandra Magnus reported that "it is all connected, it is all interdependent." (as cited in Ferreira, 2016, p. 1).

Strikingly, the overview effect does not only seem to affect the way the astronauts *see* the earth, but it also affects the way they *perceive* and *experience* it. The description of the fragile planet points to a possible inversion of the experience of the relationship between diminished self and vastness into the opposite. Once the astronauts shifted from the onlooker mode towards allowing to feel this relationship, a sense of rising care for this fragile planet evolved from a self that has abundant capacities. Astronaut Yuri Artyushkin, for example, summarized that "the feeling of unity is not simply an observation. With it comes a strong sense of compassion and concern for the state of our planet and the effect humans are having on it." (Jaffee, 2011, p. 9). Especially important for our argument that the quality of self-experience informs the quality of action, however, is the notion by space tourist Anousheh Ansari, who suggested that the overview effect goes beyond experiencing, namely that "it sort of reduces things to a size that you think everything is manageable." (Ferreira, 2016, p. 1). The one who experiences earth as a living being seems to grow in relation to it with a felt rise in capacity for action. This relates to a neurological understanding of compassion, which does not see it as an emotion only but also describes it as an activity (Singer & Bolz, 2013). Indeed, the overview effect has created lifelong changes in habits, including most of the astronauts becoming environmentalists. White explains: "My hypothesis was that being in space, you would see and know something experientially that we have been trying to understand intellectually for thousands of years." (As cited in Ferreira, 2016, p. 1)

Guidance on what fueled the profound transformation of seeing oneself beyond intellectual understanding can be drawn from Yaden and colleagues (2016):

> Images like Earthrise make that understand immediate and visceral, elevating it from something believed abstractly to something felt. The simultaneous complexity and fragility of our lives on Earth is no longer a mere concept, but a reality that can be understood personally. (Yaden et al., 2016, p. 1)

It seems that the effect of seeing oneself from the outside as part of something larger can shift anything. An interesting remaining question, however, explores how much of an impact the "effect of an in-person experience" (Yaden et al., 2016, p. 2) has if the image already creates a shift towards humanity seeing itself. Not just *seeing* a picture of the earth, but being able to *sense* a relationship led to an enlivening of the encountered other; in this case, earth. So does astronaut Yang Liu note: "I had another feeling that the earth is like a vibrant living thing. The vessels we've clearly seen on it looked like the blood and veins of human beings." (as cited in Chen, 2012, p. 288).

Yaden and colleagues (2016) conclude that the astronauts "have felt overcome with emotion, have come to see themselves and their world differently, and have returned to Earth with a renewed sense of purpose." (p.3). Importantly, although it seems that the experience of awe was involved in shifting the perception of self, others, and whole, it is probably not enough describe the quality of awareness with awe alone. Indeed, Yaden and colleagues (2016) suggests that the overview effect may have triggered "'self-transcendent' experiences (STE's)" (p. 5), which they continue to define as "temporary feelings of unity characterized by reduced self-salience and increased feelings of connection" (cf. Yaden et al., 2016, p. 5). More precisely, people experience connection with other individuals, but also with humankind as a whole, and the "entirety of existence" (Yaden et al., 2016). These sensations of unity and connectedness find resonance on a neu-

155

rological level, as they were found to be associated with a lowered activity in neural regions related to spatial awareness, which might explain why the awareness of the self steps back for the sake of the larger whole (Newberg et al., 2001; Urgesi, Aglioti, Skrap, & Fabbro, 2010).

In summary, experiences like the overview effect have led to a shift in self-identification and behavior in at least some of the astronauts (Yaden et al., 2016). The effect seems to provide us with a more profound sense of knowing that cannot solely be attributed to awe. Still, the question of what it takes to closes the knowledge-action gap (Scharmer, 2019) remains open. From a Theory U perspective, it seems that the astronauts' first-person accounts point to how significantly the experience of self and social reality is altered by accessing deeper qualities of relating to the world. On a first level (and not presented in the overview effect above), the earth would be taken as a given. On a second level, the earth is seen as a concept from the outside (i.e., seeing earthrise as a picture). Third, empathetically relating to the earth allows knowing it from within. The earth is sensed as a relational percept in the form of a vibrant living being with vessels and veins. Finally, relating to earth on the source level, one knows her as an embodiment of humankind. Astronaut Paul Cernan experiences that "That's humanity, love, feeling, and thought. You don't see the barriers of color and religion and politics that divide this world." (Yaden et al., 2016, p. 3).

Seeing, sensing, and presencing are relational categories capturing inner qualities of attending to the world and enacting different levels of action-ability. Deepening one's awareness and capacity to relate to self, others, and the world in new ways make causes and effects collapse in time and space and, therefore, become actionable. Seeing oneself as diminished in contrast to the planet's vastness may generate awe and pro-social behavioral tendencies, but it does not necessarily entail empathetic action. Sensing and empathizing with the earth (i.e., a heart-to-heart connection creating an appearance of fragility) adds a sense of urgency, potency, and response-ability but does not yet bring about a collective action ability that originates from the whole. Finally, Presencing the earth as a continually changing expression of a deeper source connects the viewer to the aliveness of a living being. The astronauts' experiences suggest that the quality of how we attend to world matters for what we believe we can do.

Integrating the Three Empirical Cases and Concluding Remarks

The commonality of the three here-discussed cases is a change in the experience of the self in relation to others and whole due to a problem (i.e., threat), emotion (i.e., awe) or experience (i.e., overview effect), the "sublime" (Burke, 2015) changes. While this is elicited by the actual threat in the first case, it is driven by self-diminishment in the second and connectedness in the third. Although the three cases are undoubtedly different, they share that they all put one's life into the perspective of eternity, which then affects attitude and action tendencies.

Similarly, one can detect the effect of a shift in awareness on action tendency in the COVID-19 case given at the outset of this chapter. While the tangible threat was certainly a driving force pushing change forward, another, less visible force was redirecting and specifying the effort. With the *flattening of the curve*-approach soon becoming the most common strategy for freeing up health care systems worldwide (Baniamin, Rahman, & Hasan, 2020), societies – including the less vulnerable subgroups –silently agreed on prioritizing the well-being of the collective before individual goals. Doing so, we all seemed to see the pandemic from the perspective of the margins, which enabled us to pause habits for the sake of others. This deceleration came from a change in perspective to protect and take care of the common good (i.e., the health care system) and the vulnerable subgroups. In its most extreme cases, the outbreak of the virus, such as the Italian region of Lombardy (Barbaro, 2020; Giuffrida, 2020), the immense suffering accompanying it, as well as the dedication of health care and spiritual professionals, seemed to guide us through an evolution from mere survival towards a longing for civilization, and life in dignity. Although we were undoubtedly challenged to deal with the crisis in a humane way (cf. Daley,

2020), we seemed to find tools of coping with it that avoided the times of darkness and cruelty seen in prior pandemics (i.e., the Black Death; Cantor, 2001). We have taken a huge leap; that is, we allowed *interiority* (Gadamer, 1960) to develop.

More specifically, while the pandemic augmented our sensual and perceptive capacities, a more profound sense of shared reality was rising from the rubble. Tho Ha Vinh, former director of the Center for Gross National Happiness in Bhutan, identified the disillusionment of independence as a core aspect of a new unfolding, shifting reality:

> The first one is the illusion of independence. For the first time in history, this crisis brings alive the experience of mutual interdependence as a reality affecting basically everyone around the globe. We have had crises much worse than this before in terms of death tolls, increase in poverty, and wars. But never before did a crunch affect literally everyone around the globe at once. Before, we always could have the impression it was not about us. It was out there in China, or Europe, or in a specific sector or with certain people. You could empathize and even help. But today, whoever and wherever you are, you are part of it as it happens. You get a sense of being part of a family that may be dysfunctional at times, but still is family, and whatever happens to one member anywhere in the world has an impact on everyone else and the whole. It is neither theoretical nor a philosophical perspective, it has become a reality. We finally get a shared first-hand experience of what it means that co-dependence is the foundation of our existence. Future development of society needs to consciously build itself on the principle of mutual dependence. (Ha Vinh, 2020)

Ha Vinh's (2020) observations portray how a shift in the configuration of social fields may be experienced from a first-person perspective. Specific configurations of the social field, as presented in cell 4 in Figure 1, enable us to turn inwards, reveal our illusions and start facing the actual reality of the workings of our social system from inside. They make us realize and attend to the true nature of our lives as humankind; that is, interdependence and impermanence. We discussed the three empiric cases to show how a change in perception of self, others, and the larger whole might affect attitudes and, eventually, behavior. However, the underlying mechanism has yet to be fleshed out in more detail to understand better what the social field is and how it may be constituted. This is what we will target in part 2. An example of how the configuration can be changed actively will be outlined in the third and final part.

Part II: The Configuration of Social Field and its Impact on the Ability to Act

In this part, we will specify the claim that the configuration of the social field determines the quality of the resulting action. To do so, we will first outline the scientific context of phenomenology, which will explain the direction of our interpretation of the social field concept in the subsequent review thereof. Next, we will discuss an understanding of social fields that acknowledges its origin in *Gestalt* psychology (Koffka, 1935; Köhler, 1925, 1967; Wertheimer, 1922, 1923, 1925), as well as its purpose to describe and change behavior (Lewin, 1943, 1951), and recent developments put forward by Theory U research (Scharmer, 2016; cf. Figure 1). Understanding that social fields can be characterized best by the underlying Gestalten (German plural form of *Gestalt* (figure, shape)), which are composed of the dynamic experience of time and space, we will then describe these two dimensions. Finally, we will close this part by briefly portraying the single fields.

Shapes as a Configuring Dynamic Component of the Social Field

Awareness-based social field research (Scharmer, Pomeroy, & Kaufer, in prep.) predicates that to shed light on how individual experiences relate to behavioral outcomes, research needs to turn inwards to the phenomenological investigation of the experience from a first- and second-person perspective. In line with

Pfuetze and Niebuhr's (1954) perception that "an increasing number of first-rate thinkers are confronting us with the proposition that man's essence is not to be found in isolated individuals, but in his bonds with his generation and his society" (p.30), we argue that we cannot fully understand action-inducing phenomena without moving research attention from single objects to relationships and the awareness underlying it. In a similar vein, Martin Buber criticized Martin Heidegger and Max Scheler for taking a perspective that "considers man in his self-being, the other of whom does consider man's relation, but regards them as impairing his real essence."(Pfuetze & Niebuhr, 1954, p. 30). Even earlier, Mead (1934) called for a study of behavior that looks at relationships, environment, and consciousness. His suggestion was as follows:

> To consider the conduct of the organism (...), and in particular 'self-conscious intelligence' within this conduct. This position implies organisms which are in relationships to environments, and environments that are in some sense determined by the selection of the sensitivity of the form of the organism. It is the sensitivity of the organism that determines what its environment shall be. (p.328).

Mead (1934) argued that consciousness "is not simply an emergent at a certain point, but a set of characters that is dependent upon the relationship of a thing to an organism" (p. 329). He understood consciousness to represent "a certain sort of an environment in its relation to sensitive organisms." (p. 329). Consequently, "anything that as a whole is more than the mere form of its parts, has a nature that belongs to it that is not to be found in the elements out of which it is made." (p.329). In its core, this understanding postulated a *nature* inhere in the whole that is not explained by its parts.

From a phenomenological first-person perspective (Varela, 2002, 2009), the shift observed in all the three above-described phenomena may be due to a redirection of attention, for which Husserl has coined the term *epochè* (Scharmer, 2000) encompassing three subsequent inner activities, which are suspending, redirecting, and letting go. Using micro-phenomenological methods (Petitmengin, Remillieux, & Valenzuela-Moguillansky, 2019), researchers have explored the inner unfolding experience of the redirection process in multiple activities and settings comprehensively.

Theory U adapted these methods. It assumes that moving from seeing to sensing implies an inner movement of redirecting attention by letting go of one's thinking and stepping into the shoes of the other (Scharmer, 2009). While this first redirection from Field 2 to 3 leads to sensing the world from the perspective of the other, a second redirection happens when moving from Field 3 to 4 on the level of the collective, such that the entirety of the collective field sees itself from the perspective of its larger context.

If we apply such an approach to the empirical cases documented above, we can at least partially explain the shift of self-experience in light of the larger whole in the awe project (Piff et al., 2015) with a suspension of one's concepts and concerns. Likewise, in the case of the overview effect, we can interpret the inner action of emptying oneself of habitual thought as the driving mechanism that brings another layer of reality into sight, which cannot necessarily be reduced to perceptual vastness (cf. Yaden et al., 2016). Indeed, Yaden and colleagues (2016) point to the fact that unlike other objects (i.e., the Grand Canyon), the "planet has an incredibly rich and broad context of meanings when viewed from above. The wholeness of the Earth makes it a symbol of almost all that is meaningful in human life." (p. 4). It seems to be physical disconnecting combined with emotional connecting that "conjures thoughts of home, of the entirety of one's world and of mankind as a whole" (Yaden et al. 2016, p. 4).

In summary, to understand a phenomenon, including the empty spaces between isolated phenomena, it seems necessary to deepen the research towards interior conditions of experience. This implies that in order to get a more researchable understanding of social fields, we need to move beyond what third-person research leaves uncovered by shifting attention from single individuals to the in-between, relational, and interior space. Underlying this argument, we assume that the "nature" (Mead, 1934, p. 329) of relationships themselves (i.e., being part of the whole, but not explained by the properties of the parts) residing in the in-between space has an impact on the quality of the whole. Whereas it does not matter now whether this nature is called configurations, patterns, or shapes, it is essential to recognize that they do not refer to the form of the visible individuals or objects but the shapes emerging from the in-between configurative space. Before we continue to describe the importance of these shapes for social fields, we will briefly review the origin of the social fields term with an emphasis on why the Gestalt-construct is essential for understanding and, finally, using it.

The Social Field

The understanding of the social field term is broad. Among the first using them, Lewin (1943) attempted to map out spatial relationships with the formula $B = f(P, E)$, implying that behavior (B) is a function of the acting person (P) and their environment (E). Based on his understanding of a field as "the totality of coexisting facts which are conceived of as mutually interdependent" (Lewin, 1951, p. 240), a *social* field means the interpersonal context including all psychological forces (i.e., perception, cognition, affect) that, in total, lead a Person P or a Party P to behave in a particular manner. Consequently, if one were to alternate a specific behavioral outcome, one would have to identify the relevant psychological forces that resulted in that behavior. Once identified, these psychological forces would then be strengthened or weakened to change an undesired behavior towards a more desirable behavioral outcome.

Whereas the conceptualization of behavior as a result of person-environment interaction, and the understanding of behavior change as the result of an altered person-environment interaction, was fundamental for conceptualizing behavior (cf. Reeve, 2008), the characteristics of a social field remained to be specified. The fact that Lewin (1943) assumed that "any behavior or any other change in a psychological field depends only upon the psychological field *at that time*"(p.294) suggests that he also expected that the interaction of person and environment would entail more than just that; namely at least a temporal component.

Indeed, Burnes and Cooke (2012) locate one of the reasons why Lewin's (1943) exceptional fieldwork had in the aftermath not always received full attention is because of his attempt to validate a Gestalt-based (Koffka, 1935; Köhler, 1925, 1967; Ref Wertheimer, 1922, 1923, 1925) idea with mathematical rigor. They argue that this effort to justify the primarily Gestalt-originated theory mathematically did not only fell short in satisfying mathematical requirements for proof but also did not fully satisfy Lewin's drive to enliven change as "a participative process and learning process" (Burnes & Cooke, 2012, p. 421; cf. Burnes, 2004). Consequently, there are at least two lines of research that, however, seem to not fully capture Lewin's (1951) original emphasis on, first, the "totality of coexisting facts which are conceived of as mutually interdependent" (p. 240); that is, the factors that create the in-between field, and, second, its effect on actual behavior. On the one hand, some scholars primarily took up the mathematical conceptualization of a field that then remained empty of the field quality in a Gestalt sense (e.g., Helbing, 1994). On the other hand, a more sociological use (e.g., Power, 1999) has helped to research subgroup relationships (e.g., McLeod, 2005) but its use has been so closely intertwined to the term *systems* that its characteristics (especially in the original Gestalt sense) remained unclear (cf. Wilkinson, 1970).

Drawing from Lewin's (1941, 1953) original work and the Gestalt tradition, Scharmer (2016) recently differentiated the social field from social systems in terms of perspective. Social fields emphasize the turn inwards to the lived experience of the acting person. Awareness-based social field research additionally points to the necessity that observing one's experience requires awareness capacity. By arguing that "social fields are social systems – but seen also from within" (Schamer, 2019, p. 1), Theory U aims to unravel a level of awareness driving the experience of mutual interdependence that one remained unaware of in Lewin's (1941, 1953) original work. As such, Scharmer, Pomeroy, and

Kaufer (in prep.) suggest that these fields compose the "source conditions" (p. 3) that guide the way we think, talk, and behave.

In an attempt to further conceptualize the social field, Scharmer (2017) describes 19 characteristics that he claims to be determining the quality of a social field. We believe that especially one of them – the idea that the quality of the social field is determined by one's awareness of time and space – is crucial for understanding how the social field determines the quality of action. We choose to focus on time as the vertical and space as the horizontal axis because they seem to set the stage for four different types of experiencing the world. Next, we will specify this awareness-experience-based understanding of the social field by going back to field theory's origin in Gestalt psychology.

The Gestalt of Social Fields

From the perspective of Gestalt psychology, social fields can be seen as Gestalten. Gestalten can be defined as "coherent wholes that have their own laws and are co-created by individual minds as reality" (Richter, 2010, p. 113). Key is the understanding of *structure*, which has originally been introduced by Dilthey (1894) as a feature of the whole. The whole can be seen as a particular configuration of its parts including the unity, which is organized by the proportional relationships between all of them. Building on the notion of Gestalt, our first take on the nature of social fields is to view them as *schemes* (Kohls & Scheiter, 2008) connecting mental (i.e., awareness), social (i.e., quality of relationships), and body-sensual (i.e., perceptions) facts of varied texture and developmental stages towards a composition that makes social reality come alive from within. As such, we suggest defining social fields as a combination of form and activity. By form, we imply socials fields are environments hosting awareness about inter-relational interdependence. By activity, we mean the degree to which an active quality of vitality is present (i.e., connection to or absence from the source).

Undoubtedly, this proposition calls for more theoretical, controversial, and empirical backing in the future. However, we want to advance this idea to reset the focus of discussion back to Lewin's (1941, 1953) original grounding of field theory in Gestalt psychology, as well as his drive to predict tangible behavioral outcomes and the change thereof.

Scharmer's (2016) Matrix of Inversion of Space, Time, Self, Collective, and Earth (see Figure 2 (adapted with permission from Scharmer, 2016, p. 238)) gives an overview of the main parameters driving distinct compositions of each social field. Moving down the table shows how increasing awareness of social space and time play out on what Scharmer and Kaufer (2013) call the three divides (Self, Collective, Earth columns on the right). From top to bottom, the experience of social reality dematerializes and reconnects self, other, and earth through the heart (i.e., Field 3) and, finally, through mere presence (Field 4).

Unit of Analysis	Social Space	Social Time	Self	Collective Emergence	Earth
1. I-in-me	One-dimensional	Disembodied Time	Habitual Self	Confirming	Dead Body
2. I-in-it	Two-Dimensional	Chronos	Rational Self	Confronting	Resource
3. I-in-you	Three-Dimensional	Slowing Down	Relational Self	Connecting	Living System
4. I-in-now	Four-Dimensional	Stillness/Kairos /Presencing	Authentic Self	Collective Creativity	Living Presence

Figure 2.

We understand Gestalten as the living essence of social fields. The nature and quality of inner activity generate "social soil" (Scharmer, 2018, p. 15). The vitality of intermediary micro-activities (such as moments of suspension, redirection, letting go) connect self, other, and whole (Versteegen, 2019) and thus cultivate a force that is either coherent with or dysfunctional for action. The work of the Social Presencing Theater research group (Dutra, 2019; Hayashi, 2017) is an example of the exploration of the pattern language underlying embodied group sculptures moving from stuck to unstuck.

Still, more research is required to identify further the quality of experience of inter-relational field shapes on a *granular level;* that is, the level of detail needed to depict the specific substance of the respective composition (cf., Petitmengin et al., 2019). For the moment being, however, we suggest to deepen our under-standing of social fields by specifying the two dimensions suggest-ed by Scharmer (2017) and that, from our perspective, represent the backbones opening up the social field.

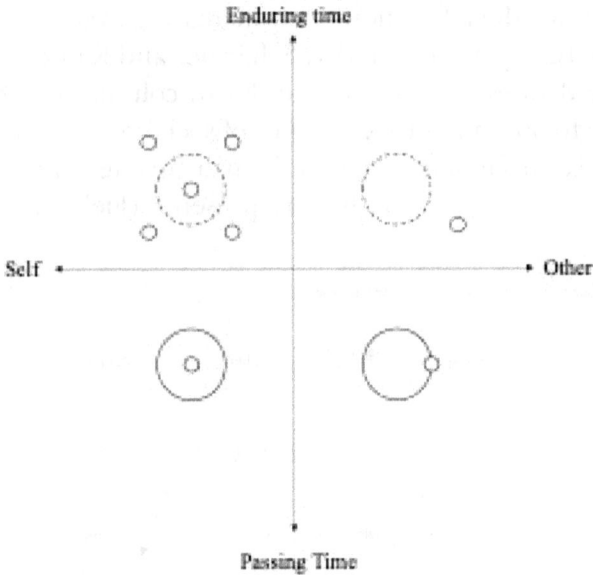

Figure 3.

The Two Axes of the Social Field.

Following Theory U's approach, building the capacity to bring oneself into the present moment intentionally is funda-mental (Goldman-Schuyler, Skjei, Sanzgiri, & Koskela, 2017). It is argued that the capacity to be aware of what is going on in one's mind, other people, and the environment is determinative for the above-discussed emergent *Gestalt* of the social field. If we aim to change towards a certain configuration, we need to become competent master observers of our experience (Scharmer, 2000; Petitmengin et al., 2019).

As mentioned above, we understand the configuration (i.e., the *Gestalt*) of any social field to be determined by two axes (see Figure 3 (Matrix of awareness-based action; adapted with permission from Scharmer, 2016, p. 242; cf. Scharmer, 2017)). The first, horizontal axis expresses the degree of social space between self and other or, as Scharmer (2017) puts it, "the split between self and other – that is, the degree of disconnect between actors in a social system" (p. 1). The second, vertical axis captures the social time in terms of absence and presence of source or, in Scharmer's (2017) words, the "body-mind split of the collective – that is, the degree of disconnect between collective action and awareness" (p. 1). Although any action certainly manifests under various conditions and in diverse forms, we argue that the nature of resulting action is determined by how time and space are experienced as a reality.

According to Scharmer (2016), the experience of reality is being modulated by three inner organs of perception, which are an open mind, open heart, and open will. By opening the mind, the experienced reality shifts from projection to an independent reality in the physical sphere perceived outside of ourselves (i.e., Field 2). Next, opening our heart connects us to the inner reality of seeing and feeling from the perspective of the other (i.e., Field 3). By putting ourselves into the shoes of the other, we redirect our attention on the horizontal axis to a co-sensing of social space. The experience of separateness (i.e., Field 2) gives way to a shared reality (i.e., Field 3). Social reality arises as a rhythmic movement of relational interconnectedness, not as a disconnected assembly of isolated things. Relating from the heart turns an object into a subject. Finally, opening the will connects us to the reality of wholeness and authentic action (i.e., Field 4). Redirecting the perspective from the parts to the whole and from passed time to timelessness creates a time-space experience of co-creation.

The vertical axis describes a collective body and mind. From bottom to top, it represents the experience of time from disembodied time to Kairos or, put differently, running time to timelessness. Time arises in our experience when we look at social reality from the perspective of its results, such as an old institution that is the manifest result of an idea invented 100 years ago. By looking at it from the outside, it appears static and dead. We externalize the visible result of an idea as something separate from us. If we, in contrast, become able to process the emergence and evolution of the idea behind it as moments of movements (Oosterling, 2005), we experience timelessness. In the social reality of perceived time-lessness, we are co-creators. In a social reality of the disembodied time, we are always late, facing the world as a finished result that we cannot participate in but become victims of.

The second, horizontal axis represents moving stages of self-other-awareness and corresponds to an opening of space moving from a manifest self to a manifest other. In moving from self to other, we are transitioning gradual shifts of inter-esse, which means the encounter with the "being" (esse) of the in-between (Oosterling 2005). Different stages of intersubjective experience have been researched from multiple perspectives (e.g., see Gallese, 2003, 2014, on the concept of intersubjectivity in neuroscience; see Depraz, 2001, 2012; Boulanger & Lancon, 2006, on intersubjectivity as alterology in genetic phenomenology; see Gunnlaugson, 2016, for an integral perspective; see Tajfel & Turner, 1986; Brewer & Gardner, 1996; Brewer & Chen, 2007, for a Social Identity Theory approach; see Buber, 1947, 1958; Friedman, 1999, for a philosophical and mystic perspective; and see Pfuetze & Niebuhr, 1954; Wilkinson, 1970, for a sociological account.)

Paradoxically, as people manage to enhance their social field quality, even complex challenges seem to get less tiring to deal with. When moving along the axes, shifting action gains speed and simplicity. As the experience of separateness mutes from Field 2 to 3 into a profoundly relational experience, Depraz (2001) suggests defining the newly emerging in-between-space as a "circular dynamic of relational mutuality" (p. 455) to capture the place between the poles of first and second person as a "plastic texture of exchanges (p. 454) rather than separate poles. Similarly, when dealing with the same paradox of how to bridge the apparent polarity on the level of the individual and the collective, Schmitz (2018) describes what could be seen as the emerging collective self in Field 4 as a plural subject:

(...) this neither creates a new subject as an additional

creature, nor a new subject as an additional creature, nor as a *fusion* of the members. The unity of the group is not the same kind of unity as the unity of an individual consciousness. It is a unity of minds, not of a mind. The collective subject is essentially a plural subject. (p.158).

When both axes collapse, perception unfolds as a distributed movement at the periphery of the whole, and each actor becomes a sensing organ. Collective self-awareness is the holding body and recipient of primary knowing. Rosch contends "that knowing capacity actually is the field knowing itself, in a sense, or this larger context knowing itself." She continues to explain that "when that happens, or when you get even a glimpse of it, you realize that we do not actually act as fragmented selves the way we think we do." (Rosch & Scharmer, 1999, p. 1; Varela, Thompson, & Rosch, 2016).

To summarize, the quality of time-space-awareness determines the degree to which we feel embodied and at home with ourselves, each other, and earth, and consequently whether we perceive the world as a friendly or hostile place. The experience of separateness (i.e., Fields 1 and 2) can be inversed by turning inwards, moving from cognizing the world as external objects to sensually experiencing it as a living movement. The essential nature of the whole expresses itself in the interaction of its parts in the in-between space. Looking for a stable world of independence, permanence, and controllability outside of oneself may be convenient but turns out to be misleading and sustains actions that contribute to fragmentation. In contrast, redirecting our attention towards our inner shared world of creativity and connectedness strengthens the sources of our collective ability to be part of the next evolutionary steps of humanity. With social fields, we have at hand a new way of understanding ourselves. They help us to see the conditions it takes to create a container for self-sustenance and well-being for all from within. Having developed our understanding of how time and space configure the conditions of connect and disconnect in our lived experience, opening up four different qualities of social fields, we will now continue by portraying those four resulting fields.

The Four Qualities of Social Fields

Quality of Action Field – Gestalt 1. One-dimensional field awareness (I-in-me; Scharmer, 2016) results in a quality of action in which one solves known problems individually. One moves along daily routines in existing infrastructures and institutional bodies. Actions on this level may reinforce self-absorbance as they feed the illusion of safety, controllability, independence, and continuity. Among the common mindsets, we assume that we need to earn more money and become more important to be able to sustain the status quo and to satisfy our need for a safe life. Although all of these are natural human features that some part of us always longs for (Maslow, 1943, 1954), this field configuration paradoxically disconnects us from ourselves. The longer we stay in this field, we dwell in our bubble and disconnect from others. Similarly, our understanding that we *can* do it all by ourselves seems to gradually turn into the experience that we *have* to do it all by ourselves. We constantly assume that we need to plan better and work harder. We start to over-extend, disembody, and compensate for the increasing disconnect from ourselves by looking for safety, continuity, and controllability in the external world (Kruglanski et al., 2018; see Kakkar & Sivanathan, 2017, for an example how perceived uncertainty affects decisions towards others). However, as we are opening the window and start looking outside, we do not necessarily like what we are seeing, which is an estranged world of people trying to gain money, safety, and predictability, and an economy promising exactly that – mirroring our mindset, but not becoming aware of it.

Quality of Action Field – Gestalt 2. The quality created by a two-dimensional field awareness (I-in-it) arises out of the social divide of me being different from you, and the realization that we compete with each other for scarce resources (Sherif, 1967). We identify with the groups we belong to (Turner, Hogg, Oakes, Reich, & Wetherell, 1987). As our group identity guides the way we see, hear, observe, and question the other (Tajfel & Turner, 1986, cf. Hornsey, 2008, for an overview), we increasingly become more aware of our rational self being distinct from the other. To give meaning to the situation, we need to make assumptions about the other, which, in turn, may re-enforce our self-identification with our view (Turner et al., 1987). As a group, we may compete or cooperate, but as we identify with ethnic backgrounds, family, profession, department, organization, or nation, there is always space left between us and the other. We are aware that the other is spatially outside and distinct from us. Meanwhile, time is flowing.

Some of the actions from Field 2 are driven by the understanding that some of the more complex challenges outside of us cannot be solved alone. Thus, we perceive the other as a resource satisfying our needs (Maslow, 1954), whom we pay to maintain the illusion of independence. As we may not trust the other, we need to make contracts, time plans, and milestones to give each other controlled outward-oriented stability. Still, in case of doubt, any action will serve our group's goals. In case of conflict, we will fight. Cooperative action, in contrast, will arise from the rational understanding that it could be useful or even necessary to cooperate. Our joint action will then be a function of what we perceive to be a balance of giving and receiving, with both of us aiming to get the most out of it. Nevertheless, we remain disconnected because of a lack of trust, and because we constantly remain and function as members of different subgroups (Tajfel & Turner, 1986)

Quality of Action Field – Gestalt 3. A 3-dimensional (I-in-you) relational space spans up the quality in Field 3. The other and we are two sides of a coin that has inversed, such that we are both aware of each other, but even more of the connection between us. This in-between space has emerged from the warmth of your otherness that we allowed ourselves to be touched by. Seeing what you feel from standing in your shoes reveals the reality you are living in behind the mask of different opinions and backgrounds. Receiving the gifts of your words and giving you my listening, we start to breathe together and reconnect to a part of us that we were not aware of. Whereas your otherness has been disturbing in Field 2, perhaps making us feeling diminished and helpless, we start sensing from our heart in Field 3. As we redirect our attention, we start sensing reality from the perspective of the impact our and others' actions have had on each of us. At first, it feels somewhat messy and clumsy to work through social reality as it is emerging anew through me experiencing your experience. However, when we stay with the old reality cracking up long enough, cause and effect will slowly turn round and present themselves in reverse order. Being in your shoes, one experiences oneself as seen from the results one's actions may have had on the other.

The inner activity of bending our concern from self to others is a grounding and enlivening experience. Paradoxically, shifting perspective from self to other and moving awareness upstream from the results of an action to its origin seems to be sharpening our sense of embodiment. The conditions in Field 3 are such that we all can hold onto staying connected to ourselves as well as face what our unskillful actions may have created for each other without blaming each other.

Reconnecting to that deeper territory enlivens us. Sensing the presence of each other and holding onto it, a little seed is growing in the in-between space. That what becomes present tells us that we are just alike; we both want to be happy and safe (cf. Pyszczynski et al., 2012). With that realization, gratitude arises and spreads in the space surrounding us. There is an emerging sense of a surrounding sphere characterized by understanding, trust, and caring. It is the reconnection of self and other that enables joint action. We start abiding by what needs us no matter what it takes.

Quality of Action Field – Gestalt 4. Finally, collective presence-in-action arises from a four-dimensional space (I-in-now) of stillness. It emerges from a 360° sense of panoramic seeing. We all see and sense what everyone sees and senses and how we are part of it. Slowing down, we attend to what is unfolding continuously. The individual awareness of each of us acts as the extended sensing organ of the not-yet-embodied whole unfolding moment to moment. We are part of one center of knowing while each of us is simultaneously functioning as a peripheral self that constitutes a common boundary holding this consciousness. To illustrate, in a mountain landscape, we would simultaneously be the deep lake in the center of surrounding mountaintops and the surrounding mountains framing that scenery. As such, we can not only see the mountain tops being reflected in us as the lake, but our collective consciousness also creates the surface reflecting back. It is thus not about the mountains or the lake but the experience of the interplay between the embedding mountains and the embedded lake, which gives us a sense of who we are. The unfolding moment is full of potentiality and co-creativity arising.

The quality of action in Field 4 is characterized by collective awareness becoming a shared social reality. We gain a panoramic sense of wholeness by seeing ourselves in view of the effects we have been co-creating. The wholeness coming into appearance may be a glimpse, skewed, cracking, or dysfunctional, but it is profoundly felt to be ours. This enables us to give meaning to a not-yet-embodied possibility that has always belonged to us, but that needed us to connect to the being of the whole to be revealed. Cause and effect, knowing and doing, collapse in time and space. As we connect the dots arising from single-minded to collective awareness, we can catch ourselves in action. Everything is. We all have a profound sense of ourselves as much as of the whole. It is hard to even think about it, and as we do, we feel the unity cracking. Selves are connected to themselves and aware of themselves as part of a distributed being of interdependence. Our individual minds and the collective mind have stilled, and may not even be two. Primary knowing comes through the field; the field knows itself and directs action (Rosch, 1997; Scharmer, 2001). We, as a distributed sensing organ, represent the whole of humankind as a living being. There is a sense of awe and wonder. As a collective body, we share mind, heart, and will, and we are aware of it. Like any being, it has temperament, vitality, rhythm, and creativity. It is truth. It is beauty. It is life itself. The Field 4 Gestalt is a profound aesthetic experience. Being, knowing, and doing are one. When collective presence becomes a social reality, anything is possible. The action arising from this social reality is effortless and playful. Making ourselves available, we are connected to ourselves, other, and source.

Conclusion

In part 1, we reported three empirical cases that show how a shift in one's experience of the relationship between self, other, and whole may alternate the attitudes one has about others (Pyszczynski et al.,2012), the way one behaves (Piff et al., 2015), or the foundation on which one is able to act (Yaden et al., 2016). Besides, we have used the example of the COVID-19 pandemic to portray how the quality of action changes due to a change in perception.

We did so because an awareness-based social fields research approach suggests that to encourage transformation, one has to shift the focus point of attention. Instead of investigating attitudinal and behavioral change in terms of isolated constructs, we have to explore the relational qualities underlying them, aiming to make the source conditions of the coherent wholes available.

Still, we argue that both approaches offer the opportunity to understand the experience of self, other, and whole, and the resulting ability for action. From a methodological perspective, social fields can be seen as operational concepts representing explicit, tacit, and self-transcending levels of knowing (Scharmer, 2001). They describe the *what* (level of action; e.g., listening, speaking, organizing), the *how* (e.g., embodiments of time-space-experience), and the *source* (source; i.e., quality of awareness) that leads to behavior. From a practitioner perspective, social fields are change tools like co-created environments (i.e., "social soils," Scharmer, 2018, p. 15), which increasingly allow actors to create a space of resonance for seeing themselves not only as individuals but as an acting whole from the outside.

Assuming that the purpose of awareness-based social field research is to understand how the quality of awareness guides action and that the drive of practitioners is to change action through awareness, we have to understand overview effect-like phenomena and how to evoke them practically. Put simply, although the overview effect (as well as the COVID-19 pandemic) seem to be excellent conditions for revealing both potentials of beauty (i.e., presencing) and destruction (absencing; Scharmer, 2016), we acknowledge the necessity for more straightforward, grounded tools to enable a shift in social field quality. Thankfully, our experience tells that certain U-related practices and process-es are able to activate such an awareness of something larger than the self, similar to the overview effect. Before that, however, it is important to examine the assumption that the leverage to the agency of change is not so much in the individual shift at first but in the inter-relational activity shifting awareness towards interbe-ing, which may create active forces of its own. By attending to self, other, and whole, they earn this kind of knowing, and by further cultivating those relationships, this intermediary space assumes existence independent from a single individual.

While the first two empirical cases, common threat and awe, are similar to the third, the overview effect, in the way that they all incorporated an altered awareness of being part of something larger than the self, they are still qualitatively different from the third. In the latter, people wake up to the deeper conditions of what it means to be human. We understand this as the final shift to a Gestalt 4 kind of field, which then enables a powerful trans-formative force. While the two former cases created the shift in a lab by the manipulations of an experimenter, Theory U practi-tioners seek to alternate these field conditions for human beings to become aware of their co-creative power and make free choices that serve the well-being of the whole better.

Whereas it is important to recognize that this drive to guide and change behavior is where we close circles with Lewin's origi-nal work (Lewin, 1941), practitioners in the Theory U tradition attempt to enable groups of multiple stakeholders to act across systems embodying human wholes or *humanity per se*. We do not do this because we aim to explain most of the behavioral outcome variance but to serve the deeper development and understand-ing of what it means to be human. As the term *development* sug-gests that there is no end to this, we understand the here-proposed advancement of the social fields terminology as a step towards understanding how an action is created and, eventually, changed. Thus, we will close this chapter by not only sharing a hands-on Theory U practice but also some questions for future research that we consider helpful in developing the quality of the social field.

Part III: Outlook

In the final part, we will first give a practical example of Theory U practice to show how awareness and action can be integrated towards a shift in social field experience. Secondly, we will share some suggestions for future research based on what has been developed in this chapter.

A Practical Example Integrating Awareness and Action

To recall, we suggested that the Gestalten of social fields shift as reconfigurations of self, other, and whole relationships unfolding within each and among the three. Each palpable configuration of relational connections across the three is a function of the combination of an inner, invisible awareness-based activity combined with an outer, visible action in the social world. The context of the following example is a 1-year-program in "Gross National Happiness: From Inner Transformation to Social Innovation" that one of us teaches with Tho Ha Vinh, (Eurasia Learning Institute for Happiness and Wellbeing, ELI[13]) and Jacoba Harm (Presencing Institute/Eurasia Learning Institute) at the Hochschule of Applied Sciences[14] in Osnabrück, Germany. The president of the university, Andreas Bertram, and Christiane Leiste, director of the university-based mindfulness leadership program, host respectively co-teach the program. The program entails four 3.5 day-long modules spread over ten months, peer coaching pairs meeting weekly to biweekly between the modules, as well as case clinic groups meeting in monthly sessions. The purpose of the program is to bring together inner transformation with outer social innovation. It provides a quality space for transformative leadership learning for 40 participants from Germany, Austria, and Switzerland, including all sectors of society.

Conceptual, experiential, group, and individual learning during the program are based on building capacity for U-Processes in the context of social change along the four pillars of Gross National Happiness (GNH; Ha Vinh, 2019). Throughout the program, participants develop a process for GNH projects in their contexts. The program asks participants to have or start building a contemplative practice as a regular part of their lives. The program is designed to experience living in harmony with self, others, and whole. This includes contemplative practices in the mornings and at night, a rhythmic organization of the days including a 1.5-hour break at lunchtime, body and arts practices, sessions of social-emotional learning (cf. Center for Contemplative Science and Compassion-Based Ethics, 2017), as well as expert teachings, and learning from each other.

In detail, this example refers to a *sensing journey* (Scharmer, 2009) undertaken in the first module. Our understanding of *sensing* as combining inner and outer activity is to deepen and widen our perception to re-connect parts and whole, as well as to make sense of the experience individually and collectively. Sensing means to deepen the perception by feeling into the phenomena we are dealing with, such that they become almost enlivened. After *deepening* the perceptual experience, we need to *broaden* it (Tho Ha Vinh, personal communication, April 27, 2020). We need to make sense of the experience individually and collectively by putting it into a larger context. Hence, sensing journeys mean to step back and forth between breathing in sensing experience (i.e., focused attention) and breathing out a quote (i.e., open awareness) repeatedly to share experiences and get into collective sense-making.

Specifically, participants gathered in subgroups and went to visit living examples of organizations, communities, and initiatives in the area that are trying to innovate around the ecological, social, and spiritual divides in agriculture, ecology, communities, special education, and health care. They were asked to interview the stakeholders involved and to collect key quotes of their most important *sensings*. When back to the program site, we first deepened co-sensing across journeys in small groups. We ended the session with a small *Jazz Combo* (Scharmer, 2000), reading quotes to each other, everyone standing up (no circle). We instructed participants to read a quote, to pause, to listen to the silence, followed by the next person reading a quote, pausing, and so on. Participants kept playing their instruments but also listened to the emerging music among them (see Scharmer, 2000, for details).

By the way the quotes were read, time slowed down and induced an expecting stillness, which then opened a new space of peripheral listening towards the quotes as unfolding footsteps of a larger, invisible movement (cf. Scharmer, 2000). As each participant did not only listen attentively to their own quote but also to the ones of others, an emerging narrative was embodied by the group before it could be named as an abstraction.

Listening to this reality emerging from amidst the quotes is a profound act of community creation. Participants slow down, attend to the emerging whole, and their authentic voice in it. The experience of time starts inversing, such that one becomes part of a collective co-creation. Every quote is a sculptural detail of some aspect of the essence of the whole, as experienced by the person who is quoting it. By voicing authentic individual sense experience quote by quote, patterns of collective experience move through all of them and become alive as the living forces forming the Gestalt of the emerging whole. As the whole starts to get a hold in the community, the time-space-configuration is shifting, and with it comes a new sense of reality and understanding.

Critically, as this happened on the first module's first day of the program, nobody knew anyone else. The shared experience of sensing the whole created a tight bond amongst participants, though not knowing each other. Some would tell us at the end of the second module that they still had not met every single co-participant but felt comfortable and safe. Approximately 25% of the participants came from the Osnabrück region. Some shared with us how profoundly this experience had changed their perspective on their home base. They had started to see the well-known with new eyes. Conversely, non-locals observed that the place moved from feeling strange to feeling familiar.

In summary, our takeaway from this example is that cultivating sensing as an inner dual activity of breathing in sensory perception and breathing out sense-making *reframes the configuration* of part and whole, as well as self and other in space and time. This example makes it possible to see how the lens of experience elicits how a Gestalt as a configuration of hidden relationships metamorphoses across the four fields.

In the Field 1 Gestalt, we are undifferentiated unities, such that everybody brings their ideas about the region of Osnabrück. In the Field 2 Gestalt, we are both parts of a non-existing unity, such that we can differentiate between participants from Osnabrück and those coming from outside. In the Field 3 Gestalt, we are both part of an inter-relational being (Buber, 1958) and start becoming aware of a shared social body. Finally, in the Field 4 Gestalt, we, co-enacting the region by our quotes, start to see the region as a living being. Our authentic quotes become the mirror cells of the collective mind becoming aware of and seeing itself. Mirroring our collective self, we may come to see that it is not only us in need of the earth. In contrast, we may see the reverse, namely that the earth is a living being with a biography of its own in need of us to make its next evolutionary step.

Questions for Future Research

This chapter attempted to describe the social fields concept in more detail. Specifically, we discussed social fields in relation to the matrix of awareness-based action (Scharmer, 2016) and the quality of each social field. Although understanding each of these concepts certainly deserves more attention in future research, we deem it necessary to study how the single concepts are related, and, more importantly, distinct from each other. A key part of this line of research would be to disentangle the components within awareness-based social fields research that requires an integrated perspective (i.e., that need to be explored in relationship to understand the full quality of the concept under discussion), and which components can be differentiated from each other. Whereas it would, for instance, have little meaning to examine the two dimensions self-other and body-mind within the matrix of awareness-based action (Scharmer, 2016) in isolation from each other, it could be worthwhile to organize the distinctiveness of overarching concepts more clearly.

A first project would establish a comprehensive list of all concepts under discussion (e.g., social fields, the matrix of awareness-based action, social reality, three divides), and explore potential content overlap thereof. The aim of this is to get a clear impression of the constructs needed to understand behavior change and to streamline their use a bit more.

Another project would then attempt to explore the temporal

and spatial positions of the single constructs. Again, the goal of this approach would not be to isolate the constructs. However, if we are keen enough to postulate a clear sequential order by claiming that action follows awareness (cf. Scharmer, 2016), then we should also try to maintain this clarity within our constructs. Right now, for example, we would speculate that the matrix of awareness-based action (Scharmer, 2016, p. 242; cf. Figure 1) is what opens up the social fields. These social fields, in turn, make us experience the relationships between self and self, self and other, and self and nature as divided or healed. Finally, depending on whether we experience them as divided or healed, we become able to act (see Figure 4).

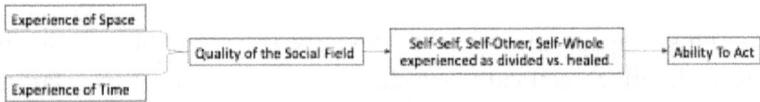

Figure 4.

A third project could investigate the claimed relationships more rigorously. For example, it would be interesting to examine if the quality of the social field is indeed sufficiently described by the interaction of the two suggested dimensions. If this is the case, field experiments using four separate groups representing each dimensional expression should be able to predict the proposed quality of each field, respectively. Such a project would not only offer a better theoretical understanding but give clear suggestions for what U-practitioners have to alter when aiming for action change.

Conclusion

We opened this chapter with the COVID-19 pandemic to raise a practical example for the argument that the quality of action depends on the social field creating it. Using three empirical cases, we described additional content from which we could then derive an advanced understanding of the social field. Based on the origins of social field work in Gestalt psychology, as well as more recent developments in awareness-based social field research, we suggested advancing our understanding of social fields as a Gestalt evolving from our experience of social time and social space. We closed the chapter with a practical example showing how the quality of a social field becomes apparent, as well as sharing some questions for future research; both revolving around the question of how collective action can be facilitated out of free consciousness when a pandemic is not at hand.

References

Alon, T. M., Doepke, M., Olmstead-Rumsey, J., & Tertilt, M. (2020). The impact of COVID-19 on gender equality (No. w26947). *National Bureau of Economic Research.*

Appuzzo, M. & Kirkpatrick, D. D. (2020, April 14). Covid-19 Changed How the World Does Science, Together. *New York Times.* Retrieved from https://www.nytimes.com/2020/04/01/world/europe/coronavirus-science-research-cooperation.html, April 25, 2020.

Baniamin, H. M., Rahman, M., & Hasan, M. T. (2020). The COVID-19 Pandemic: Why are Some Countries more Successful than others? *SSRN,* 1–23. doi: 10.2139/ssrn.3575251

Barbaro, M. (2020, March 17). It's Like War. [Audio Podcast]. *The New York Times.* Retrieved from https://www.nytimes.com/2020/03/17/podcasts/the-daily/italy-coronavirus.html, April 25, 2020.

Blasberg, M., Fahrion, G., Sarovic, A., & Schaap, F. (2020, April 10). A Nasty Competition Emerges in Hunt for Corona Protective Gear. *Der Spiegel.* Retrieved from https://www.spiegel.de/politik/ausland/eat-or-be-eaten-the-global-medical-products-market-has-gone-feral-a-e6f65515-c913-4837-a121-be6567372c42, April 28, 2020.

Boulanger, C., & Lançon, C. (2006). L'empathie: réflexions sur un concept. *Annales Médico-psychologiques, Revue Psychiatrique,164,* 497–505. doi: 10.1016/j.amp.2006.05.001

Brewer, M. B., & Chen, Y. R. (2007). Where (who) are collectives in collectivism? Toward conceptual clarification of individualism and collectivism. *Psychological Review, 114,* 133–151. doi: 10.1037/0033-295X.114.1.133

Brewer, M. B., & Gardner, W. (1996). Who is this" We"? Levels of collective identity and self representations. *Journal of personality and social psychology, 71,* 83–93. doi: 10.1037/0022-3514.71.1.83

Buber, M. (1947). *Between Man and Man*. New York, NY: Routledge.

Buber, M. (1958). *I and thou*. In R.G. Smith (Ed.). I and thou. New York, NY: Scribners.

Burke, E. (2015). A Philosophical Enquiry into the Origin of our Ideas of the Sublime and the Beautiful. In P. Guyer (Ed.). Oxford, UK: Oxford World's Classics.

Burnes, B. (2004). Kurt Lewin and the planned approach to change: a re-appraisal. Journal of Management Studies, 41, pp. 977–1002. doi: 10.1111/j.1467-6486.2004.00463.x

Burnes, B., & Cooke, B. (2012). Kurt Lewin's Field Theory: A Review and Re-evaluation. *International Journal of Management Reviews, 15*, 408–425. doi: 10.1111/j.1468-2370.2012.00348.x

Cantor, N. F. (2001). *In the wake of the plague: the Black Death and the world it made*. New York, NY: Simon and Schuster.

Center for Contemplative Science and Compassion-Based Ethics (2017). *See Learning. Social, Emotional, and Ethical Learning. Educating the Heart and Mind*. Emory University, US.

Chen, S. (2012). *A documentary on Shenzhou-9*. Hu-nan, China: The Science and Technology Press of Hunan.

Daley, J. (2020, March 20). How to Triage Patients Who Need Intensive Care. *Scientific American*. Retrieved from https://www.scientificamerican.com/article/how-to-triage-patients-who-need-intensive-care/, April 25, 2020.

Depraz, N. (2001). The Husserlian theory of intersubjectivity as alterology. Emergent theories and wisdom traditions in the light of genetic phenomenology. *Journal of Consciousness Studies, 8*, 169–178. doi: 10.1007/s11007-012-9223-z

Depraz, N. (2012). Empathy and second-person methodology. *Continental Philosophy Review, 45*, 447–459. doi: 10.1007/s11007-012-9223-z

Dilthey, W. (1894). Ideen über eine beschreibende und zergliedernde Psychologie. In W. Dilthey (Ed.), *Gesammelte Schriften, V. Band*. Stuttgart, Germany: B. G. Teubner Verlagsgesellschaft Stuttgart.

Dutra, R. (2019). Social Reality Contemplation: a Performance-Led Approach to Making Visible Deeper Layers of Social Fields. *Presencing Institute Blog*, retrieved from https://medium.com/presencing-institute-blog/social-reality-contemplation-a-performance-led-approach-to-making-visible-deeper-layers-of-social-5ea4627418fc, April 30, 2020.

Evans, C., Lawson, H., Fenton, S., & Donovan, K. (2020, April 14). Factbox: Global economic policy response to coronavirus crisis.

Reuter Polls. Retrieved from https://www.reuters.com/article/ us-health-coronavirus-economy-factbox/factbox-global-econom- ic-policy-response-to-coronavirus-crisis-idUSKCN21W2AJ, April 25, 2020

Jaffee, R. (2011). Anthropogenic relation to other biota: Connections to Disorders and Crises of our Time. Interpretation of 21st Century Punctuated Equilibria and predictive Perturbations. Implications for sustainable and affordable survival (Unpublished manuscript). Health studies Collegium, Ashburn, VA.

Ferreira, B. (2016). Seeing Earth from Space Is the Key to saving our Species from Itself. *Vice*. Retrieved from https://www.vice.com/ en_us/article/bmvpxq/to-save-humanity-look-at-earth-from-space- overview-effect, April 25, 2020.

Friedman, M. (1999). The interhuman and what is common to all: Martin Buber and sociology. *Journal for the Theory of Social Behaviour, 29*, 403 – 417. doi: 10.1111/1468-5914.00110

Gadamer, H.-G. (1960). *Truth and Method*. London, UK: Bloomsbury Academic

Gallese, V. (2003). The roots of empathy: the shared manifold hypoth- esis and the neural basis of intersubjectivity. *Psychopathology, 36*, 171–180. doi: 10.1159/000072786

Gallese, V. (2014). Bodily selves in relation: embodied simulation as second-person perspective on intersubjectivity. *Philosophical Transactions of the Royal Society B: Biological Sciences, 369*, 1–10. doi: 10.1098/rstb.2013.0177

Giuffrida, A. (2020 April 8). Coronavirus Italy: Lombardy Province at Centre of Outbreak Offers Glimmer of Hope. *The Guardian*. Retrieved from https://www.theguardian.com/world/2020/apr/08/ coronavirus-italy-lombardy-province-at-centre-of-outbreak-of- fers-glimmer-of-hope, April 25, 2020.

Goldman-Schuyler, K., Skjei, S., Sanzgiri, J., & Koskela, V. (2017). "Moments of Waking Up" A Doorway to Mindfulness and Presence. *Journal of Management Inquiry, 26*, 86–100. doi: 10.1177/1056492616665171

Gunnlaugson, O. (2016). Uncovering Four Levels of Leadership Presence: A Dynamic Presencing Journey. In O. Gunnlaugson & M. Brabant (Eds.), Cohering the Integral We Space. Engaging Collective Emergence, Wisdom and Healing in Groups, *(pp. 115–130)*. US: Integral Publishing House.

Hallam, M. (2020, March). Coronavirus: Treating European Patients in Germany. *Deutsche Welle*. Retrieved from https://www.dw.com/en/

coronavirus-treating-european-patients-in-germany/a-52943695, April 28, 2020.

Ha Vinh, T. (2019). *Der Glücksstandard. Wie wir Bhutans Bruttonationalglück praktisch umsetzen können*. München, Germany: Droemer Knaur.

Ha Vinh, T. (2020, March). *Reflections on the Corona Pandemic*. Presentation given at the Eurasia Learning Institute for Happiness and Well-Being. Lausanne, Switzerland, March 2020.

Hayashi, A. (2017). *Social Presencing Theater*: Listening to our body-knowing to access the wisdom that lives in us? Presentation given at the Wisdom Together Conscious Leadership Conference, Oslo, Norway, October 2017.

Helbing, D. (1994). A mathematical model for the behavior of individuals in a social field. *Journal of Mathematical Sociology, 19*, 189–219. doi: 10.1080/0022250X.1994.9990143

Hirsch, C. (2020, April 3). European Citizens Support Strict Coronavirus Lockdown, Say Polls. *Politico*. Retrieved from https://www.politico.eu/article/citizens-in-favor-of-even-stricter-measures-to-fight-coronavirus/, April 25, 2020.

Hornsey, M. J. (2008). Social identity theory and self-categorization theory: A historical review. *Social and Personality Psychology Compass, 2*, 204–222. doi: 10.1111/j.1751-9004.2007.00066.x

Irwin, J. B. (1973). To Rule the Night. The Discovery Voyage of Astronaut Jim Irwin. Philadelphia, PA: A. J. Holman Company.

Koffka, K. (1935). Principles of Gestalt Psychology. London, UK: Routledge.

Köhler, W. (1925). Gestaltprobleme und Anfänge der Gestalttheorie. *Jahresberichte über die gesamte Physiologie und experimentelle Pharmakologie für das Jahr 1922, 3*, 512– 539.

Köhler, W. (1967). Gestalt psychology. *Psychologische Forschung, 31*, XVIII-XXX. doi: 10.1007/BF00422382

Kakkar, H., & Sivanathan, N. (2017). When the appeal of a dominant leader is greater than a prestige leader. *Proceedings of the National Academy of Sciences, 114*, 6734–6739. doi: 10.1073/pnas.1617711114

Keltner, D., & Haidt, J. (2003). Approaching awe, a moral, spiritual, and aesthetic emotion. Cognition and Emotion, 17, 297–314. doi: 10.1080/02699930302297

Kohls, C., & Scheiter, K. (2008). The relation between design patterns and schema theory. *PLoP 2008: Proceedings of the 15th Conference on Pattern Languages of Programs, 15*, 1–16. doi: 10.1145/1753196.1753214

Koelbl, S., Lüdke, S., Peters, K. G., Pitzke, M., & Stöhr, M. (2020, April 2). People Are Finding Creative New Ways to Support Each Other. *Der Spiegel*. Retrieved from https://www.spiegel.de/international/world/corona-how-people-around-the-world-are-supporting-each-other-a-9d6b1e7d-b12b-432e-aad4-e814802243b4, April 25, 2020.

Kruglanski, A. W., Jasko, K., Milyavsky, M., Chernikova, M., Webber, D., Pierro, A., & Di Santo, D. (2018). Cognitive consistency theory in social psychology: A paradigm reconsidered. *Psychological Inquiry, 29*, 45–59. doi: 10.1080/1047840X.2018.1480619

Lewin, K. (1941). *Defining the Field at a given Time*. Paper given at a Symposium on Psychology and Scientific Method, University of Chicago, September 1941.

Lewin, K. (1943). Defining the 'field at a given time.' *Psychological Review, 50*, 292–310. doi: 10.1037/h0062738

Lewin, K. (1951). *Field theory in social science: selected theoretical papers*. In D. Cartwright (Ed.). New York, NY: Harpers.

Mækelæ, M. J., Klevjer, K., Reggev, N., Tamayo, R. M., Dutra, N., Briganti, G., & Pfuhl, G. (2020). Perceived efficacy of actions during the early phase of the COVID-19 outbreak. *PsyArXiv Preprints*, 1–19. Preprint doi: 10.31234/osf.io/ce4n3

Maslow, A. H. (1943). A theory of human motivation. *Psychological Review, 50*, 370–396. doi: 10.1037/h0054346

Maslow, A. H. (1954). *Motivation and Personality*. New York, NY: Harper Brothers.

McLeod, J. (2005). Feminists re-reading Bourdieu: Old debates and new questions about gender habitus and gender change. *Theory and Research in Education, 3*, 11–30. doi: 10.1177/1477878505049832

Mead, G. H. (1934). *Mind, self and society*. Chicago, IL: University of Chicago Press.

Newberg, A., Alavi, A., Baime, M., Pourdehnad, M., Santanna, J., & d=Aquili, E. (2001). The measurement of regional cerebral blood flow during the complex cognitive task of meditation: A preliminary SPECT study. *Psychiatry Research: Neuroimaging, 106*, 113–122. doi: 10.1016/ S0925-4927(01)00074-9

Oosterling, H. (2005). Ma or Sensing Time-Space. Towards a culture of the inter. (Unpublished paper presented at Transmediale). Haus der Kulturen, Berlin, Germany.

Partington, R. (2020, March 20). UK government to pay 80% of wages for those not working in coronavirus crisis. *The Guardian*. Retrieved from https://www.theguardian.com/uk-news/2020/

mar/20/government-pay-wages-jobs-coronavirus-rishi-sunak, April 25, 2020.

Petitmengin, C., Remillieux, A., & Valenzuela-Moguillansky, C. (2019). Discovering the structures of lived experience. *Phenomenology and the Cognitive Sciences*, *18*, 691–730. doi: 10.1007/s11097-018-9597-4

Piff, P. K., Dietze, P., Feinberg, M., Stancato, D. M., & Keltner, D. (2015). Awe, the small self, and prosocial behavior. *Journal of Personality and Social Psychology*, *108*, 883–899. doi: 10.1037/pspi0000018

Pfuetze, P.E. & Niebuhr, H.R. (1954). *The Social Self. Library of Current Philosophy and Religion*. New York, NY: Record Press.

Power, E.M. (1999). An Introduction to Pierre Bourdieu's Key Theoretical Concepts. *Journal for the Study of Food and Society*, *3*, 48–52. doi: 10.2752/152897999786690753

Pyszczynski, T., Motyl, M., Vail III, K. E., Hirschberger, G., Arndt, J., & Kesebir, P. (2012). Drawing attention to global climate change decreases support for war. *Peace and Conflict: Journal of Peace Psychology*, *18*, 354–368. doi: 10.1037/a0030328

Reeve, J. (2008). *Understanding Motivation and Emotion*. Hoboken, NJ: John Wiley & Sons.

Richter, I. (2010). Organization Development as a Source. In J. Ubels, N.-A. Acquaye-Baddoo, & Fowler (Eds.), *Capacity Development in Practice* (pp. 101–115). New York, NY: Routledge.

Rosch, E. (1997). Transformation of the Wolf Man. In J. Pickering (Ed.), *The Authority of Experience. Essays on Buddhism and Psychology*. Surrey, UK: Curzon.

Rosch, E., & Scharmer, C. O. (1999). Primary knowing: When perception happens from the whole field. Interview with Elanor Rosch. *Presencing Institute* (Personal Communication), October, 2005. Retrieved from https://www.presencing.org/aboutus/theory-u/leadership-interview/eleanor_rosch, April 30, 2020.

Sacks, S. (2011). Social Sculpture and New Organs of Perception: New practices and new pedagogy for a humane and ecologically viable future. In C. Lerm Hayes & V. Walters (Eds.), *Beuysian Legacies in Ireland and Beyond. Art, Culture and Politics* (pp. 80–97). München, Germany: LIT Verlag.

Scharmer, C.O. (2000). The Three Gestures of Becoming Aware: Interview with Francisco Varela Paris, France January 2000. Retrieved from www.presencing.com/dol/varela, April 30, 2020.

Scharmer, C.O. (2001). Self-Transcending Knowledge: Sensing and Organizing Around Emerging Opportunities. *Journal of Knowledge*

Management, 5, 137–151. doi: 10.1108/13673270110393185

Scharmer, C. O. (2009). Theory U. Leading from the Future as it Emerges. San Francisco: Berrett-Koehler Publishers, Inc.

Scharmer, C. O. (2016). Theory U. Leading from the Future as it Emerges (2nd ed.). San Francisco, CA: Berrett-Koehler Publishers, Inc.

Scharmer, C.O. (2017) The Blind Spot: Uncovering the Grammar of the Social Field. *Huffington Post Blog*, retrieved from https://www.huffingtonpost.com/otto-scharmer/uncovering-the-grammar-of-the-social-field_b_7524910.html, April 25, 2020.

Scharmer, C.O. (2018). The Blind Spot. In *The Essentials of Theory U: Core Principles and Applications* (pp. 3–15). San Francisco, CA: Berrett-Koehler Publishers, Inc.

Schamer, C.O. (2019). Social Field Resonance: How to Research Deep Structures of the Social System. *Presencing Institute Blog*, retrieved from https://medium.com/presencing-institute-blog/social-field-res-onance-how-to-research-deep-structures-of-the-social-system-544d68654abf, April 30, 2020.

Scharmer, C.O. & Kaufer, K. (2013). *Leading From the Emerging Future. From Ego-System to Eco-System Economics*. San Fransciso, CA: Berrett-Koehler.

Scharmer, C.O., Pomeroy, E., & Kaufer, K. (in prep.). Awareness-Based Action Research: Making Systems Sense and See Themselves. *Handbook of Participatory Research and Inquiry 2021*. Unpublished manuscript, Massachusetts Institute of Technology & Concordia University.

Schmitz, M. (2018). Co-subjective consciousness constitutes collectives. *Journal of Social Philosophy, 49*, 137–160. doi: 10.1111/josp.12228

Sherif, M. (1967). Group conflict and co-operation: Their social Psychology. London, UK: Routledge and Kegan Paul.

Shiota, M. N., Keltner, D., & Mossman, A. (2007). The nature of awe: Elicitors, appraisals, and effects on self-concept. *Cognition & Emotion*, 21, 944–963. http://dx.doi.org/10.1080/02699930600923668

Singer, T., & Bolz, M. (2013). *Compassion: Bridging practice and science*. Max Planck Institute for Human Cognitive and Brain Sciences.

Thompson, L. A., & Rasmussen, S. A. (2020). What does the coronavirus disease 2019 (COVID-19) mean for families?. *JAMA Pediatrics*, 1–2. doi: 10.1001/jamapediatrics.2020.0828

Tajfel, H., & Turner, J. C. (1986). The social identity theory of inter-group behavior. In S. Worchel & W. G. Austin (Eds.), *Psychology of Intergroup Relations* (pp. 7–24). Chicago, IL: Nelson-Hall Publishing.

Turner, J. C., Hogg, M. A., Oakes, P. J., Reicher, S. D., & Wetherell, M. S. (1987). *Rediscovering the social group: A self-categorization theory*. Oxford, UK: Blackwell.

Turner, J. C., & Oakes, P. J. (1986). The significance of the social identity concept for social psychology with reference to individualism, interactionism and social influence. *British Journal of Social Psychology, 25*, 237–252. doi: 10.1111/j.2044-8309.1986.tb00732.x

Urgesi, C., Aglioti, S. M., Skrap, M., & Fabbro, F. (2010). The spiritual brain: Selective cortical lesions modulate human self-transcendence. *Neuron, 65*, 309–319. doi: 10.1016/ j.neuron.2010.01.026

Varela, F. (2002). *The View From Within. First-Person Approaches to the Study of Consciousness*. London, UK: Imprint Academic.

Varela, F. (2009). *Ten Years of Viewing from Within. The Legacy of Francisco Varela*, (C. Petitmengin, Ed.) Charlottesville, VA: Imprint Academic Philosophy Documentation Center.

Varela, F., Thompson, E., & Rosch, E. (2016). The Embodied Mind. Cognitive Science and Human Experience (2nd ed.). Cambridge, MA: MIT Press Ltd.

Versteegen, U. (2019) Soziale Bodenfruchtbarkeit. *Punkt und Kreis, 58*, 11–13.

Viner, R. M., Russell, S. J., Croker, H., Packer, J., Ward, J., Stansfield, C., ... & Booy, R. (2020). School closure and management practices during coronavirus outbreaks including COVID-19: a rapid systematic review. *The Lancet Child & Adolescent Health, 4*, 397–404. doi: 10.1016/S2352-4642(20)30095-X

Wertheimer, M (1922). Untersuchungen zur Lehre von der Gestalt. *Psychologische Forschung, 1*, 47–58. doi: 10.1007/BF00410385

Wertheimer, M (1923). Untersuchungen zur Lehre von der Gestalt. *Psychologische Forschung, 4*, 301–350. doi: 10.1007/BF00410640

Wertheimer, M. (1925). Experimentelle Studien uber das Sehen von Bewegung. Drei Abhandlungen zur Gestalttheorie (pp. 1–105). Erlangen, Germany: Verlag der Philosophischen Akademie.

White, F. (1987). The Overview Effect: Space Exploration and Human Evolution (3rd ed.). Reston, VA: American Institute of Aeronautics and Astronautics.

Wilkinson, K. P. (1970). The community as a social field. *Social forces, 48*, 311–322. doi: 10.2307/2574650

Yaden, D. B., Iwry, J., Slack, K. J., Eichstaedt, J. C., Zhao, Y., Vaillant, G. E., & Newberg, A. B. (2016). The overview effect: Awe and self-transcendent experience in space flight. *Psychology of Consciousness: Theory, Research, and Practice, 3*, 1–11. doi: 10.1037/ cns0000086

CHAPTER 8

The Four Fields of Dynamic Presencing

Olen Gunnlaugson

Introduction

As a process framework, *Dynamic Presencing* (Gunnlaugson, 2020) focuses in depth on five foundational journeys that develop our capacities for presencing mastery, leadership and flow. To attain this aim, each journey introduces a series of key updates to the presencing theory and practices described in *Theory U* (Scharmer, 2007), introducing an updated set of in-depth practices, subtle distinctions and ways of engaging presencing that gradually bring to life an overall transformed understanding of presencing in one's day to day life.

The fourth journey of primary communicating marks an important turning point in Dynamic Presencing. Where the first two journeys focus on uncovering and excavating our presencing nature, in primary perceiving, we explore how to access and sustain presencing awareness at the level of our felt arising perception. As we begin primary communicating, we turn our attention to engaging the interior dimensions of the presencing field. In Theory U, presencing is presumed to take place exclusively in the social field. Dynamic Presencing takes a different approach and introduces four new phenomenological locations to access the hidden presencing field: our own "i-space", another's "you-space", the group's "we-space" and the greater collective "all-space."

As a field template to assist our presencing, each of these four field locations serve as distinct interfaces to the presencing field. If we practice presencing on our own, we work with accessing our individual i-space. If we are presencing with another colleague or client, then we engage with their you-space. If we are presencing in a group, then we shift into our shared we-space, whether in dyads, triads or a larger group. Finally, if our intent is to connect with the greater more-than-human context, either alone or with others, we engage presencing in the all-space.

Each of the four regions (figure 1.0) offers a particular field-perspective as well as a subtle yet invisible field-structure that when activated, supports the presencing process in distinct ways. With the update of one individual and three collective field locations, primary communicating offers a field template to help synchronize our presencing process with the context of everyday communication. In being more precisely fitted to each situation, the interface of each field-space brings us into closer alignment with the overall presencing process as it unfolds through conversation.

Overall, the four field locations bring an updated subtle geography that is supported by the findings of field-theory research traditions in social psychology, sociology, communication and consciousness studies among other disciplines. Phenomenologically speaking, each of the four field locations are similar in quality yet have distinct features, forms of engagement and are accessible through the subtle dimensions of our direct experience in any moment when key conditions are present.

Practically speaking, the four locations serve as a comprehensive presencing field map and more importantly for the purposes of Dynamic Presencing, as an experiential guide of practice. Once we connect to the interface of any of the four field-spaces, each has its micro-context and culture of presencing that directs our presencing awareness and perception in particular ways.

Whether each field-space is taken up individually or as a larger flowing core movement (explored in greater depth at the end of the chapter), the four field-spaces provide an inner pathway that coheres and calibrates our presencing practice both individually and collectively to new levels of subtlety, precision and comprehensiveness.

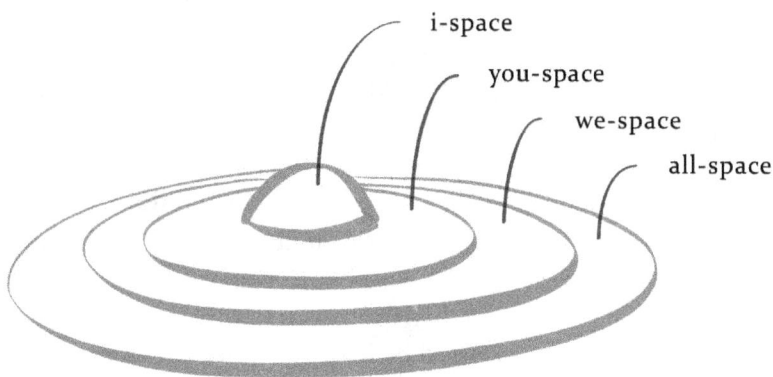

Figure 1.0 The four presencing field-spaces

The nested interconnected nature of the four field-spaces

The above illustration depicts our individual i-space and the three collective locations. Generally, the immediate presencing context we are in informs which field location will be our focus. If I am alone, I am exploring presencing through my individual i-space or the greater all-space. As I am alone, another's you-space or a collective we-space are not available to me, at least not in a direct or immediate way. If I am with others, presencing can be explored in their you-space, our we-space or the all-space together, depending on the intent, purpose and particular needs of the collective situation.

Again, this field map offers coordinates that keeps our presencing awareness subtly aligned and in synch with the underlying spatial context of our communication. As a subtle interface, each field-space informs our attention once the presencing process is underway. As a felt-based reference point and guide, the space and structure of each presencing field location assists us in more seamlessly accessing and discerning the inner regions of the presencing field we are engaging.

The depiction of the four field-spaces as a series of concentric, encompassing realms reminds us that each location is not separate from the other locations and the greater presencing field. The embedded interconnected relationship between the four locations can be understood in the following way. Learning to engage with presencing in another's you-space draws upon insight we have uncovered in presencing through our i-space. We-space facility is supported by learning from presencing in the i- and you-space. Finally, all-space proficiency draws from the presencing skillful means we have cultivated from work with the i-, you, and we-spaces.

There is an iterative filling out of a contextual capacity for skillfully accessing presencing that takes place as we move from the most sovereign i-space to the most encompassing all-space. And while these four locations presume distinctness, again they do not presume separateness. This is a crucial point, for the four field geographies are simply mapping our contact with the greater underlying presencing field that is always available. Each location brings into focus structurally the contextual region that is most aligned or suited to our immediate experience and communication situation.

The foundational role of our presencing self in primary communicating

In primary communicating, we drop into any of the four field-space locations by first connecting with our presencing self. By initially accessing our presencing self, we are able to move into a more permeable, choiceful and fluid relationship with the presencing field. Connecting with one of the four presencing field-spaces from our presencing self serves a number of functions.

First, our presencing self becomes as an embodied reference point for connecting with our presencing awareness in a more effective manner. As our presencing self contains a discernable self-sense, this helps ground our presencing awareness in our immediate experience. Secondly, it provides a more seamless means to connect with the presencing field location we are in. If the focus on presencing is on accessing the field, practitioners typically overlook the role our presencing self plays in accessing the presencing field. When the focus shifts to the place where our presencing self and field connect and synchronize, we enact conditions that help us sustain the presencing process alone and with others. Thirdly, this synchrony offers a nexus point through which we can align, adjust and optimally engage our presencing awareness in. Accessing the presencing field in this connected relational manner ensures that we are each individually not falling back to our familiar ego-based self when engaging any of the field-spaces of presencing.

It is important to clarify that each of the five journeys of Dynamic Presencing is developing our presencing self in particular ways. As it is presence-based and emergence-led, in primary communicating our presencing self supports, catalyzes and stewards the presencing process within our individual field location as well as across each collective field location. When we engage any of the three collective field-spaces, we learn to ground and synchronize our presencing self in the collective field location we are in. This ensures that we are functioning from a state of optimal presence-generating influence when working with others in any of the collective field-spaces. Engaging our presencing experience in this way also ensures that each practitioner is doing their part to support the generative conditions for communication within and across the three greater collective field-spaces.

De-mythologizing the presencing field

A number of Theory U inspired groups[15] in recent years have described the social field as a "circle being", "we-being", "a field or entity that wasn't me", "knowing field" among other anthropomorphic descriptions. Depicting the presencing field as existing apart from or beyond the presencing self with a "higher" or more exalted spiritual connotation tends to overlook our presencing nature and can become problematic in practice.

For the purposes of Dynamic Presencing, the focus lies with engaging the actual inner dimensions of where our presencing nature interfaces with each presencing field-space. This requires observing, suspending and bracketing any tendency to ascribe sentience or anthropomorphic weight to the presencing field. Relating to the presencing field in this manner opens and refreshes our presencing awareness at its source through ongoing contact with what-is and what-is-emerging as the gateway to discerning the arising new.

In primary communicating, each presencing field location is a discernable space or inner environment where presencing is active collectively and/or individually. Exploring the presencing field geography through these inner regions helps practitioners access the presencing field in a more immediate way. From our presencing nature, we work with a process of active felt-sensing and connecting with the field-space of consciousness that is arising in the particular location we are in.

In primary communicating, what-is is the gestalt of presence that is sensed and accessed directly inside the presencing field. Contact with what-is draws us into a deeper enfolded connection with *is-ness* or the underlying essential nature of reality that is always present and available to us on a sensory level of our experience. What-is contains both the visible "explicate" and invisible "implicate[16]" dimensions of reality that resides in each field-space. Learning to work directly with the interior conditions of the presencing field puts our attention in service of attuning to what-is as our perception entrains with what-is-emerging in order to discern the arising new. Again, if we relate to the presencing field in a way that projects, colors or mystifies what is coming through or interprets it in an anthropomorphic fashion, there is a risk of missing the opportunity to actually see and behold the creative movement of what-is-emerging in its fullness and actuality.

Establishing a rich sensory felt-contact with the space of each field through the inner body of our presencing self, which is now active, we can effectively observe, suspend and bracket our projections, idealizations and hoped for wishes which tend to narrow, condition, or otherwise block the subtlety of the arising new. Retaining our commitment to uncovering and being with what-is keeps the interior space of each presencing field clear of these metaphysical constructs, cultural filters and beliefs, supporting a continuous and direct exploring of the presencing process itself. This keeps us more closely calibrated to the fullness and actuality of the arising new as it arises.

Staying attuned to what-is on the felt-level of our experience ensures that we retain contact with the field-space we are in. As presencing becomes more familiar and second nature to us, we are able to more effectively discern the arising new in each field location. In learning to discern emergence with more exacting precision and skill inside the presencing field-space, our presencing awareness in turn grows and develops without the former socio-cultural filters conditioning, directing or limiting our perception.

Clarifying our presencing self-field boundaries

To access any of the four field locations, we relax into and move across the subtle inner boundary or membrane between our presencing self and particular field-location. Because our presencing self is the gateway through which we access the other field locations, this ensures that connecting and relating inside the presencing field is referenced through our individual presence, agency and voice.

As an example, I am with colleagues and my intent is to connect with them in our we-space. In Dynamic Presencing, this subtle action is mediated through my presencing self. Entering the we-space in this way ensures that my presencing faculties are fully active as I join others in the collective process presencing in a way that honors my individual presencing perception in relation to the collective process with others in the field.

This approach of initially leading forth from our presencing self stands in contrast to collective methods that begin with moving away from our individual location or "agency" by letting go of our egoic or separate sense of self as we move into full "communion" with the social field. Because this later approach overlooks the significance of our ground, voice and critical agency, there is a need to re-establish our individual presence within the collective.

This ensures a filling out of both the interiority of our presencing self and field are taking place in a way that supports relational mutuality and individual empowerment. In doing this, we open into service of a more complex and nuanced movement of presencing collectively that at some subtle level is still in contact with our agency, voice and individual location. This empowers presencing practitioners to shift into a more choiceful way of engaging ourselves, others, and each of the four field locations in both a sovereign and relational manner.

It is also important to point out that in engaging the presencing field, the boundaries of our presencing self are not static. There is an ongoing need to sense, shift, modulate and adjust these boundaries in a fluid manner that best accommodates each particular field situation in primary communicating. Sometimes a certain way of holding our self-field boundaries is too rigid or too open and is no longer serving the presencing process alone or with others. As such, we need to be mindful of our presencing self-field boundaries in order to optimize the presencing process across each of these field locations.

Within each field, our presencing self assists us in becoming a transparent instrument in discerning the arising new through felt-shifts and felt-openings in the space of each presencing field. Through our presencing self, our inner body merges and becomes co-extensive with each field-space. Inside this nexus point, there is no longer a gap between our inner body and the phenomenological space of each presencing field location. The two simply merge and begin to synchronize.

Much like an audiophile music system reduces and removes

unwanted noise and static so that the listener can appreciate how the music sounds closer to its source, when the inner dimensions of our presencing self and field move into a state of coherent alignment, on very subtle levels of our perception this removes any "static" or "interference" between the source and the presencing information we receive from it.

As our boundaries become more permeable, this allows presencing awareness to be accessed more richly inside each presencing field-space. As an attentionally-mediated process rather than a psychologically-based structure, the inner body of our presencing self can move into a seamless relating and alignment with the inner space of each field location. This further catalyzes energy, attention and presencing awareness across these previously separate regions of our presencing experience, inviting a seamless synchrony with the presencing field.

The I-Space

The journey of primary communicating begins with a depth activation of our individual i-space. The i-space is otherwise known as the inner dimension of the individual presencing field, individual "field of the soul"[17] (Beaumont), "phenomenal field"[18] (Jacobs), among other descriptions. To activate our i-space, we begin by connecting with our presencing self and then allow our immediate presence to expand more peripherally into our presencing field location. As this fills out, our i-space offers a new co-extensive presencing self-sense that is in touch with the inner condition of the presencing field as a dimension of our own interiority and expanded presencing self-sense.

While Theory U does not address the individual presencing field, it is helpful to understand the presencing process through our i-space for several reasons. Connecting with our i-space activates presencing awareness through our inner body inside the presencing field. In this way, the i-space helps us access a more stable, coherent and embodied presencing awareness on our own and when in solitude. In turn, this builds our capacity for presencing in any of the three collective field locations.

When the i-space is overlooked, there is a tendency to privilege as well as develop a psychological dependence on the collective field locations. When our i-space is overlooked, presencing is typically presumed to take place outside ourselves: beyond in the emerging future or in the social field. This conventional understanding is problematic however, in that it overlooks the generative capacity of our presencing nature within our i-space and instead, projects this upon the social or other collective fields. In workplaces and communities, this leaves practitioners prone to groupthink tendencies within the group, team or organization.

Comparatively speaking, in Dynamic Presencing our presencing practice is underdeveloped to the extent that we ignore or overlook our i-space. Engaging a collective field location without a sound understanding of how to work with our i-space leaves our presencing skills developed in a partial manner, making us prone to developing a tacit dependency on others or the collective social field to become the principle catalyst and main driver of our presencing practices.

This habit tends to play out in groups and teams that privilege the group through an emphasis on collective presencing over the individual through the movement from the "I" to the "We", with the collective field being perceived as a more authoritative source of presencing intelligence, wisdom and so forth. In practice though, such groups may lack a sufficient grounding and understanding of how their individual fields of presencing serve the greater social fields, particularly in a more differentiated as well as integrated manner.

The tendency to conflate individual and collective agency is reduced, however, when our field capacity and literacy expands to include these distinct yet essential geographies of presencing. Because privileging collective agency over individual agency, in cases where the i-space is overlooked or diminished tends to quickly devolve into subtle forms of collusion or more obvious expressions of groupthink, the importance that the i-space plays in laying the groundwork for collective presencing contexts cannot be overstated.

As the first field-space in the journey of primary communicating, the i-space serves a foundational role that opens a more integrative path for building one's capacity and skill to navigate the collective field locations. By acknowledging the individual interior dimension of presencing, the i-space empowers practitioners to work more skillfully and perceptively within the presencing field.

The You-Space

When we engage with another person in a presencing conversation, for example in a coaching session, our focus shifts to connecting with the inner environment of their presencing field or the interface of the you-space. The you-space is a reference for the "client field" (Gilbert & Evans)[19], "interpersonal space" (Lloyd)[20], "client environment" (Wright)[21], "I-Thou relation" (Buber)[22] and describes the phenomenological region of another person's presencing field location.

In helping professions such as coaching, teaching or therapy, distinguishing the inner environment of one's client or student is needed to uncover optimal conditions to support, challenge and in essence, help them grow and develop. Distinguishing the phenomenological location of our client's field and giving it ontological status clarifies subtle perceptual, energetic and relational boundaries that have a bearing and influence on the presencing process when working with another.

Speaking more technically, to engage with another's location in the presencing field involves establishing a felt-sensed contact with the inner dimension of their field-space and presencing selves. In this you-space location, important social, emotional, relational information becomes available. Additionally, the energetic quality of the subtle field structure of another's you-space is important in that it sets the client's presencing space as distinct from both our shared we-space and individual i-space locations, in turn opening a new practice domain for presencing to develop.

This becomes particularly useful in coaching where supporting the development of key capacities and empowerment of another practitioner is of central importance. If I am oblivious to another's field-space when presencing with them or treat their field-space as a general social presencing field, in other words, as our we-space, this can be an ineffective or worse, inappropriate way of engaging them—particularly in coaching contexts. In the case of interpersonal communication, if I am a coach and I am oblivious to your presencing field, then I am overlooking a key means for supporting and serving your development and learning.

In primary communicating, another's i-space becomes a you-space through "our eyes," reminding us of the greater significance of interpersonal boundaries as well as the optimal conditions for leveraging presencing with another person. In a conversation among colleagues, being aware of one another's you-space clarifies the field dynamics of our relating. Describing this process gets a bit technical, but they will be able to tell that our attention is now being directed towards tracking and being with their presencing process exclusively with and inside their location in the presencing field.

This is a marked contrast to either 1) attempting to serve their presencing process through our i-space, which is self-serving and generally ineffective or 2) being in a shared we-space with a colleague, and attempting to help them from a place of mutuality and shared resonance and meaning, which can also be self-serving and less effective than simply presencing their field location directly. Location wise in the first instance, there is a shift from being inside my own i-space to interfacing and in turn, more effectively serving my colleague's learning and development. And in the second instance there is a shift from being inside our shared we-space to interfacing my colleague's you-space.

As these boundaries get clarified in the primary communicating journey training, it helps our presencing practice by being more aware of how our field location influences the presencing process. Again, if I am coaching my client but not interfacing their you-space but either superimposing my i-space or conflating it with our we-space, I am doing them a disservice by unskillfully engaging our presencing process together. Working with precision in and across each field location helps us more effectively discern the commonplace distortions that inevitably surface when presencing is explored collectively. Following from this point, with clients, colleagues, students, friends and so forth—it helps cohere, clarify and empower another's presencing process by relating directly to their presencing field. With the territories of the i-space and you-space delineated, we can attend more clearly and precisely to when our listening and speaking are engaged within our own i-space, versus another's you-space or in our we-space, inviting us into a more precise contact with ourselves and others inside the overall presencing process.

Much like having clear interpersonal boundaries contributes to a more skillful management and health of relationships in one's professional and personal life, referring to each specific presencing field location helps us assume different presencing postures depending on the social context we are in. Being unaware of the connection between the underlying subtle structure of each field location and the subtle dynamics this plays in our communication with colleagues or clients across different presencing contexts, we in turn lack understanding of how and where to leverage our attention and presence in ways that can more optimally support the presencing process. Learning to direct our listening and speaking within and across the individual, interpersonal, collective and more-than-human presencing field-spaces increases the coherence, clarity and insight, further helping the presencing process flow in more differentiated, integrated and comprehensive fashion.

As a further clarification of this point, whenever my presencing self is active, I have a reference point and ground to draw from when connecting with another's you-space. The presencing self again plays an important role in helping me navigate within and across different field-space locations. Also, if my presencing capacity is low or not well developed, I will lack a more stable access to the arising inner wisdom and intelligence of my presencing self. This has implications for how I engage another's you-space in that to serve another's presencing process requires drawing actively on my presencing self in resourcing and stabilizing the process.

If both my and their presencing self is neglected in the process of working with another's you-space, we lose contact with our ground access to presence and the subtle field-structure. If I am coaching my colleague, then the presencing process is more optimally served by engaging her you-space by resourcing myself from my presencing self and ground. Following from these points, it is one thing to work with presencing in solitude and quite another to learn to support another's presencing process collectively—an area of emerging research that will certainly have important relevance for leaders, coaches and managers in the coming years.

The We-Space

A third phenomenological location opens in the presencing field when our focus moves into the interior shared dimensions of what is emerging collectively (with collective being defined as two or more individuals). Here we arrive into the shared "inside" of our collective location in the greater presencing field. The we-space is in essence, the inside of the "social field" in Theory U. This shared inner dimension of the presencing field has also been described as a "group field" (Bache)[23], "ba" (Nonaka and Konno)[24], "dialogue circle" (Bohm)[25], "interhuman sphere of between" (Buber)[26], "field of collective wisdom" (Briskin), "we-space" (Gunnlaugson)[27] among others.

To connect with the we-space, we first connect through our presencing self, and in turn with the space of shared presence of the group that surrounds us. Beginning with our presencing self is initially important as this creates a stronger energetic base from which to engage the presencing field collectively. Again, the quality of our contact with the we-space is influenced by the quality of our resourcing in our presencing self. Each mutually informs the other within this dynamic polarity.

In arriving into the we-space through our presencing self, we bring forth essential field-stabilizing conditions for a collective individualism to take root and support the overall presencing process in the team or group. By inviting everyone in the we-space to connect from their presencing selves, this helps us all to come into our full presencing activation and expression. At some point, a shift occurs where the presencing selves of participants and the collective we-space merge. For many presencing practitioners, it is not uncommon to experience this as a kind of emerging purpose, an existential imperative that inspires a new way of engaging collectively that optimally draws from a mindful integration of our individual co-authorship and articulation.

In group, team and organizational life, the we-space establishes an important collective interface and container to drive the presencing process. It also develops our individual presencing selves that are building the capacity and skillful means to serve this unfolding. As we each engage the we-space from our presencing selves, we move into a shared phenomenological territory of mutual exploration and discovery of the arising new.

The we-space in this way, introduces a renewed social basis for shared depth, meeting and co-created community that is relationally oriented and aware, opening groups into a way of being together that guides the communication and inquiry process in unforetold ways. By providing collectives with a tangible shared reference point for uncovering a presencing way of thinking, learning and being together, the we-space opens new possibilities for collective co-creation.

Unlike the you-space or i-space, the we-space is the first collective field that relies initially on a facilitator in order to collectively establish the presencing norms within the specific group. Within an organization, team or community that is exploring presencing, it can be helpful to clarify and establish norms and commitments for engagement. For those who are new to Dynamic Presencing, there will be a period of becoming acclimated to the distinct ways of engaging and uncovering a collective basis of communicating and leading from the we-space as a collective interface.

Initially it can be helpful to work with one or several facilitators concurrently. That said, the objective here is to establish and seed conditions for individuals to find their way of connecting and staying in synch with their presencing selves in the we-space. This is important in order to bring about conditions for a flourishing collective individualism, where the weaving of presencing contributions move to being guided collectively through a subtle participation with the we-space as the group or team's shared generative interface.

In practice, it is advisable that the facilitator strive to work at serving this leadership role as described above. It can also be helpful to have a process where the group clarifies what their presencing norms for engagement are—whether they wish to engage a common shared process or work with a more emergent, eclectic process. In either case, experimentation is needed to establish helpful objectives and guidelines that support the emergence of a flourishing collective practice within the we-space.

As the we-space offers groups a tangible collective reference point from which to stay anchored in the presencing process collectively, as a shared process, this has the effect of helping keep participants grounded in their presencing selves. This also opens groups into accessing the flow channel within the field together. As our collective presencing attention becomes cohered and embodied inside the we-space, each individual explores uncovering a new ground of collective communication that is entrained with the field.

The we-space tends to help individuals relax into a broader and deeper scope of presencing awareness, as perspectives and perceptions flow in with less individual identification and attachment. Again, as each practitioner is engaged in presencing as a way of being related to their experience, whatever is shared in the space of the we-space is held, met and engaged with in a generative way. Just as the i-space and you-space provided a bridge into the flow channel in the presencing field, the we-space is no exception.

Engaging the we-space effectively in groups of two or more requires ongoing practice. However, once groups learn how to find and sustain flow in the way they engage the we-space, this creates conditions for collective thinking and a new ethos for a collective way of being and learning together. As our self- and -field boundaries become more translucent and permeable, the connectivity between our presencing self and the we-space grows and develops.

In maturing into a more distinguishable "form" for our presencing self to engage with, the quality of our presencing awareness becomes clearer and more lucid, stirring awake the collective intelligence and collective wisdom held implicitly by the group. As the we-space heats up, individuals tend to experience less separation between themselves, activating a deeper collective source of intelligence and wisdom, something we become more receptive to as work in the we-space deepens.

By touching into and activating the always already present ground of inter-relatedness that precedes our individual human subjectivity, the we-space offers a means for contacting this elemental if not primal foundation of interbeing. On the human level, since time immemorial the longing to commune with and from this ground has been an essential dimension of who we are as a species. Transposing this perennial longing into we-space practice opens groups into contact with the primordial originating ground of who we are. When groups, teams and collectives come to understand how to access these primary grounds of interrelatedness, a new means for experiencing collective presencing intelligence and wisdom begins to emerge.

As the we-space grows to become a reliable container for supporting collective presencing, this brings participants an expanded basis of identification and broader inclusive sense of selfhood that grows from our initial work with our i-space and you-space. With sustained practice, this nurtures an ethos that is relationally oriented and aware yet also capable of serving the deeper generative unfolding of Dynamic Presencing. As the we-space becomes more accessible to practitioners, again the sense of separation we ordinarily experience between ourselves and the field dissolves, opening new possibilities for collective presencing.

Touched upon earlier in this chapter, I pointed out that as we connect with the we-space, we each have the responsibility for learning how to stabilize and sustain access to it through our presencing selves. This presents a challenge in that an initial surrender is needed to access the shared inner realm of the we-space. If the self-surrender is too deep, we can temporarily lose our footing in our own agency and voice and find ourselves overly identified with the we-space or collective. Conversely, if our surrender is not strong enough to relax the sense of separation that ordinarily exists between us and the we-space, we find ourselves outside the collective group process, looking in as an observer. Hence the importance of an initial process of facilitation, as well as inner self-management that brings our presencing self into synchronization with the we-space.

In this sense, learning to develop a sustained access to serving the presencing process inside the prior i-space and you-space helps practitioners transfer the abilities and know-how knowledge into their work within the we-space. This is essential. Our collective presencing practice is diminished to the extent that we have not yet learned how to develop a more sustained and regenerative ability to engage Dynamic Presencing with others in the we-space.

The All-Space

- Unless we live our lives with at least some cosmological awareness, we risk collapsing into tiny narcissistic worlds. For we can be fooled into thinking that our lives are passed inpolitical entities, such as the state or a nation; or that the bottom-line concerns in life have to do with economic realities of consumer lifestyles. In truth, we live in the midst of immensities.~ Swimme, Brian[28]

Before introducing the all-space, let us first retrace our steps back through the three prior field-space locations. Connecting with our presencing self brings forth a gentle expansion, a de-centering and filling out of our presence through our inner body. From here, we explored connecting with our individual i-space and the collective presencing field locations of the you-and we-space.

Across each of these field-spaces, this expansion of presence connects us with distinct horizons of each field that envelope and fill out the space around us in greater orbs of inclusivity and connection. As we explore expanding into each field location in an encompassing manner through the core movement of primary communicating, this makes it possible to contact, hold and engage presencing awareness within and through each field geography.

Having explored these three human-centered field locations of presencing opens a panoramic spaciousness as the interior dimensions of each field-space are connected with the felt levels of our perception and presence. As the process of connecting with each field-space of presencing becomes more second nature to us, there is a growing field capacity that begins to emerge.

Through the synergistic coupling of our presencing self and field, there is an enhanced connectivity with presencing awareness. In accessing each field location, we practice letting go of what is obscuring our perception of new emergence, and in its place, there arises a fluidity and extension of our own interiority, opening us into a more expansive sense of our presencing self that includes the presencing field as integral to its constitution.

In this sense, the journey of primary communicating opens us into the experience of both sovereignty and inter-relatedness, restoring our connection to presencing in the field as a function of sovereign mutuality. At the junction point between the we-space and the all-space, there is a shift into connecting with the interior dimensions or space of the greater macro contexts of presence, which in primary communicating are languaged in the form of nature, culture, the earth and the universe. While the three prior field locations focused more on the individual and collective "human" expressions of presencing, the all-space opens our sightline into the largest background contexts that hold the whole of human experience and are integral to life and existence as we know it.

Given the broad scope and magnitude of the all-space, this final field location invites us into a participatory way of relating with the larger communities that our lives intimately depend. In the all-space our presencing identity is invited to expand beyond our scope of human identifications into a broader post-personal and post-human perspective. Within field theory, the all-space is otherwise referred to as the inner region of the "morphic fields" (Sheldrake)[29], "akashic field" (Laszlo)[30], "earth body" (Hayashi)[31], "interbeing" (Nhat Hahn)[32], "gaia-field" (Nichol)[33], "council of all beings" (Macy)[34] among other references.

With the arrival of the all-space, there is the opening into a qualitatively different presencing inscape in two ways. First, it extends us beyond the location of the intersubjective human social field of the group-based we-space. And secondly, it connects us to the invisible interior dimensions of the larger more-than-human contexts to which again, twenty-first century life increasingly depends. The imperative for a more fundamental re-casting of our self-reality boundaries within the greater collective context has become increasingly apparent in recent years with the advent of climate change and other global disruptions. In this way, the all-space plays an indispensable role in rising to meet and support our efforts towards including this realm of life as essential to our overall presencing process.

What has been to date lacking in the social field literature is a relationally-responsive orientation that places us into a very subtle yet meaningful form of participation, sensemaking and communion with the greater macro dimensions of reality. To invoke the language of Martin Buber, there's a growing imperative to learn how to effectively make the shift in orientation from an it to a thou in our way of being and relating with the interior dimensions of the all-space, where it becomes possible to explore a movement of reciprocity and co-responsibility with and for these dimensions of reality.

When this larger dimension of the all is related to as an it or object, we fall out of an interior relatedness to these essential facets of reality and life as a whole. But more than this for our purposes here, we lose touch with the ways these fundamental macro dimensions of reality (i.e. nature, culture, the earth and the universe) mirror and enfold the deeper micro levels of presence that our presencing selves intimately depend upon. This move risks reducing the scope of our presencing work to an unconscious default of privileging the human over the more-than-human, but also diminishing our sensitivity to the ways in which both these macro and micro dimensions of presence are interdependent, interwoven and deeply supported by one another.

Once the all-space becomes sufficiently active, presencing this macro context helps us open to a wider relational orientation that unlocks the wisdom and intelligence held within these dimensions of reality. As the inner bonds between our presencing self and this field-space grows, this gives rise to developing a more comprehensive ethic of care. By letting our sensemaking contact these dimensions of reality, our apprenticeship into presencing deepens, extends into and eventually includes the interests of each of these domains of life as integral to shaping and informing our path of presencing.

Where the i-, -you and we-spaces might be thought of as gateways to engaging the human dimensions of our presencing lives, the all-space becomes the gateway to re-engaging the more-than-human dimensions of our lives and current world. Traditionally this plays an integral part to understanding one's purpose and function within the whole of life, as explored by the domain of cosmology, and more perennially by the world wisdom traditions. If the promise of the we-space lies with establishing a collective means for thinking, learning and leading together, the call and promise of the all-space is in its further opening of the "human" scope of our concerns to the larger contexts that inform each decision and action, regardless of how seemingly insignificant at first.

By redirecting and expanding both our individual and collective scope of identification, accessing the all-space involves a subtle way of "turning towards" and "tuning into" the tacit dimensions of the world and kosmos that all of life depends. Exploring the possibility of presencing in the all-space interrupts a prevailing tendency to have these greater macro dimensions continue to be currently outside our scope of identifications and deemed as "other", "foreign" or "it" to the extent that we are not in touch with them. Engaging our presencing from the all-space opens us back into connection within and between each of these essential contexts as a "thou."

In the all-space there is no longer a "we," but an expanded felt connectedness that expands to include the "all," as the field opens in both depth and breadth, shifting us into a place of exploring and connecting with the whole of reality. Learning to open our presence into meeting and contacting these greater grounds at very subtle felt levels helps us re-set the scope and nature of our presencing self-boundaries and identifications.

Work in the all-space brings about a gradual dissolution and reconfiguration of boundaries held in place by our long inherited modern condition of separateness from nature, culture, the world and greater universe. Where our focus in the initial journey of primary presence was on reclaiming the inner ground of our presence within and between one another, the focus of primary communicating in the all-space extends to reclaiming the inner dimensions of the larger grounds from which our presence depends. Through this dual process of reclaiming the ground of our presence deeply within and expansively without, we reconnect to the fullness of who we are in service of this burning emerging leadership imperative of twenty-first century life.

In connecting with the expansive presence of the all-space, we are drawn into greater synchrony with the presence of one another as we open ourselves to accessing and learning from these greater contexts. Contact with the all-space inspires possibilities for a new level of emerging purpose, bringing with it what is traditionally considered to be a more activist or spiritual imperative as there is a growing urgency to interrupt the prevailing global narcissistic narrative and restore the health and well-being of our relationship to each of these dimensions of reality.

Expanding the scope and reach of our presencing practices in this manner inspires new forms of collective communication and leadership that in their extended embrace, leave no one, thing or facet of life outside our scope of care. In this sense, the all-space keeps us more closely attuned to the greater contexts that our lives are intimately apart of and depend upon. The all-space catalyzes connection with the greater life contexts that are increasingly becoming an ethical and leadership imperative in our time.

By uncovering new presencing pathways into engaging these macro dimensions of life and the kosmos, the all-space also opens up new ontological grounds and horizons to work form. In this sense, the all-space is a prime embodiment site for growing and nurturing what Scharmer and Kaufer (2013) describe as the next emerging purpose of presencing, which is to foster the shift from ego- to ecosystem awareness that is committed to serving the well-being of the whole. Because the all-space works primarily with the interior dimensions of presence that constitute these systems, Dynamic Presencing provides a more ontologically-guided (rather than systems-awareness based) process that gives presencing practitioners an immersion into eco-system awareness as a living experiential enactment. With practice, this ecosystem awareness gradually fills out and takes root in practitioners as a living wisdom that informs our presencing awareness. As we transition from leading from what-is into learning how to steward and lead from the whole of life, the all-space holds possibilities for a more mature and comprehensive order of presencing.

The core movement of primary communicating

The core movement of primary communicating works with developing our capacity for engaging the presencing field in a more immediate, discerned and comprehensive way. This takes place by honing our ability to access and navigate our communication from presencing awareness directly in both individual and collective contexts, as well as arrive at a more nuanced understanding of the subtle nexus of our presencing self as it engages the individual and three collective field locations.

The core movement works with a step-by-step activation from the i-space, you-space, we-space and all-space that connects us more powerfully with each field geography from the inside out, as well as opening us up to four new presencing horizons or inscapes for generative exploring. At its heart, primary communicating is about learning to communicate from presencing awareness directly, both listening and speaking in a way that integrates our presencing self in the field location we are in. Navigating our presencing awareness in this way opens us into contact with dimensions of presencing reality that were previously not possible with the social field alone.

In primary communicating, the core movement can be explored in one of three following ways. First, it takes place serially as one flowing movement of perspectives from the i-space to the you-space, we-space and finally the all-space. This initial step-wise movement is critical to develop familiarity and basic skill in working with each presencing field-space in relation to the other.

Second, the core movement can take place emergently, where we shift into different field-spaces depending on the arising needs of the presencing situation as it presents itself. This secondary movement develops more naturally once we have developed enough familiarity and skill with accessing each of the four geographies within the greater presencing field.

Thirdly, we can engage the core movement more dynamical-

211

ly, deploying our presencing awareness to be in contact with two or more locations at the same time, giving rise to a new comprehensive seeing and engagement with more of the presencing field territory. This emergent stance in turn fills out of our deeper presencing identity, stretching our perception to connect with different field-spaces simultaneously, in turn open up new creative ways of engaging the overall presencing field.

As each field-space is connected with an actual phenomenological location, individually and collectively connecting with these locations as generative interfaces ensures our presencing process is connecting with the actual context of the situation we are in. When these four field locations are not active in our awareness, there is a tendency for our way of engaging presencing to collapse into the social field as a default mode of presencing engagement and to overlook the presencing information that otherwise arises through contact with these interfaces.

As covered earlier in the chapter, our efforts to master the presencing process are limited to the extent that we do not recognize the presencing field location we are in. With this framework update, there is a new understanding of how presencing is enacted across these main individual and social contexts. Working in depth and breadth with these field locations and geographies ensures that we are developing a generative capacity and skillful means for accessing the respective regions of the whole presencing field in its fullness and entirety.

With practice, this develops a more nuanced and differentiated leadership stance, as well as a more refined field acuity and ability to work skillfully within and across each of these respective field geographies depending on the contextual factors of our practitioner situation—i.e. this typically varies across different professional roles and situations.

In addition, without this fourfold field-space awareness, different habits, blind spots and tendencies tend to develop in our presencing practice, creating imbalances in how we work with the presencing field as a whole. When it is presumed that our individual presencing capacities are being developed indirectly through our collective presencing practice in the social field, key embodied capacities to discern, ground, and access presencing intelligence directly in our experience tend to be overlooked.

Collective presencing practice requires a grounding and rooting at the very core levels of our inner experience and i-space. Sufficient realization and access to our post-identified presencing natures (i.e. our presencing self), without the support and anchoring of a robust individual presencing practice that works with our i-space overlooks the core source of our immanent embodiment of presence and the presencing process. When our presencing selves are overlooked when engaging the presencing field, we skip over a foundational part of the presencing process.

Instead of bypassing the wisdom and intelligence of our presencing nature, in the journey of primary communicating, the presencing self is brought into a new symbiotic role with each of the four presencing field locations. This opens up new ontological leadership territory for us to explore a more complex and adaptive presencing self-system that is capable not only of substantive presencing awareness without, but more importantly understanding the interior basis and means for learning to lead and live from that very presencing awareness as a way of being and communicating.

This brings a critical update to the practice of presencing by opening up new territory first by honoring the crucial role that the presencing self plays in engaging each of the presencing field locations and second, by acknowledging the indispensable roles that each of the four field-spaces of presencing play. Especially as we move towards unfolding a new mode of dynamic presencing that is relationally-attuned and contextually-precise in its overall orientation and service in stewarding the arising new.

Working with the four field-spaces as interconnected territories that can be accessed in any communication situation, and more dynamically in a simultaneous manner introduces a new set of embodied interfaces that allows for a new cross pollination of presencing perspectives. This makes it possible to engage presencing in a more choiceful, precise and encompassing way "within" and "across" these field horizons, filling out any presencing blind spots or preferences we might have. Once again, privileging the social field or we-space over other field locations is highly problematic in that each has its respective presencing contribution.

While a particular presencing conversation may take place predominantly in one of the three collective field locations, the core movement reminds us of the limitations of our own partial presencing perspective (i.e. too much reliance on one particular field-space) as well as possible blind spots that we may unintentionally fall into through an over-emphasis on one field horizon over the others. Also, the core movement reconnects us interiorly with each of the field locations that begin from our individual presence right through the interpersonal, collective and more-than-human dimensions of reality.

Finally, the core movement opens us up to the possibility of a dynamic movement that orients from two or more geographies simultaneously, assisting us in perceiving the greater whole of the presencing field in a manner that is more precise, engaged and encompassing. Learning to working with each field location as a larger flowing core movement brings us a richer breadth of presencing awareness as well as a more attuned process for dynamically connecting with the contexts that inform each of the four presencing field regions.

On the whole, the journey of primary communicating establishes a generative infrastructure for exploring a dynamic expression of presencing that is richly attuned to the complexity of the contexts, life conditions and communication needs of this early twenty-first century moment.

CHAPTER 9

Contemplative Being, Becoming, and Knowing:

The "Work" at the Bottom of the U in a Graduate Program in Contemplative Inquiry

Charles Scott

Introduction: Our Complex World

As a model of both understanding and addressing the considerable challenges we face on both local and global levels, Theory U (Scharmer, 2009) has emerged as a way forward in a world that is, at both levels, increasingly complex, ever more rapidly changing, increasingly connected, and challenged with a lack of sufficient opportunities to reflexively explore values and the meanings of our lives in depth. We need the capacities to discern not only what is present—a challenge in its own right—but also what is emerging or wanting to emerge. Being able to discern what is emerging or wanting to emerge is a more sophisticated challenge; reason alone, and educational systems that focus primarily on the sole development of reason or narrow conceptions of 'critical thinking' are likely not going to prepare students sufficiently to meet and address the emerging future.

Despite the rapid change and complexities of contemporary society, the work of Theory U offers us viable pathways forward into the future. As Scharmer and Kaufer (2013) have noted: "It's a future that requires us to tap into a deeper level of our humanity, of who we really are and who we want to be as a society. It is a future that we can sense, feel, and actualize by shifting the inner place from which we operate." The key, then, is this 'deeper level of our humanity,' along with our abilities, in educational settings, to explore this deeper level. What is also significant about their words is the reference to our humanity: this is work that involves the whole being, not just the intellect. This is work that engages every part of our being to explore, as deeply as we are able, the very core of our being. That work at the core of our being represents the vital work done at the bottom of the U. It is in essence a contemplative form of work. It is, or becomes, a contemplative way of being.

The Need for this Contemplative Space

The value for individuals and organizations of the work that Theory U advocates has been well established in the past decade. More recent work by Joseph Jaworski (2012) and Gunnlaugson (2019) has focused on a critical part of work along the bottom of the U. Jaworski refers to Source as an inner store of knowledge and outlines four principles for understanding and working with Source. The third and fourth principles are "There is a creative Source of infinite potential enfolded in the universe" and "Humans can learn to draw this this infinite potential of the Source by choosing to follow a disciplined path toward self-realization and love, the most powerful energy in the universe" (p. viii). I suggest this process of drawing from Source involves the contemplative work to which both Jaworski and Gunnlaugson refer. In this chapter, I will outline a graduate program in contemplative inquiry that represents an institutionalized commitment to the creation of space and time in which individuals are exploring this emerging contemplative territory. In my view, this program and the work faculty and students are doing within it represent an example of the transformative work that both Jaworski and Gunnlaugson call for.

As Jaworski (2012) points out, as we change our fundamental inner understandings and ideas, we then effect change in the world; inner changes lead to outer ones. While Jaworski's work does focus on Source as being 'enfolded in the universe," Gunnlaugson (2019) builds on Jaworski's work with the ground of presence. Gunnlaugson focuses explicitly on bringing Source into the self ontologically, and more specifically, into our own grounded, lived, phenomenological experience. Or, to put it another way, to have Source emerge into and inform our presence directly from within. While two scientists Jaworski cites argue that Source is "largely insulated from human experience, representation, or even comprehension" (p. 3), it is in fact available to us. We can experience it, and as Gunnlaugson (2019) stresses, the pathway to this experience lies, at least initially, within.

From either perspective—a focus on Source as omnipresent or as within—attunement with it is a grounding in Being. Such personal, inner grounding is a subtle but important distinction, for it focuses our attention and work on subjective and intersubjective work, rather than drawing out attention outward. This work, then, is the deep, focused work at the bottom of the U that is essentially contemplative in nature and requires a contemplative orientation and set of practices to sustain and deepen it. It is the epistemological shift of gaining access to and developing this at the level of our knowing and then the ontological work of more fully developing being-ness, our felt connection to what Jaworski and Gunnlaugson both refer to as "Source," to what Jaworski refers to as that deeper region of consciousness. In sum, the work involves the whole being in an integrated fashion: body, mind, emotions, aesthetics, and intuition. Dwelling in being and the knowing that emerges out of that connection with Source provides the impetus for discerning, wise action as we emerge out from the bottom of the U. As Gunnlaugson (2019) writes:

Given the challenges of sustaining presencing in many

work places, what shifts are needed for it to take root and serve as a powerful resource for learning and innovation rather than fleeting point of reference and ephemeral ground? How to unlock the deeper source codes of presencing within practitioners that make it possible for it to flow as a palpable way of being and leading in our lives?

These deeper source codes are unlocked in the contemplative presencing work that occurs at the bottom of the U. In this chapter, I will focus on the nature of the bottom of the U and the contemplative work involved there. My contention is that rigorous, repeated, systemic contemplative practice and inquiry allow us contact and connect with what Gunnlaugson (2019) calls "the deeper grounds of our embodied presence," to allow us to skillfully engage this wisdom ground. Jaworski's work with Source builds on the bottom of the U, and Gunnlaugson's work in Dynamic Presencing has offered us a rich examination of the contemplative processes that are enacted there.

Uncovering the Work at the Bottom of the U

Plumbing this deeper wisdom ground is the contemplative work at the bottom of the U that develops both discernment and more relational ways of being in the world. Gunnlaugson and Walker (2013) point out that presencing fosters our abilities to "engage our awareness with viable creative possibilities that have not emerged" (p. 130). Although these possibilities may not have emerged outwardly, they are still present and able to be cognized. The work at the bottom of the U is the subjective and intersubjective work (co-presencing) that brings us in contact with these possibilities, potentials, and the unmanifest. It offers what Reams, Gunnlaugson, and Reams (2014) refer to a means of accessing "stillness, discernment, and generative action" (p. 41). As well, this contemplative work reveals to us the deepest, most fundamental levels of our being, connecting us to Source and the deeper dimensions of presencing. The (inter)subjective dimensions of the work lead us to notice more deeply, to suspend our assumptions of the ways things are, and to open to creative, generative forces and possibilities. The deeper presencing work of Dynamic Presencing involves these contemplative practices, carried out regularly over a sustained period of time, that connect and deepen our access to Source.

Gunnlaugson (2019) makes a vital point: that the work of Dynamic Presencing is both epistemological, yet also ontologically driven. It involves not only the attunement, unfolding, and creation of knowing and ways of knowing (the work of epistemology), but also the attunement, unfolding, and creation of our very beings (the work of ontology). It thus offers an "epistemological and ontological renewal" (p. 134).

Dynamic Presencing work of Gunnlaugson

Gunnlaugson (2019) outlines five journeys as the main process method of "Dynamic Presencing." The initial journey of *Primary Presence*, focuses on "restoring our subtle relationship to this ground of presence." The focus of the work here is revealing or making the underlying ground levels and locations of being our inner, phenomenological *lifeworlds* tangible to practitioners. Understandably, the work here is ontological in nature, the work of being-ness. As Gunnlaugson (2019) writes, this work involves establishing, through practice, the ideas of Theory U in the various aspects of our being; he refers to this as helping presencing practitioners establish an ontological lived-through experience of the *Theory U* ideals, with the focus being on the development of our emerging presencing self. The work here is that of uncovering, realizing and embodying core dimensions of our implicit presencing nature.

The second journey of *Primary Knowing* focuses on a knowing *from* being. Making contact with the generative ground of being allows what Gunnlaugson calls the "wisdom way of knowing" to emerge. It is a contemplatively active move into 'letting be,' allowing us to rest into being and the knowledge that emerges out of that resting. Gunnlaugson identifies letting be as the main previously hidden contemplative way-station between the movements of letting go and letting come outlined in Theory U.

Primary Perceiving is the third movement, described by Gunn-laugson as expanding "our existing presencing practice further into the subtle territory of where our inner embodied perception meets not-yet-manifested reality. This gives rise to a way of engag-ing presencing as a process of *embodied* inner seeing" [emphasis added]. This aspect of Dynamic Presencing brings attention to our perceptions: our felt, embodied experience. The focus is on the embodied refining of our perceptions, what Gunnlaugson refers to as a "nuanced sense-making process."

The journey of *Primary Communicating* brings the work into new social and collective fields while realizing that both *I* and the *other(s)* remain vitally important. Thus, Gunnlaugson outlines four interactive field spaces: the I, you (being and working with one other), we (being and working with several others, and all (all of us) space. The final journey of *Primary Leading* consolidates and integrates the previous journeys into uncovering our pres-encing nature in the field. As well, we "let go into an improvised, integrative and unitive way of engaging presencing as an overall path of engagement and leadership." We are engaging and learn-ing to lead from the bottom of the U.

The fundamentals of Dynamic Presencing and its work are a focus on presencing as a way of being; as way of knowing that arises out of being; as a way of perceiving arising out of our attunement with felt, embodied experience; as a way of commu-nicating that honors new intersubjective fields of self and others; and as a way of leading arising from the integration and applica-tion of these four previous, subjective and intersubjective con-templative movements.

Contemplative Inquiry and Practice: A Perspective

I draw here from my own experiences with contemplative practice of 45 years in the classical Raja yoga tradition. I was drawn to contemplative practice as a means of self-discovery, as a spiritual path. Contemplative inquiry has been for me primarily and almost exclusively a method of spiritual inquiry (Bai, Morgan, Scott, & Cohen, 2016; Ergas, 2016); any other benefits, such as stress relief or a focused mind, were secondary. I found the Raja yoga teachings appealed to me as a coherent, cohesive, comprehensive, and integrated system of both spiritual development and contemplative inquiry; the teachings worked on all lines of development (Wilber 2006, 2016, 2017). I found these particular teachings appealing in that they seemed logical and emerged out of a classic tradition that had literally thousands of years of supportive evidence, both in attendant literature and personal testimonials. What convinced me to continue was that a few months of regular practice brought results in the forms of spiritual insight and deeper, more authentic ways of being: my own phenomenological experience convinced me contemplation worked powerfully also as a means of deeper spiritual inquiry.

The contemplative work I have engaged in is exactly what Gunnlaugson describes as the ontological, epistemological, perceptual, and intersubjective inquiry that informs Dynamic Presencing. This is the work and inquiry into the ground of being and presence; the work of allowing the waters of consciousness to settle so that in stillness our deeper wisdom way of knowing can emerge. This is the work where presencing as a process of embodied inner seeing is a reality, where I can bring that full presence into generative dialogue with another being or beings (Scott, 2011, 2014). Finally, this is the work that allows leadership to emerge out of a greater sense of presence, a leadership that is ontological and vision-based.

I suggest that the Dynamic Presencing work at the bottom of the U is contemplative and spiritual in nature insofar as it concerns matters of being, knowing, and relating. What I have found in my experience is that effective contemplative inquiry is based in regular (daily) and committed practice, and is supported by a comprehensive spiritual and ethical teaching that can serve to guide the contemplative inquiry and ground it in principled ways of being in the world. The detailed, collective teachings of the wisdom traditions emerge out of thousands of years of cross-cultural testing and practice. All of these traditions have both ancient as well as contemporary experts who offer a rich legacy of guidance. In my experience, it works best to find a teaching that resonates with one's heart and mind and then stick to it.

As Thoreau (1962) comments in the final chapter of *Walden; or Life in the Woods*

> Direct your eye right inward, and you'll find
> A thousand regions in your mind
> Yet undiscovered.
> Travel them, and be
> Expert in home-cosmography. (p. 341)

As well, committing to practice without expecting particular results at any particular time is more effective than having continual expectations of one's practice; paradoxically, not expecting or looking for results brings the best results. What is also significant is the embodied nature of the movement of *Primary Perceiving*. David Abram (1996) points out that we must become open to our "spontaneous experience of the world," and its being charged with "subjective, emotional, and intuitive content" (p. 34); these lie beneath and form the ground of our more rational ways of knowing. We need to contemplatively attune ourselves, in and through the body and its organs and senses, to the world as it is "experienced in its felt immediacy" (p. 35). Attunement with and through this phenomenological experience requires practice with contemplative practices that are work in the body, recognizing it as a source of knowledge (Bai, Morgan, Scott, & Cohen, 2016). What we are seeking is what Wilber (2016) refers to as a deeper integration of mind and body, thoughts and feelings.

A final point I would make is that the contemplative practices, especially as they have been developed over millennia of research, both ancient and contemporary, are powerful "technologies of the self," as Foucault (2001) frames them. They have the ability to take one into the deep states of consciousness that are representative of the journeys of *Primary Being* and *Primary Knowing* (Gunnlaugson, 2019). In embarking on these journeys, one needs a reputable and trustworthy guide: one needs guidance from a tradition that has thoroughly mapped out these terrains of consciousness. There are a "thousand regions in your mind," and the guidance of those who have traversed these regions is of incalculable value in getting where one needs to go and in avoiding pitfalls and detours along the way.

I will now turn to a discussion of how aspects of this Dynamic Presencing and Theory U work is being enacted in a university graduate studies program. Being part of the program below has allowed me to bring my own contemplative inquiry into an educational setting, creating curricular and pedagogical approaches out of that contemplative ethos.

Presencing in Action in a Graduate Program in Contemplative Inquiry

Education as an institution obviously offers us opportunities to enact the ideas and promises of Theory U. I have pointed out that the work at the bottom of the U is primarily contemplative. Universities have always (albeit in varying degrees) offered contemplative spaces for inquiry; as Hadot (1995) and Foucault (2001) and Foucault, Martin, Guttman, & Hutton (1988) have made clear, philosophical or various forms of academic inquiry are or can be contemplative in nature. Graduate studies in education provide excellent opportunities to enact the contemplative inquiry work of Dynamic Presencing that is carried out at the bottom of the U, and there are now several undergraduate and graduate courses and programs in Contemplative Inquiry in several North American universities.

The Master of Education (M.Ed.) in "Contemplative Inquiry and Approaches in Education" at Simon Fraser University was first launched in 2014 and is designed to fill the growing hunger for contemplative perspectives and practices in our educational institutions, communities and world at large. The program was initiated and developed by Drs. Heesoon Bai and Laurie Anderson. It is intended for educators, leaders, service-providers and decision-makers in both public and private settings who are seeking deeper levels of inquiry and transformation to apply contemplative theory and practices in their respective institutions. In an interview, Bai noted "Having students pay attention to what's going on in the present moment gives them a much more expansive perspective on what they're doing with education and knowledge and maybe what they're doing with their lives" (Johnson, 2014, para. 3). She adds "A graduate program is the perfect place for examining sociological and philosophical assumptions behind what constitutes knowledge and reality. There are really big questions that we can get at and see how our understanding is not just changing the way we live but also the way we perceive life and what it means to live well" (para. 5)

The program aims to help participants develop mindful awareness but also compassion, resilience, empathy, and emotional intelligence, along with enhanced teaching and learning skills. These are examples of the contemplative work performed at the bottom of the U. A core objective is the cultivation of a "foundational humanity." Theoretical and contemplative exploration of the key concepts and practices, such as mindful awareness, mind-body integration, well-being, ethical integrity and authenticity, and compassion are based in curriculum as "living inquiry." The program includes courses on moral and social philosophy, embodiment and curriculum inquiry, current issues in curriculum and pedagogy, developing educational programs for diverse settings, curriculum and instruction in individual teaching specialties, a fieldwork course and a comprehensive exam. The latter two courses are designed to allow students to integrate their learning across the program, focusing on their particular contemplative and educational interests.

Aside from regular coursework and assignments, students develop a portfolio, usually digitally-based, that serves as a space for housing any of the work they are doing, but more importantly as a reflective space where they can integrate all the work they carry out during the program.

The program is cohort-based, each cohort having approximately 20 students; the third cohort began the two-year program in September 2017. Students in the three cohorts have come primarily from the public K-12 education sector, but we have also had students from the physical and mental health fields, from postsecondary education, from the fields of social service and social activism, environmental education, and arts education.

Pedagogical Practices Contributing Toward Dynamic Presencing

Most students who come into the program already have established contemplative practices, including mindfulness, other meditative practices based in the various wisdom traditions, arts-based contemplative practices (Eppert, 2008; Grace, 2011; Gradle, 2011; Margolin, 2014; Mullen, 2002; Saarnivaara, 2003; Walsh, Bickel, & Leggo, 2015), and intersubjective forms of contemplative inquiry (Gunnlaugson, Scott, Bai, & Sarath, 2017, 2018) that involve both human and more-than-human realms.

Faculty aim at developing a caring, supportive environment where authentic dialogue can emerge; a good deal of attention is placed on creating the container for meaningful dialogue. Classes are set up to encourage dialogical exchange, with students and faculty sitting in a circle. Classes usually begin with periods of silent meditation followed by a 'check-in' period, in which those present can share where they are at. Conversations around readings and other resources occur in both small group dialogue and with the entire class; students are encouraged to bring their own personal experience to the conversations along with the mindful engagements with the resources. Students are given numerous opportunities to present their insights and are encouraged to share their own contemplative modalities; student presentations include performative pieces that include dance, movement, music, and storytelling; and visual arts such as painting and photography; occasional presentations embody mixed-methods. Métissage—working and weaving in the intervals and liminal spaces between cultures and expressive modalities where genres and identities are merged and blurred (Chambers, Donald, Hasebe-Ludt, 2002; Kelly, 2012)—is encouraged, especially in the courses taught by Vicki Kelly and in the students' portfolio work. Ample opportunities are given for outdoor inquiries in forests, by the ocean, in a traditional Chinese garden, and botanical gardens.

Student Feedback: Journeys of Primary Being, Knowing, Perceiving, Communicating, and Leading

Comments from the students attest to the transformative nature of their experiences in the program. With respect to the movements of *Primary Being*, one student writes about a newly developed sense of ontological grounding:

> I understand my life as it is, not as I want it to be. I don't push away experiences that are painful. I walk right into them, knowing that praxis, embodiment and connection will hold me up if and when I falter.

The student goes on to mention a further grounding that allows her to then move into an integrated and relational sense of being; out of this move, connectedness with others, a more integrated way of being in the world, and a deeper capacity for leadership emerge.

> I think that at the heart of this program is interconnectedness. Through readings, writing and discussions, this Master of Education in Contemplative Inquiry has revealed the practices I need to undertake to balance my interior life with my exterior life, or my feelings, thoughts and intuitions, with my work, home and family. I honour the harmony of science and art, poetry and data, the written and abstraction.

The student adds an interesting point about coming to a new attitude toward herself: "To genuinely listen to and see other people, I have to treat myself with the same respect. I am not just less judgmental with others but also with myself. I added Loving Kindness meditation to my meditation practice." This is a significant move into the ground of one's being and testifies to the reality that ontology influences epistemology: her grounding in compassionate being develops the ability to see and hear others and to do so with that awakened compassion.

Another student makes a similar comment about a fundamental shift in being that grounds the self in primary being, allowing her to move into compassionate, relational being:

> My experience of this program is one deeply rooted in compassion and healing. This program was a soothing balm to the parts of me that have been harmed, shut down and silenced by our educational institutions. With focus on the inner life, on connection with self, others and the earth, on wholeness, and on listening it is subtly subversive to the ways our minds and hearts have been colonized by systems that force us to rush, to life from the shoulders up, and to seek competition rather than collaboration.

Yet another student writes, simply "For me, the program was a process of distillation: my essence, who I am, has become clearer and more concentrated. I have become more connected to my roots." The contemplative nature of the program offered space, time, and support for resting and sinking down into the depths of primary being: a distillation of the essence of being, a connection to primary roots. A similar comment is offered by another student, where she touches on the authenticity and congruence that emerge out of connection with primary being; again, we see the development of an integrated sense of self. Again, the grounding in primary being leads to leadership grounded in a deep calling.

> A theme that has arisen many times throughout my journey in relation to this story is the congruency of the interior and exterior as an expression of authenticity. One is propelled to act from a deep calling, an expression of authenticity .... I continue to explore internal callings as I develop a relationship with myself—my whole self—body, spirit, mind and heart.

From another student we can see the changes in a sense of both being and knowing and, as well, how these were made possible by being open. It is interesting to note she claims the philosophies and practices found her; what is also possibly the case is that her openness allowed her to discover them within herself.

> Throughout my journey, I've come to understand my au-
> thentic self by developing greater capacities for intention-
> al presence, gratitude, empathy and compassion. ... I
> have been changed in immeasurable, intangible ways that
> I cannot fully describe. In hindsight, it is as though foun-
> dational philosophies and practices found me along the
> way. I merely showed up for the ride with an open heart
> and mind.

Similar, fundamental and increased attunement with *Primary Knowing* was noted by one student, who wrote "In this program, what began as an exploration of intrapersonal and interpersonal connection through a research based lens, has evolved into a way of seeing and being reflecting a tapestry of Indigenous wisdom, contemplative embodiment and artistic expression." It is worth noting her connection of being and seeing and the embodiment of her contemplative practice as a possible reflection of *Primary Perceiving*. A fellow student writes that "Depth and reflection become central to every activity as contemplative approaches permeate everything," reflecting a deeply contemplative way of seeing. Another student mentions that through her contempla-tive practice, she is more aware of those experiences that have "informed my worldview, including my blindspots"; she has a deep meta-awareness of her own epistemological situatedness, a pre-condition of being able to let come.

Also with respect to *Primary Perceiving*, a student comments that artistic practices help in developing sensitivity to embodied ways of knowing; in her contemplative practice, she became more attuned to *felt* perceptions as expressions of her knowing. Two students commented on the impact the contemplative approach-es had on their movements toward *Primary Communicating*. One writes:

> Together with my fellow cohort members, we explored
> what it means to listen, to really listen, to the point that I
> believe it would be possible to spend all of elementary

school working on listening and nothing else. I understand the significance of giving someone your undivided attention. Really listening has opened me up to stories. I have learned more about the lives of people around me, at my work and in my community, than I ever imagined, just because I hold the space to listen and honour. The ongoing effort required to create this environment is enough work for a lifetime.

Another notes her connectedness to all around her, an ontological, empathic pre-condition of primary communicating; her ability to communicate with others emerges out of her grounding in relational being:

When I applied to the program, I thought of myself as one person, on my own. Now, I recognize all the interconnectedness that holds my life up. I am part of a tribe, part of a beautiful city, part of a school library, part of a cohort, part of the wind that blows and part of the falling Sakura petals on my way to work.

We can see in these comments the I, you, we, and all fields being engaged. A similar comment from another student:

I feel more connected to those around me and braver in approaching those whose values and opinions I do not share.... I share a bond with my fellow students and lecturers that is hard to explain. I like to think we created a micro-climate where diversity is appreciated and understood as strength and beauty.

Out of these four movements come the move to *Primary Leading*, the way of enacting presencing in the world. It is worth noting this comment from a student in realizing where real change begins. "It is the quietest revolution possible. But the commitment is large and practice makes you understand the central lesson: there is no real change beyond changing yourself." She goes on to add:

My main focus in life and work is modelling this approach to being.... I now know how to attend to [my students], to be present in their lives, to hold their stories. If the only way to change the world is to change yourself, it is contagious to be around so many people doing that work.

Another student shares her efforts, referring to the legend of the hummingbird, Dukdukdiya, among the Quechuan peoples of Ecuador, and her message of trying to save the burning forest by bringing drops of water:

The beads of water that I continue to drop [in my work in the world] are expressions of my truth and this truth permeates my gestures, actions, words, and intentions in the form of embodiment. With every drop that is shared, I hope there are ripples emanating from each bead. I try not to be concerned about the outcomes. Instead, I do my best to focus on my commitment in honouring my interiority and trusting in the process.

Finally, a student offers humility in sharing her outlook: "This program is simultaneously rooted in the reality of our broken world and deeply respectful to what is possible."

The students' comments demonstrate that the program serves to allow both students and faculty to embody the contemplative work characteristic of engagement at the bottom of the U; we see the work of primary being, knowing, perceiving, communicating, and participants move to manifest primary leadership in their ways of being, knowing, and communicating. The students' can take what they have learned over two years into their communities of practice.

We have found a need, especially because the program is relatively new, to be responsive to community needs; students have offered helpful feedback and suggestions for both curriculum and pedagogy. Having a responsive, adaptive approach to curriculum (Aoki, 1993, 2003; Davis & Sumara, 2007; Luo, 2005; Snowber, 2004) is vital, as is a dialogical approach to pedagogy.

This two-year program in contemplative inquiry offers a

training ground that is focused on both the theory and practice of contemplation, situating both in the realities of today's local and global contexts. The program offers a comprehensive approach to contemplation, allowing each student to both find the theories and practices that work for them and to also devote time to practice, both in and outside the classroom. We find that the practice makes it all work, and the times in the classroom offer both time for practice and for meta analyses of subjective experience, dialogues that probe the intersubjective, and additional, supportive conversations around how to bring the knowledge gained in practice forward into our lives. The student comments, along with our own experience and conversations as faculty, demonstrate to us that presencing can and does become a way of life to the degree that one might say "How could it not be central to my life?" In addition, we can see that the work with each cohort appears to be building up a collective field that serves as container for the wisdom and lived experience; the container seems stronger as we move forward.

Although the program is still young, there is evidence that we have been creating a collective container of consciousness that nurtures and advances participants—both students and faculty—as we progress along together. In referencing Scharmer's work, Gunnlaugson (2007) writes:

> First of all we need individuals who are strong containers. That means people who take responsibility for their emotions, their bodily energy fields, their thoughts, their own wills. People who are containers for themselves. Individuals who can witness all this, even when the charge is high. In a group, we need the same: strong group fields that can hold, can contain strong energies. The available energy in a group reflects the collective potential of the group. But with higher potential there is more at stake, so emotions can get very charged. Therefore, groups with a strong vision and a high potential need to invest in building strong, yet flexible containers. (p. 168)

Leaders, especially, need to contribute by bringing trust, insight, compassion, and, perhaps most of all, their own presence into developing and supporting the container; the container itself must reflect a supportive, caring ethos. We can now see that our collective container has been developing strength and an intangible wisdom. We are finding that our third cohort (including faculty) is making more rapid progress as they begin their collective journeys along with us.

Conclusions

Our graduate program addresses the challenges we face in both the present and future with an increasingly complex, connected, changing, and sometimes chaotic world. The required response, as Scharmer and Kaufer (2013) suggest, is one sourced from a "deeper level of our humanity." As Scharmer (2009) writes, presencing involves connecting from the "Source of the highest future possibility" and bringing it to the present (p. 161). Jaworski (2012) adds that the big decisions require access to the deeper regions of consciousness where an inner wisdom can emerge.

Educational programs like ours are increasingly relevant in offering that very possibility. They offer what is necessary: the contemplative movements required at the bottom of the U that can prepare and propel us forward into acting "from one's highest future potential" (Scharmer, 2009, p. 163). If we are to lead from our emerging self and future, as Gunnlaugson (2019) argues we must, then we need the opportunities, space, and time for the grounding, ontological, and epistemological work in the present, as represented by the work at the bottom of the U.

This graduate program offers both students and faculty to engage in the work that finds a theoretical foundation in the movements of Dynamic Presencing. A graduate program like this very much represents what Gunnlaugson (2019) calls on us to offer: a "more robust and capable presencing that is well sourced and resourced in the *true, the good and the beautiful* movements and intimations of our deeper wisdom nature." As Michael Ray of the Stanford Business School told Otto Scharmer (2009), his success lay in creating "learning environments ... that allow people to address and work on the two root questions of creativity: 'Who is my Self?' and "What is my Work?'" (p. 164). These are in a sense the very inquiries at the heart of our program.

The program might be seen as an expression of an approach that recognizes human beings as what Scharmer (2009) refers to as "evolving selves" who have the capacities to connect with and work from deeper sources of the self. In a way, the program is an explicit rejection of educational models that are primarily intellectual and ignore the calls to connect with the deepest parts of our beings ... and from there to others and the world.

There are three reasons a program like this offers a viable way forward. First, it is set within the institutional settings of higher education that are slowly becoming more responsive to such contemplative initiatives (Gunnlaugson, Sarath, Scott, & Bai, 2014). Second, students entering graduate programs like this one tend to bring with them maturity, life experience, and the deeper philosophical and personal inquiries that make them open, receptive, and willing to engage the hard, nuanced, holistic, and disciplined contemplative work. Third, a two-year program offers the necessary time required to engage in the kinds of contemplative work required. This work cannot be accomplished over a weekend, a few weeks, or a couple of months. It requires regular, committed, and disciplined study and practice over an extended period. As Jaworski (2012) points out, this work requires time, patience, and courage. We are, I think, enacting Jaworski's fourth principle: drawing from Source through a disciplined path of self-realization and love.

In the students' disciplined work and experience, we can see the movements of Dynamic Presencing. We see the work of Primary Being manifest in living more fully, more authentically, with the courage to remain more open to life and the challenges of these contemplative movements. We see an integration of "body, spirit, mind, and heart" that allows students to dwell in Primary Being and all that flows from the movements of Primary Being. We see a shift to a more understanding, expansive, relational self, and an embodiment of both wisdom and compassion. The work we engage in is what Gunnlaugson (2019) refers to as "a more nuanced and embodied way to learn to live from the deeper realms of consciousness and source itself *as a researcher, practitioner, and human being*" [emphasis added]. What we notice is the deepening, grounding, and integration of the self. It is a self that is more able to "be with what's here," as Gunnlaugson and Biggs (2017) put it, a self that is more able to be fully engaged with others and the world.

Primary Knowing is represented in students integrating their various ways of knowing into, for example, a "tapestry of Indigenous wisdom, contemplative embodiment, and artistic expression." Students' knowing becomes more relational, connected, and integrated. They come to see that contemplative approaches permeate everything with respect to their ability to know and understand, including the abilities to work reflectively with a meta-cognitive awareness.

The work of Primary Perceiving shows up in becoming more attuned to felt perceptions through the somatic work that is woven throughout the program and in students' reported deeper abilities to listen to others and the world with an increasingly open heart. Attention to the body and to somatic and sensory awareness is central and ongoing throughout the program.

The abilities to listen with undivided attention, respect, and confirmation of the other are examples of students' engaging in Primary Communicating. We see in the students an increased ability to communicate more deeply and with more compassion, an ability that emerges out of an ontological grounding in relational being and an epistemological grounding in relational knowing. As one teacher put it, this manifests as her ability to be "attending to my students" more fully.

There is an increased awareness among students that Primary Leading must begin with the transformation of one's ways of being, knowing, perceiving, and communicating. These movements offer a greater grounding, a greater development of presence where modeling the change becomes an integral and necessary part of enacting leadership. There is also a subtle but important shift in focus away from outcomes to a "focus on my commitment in honouring my interiority and trusting in the process." We see, too, a newfound ability to engage with those who are Other and to work with and through diversity. Moreover, working collectively in a more generative fashion allows the students to access a wider reality, a "picture of the whole" (Jaworski, 2012, p. 92) required by leaders. What makes this access to the wider reality of presencing is the careful and care-filled attention to the collective container.

There is an important recognition that contemplation in its depths represents not a technique or approach but a lived way of being; it represents what Gunnlaugson refers to as "an embodied methodology for sustaining presencing as a way of being."

What I witness in working with the students in this program is the transformation Gunnlaugson (2019) points to in the work of Dynamic Presencing: it is that the move to the bottom of the U "shifts the nature of who we are and the work and challenges we are seeking to transform." Students *do* shift in who they are and they *do* come to see a sometimes radical re-alignment in their work as teachers, activists, artists, counselors, or health practitioners. I concur with Gunnlaugson here that "it is not really possible to experience the bottom of the U without being changed by it in a more fundamental way."

We have been fortunate in having a faculty that has supported this bold move. It was an untried risk. The nature of contemporary challenges, however, supports such risk taking. We feel the program serves as an example of how a collective can work together at the bottom of the U such that participants are ready for the moves up the U into outward action and leadership.

Our program emerges out of the understanding that, as Ergas (2018) asserts, consciousness is curriculum in its own right. It is a consciousness that is "infinitely deep, constantly shapes us whether we are aware of it or not, and is always waiting to be acknowledged through serious engagement with contemplative practices" (p. 443). At the same time, our work has a core 'nitty-gritty' feel to it. A core understanding is that our contemplative work is fundamentally connected to our everyday lives, lives that are now lived out in changing, complex, and sometimes chaotic conditions. We are situated beings, and our work must connect us to our multifarious contexts. Gunnlaugson (2019) maintains that the focus of Dynamic Presencing is "to help practitioners more effectively embody their existing presencing practices as a core way of being and leading that can be accessed in any day to day context, situation or moment that it is needed." Ultimately, this is what our students are hoping for, and we have found that this contemplative work at the bottom of the U not only allows them to access their deepest Self but also to engage more fully and wisely with the communities that require this emergent wisdom and the actions that arise from it.

Acknowledgment

Human subject research reported in this chapter was funded by the *Institute for the Study of Teaching and Learning in the Disciplines* at Simon Fraser University, which also provided ethical review of the research protocols.

References

Abram, D. (1996). *The spell of the sensuous: Perception and language in a more-than-human world*. Vintage.

Aoki, T. T. (1993). Legitimating lived curriculum: Towards a curricular landscape of multiplicity. *Journal of Curriculum & Supervision, 8*(3), 255–268.

Aoki, T. T. (2003). Locating living pedagogy in teacher "research": Five metonymic moments. *Counterpoints, 193*, 1–9.

Bai, H., Morgan, P., Scott, C., & Cohen, A. (2016). Prolegomena to a spiritual research paradigm: Importance of attending to the embodied and the subtle. *Toward a Spiritual Research Paradigm: Exploring New Ways of Knowing, Researching and Being*. In J. Lin, R. Oxford, & T. Culham (Eds.), *Towards a spiritual research paradigm: Exploring new ways of knowing, researching and being*, (pp. 77–96). Information Age.

Chambers, C., Donald, D., & Habese-Ludt, E. (2002). Métissage. *Educational Insights, 7*(2). Retrieved from http://einsights.ogpr.educ.ubc.ca/v07n02/metissage/index.html

Davis, B. and Sumara, D. (2007). Complexity science and education: Reconceptualizing the teacher's role in learning. *Interchange, 38*(1), 53–67.

Eppert, C. (2008). Fear, (educational) fictions of character, and Buddhist insights for an arts-based witnessing curriculum. In C. Eppert & H. Wang (Eds.), *Cross-cultural studies in curriculum: Eastern thought, educational insights* (pp. 55–108). Routledge.

Ergas, O. (2018). Response to William Pinar's review of reconstructing 'Education' through mindful attention. *The Curriculum Journal, 29*(3), 443–444.

Ergas, O. (2016). Knowing the unknown: Transcending the educational narrative of the Kantian paradigm through contemplative inquiry. In J. Lin, R. Oxford, & T. Culham (Eds.), *Towards a spiritual research paradigm: Exploring new ways of knowing, researching and being*, (pp. 1–23). Information Age.

Foucault, M. (2001). *The hermeneutics of the subject: lectures at the Collège de France, 1981-1982.* (G. Burchell, Trans.). Picador.

Foucault, M., Martin, L., Guttman, H., & Hutton, P. (1988). *Technologies of the self: A seminar with Michel Foucault.* University of Massachusetts Press.

Grace, F. (2011). Learning as a path, not a goal: Contemplative pedagogy: Its principles and practices. *Teaching Theology & Religion, 14*(2), 99–124.

Gradle, S. A. (2011). A university course in mindful viewing: Understanding art and self through contemplative experience. *International Journal of Education through Art, 7*(2), 137–151.

Gunnlaugson, O. (2007). Dialogue education: A response to working with diverse perspectives in the post-secondary classroom. Proceedings of the 7th International Transformative Learning Conference—*Transformative Learning: Issues of Difference and Diversity* (pp. 168 – 173), October 24-26, 2007 Albuquerque, New Mexico . Retrieved from: https://meridianuniversity.edu/images/tlc/proceedings/2007%20Transformative%20Learning%20Conference%20Proceedings.pdf#page=179

Gunnlaugson, O. (2019). *Dynamic Presencing: A Journey into Presencing Mastery, Leadership and Flow.* Trifoss Business Press.

Gunnlaugson, O., Sarath, E., Scott, C., & Bai, H. (2014). *Contemplative learning and inquiry across disciplines.* State University of New York Press.

Gunnlaugson, O., & Biggs, W W. (2017). *Dynamic presencing in the we-space.* Presentation at the online We-Space Summit, October 9-13, 2017.

Gunnlaugson, O., & Walker, W. (2013). Deep presencing leadership coaching: Building capacity for sensing, enacting, and embodying emerging selves and futures in the face of organizational crisis (pp. 128–137). In O. Gunnlaugson, C. Baron, & M. Cayer (Eds.), *Perspectives on Theory U: Insights from the Field.* IGI Global.

Gunnlaugson, O., Scott, C., Bai, H., & Sarath, E. W. (Eds.). (2017). *The intersubjective turn: Theoretical approaches to contemplative learning and inquiry across disciplines.* State University of New York Press.

Gunnlaugson, O., Scott, C., Bai, H., & Sarath, E. W. (Eds.). (2018). *Catalyzing the field: Second person approaches to contemplative learning.* State University of New York Press.

Hadot, P. (1995). *Philosophy as a way of life: Spiritual exercises from Socrates to Foucault.* Blackwell.

Jaworski, J. (2012). *Source: The inner path of knowledge creation.* Berrett-Koehler

Johnson, G. (2014). Get a degree in mindfulness at Simon Fraser University. *Georgia Straight,* January 22, 2014. Retrieved from https://www.straight.com/life/571946/ get-degree-mindfulness-simon-fraser-university

Kelly, V. (2012). A Métis Manifesto. In C. Chambers, E. Hasebe-Ludt, C. Leggo, & A. Sinner (Eds.), *A Heart of Wisdom: Life Writing as Empathetic Inquiry* (pp. 363–368). Peter Lang.

Luo, L. (2005). Letter to my sister about Doll's 4 Rs. *TCI (Transnational Curriculum Inquiry), 1*(1), 28–42.

Margolin, I., (2014). Collage as a method of inquiry for university women practicing mahavakyam meditation: Ameliorating the effects of stress, anxiety, and sadness. *Journal of Religion & Spirituality in Social Work: Social Thought, 33*(3-4), 254–273.

Mullen, C. (2002). A pedagogue's poetic meditation. *Teacher Education Quarterly, 29*(4), 16–17.

Reams, J., Gunnlaugson, O., & Reams, J. (2014). Cultivating leadership through deep presencing and awareness based practices. In K. Schuyler, J. Baugher, K. Jironet, & L. Lid-Falkman (Eds.), *Leading with spirit, presence, and authenticity* (pp. 39–58). Jossey-Bass.

Saarnivaara, M. (2003). Art as inquiry: The autopsy of an [art] experience. *Qualitative Inquiry, 9*(4), 580–602.

Scharmer, C. O. (2009). *Theory U: Leading from the future as it emerges.* Oakland, CA: Barrett-Koehler.

Scharmer, C. O., & Kaufer, K. (2013). *Leading from the emerging future: From ego-system to eco-system economies.* Berrett-Koehler.

Scott, C. (2011). *Becoming dialogue; Martin Buber's concept of turning to the other as educational praxis.* Unpublished doctoral dissertation, Simon Fraser University, Burnaby, Canada.

Scott, C. (2014). Buberian dialogue as an intersubjective contemplative practice. In O. Gunnlaugson, E. Sarath, C. Scott, & H. Bai (Eds.), *Contemplative learning and inquiry across disciplines* (pp. 325–340. State University of New York Press.

Snowber, C. (2004). Chapter 11: Leaning absolutes. In D. Denton & W. Ashton (Eds.), *Spirituality, action, & pedagogy: Teaching from the heart* (pp. 124–135). Peter Lang.

Thoreau, D. (1962). *Thoreau: Walden and other writings* (J. W. Krutch, Ed.). New York, NY: Bantam.

Walsh, S., Bickel, B., & Leggo, C. (Eds.). (2015). *Arts-based and contemplative practices in research and teaching: Honoring* presence. Routledge.

Wilber, K. (2006). *Integral spirituality: A startling new role for religion in the modern and postmodern world*. Shambhala Publications.

Wilber, K. (2016). *Integral meditation: Mindfulness as a way to grow up, wake up, and show up in your life*. Shambhala Publications.

Wilber, K. (2017). *The religion of tomorrow: A vision for the future of the great traditions–more inclusive, more comprehensive, more complete*. Shambhala.

CHAPTER 10

Ready for U: A facilitator's reflective offerings

Amy Barnes

Introduction

Writing this chapter has been a journey in itself. I was motivated to write because of a desire to share what I do with others in the service of expanding the field. In the course of writing this chapter, I noticed the writing process itself followed a U-process and that the process led me to a number of surprising insights about the concept of Letting Come.

In reflecting on practice, I have drawn from my last 15 years of facilitating U-type processes. I say 'U-type processes' because I suspect, like many practitioners across various disciplines, that the U-shape curve applies whenever we are engaged in facilitating work that involves reaching beyond what is on the surface, not just in sessions characterised as being Theory U processes. My learning journey started in 2003 when I exited in-company Organisation Development roles and realised I did not really understand 'change'. My enquiry took me to many different settings; from Human Interaction Labs at the NTL Institute in

Maine, to Gestalt Psychotherapy training in London, to Biodynamic Massage Therapy training in Cambridge and to a re-con-
nection with art. I combine these influences with in-company
executive experience and with knowledge gained from MBA
studies in different ways when I work in the different spaces of
Organisation Development (OD), Organisation Effectiveness
(OE), personal development intensives, executive coaching, dialogic therapeutic work and personal growth work, including
direct hands-on work with the body. At the core, I am a practitioner. With that in mind, what I offer here is an exposure of the
inner workings of facilitating U-type processes where significant
shifts are desired by individuals or groups. I hope that by my
doing so, others might also feel invited to reveal how they work
and that together, we can collectively contribute to expanding
and extending the field as a whole.

Core Practices that contribute to the creation of conducive field conditions for working with U processes

Why are field conditions important for U processes?

After a hiatus of several years, I attended a Social Presencing
Theatre (SPT) basic course in Oxford in the spring of 2017. I had
attended early versions of SPT in 2008, then called Embodied
Presence Practices. After a brief introduction, we proceeded with
various experiential exercises and practices which are now part
of SPT. Although the group climate was open I somehow felt
something was missing. It was the quality of energetic focus or
collective presence that was not quite there in our group field. It
eventually dawned on me that we were not spending any time in
group meditation, which in 2008 had been intrinsic to Embodied
Presencing Practices. During our whole group debrief at the end
of the first day, I asked the workshop leader, Arawana Hayashi[35],
about meditation and she said she was open to incorporating it if
it was acceptable to the group. The group agreed. The second

day started with a short group meditative practice. The quality shift in the room during and after meditation was palpable. I would describe the atmosphere as 'deep and open stillness' and within that space, we too seemed softer and stiller in our presence. Our energetic field could be described as open and gathered at the same time.

This phenomenon brought to mind the significance of field conditions within which U processes take place. When conducting deep work, particularly Theory U processes where we are intending to connect with 'source', our 'highest potential' or our 'highest future' (Scharmer, 2016), it is helpful if the space is a sourceful space. In Gestalt Phenomenological Field Theory, we are said to be of the field. That is, we shape and are in turn shaped by the field of which we are an intrinsic part, while at the same time the field is an intrinsic part of us. Seen through this lens, the condition of the field is highly relevant to U processes. Terms such as 'holding space' and 'creating a strong container'[36] are often used to describe what is needed for creating the conditions for deep work to be done. Although it is possible for group members to be member-facilitators, in many instances, the initial creation of this field is the task of the group facilitator who also assumes the role of process leader.

As illustrated in the example of the SPT workshop, group meditative practices can be helpful. What else might be helpful for a facilitator to create a sourceful space? Below I offer some core practices. Each one is refined in an ongoing way and could be practised in contexts other than during facilitation. Over time, they collectively provide capability and capacity for working with U-type processes.

Core Practice 1: Sensitised and sensitive sensing

Sensing is core to Presencing and any work that requires deep listening. What can we practise to develop, refine and heighten our sensitivities?

Two modes of sensing

There are two broad modes of sensing that I call 'diffused' and 'focused', and as a facilitator, I tend to shuttle between the two while I work. In diffused sensing, I engage the five senses, seeing, hearing, smelling, tasting and touching, in a relaxed and open state. My capability in sensing in a diffused way was greatly enhanced by Arawana Hayashi in her earlier version of SPT called Embodied Presence Practices. I remember at the end of one of our exercises when we were moving from lying down to standing up, we were encouraged to open our eyes very slowly and 'let the world come to you'. In diffused sensing I am not focused on any one thing in particular but instead I am opening my awareness to the multiplicity of stimuli. This includes awareness through my peripheral vision and even of what is behind my back. Blending the principle of equalisation or horizontalism (Joyce and Sills 2001) from phenomenological field theory, I treat everything coming to meet me as being equally important.

This mode of diffused sensing can be accompanied by simply allowing energies and impressions to 'have their way with me' without feeling the need to do anything. I am trusting that somewhere within me the impressions will land. From meditative practices, I may let these first impressions float for a while and continue to pay attention to how things settle. By nature, diffused sensing is expansive. This is very helpful in getting a fuller sense of the overall field climate. It enables a 360 degree alertness. It cultivates an awareness of my presence both as an aspect of the field environment as a whole, and my relationship with it. Diffused sensing can also be helpful in putting us in touch with non-solid aspects of nature such as energies, vibrations, light and sound and their subtle qualitative expressions in textures and density which are often out of our awareness.

Diffused sensing is usually accompanied by the second mode, focused sensing. As energies continue to arrive, I will start to notice feelings arising within me. These are sensations. Often, emotions and thoughts will accompany those feelings although, through practice, I may notice more space between sensations, emotions and thoughts. As Gestalt practitioners, we are trained to be mindful of figure and ground and how they relate to one another. In simplistic terms, against an amorphous background of undifferentiated mass, something becomes differentiated and stands out from the mass as 'figure'. Figures can be immediate; something that catches my attention, random thoughts, unresolved history, imagined futures, or something new and novel. Sometimes, figures contain needs. The extent to which we are able to fully meet this figure will determine the extent to which it can be dissolved to make space for the next figure. When we are dissatisfied with how we have dealt with figures, those figures will remain in us. These 'unresolved issues' take up energy and will retard our capacity to deal with new figures as we interact with our context. We rely on focused sensing to notice what is figural and, of the figures, which one is pulling on our attention the most. And, given the range of possibilities which each figure might contain, we stay connected to this figure in order to chew on it and work out what is inside it. Focused sensing is useful in attending to a figure, engaging with it, and fully exploring it. We use focused sensing to develop an intimate understanding of what it is that is unfolding.

Shuttling between the two modes is helpful in developing an understanding of the relational dynamics between what is unfolding and the field climate. It is also an effective way to ensure I do not lose sight of context, by retaining a degree of situational awareness.

Whole body sensing

Both diffused and focused modes of sensing are dependent on highly sensitised portals of our body-mind. Listening has been widely written about, but the other senses seem to have been somewhat overlooked. For instance, we rarely read about smell. We know from neurobiology that the olfactory has a direct link to the limbic system responsible for mood, memory and emotion. When we say 'something doesn't smell right' it might actually reflect a deeper connection between smell and instinct. Smell is a source of information. I took part in an experimental development session where we were encouraged to meet one another through smell *first*. It was a very interesting experience not only because it was novel but because smell is very subtle and has many layers. To fully appreciate each person, it was necessary to spend some time with them, much longer than the usual handshake or 'hi', and to take long breaths in order for someone's smell to register. In that exercise, any perfume or artificial smell acted as a metallic barrier to the subtle smells of the person. Because of social norms, it is not usually possible to smell people in this way. But, what the exercise did was to open up the possibility for me to take more time and use my breath to take in someone or a situation more deeply.

Touch is increasingly controversial in our current context of sexual harassment and heightened concern about the appropriateness of any touching. Some people say it is never appropriate to touch another person without consent. Some people suggest it is never necessary to touch another person at all[37]. With a gesture like a hug, in therapeutic circles, it is standard practice to consider why I want to give or ask for a hug, to articulate what sits behind that intention, to ask someone for their consent and to be unattached to whatever the answer is. As a facilitator, I regard my tactile sense organ as a crucial aspect in sensing. Our skin has many roles such as boundary maintenance, filter, receptor and signaller. For the purpose of Presencing, I will take the liberty of extending our sense of touch to include our entire structure, that is tissue, muscles, nerves and bones, as a combined unit. Sensations through skin and touch affect impulses and responses. Touch provides information that feeds into Presencing work; how different touch is interpreted, how we feel touched non-physically as well as physically, how we instinctively touch our own bodies such as putting our hand over our heart in response to what we have heard. Our ability to touch and be touched provides the basis of bonding, closeness and trust: the glue that holds together our invisible human network of relationships. Given the sensitivities around touch, I am not sure whether we can easily reconcile the importance of touch and how we can use touch in a way that is respectful and spontaneous. From a personal development perspective, facilitators could consider bodywork and practices such as contact improvisation[38] as vehicles to help us be more connected and more confident with this sense organ. From a facilitation perspective, given how loaded touch has become, I have recently started to more deliberately use my eyes and words as substitutes for direct touch. Varying the way I look at someone by varying the energy, focus, duration and distribution of gaze, it is possible to convey different intentions in how I want someone or a group to be held. Not only is this what I do as a facilitator, I also teach this when I am asked to run workshops on topics such as 'presenting with confidence' and 'assertiveness' where we experiment and play with different ways of looking at each other and how to do this in a group setting. Similarly, tone of voice and choosing to use words that resonate and enable can significantly alter the quality of the relational field.

We do not see only with our eyes although we often equate seeing with eyesight. In earlier versions of SPT practices with Arawana Hayashi, we practised using exercises to include and extend our peripheral vision and to incorporate our backs in our "seeing". An important point of practice for me is to disconnect seeing with knowing and understanding. This requires conscious effort, particularly when we are familiar with a phenomenon. Not only do we need to handle our seeing with care, such that we look to learn, it is also helpful to consciously de-couple the phenomenon 'as it is' from our interpretation of it. Joyce and Sills (2001) refer to this type of de-coupling as a process of discerning what I am noticing, what I am perceiving and what I am experiencing from my preconceptions and judgements. They regard this way of discerning and following phenomenon as core aspects of adopting a phenomenological method of enquiry within Gestalt. In Biodynamic bodywork[39], we sometimes work with a 'matter of fact' intention to simply affirm the actuality and presence of client and self. I recall the use of this 'matter of fact' way of reporting by observers at an SPT interval. Observers said 'I can see X sitting behind Y and Y being held by X. X and Y are sitting away from the rest of the group.' There was a distinct lack of qualifiers such as 'held tightly' or 'sitting far away...'. This way of seeing and reporting is more faithful and spacious because we are not over-laying it with our own 'stuff'. When we practice seeing in this way, we are attending to phenomena as they are, not as we think they should be. Practising discernment and decoupling what I am noticing from preconceptions and judgment enables me to intervene in a clearer and more choiceful way.

So much has been written about listening that it is hard to know what to say that has not already been said. In Presencing or deep work, like many others, I am listening to what is being discussed as well as what is not being discussed. I am listening to the content, and increasingly in my work I am listening to other aspects; the choice of words, use of words, sound of words and sentences, energy of delivery, energy carried, impact, tone, resonance, flow, gestures, movement and themes. From the field of body psychotherapy, Westland (2015) uses the word 'rooted' to describe ways of talking that arise from the body. She makes a distinction between talking in a way that is disconnected with bodily sensations and talk that comes from bodily sensations. In the latter, '...words resonate with and are directly expressive of their movement of life'. From my own experience, rooted talk is often slower with many pauses as the person searches for ways to give expression to what is being felt. How we talk and where we are talking from directly impact the field we co-create.

By engaging more of ourselves through our senses, not only are we increasing our awareness, our presence and our availability to ourselves and others, the field is also larger and more sourceful by virtue of our encompassing more within the space we hold. Kepner (2003) in his article The Embodied Field made explicit links between the depth of a facilitator's embodiment and the quality of the experiential field created.

Core Practice 2: Feeling feelings

Whole body sensing is not sufficient if we do not know how we are affected by what we take in, and what happens when we are affected. A second core practice is to notice what feelings arise 'in here' when we take in information 'out there'. In other words, we are shuttling backwards and forwards between paying attention to our own physiological changes and paying attention to the environment, as both unfold. As I mentioned previously, by adopting a phenomenological stance to field theory, a Gestalt perspective allows us to include everything as equally useful. In this context, I give my own physiological changes due attention in relation to what is going on in the environment. This means I am interested in internal shifts and changes; flat, dull, calm and so on, as they are indicated by physiological feelings. Central to Focusing, an approach developed by Gendlin (2003), is for each of us to contact our 'felt sense' which he describes as our 'body-sense of meaning'. He suggests that our felt-sense is an internal feeling of a problem or situation which usually appears fuzzy and vague, but by focusing and attending to it and the process of its movement from formless to form, our body will find its own way and its own answers and the process itself will deliver change. I think what Gendlin describes is built upon our ability to feel our feelings and from that foundation, we develop and broaden our awareness to feeling processes which give us an ability to enquire when we notice ourselves registering a feeling about something. When working in groups, I am aware of both usual and unusual feelings that arise. I pay particular attention to the latter as I am often curious as to what information these unusual feelings provide. Depending on what I think it might be, this source of information could be utilised in the moment to help raise awareness for self and others. In order that we can feel feelings, differentiate between them and name them, and for us to trust our feelings as a rich source of information, we need to embark on a continuous journey of awareness development.

Like Gendlin, I make a distinction between feelings and emotions but unlike Gendlin, I use the word 'feelings' as primarily physiological sensations rather than 'emotions' which is a descriptor that may or may not be connected to experience. Applying the Gestalt 'figure and ground' approach, feelings could be regarded as the ground of emotions and thoughts. Feelings and thoughts inform action and as we take action, feedback is returned to us via feelings to provide contextualised meaning. This meaning-making process in turn shapes our capacity for future action. Understanding how this process works within ourselves informs us in the way we interact with the world. Continuous reflection can give rise to a deeper understanding of many relational dynamics between self and environment. This working theory is informed by the work of Damasio (2000), Freeman (1999) and Stacey (2003).

In many corporate settings where I have spent a lot of time facilitating groups and individuals, feelings and emotions are often excluded as if they are dangerous diseases. Yet how we feel is so inextricably connected to decisions and actions that if we want to understand and connect with 'source', a good starting point is to be able to connect with our feelings. In this sense, it does not matter if I have some people in the room who cannot access their feelings or people who are sceptical. By inviting people to share their feelings and lack of feelings and where possible, to talk about what lies within those feelings, more is revealed and the field expands. What is important is how comfortable I am as a facilitator in working with feelings. The more comfortable I am, the more spacious I can be, the more holding and safety I can provide, the more everyone feels it is alright to contribute, the more secure the space becomes and when this happens, the more everyone becomes ready to co-create.

As I become more attuned to my own feelings and the action-meaning cycle, I bring more sensitivity and a more reliable barometer to the field. Depending on the nature of the work we are doing, it is sometimes appropriate to share and offer our feelings as a way to access or reveal more of what is out of awareness. This in turn can lead to other people revealing more, and the field expands.

Core Practice 3: Somatic resonance

This might be an appropriate point to bring in the idea of somatic resonance, which I first encountered in a Gestalt coaching training group led by John Leary-Joyce. An aspect of our exploration involved working with a partner, sitting back-to-back with our eyes closed. One of us would describe an experience while the other listened. Our task was to listen to what our partner was describing with our whole being, to tune in and to allow feelings and any imagery to arise. By tuning in through hearing the words and allowing the vibrations of the words being felt through direct bodily contact, we were able to enter more fully into each other's stories. My partner described a conversation with his father while out walking. By allowing the vibration of his words to reverberate through my body, images came into view for me, images of a beach, of crashing waves and soft, peachy late afternoon light. In the debrief, I shared the imagery with my partner and he was amazed by the accuracy of the scene; the walk and the conversation with his father took place late in the afternoon on a beach, and in his mind, the scene of crashing waves was a vivid aspect of the scene. These details were not in the content of what he said, and yet they were conveyed to me.

According to Westland (2015), somatic resonance is the direct experience of someone's body with another person's feelings, experiences and thinking and it is part of embodied relating. That is, one bodymind relating to another bodymind. Somatic resonance, feelings and whole-body sensing work together in a way that helps me and the group contact important issues as they arise. These issues often lead to 'pop ups' which I will describe within the Letting Go process.

Core Practice 4: Energy

In many ways, I regard energy as the gateway to facilitating U processes. The importance of attending to and working with energy can be seen through several lenses. Seen through the lens of presence, an awareness of our own energies can alert us to the quality of presence we are bringing to a group space. There are many ways of connecting with energetic flow as well as many energy practices available to us such as Chi Gung (Qigong), yoga, breathwork and bodywork to name but a few. At a personal level, we are increasingly aware of the centrality of energy in our lives as evidenced by the growing fitness, health and wellbeing movements. However, much of the current awareness is focused on personal energy management. Less emphasis is placed on self-care, where I am tuning in to my energetic cycles and flow, paying attention to how my energetic movements exchange with our environment, and acting to restore and sustain energetic flows by working with how I am flowing rather than to overcome it or by working against it. Gerda Boyesen in Biodynamic Body Psycho-therapy referred to body streamings and pulsations as in-body sensations of our own life-force. Part of our self-care might also include regular 'emptying', as described in core practice 6, as well as what Julia Cameron[40] calls 'refilling the well'. We can replenish our energy through contact with nature[41], with inspirational ideas, with beauty, with food and with simple tasks that give us joy. In our consumption-oriented cultures, I cannot help but wonder whether replenishing needs to be accompanied by the previous core practices, because without them, we might just be consuming without awareness of how that consumption is absorbed. Therefore, I wonder how well we understand when and how replenishment turns into nourishment.

Using the lens of field creation and co-creation, Parlett and Lee (2005) quoted the insight of Kepner (2003), that 'the energetic field of the therapist, group and environment is crucial to support or mitigate certain kinds of experience', and that an understanding of how energetic fields are created is essential in understanding how we create experiential fields. What this looks like in practice is paying attention to our feelings and energies from the moment we have initial contact with a client. We can pay attention to how those feelings and energies shift and flow as our contact with the client continues. We can pay attention to our energies as we enter the venue and throughout our preparations. We can meditate on our energy as we wait for the group to arrive. I was once told by my Biodynamic clinical supervisor, that 'you can feel your client coming'. I have to admit, initially I thought she was crazy! But I frequently experience this now. Recently, I not only felt a client arriving, I also 'saw' her retracting her foot abruptly from what looked like a pavement. She later confirmed that as she was arriving, her bus had broken down. All the passengers had to get off the bus in the middle of the road and, just as she was about to get off the bus, she had to pull her foot back sharply to avoid a car. I think this type of energetic sensing has much to offer 'pre-sensing' (Senge, Scharmer, Jaworski, Flowers

2005), connecting with source and in Letting Come.

Developing skills to work with energy is also directly applicable to how we can facilitate U processes. A core idea in Gestalt is the interaction between organism and environment (Perls, Hefferline, Goodman 1951). When we are unimpeded, we interact freely with our environment and bring in elements from the outside to meet what we need, eliminate what is no longer needed, and integrate whatever is new. This cycle is often referred to as the 'cycle of experience' (Joyce and Sills 2001) and is a helpful tool in terms of following our energies. When we can have our needs fully met, our energetic cycle peaks at the point of exchange, followed by a gradual decline of energy as what is external to us is being brought inside to be digested, assimilated and discarded. These processes can be felt as energetic waves and they are present all the time. How these waves build and move, and the intensity and concentration are often indicators of whether something is important or not. In fact, I think it is more accurate to say from experience that energetic charge or intensity is a reliable indicator of whether something matters.

By locating and fully contacting what matters we can often unlock an important gateway towards connecting with source. This gateway could be stuck patterns, past unfinished business, an idea, an unexpressed need, or a past wound. By contacting it and enabling the energy to complete, we release more space and energy for what is new. It is a way of enabling Letting Go. Energy is also an indicator of aliveness and vibrancy. By paying attention to where the group or the system is spending energy, we can see where things are most alive. Therefore, bringing awareness to the issues on which energy is placed can open a lot of potential for the group. For instance, an espoused corporate value might be 'innovation', but if most of the energy is spent in cost control then it is cost control that is more alive. Another example is that sometimes there is a distinct lack of energy 'in the room'. We can choose to ignore this and pretend it is 'nothing' and hope it goes away soon enough. However, working with energy means the lack of energy is an important indicator of group aliveness. Therefore, instead of ignoring it, one option is to share this observation with the group in a 'matter of fact' way. Often, by sharing my sense of the lack of energy in the room, I enable the group to open up about how they feel. In some instances, group members admitted to feeling tired and that in turn led to a variety of options generated, such as taking an unscheduled break, sub-group work, and the surfacing of 'undiscussables'.

In short, facilitative work in U processes can be focused on tracking, following and enabling energies by paying attention to their formation, contact and withdrawal patterns. Groupwork taught by Carl Hodges works along these lines, in that the group itself is regarded as a gestalt with its own life. Within a given event, the group will have its own cycles of experience (Hodges 2003). Seen through this lens, the task of group members is their contribution to the energetic ebb and flow of the group-field as an organic whole.

Core Practice 5: Emptying

Fritz Perls introduced the idea of a 'zero point' of nothingness which, if we were to enter it, becomes the 'fertile void' (Clarkson, Mackewn 1993). A zero point describes a period when there is nothing figural and we are in repose. In plants, the dormant period is often the time when they are conserving their strength for growth.

Emptying involves clearing space in body and mind. It could also involve extending the natural point of rest, the gap between one thing and another. Practitioners of Theory U and Presencing are often encouraged to engage in meditative practices to still the mind. In addition, I find it helpful, as part of the path that leads up to meditation, to ground myself. I do this by feeling the connection of my feet and my rootedness to the ground and to use body-scanning by placing awareness on each part of my body in turn to bring myself to myself. I also use breath-work whereby we are actively engaged in expanding the movement of our diaphragm and ribcage in both the in-breath and the out-breath. Diffused sensing, as described in Core Practice 1, can assist in this practice. Diffused sensing can work by my becoming aware of all that is 'out there' while maintaining my energetic focus and attention on my centre or core. I use my out-breath to assist in gently pulling my focus inwards. This way of emptying can be very helpful when I struggle to still my mind with eyes closed or when it is not appropriate to close my eyes. Sometimes, I use this approach as a prelude to meditation so I can drop naturally into a more meditative state.

Emptying is a vital part of personal energy management and the management of space for holding deep work.

Core Practice 6: Experiments/Play/ Try-on

Playing, trying things and experiments are all enablers to free up energy. This is a core ingredient in many of the truly transformational experiences and is very much encouraged in art making. Without the weight or loading of expectations, we feel free to explore and create. When we do that, we are open to all possibilities. Whether in personal development work, executive coaching, or clinical work, it is often in experiments that breakthroughs occur. Sometimes experiments can be used more specifically, such as experimentation in Gestalt, which serves the more specific purpose of insight development because it is part of phenomenological exploration. When used in this way, experiments need to be combined with focused and systematic awareness so that we are conscious of process. Experiments can also be used to develop an awareness of the process of awareness itself (Yontef 1988). This type of double layered learning can be combined with double-loop learning (Argyris and Schön, 1974). According to the authors, we can only truly improve our effectiveness when we open ourselves to information and challenge from others and for others to offer these freely. When they do this, our assumptions and expected results from the actions we take can be openly and jointly tested in an on-going basis without coercion. I think their work in 1974 still has relevance today as facilitation can so easily and unintentionally drift into coercive territory where our main focus is on results at the expense of discovery and learning. What might combining Gestalt with Argyris and Schon's double-loop or 'Model II'[42] learning look like in practice? One possibility is for the facilitator to invite individuals to contact and explore what is present by using experiments, play, simulations and other types of try-ons through a co-creative and open-ended process. By co-designing experiments we can ensure whatever we do can accommodate the fullest range of engagement levels and welcome instances when experiments are 'not working'. In those moments, a decision can be jointly made to stop, to modify or do something else. Suffice to say, we all learn something from the experience especially when we are faced with some form of disconfirmation. In personal and leadership intensive sessions, we often invite people to create scenes. This method is informed by improvisation, embodied practices, psychodrama and systemic constellation methods[43]. We play to explore, play to express, and play to create. How we play and what we use can be co-determined with group members, using all that is available. Following on from core practice 4, working with energy, the more we can work with immediacy and design experiments when the energy is present, the better we are able to capitalise on that wave. From art making as a creative process, my learning is that riding the wave in play may not in and of itself contain a solution, but the process might reveal something that was previously out of awareness. It is not as important to make experiments perfect as it is to create an experiment that delivers as close to what is desired as possible. If what is desired is completion of unfinished business, then whatever can be brought together to deliver a 'good enough' completion will suffice. The acid test as to whether something 'works' or not is how people feel and where their energies go.

A critical aspect of experiments, play and try-on is that they do not have to be forever. This can be very releasing for self and others as it offers space and lightness for mistakes and failures. In comedy improvisation (improv), mistakes and failures are welcomed and treasured. In contact improvisation[44], playing with weight and gravity alone leads to multivarious original movements and sequences.

Julia Cameron[45] in her short video 'Artist Date' speaks about the need for play as an essential aspect of 'refilling our well' for everyone involved in creative work. In her description of play, she describes feelings of enchantment and 'wooing', words that conjure up possibilities not usually associated with work. She likens refilling our well as 'refilling our consciousness'. We become source-full.

As I mentioned in the introduction, an unexpected insight in writing this chapter is the realisation that Letting Come is a very different process than Letting Go. The insight was brought about by this core practice of experiments, play and try-on.

Core Practice 7: Working in the here and now

In the last consulting practice I co-owned and co-led, a strapline we often used was 'real people, real issues, real time'. In Gestalt practitioner circles, we are accustomed to differentiating between 'there and then' talk and 'here and now' talk. The difference is sometime also expressed as 'talking about', which usually involves talking about something that has happened in the past rather than describing how things are in this space, with this group, with you, now. From my own practice, the difference is not so much the content as the location of energy.

An example using 'there and then' talking might be 'I always find it difficult to express what is truly inside me. For instance, when I had to write a dissertation, it took two months of solid work and when comments came back to me from my supervisor, I knew to continue would only produce a mediocre piece of work. I decided to start again from scratch....'. While the story might be interesting, it is different from the here and now which is 'as I listen to the tapping of the keyboard and the words appearing in front of me, on the screen, individual letters that come together to make words and those words taking a life of their own, I can feel myself being drawn into the process of word-making in a way I have never experienced before. As I continue to be drawn into the miracle of this process, I am partly thinking about what the next word is, where I want to go next but a large part of me is just flowing now, flowing with where the words want to go next and the words that want to come through into the light. I am not controlling anymore but now, more freely, flowing with just what wants to come through.' Had I spoken those words with you listening to me in person, you would have heard the difference in the location of energy. In the first instance, I was busy recalling the key stages of the event and including all the parts that made up the story. The story was the primary focus. Because it was a story I have told others before, I am actually quite bored with it but it's a 'good' story in the sense that people seemed impressed by it in the past. In the second example, I did not have a particular story in mind, but instead I was focused on what was going on in each moment and with being connected with the process of word-making. Process was my primary focus. While the 'there and then' way of talking about things can serve the noble purpose of creating safety, it is also a way of avoiding contact with what is fresh or, using the frame of reference in Theory U, a barrier to 'seeing' (Scharmer, 2016). As a facilitator, I often need to intervene to bring attention into the here and now by offering my observation, by redirecting people's attention to what is going on 'in here', and by inviting people to carry out sub-group work to make it possible to share individual experiences of the story and so on.

Presence and working in the here and now are two sides of the same coin. It is demanding and requires courage and comfort in the discomfort of being alive to this moment, as I am, as people are, as things are and to the potential too, from something else. Paradoxically, this means preparation for any group event is very important. Here is a case story as illustration.

I was co-facilitating a large corporate group event at which the client team brought together their top managers from a newly created entity in order for them to connect with their new culture and values, and to see what changes might be needed to bring these to life and not just remain as empty words. Workshops and discussions on culture and values were regular occurrences prior to the formation of the new entity but with an influx of new managers who came from other organisations, the senior leadership felt it was important to re-engage everyone around this and for all managers to take ownership going forward.

The event was held over two days. It was not the first event we facilitated nor the largest gathering of people. What was different was the inclusion of a greater mixture of managers from different levels of the organisation which was a direct result of sharing our earlier observations with the senior leadership team. The official first day concluded with a team event with the 'after party' continuing until the early hours of the following morning. The flow from an official business event to informal partying was entirely 'business as usual' and in keeping with cultural norms. The following morning, at the scheduled start time, the room was significantly emptier than the day before. In the design plan, the second day was to be more business focused and the intention was to look at how the new culture would support business strategy. The second day started with a debrief of the previous evening's team event. Although people took some time to get going, they soon became engaged in small group discussions. However, the session was continuously punctured by people joining the meeting looking the worse for wear, and by people leaving the room. The energy was scattered and low.

At the end of the debrief, we took the opportunity to flow with the (lack of) energy and suggested a short break so people could gather themselves. During this time, we spoke briefly to the senior team to see whether it was appropriate for people to turn up late. They said they had not noticed and it was important for people to be present. After the short break, the meeting restarted with a senior team presentation on strategy. The presentation was again punctured by people joining, and each time someone joined the large door opened with a creak and a bang. As I watched this scene, I became curious as to what might be going on for each senior team member as they looked at the empty seats, managers joining over an hour late, and very tired looking people dotted around the room. It all started to feel as though we were going through the motions. After the presentation, we again called a short break to regroup with the CEO. I felt this was an opportune moment for the CEO to engage with everyone present on their culture as it was presented in the here and now. I could see how, by facilitating a dialogue, we could help everyone explore their norms, as well as the implications for themselves as leaders and as a leadership group. We took on different stakeholders to discuss our emergent design. Even now, a few years after the event, describing what happened is bringing on an ache around my neck and shoulders which I always experience when

I feel tense. As I checked in with my co-facilitator, I was told the CEO was ready to tackle what was happening and would be doing something at the start. As people settled for the next segment, the CEO stood up and said it was unacceptable for people to be late, and that the door would be locked for the next segment. The atmosphere in the room changed in an instant. It was as if everyone was lolling around, a drill sergeant suddenly said 'ten-shun' and everyone's attention snapped into focus. I was left wondering what prompted that action and what that action was intended to deliver.

At the next break, both of us as facilitators felt we needed to regroup with the CEO but we differed in what we felt was required. I was still feeling it was important to facilitate a dialogue, but my co-facilitator said it was probably better to follow the agenda although if I felt strongly about it, it was up to me. I went up to the CEO and said we could still facilitate a dialogue about people arriving late because it would enable an exploration of their cultural norms in real time. He looked at me straight in the eyes and said 'no, we should move on'. At the start of the next segment, he asked for the door to be opened with no explanation given. The remaining people came in and all the seats were filled. The rest of the event went ahead as planned, but the feeling of 'going through the motions' was the dominant figure for me until the end of the event. The output from the event was a set of action points for making changes to enable the new culture to be embedded. People were organised into working groups. It did not surprise me to learn that those working groups melted away soon after the event.

A key learning from this incident was the lack of the right kind of preparation prior to the event to work in the here and now. It is sometimes part of Organisation Development (OD) practices to gather information as part of event design. Sometimes a great deal of effort is used in designing events and interventions to enable desired changes to occur. In many cases, clients want to know ahead of time what is going to happen. In those instances where client anxiety is high and fear of 'failure' is high, the need to submit a proposed design tends to ameliorate the anxiety of both the client team and facilitators. But I find the more an event has a pre-determined design, especially in the form of a set agenda, the more difficult it is to work with what surfaces. It is of course possible to still work in the here and now but the nature of working in the here and now is that the direction of flow, if it relates to immediacy, is unpredictable. Unless all parties involved are prepared to ditch the plan completely if need be, the true power of working in the here and now is lessened. In this case, the usual way of gathering information left all of us, especially the senior team, completely unready and ill-equipped to engage with what was unfolding. What kind of preparation would have been effective? Would it have been individual and team coaching? And if so, coaching to do what and for how long? Would it have been helpful to schedule some unstructured group time to practise some of the practices suggested by Theory U (Scharmer, 2016)? Had the management team been more courageous, could they have stepped into the void? Was it reasonable to trust that by getting on a steep learning curve we would learn something together? Maybe if our facilitating team had been more united and courageous we could have been more sourceful and generated different options to capitalise on what was unfolding. Working in the here and now is demanding for both facilitator and group members, and we need to understand the kind of preparation that is effective and the type of preparation that is not.

We also need to bear in mind we do not always get it 'right'. This is when the four principles of Open Space Technology offered by Harrison Owen (1997) are so helpful:

'Whoever comes is the right people.
Whatever happens is the only thing that could have.
Whenever it starts is the right time.
When it's over, it's over.'

Conclusion of core practices

As we work on these practices, refine them individually and collectively, and combine them in different ways to create conducive field conditions and facilitate deep experiences, we are enabling ourselves to connect and contact an ever-expanding range and depth of possibilities.

Having described the core practices which are applicable whenever we are working with U-type processes, I will now focus on specific aspects in the Letting Go process that have helped me facilitate effectively.

Letting Go process

Reflecting on the work I have been doing, I have identified some specific ways of working that have helped me in facilitating Letting Go processes. I have realised that a large part of my training and facilitation work has been in helping individuals and groups to let go of the past, whether this is unfinished business, past wounds, stuck patterns, critical incidents, traumas, injustices lodged in the memories of people and groups, or simply a time when teams and groups have 'hit a wall'. Half of what I describe below derives from Gestalt practices and half is extracted from examining my direct experience in how I approached moments when an individual or a group is ready to let go. Below are specific techniques I use in combination with the Core Practices already described.

Tracking

Tracking is a skill I have been practising since the start of my therapeutic training. It is being able to register and remember in a moment-by-moment way how a phenomenon unfolds. It requires total attention to what is going on, in order that each moment can enter my system. It might sound difficult and at times it is, particularly when there is a lot going on. However, it is surprising how much information can be retained if we provide both focus and spacious letting in, without interfering with what is unfolding or letting our own thoughts and reactions take up our attention. This means I am simultaneously parking my own thoughts as they arise, a practice in therapeutic circles sometimes called 'bracketing'.

What this means in practice is, much like meditation, as my own thoughts arise, rather than following those, I notice them and put them 'on the shelf' knowing I can return to them if those thoughts remain, so that I can stay with what is unfolding before me in 'the other'. As a trainee therapist, I was discouraged from taking notes since that is a distraction and could trigger anxiety in the client. Instead, we were encouraged to focus, listen and stay open and remain able to track how things unfold. This has given me an ability to recall the order in which things happen. Somehow, this moment-by-moment tracking enables me to build up an internal picture. This picture consists of what happens, when something happens and how something happens, rather like a movie.

This picture also includes the intuitive and hypothetical connections that start to emerge. These are relationships between events and actions that are contained in the narrative that is being told and by the way words and ideas are picked up and built upon by each person as they weave their experiences to develop a simultaneously individual and collective invisible net. In group work, these exchanges can be seen to be part of container building. In my previous description of Core Practice 7, Here and Now, I mentioned a unique perspective offered by Hodges (2003) of treating the group as a gestalt and group members as vehicles through which the group forms, develops and completes its own gestalt. Using this frame of reference, tracking the formation and development of the invisible net, the themes carried within interactions can provide me with an indication of what the collective or 'the field' might want to accomplish. What this whole group-field wants to accomplish may or may not be directly related to the topic in hand, yet without this work being done, the topic in hand might not be tackled because there is something about the field structure or condition that is not ready or stable enough for the topic to be held and handled safely.

Staying with

It seems paradoxical that staying with something enables letting go. Staying with something, particularly with 'stuck', can be very helpful. What this means in practice is when we experience a block, instead of turning away, we continue to contact it, to enter into it, to continue to explore it in order to better understand it. In Gestalt, this way of engaging with stuck can be attributed to the 'paradoxical theory of change', an idea put forward by Beisser[46]:

'...that change occurs when one becomes what he is, not when he tries to become what he is not. Change does not take place through a coercive attempt by the individual or by another person to change him, but it does take place if one takes the time and effort to be what he is - to be fully invested in his current positions. By rejecting the role of change agent, we make meaningful and orderly change possible.'

In the Social Presencing Theatre basic training I attended in 2017, Arawana invited an individual or group to embody the feeling of our 'stuck' and to give it expression by creating body sculptures from 'stuck 1' to 'stuck 2'. In gestalt, individuals and groups are invited to be all the aspects contained within a stuck in turn. As described above in Core Practice 7, sometimes in development intensives, these methodologies are used where those participating in stuck 'scenes' enter into a scene, co-create by being an aspect of the scene and speak from their experience at the 'step out' or debrief. Let us say the current situation is described as a car stuck in heavy mud. A scene could be constructed where people are the mud, some are wheels, some are the car and others might be in the car. Each can be invited to speak or dialogue with the other, not to change anything but simply to understand how things might be experienced within that place and from that perspective. These creative ways of 'staying with' a situation can be part of a process to develop a more intimate understanding of the status quo, trusting that when whatever is needed has been fully met, moving on will naturally occur.

Pop-ups

Sometimes I notice recurring feelings, imagery, thoughts or metaphors which might suggest there is something forming in the field I am picking up. By noticing these occurrences and combining this with tracking, I am aware of when internal shifts are happening in individuals and in the field. I can then offer these to the individual or the group.

It is often the case when strong metaphors pop into my mind that these are relevant in some way to the group. They often act as connectors to enable something more to be revealed. By something more, I mean aspects of context that might not have been explicitly brought up, hidden issues or 'sacred cows' that people find awkward to bring up. At other times, these 'pop ups' act as gateways to deepening connections. They might take someone back to a critical feelingful moment in their narrative and with this, they feel able to more fully connect with their feelings, emotions and thoughts. When they move closer to themselves, they can move closer to what really matters, which I call 'the core'. The extent to which I trust pop-ups has a great deal to do with the Core Practices, particularly whole-body sensing, somatic resonance and continuously working on discerning the connections I make in the ongoing feeling-thinking-action-meaning loops as previously described in Core Practice 1,2 and 3. An intimate understanding of 'usually like me' and 'usually not like me' serves as a useful reference for the accuracy of pop-ups.

In their work on examining the process of presence, Chidiac and Denham-Vaughan (2007) used the term coined by Bollas (1987) 'unbidden un-thought knowns' to describe the 'coming together of externally gathered sensory information with internally generated sensory images, to give a vivid, synthesized view of self with other. Sometimes this could be experienced as an almost palpable sensation in the abdomen, which seemed to vibrate and act as a source of coalesced sensations which were then cognitively interpreted and fed back to the other as either a gesture or verbal statement.' Although their description offers a close approximation to my personal experiences I wish to emphasize the crucial ingredient of surprise in the way these pop-ups present themselves. Sometimes they are so 'far out' that I park them for a while in case they are random creations of mine. But experience over time shows that the more far out they are, the more they tend to have some relevance. It then becomes a case of when I feel it is appropriate to offer what has popped up in me and the way these pop-ups are offered. Again, through Gestalt training, I learned to share and offer lightly. This is sometimes known as 'creative indifference' by Gestalt practitioners such as Joyce and Sills (2001).

Core

I think the core can best be described as an energetic center. In Gestalt-speak, it is most likely to be unfinished business (Perls, Hefferline, Goodman, 1951), an open gestalt that is still taking up attention and energy, whether the person or group is aware of it or not. This core could also be a closely-held desire or an intimate knowing of a 'truth'. It is the heart of the matter. The core can be regarded as the nub of a given situation, requiring a release of energy to allow a letting go or letting come, whichever is applicable.

It is often different in group events where the focus of transformation is at the level of the group. In the context of a group being an organic whole, core can best be described as repetitive themes, expressed in various ways by individuals in different moments, which are nevertheless along similar lines. These themes can be offered as possibilities for group members to explore together or in sub-groups. How do we know when a theme is fully explored to a satisfactory completion? From experience, we can track flows of energy as surges of varying intensities, from full flow to a gradual reduction in energy. Completion usually has an energetic withdrawal, an ebbing, followed by an open and relaxed group space and a feeling of completion within individuals.

If I am very close to the unfolding phenomena, I will feel the charge or quality of space changing when we approach the core and a release as the core is resolved.

Merger

In individual one-to-one or small group work, getting to the core requires entering and joining the person for a short time, mostly through being able to sensate through feelings with them. I think it might be similar to what Scharmer (2016) describes as 'empathy' in Theory U[47]. I am not sure whether this type of merging is encouraged at all in any facilitative training. In fact, it is probably discouraged! In Gestalt psychotherapy, it is frowned upon as 'confluence' where there is a 'boundary collapse'. In practice, I find that a temporary merging with another person provides a way of entering into the same channel of flow. This way of flowing and experiencing is probably an intense version of empathy. It might be explained as being able to tune in my vibration, so that for a short time I am very close to the vibration of the other person. When I am better able to see through the eyes of the other the interventions I offer tend to resonate with the other in a way that is 'just right'. I often imagine this is what is sometimes referred to as grace. Denham-Vaughan (2005) incorporated the work of Roberts (1999) to provide a description of grace as a phenomenon of co-emergence through our receptivity to the organising field force. She further suggested that the extent to which we are receptive to this field force has a direct effect on the quality of contact we have with the environment field. So, it is probable that in passages of work, when I seem to enter a zone where suggestions effortlessly suggest themselves, I am highly attuned and receptive to co-emergence. I have found that in most cases, these moments are usually irreversible moments where there is a complete reorganisation of the field such that relationships are fundamentally reconfigured.

Letting Come process

Much investment, personal, financial and energetic, has been ploughed into the Letting Go side of the U curve. A great deal of my executive education, Gestalt therapeutic training, and even meditation, with roots in Buddhism, have tended to lend themselves to enabling Letting Go. Letting Come as a process has had less attention.

In parallel, I am connecting to the core desire at the heart of Theory U to 'listen to the highest future' (Senge, Scharmer, Jaworski, Flowers 2005) and beginning to go through in my mind, experiences where 'the highest future' came about. In doing so, I became aware I may have experienced an alternative U. For some people and some groups, 'the highest future' is indeed about letting go of the past. Frequently, this necessitates the completion of an open gestalt or unfinished business. In this context, the absence of unfinished business that holds our energies back from being able to engage more fully with the present is already the 'highest future' possible in this moment. In conflict-ridden communities and regions of the world, reconciliation and forgiveness resulting in an *absence of conflict* is significant beyond measure.

As important as Letting Go is, it is not the whole story, because in Theory U the other movement in the Presencing zone is Letting Come. I began to look for examples of Letting Come from work with individuals and groups, and in my personal development, where we experienced significant and, at times, surprising shifts. A few things struck me about those experiences. Firstly, they were not necessarily contained within a U process. Secondly, they occurred in very open and spacious states. Thirdly, they occurred via a different process. As I entered more fully into exploring these three aspects, it dawned on me that Letting Come is possibly an entire process in itself. Furthermore, in the examples I held in mind, the direction of travel was entirely different, that is, from right to left of the U as depicted in Theory U. I will now use three different examples to illustrate how Letting Come might be a distinct process in its own right.

Example 1: Letting Come from small group work

The first example is drawn from small group work. We were asked to facilitate a gathering for a Management Board with whom we had worked for a few years. They had been a team for several years and worked well together. I would describe them as a group of talented and highly independent individuals who were warm but 'at arm's length'. Each person felt they and the company needed to take a bold step and each had some ideas as to what the options were. They were highly informed, commercially savvy, reflective and very capable of doing radical things as a team. One of their patterns was to have a long digestion and gestation period, but once a decision was made, they acted in a flash and often in unexpected ways.

The facilitation challenge from my perspective included working with a small group who were familiar with each other, who spent many hours talking about the business together, who were not particularly expressive and who were hard to read because energies were relatively held back. As an experiment and as a vehicle for facilitating expression other than talk, I thought of bringing some art materials into the room. I hoped this would give an opportunity to do things differently. It felt risky to me: I imagined being ridiculed, or that the group would half-heartedly do something but that they would think less of me because art is fluffy and pointless, or that they would produce lovely drawings that led to nothing. Yet, over the years, I have come to accept that my own feelings of risk and fear associated with difference are to be embraced and trusted. Clinical experiences and Gestalt ways of working in the here and now provided a capacity for rolling with surprises as they manifest. So, I decided to make the art materials available.

The first half of the event was smooth, and the atmosphere was relaxed. There came a point when the conversation took us to the company's future and suddenly, I felt we were standing on the edge. One road was to talk about the future and the other was to express and explore. I pointed to where the art materials were and invited them to produce a picture of their desired future for the company. I did not know what their reaction would be. As I am writing it now and reconnecting with that moment, I can feel my body turning cold. To my surprise, they all gravitated to the table with no push-back, and a couple of people took to the task with great enthusiasm and gusto. Building on this wave, I suggested to the group that each person took time to describe their picture of the future. For those listening, they were there to receive the picture and join in with the exploration by asking questions that would encourage more[48]. In other words, not to challenge and narrow down but to support, join and expand. It was an expansive and rich session and it took some time. Somehow, this process culminated in a point of absolute agreement between everyone on a common course of action that, in their 'heart of hearts' they all wanted and that they all recognised was *the* step-change for the company. The gathering of energy that led up to the decision moment was swift but almost imperceptible. The decision moment felt connected and grounded. After the decision point, there was a visible difference: everyone looked shiny and a sense of excitement was radiating from each person. We had no doubt they would take things forward. In fact, their decision was wholly realised within 18 months and the step-change for the company was something they all executed together.

I mention this example because it shows it is possible by fully entering the energy of a desired future state we Let Come into being what is wanting to be born and allow the Letting Go process to take care of itself. The team knew it was a 'bet the ranch' decision. They were neither interested in incremental toe-in-the-water testing nor did they feel that incremental options would be conducive to what the company truly needed. I am proposing that what this team did and how change came about was through being in the right arm of the U and staying there. They journeyed to the bottom of the U when their collective vision was realised. What to let go and how to let go became apparent as their new reality unfolded. In facilitating the event, I did not place my attention nor was I consciously engaged in letting go. My curiosity was how to help them unearth their futures, to enter into their futures as fully as possible and to allow us to be taken forward by whatever had energy and was alive for them.

Example 2: Letting Come from 1:1 coaching

The second example of the Letting Come process is drawn from one-on-one work. During an individual development intensive, the client realised that despite being a member of the senior leadership team for her company, she had not stepped into that role at all. In fact, it was as if she was still in her 'old role' while everything about her context had changed. She realised her effectiveness required her complete investment in her new reality. That necessitated her jumping completely into her new role and from there, to see what, if anything, from her old role she needed or wanted to keep. She also realised that even if her decision was to leave the company because the reality of her new position was not what she thought being a member of the senior leadership team would be, she could not possibly make that decision without being fully in it and doing the job as it needed to be done in its fullest sense. A natural consequence of fully and *freely* stepping into her 'new world' was an appreciation of the need to pay attention to different things, such as shareholders, and gain a broader perspective. To effectively deal with the business required her to let go of many aspects of how she handled people and situations both in terms of her now-peers, her then-peers and her direct reports. To her, what she needed to let go of was 'obvious' from her new vantage point. But she needed to jump fully into Let Come first, and only then could she know how to Let Go.

Example 3: Letting Come from art making

My final example to illustrate how Letting Come can be a different process is from a personal development experience through art making. It started with an art workshop I attended in August 2017 which sparked off many ideas and possibilities for exploration. One evening, I picked up a packet of unused oil pastels and on making contact with their texture, a great urge arose to experiment with them. One thing led to another and I suddenly remembered a scene from Tenerife I had been wanting to express for a few years. I recovered a short video I had shot from my phone and proceeded to make a drawing of it.

Figure 1 Oil pastels on paper, Buena Vista del Norte, Tenerife

I enjoyed creating the movements of the waves, particularly the meeting of the waves against the rocky coastline. I liked the texture of the pastels and the way the colours could be worked with on paper by hands and fingers. The medium made it possible to connect with the movement expressed from inside me through my fingers to the paper.

'That looks great Amy! Carry on experimenting…. Alongside what you are doing - have you tried painting just how it feels rather than how it looks, as large as possible?'

The invitation from Lorna, the art facilitator-teacher[49] reminded me to take myself away from the confines of form and to enter more fully into feelings. The 'as large as possible' took me to an art store where I stood in front of canvases of many different sizes for over an hour. These were blank canvases. As I stood in front of each one, I was noticing whether I felt anything arising in me. Had I gone for one which I thought would be 'as large as possible' relative to the sizes I had been using, it would have been a canvas about 110cm wide. But in terms of feelings, I only actually started to feel stirrings of fear and excitement when

I was standing in front of a large canvas 170cm wide. It was too big to take home in the car! But undoubtedly it was the only one where I felt something moving inside me.

The next part of the exploration was connecting with 'how it feels'. The northern part of Tenerife is exposed to the power of the Atlantic. In the winter, there is a constant deep rumbling vibration, like the 'thud' of a helicopter. As I stood near the giant waves, I felt waves of fear and excitement inside me and I could see colliding lines and flow as waves crashed against the rocky shoreline. While in transit, I decided to buy a small notebook and a small packet of crayons, so I could play with the emerging feelings while travelling. I started by connecting with the colours of the crayons and with the picture of Tenerife in my mind. Straight away, I found I wanted to experience lines of incoming force hitting a jagged static line.

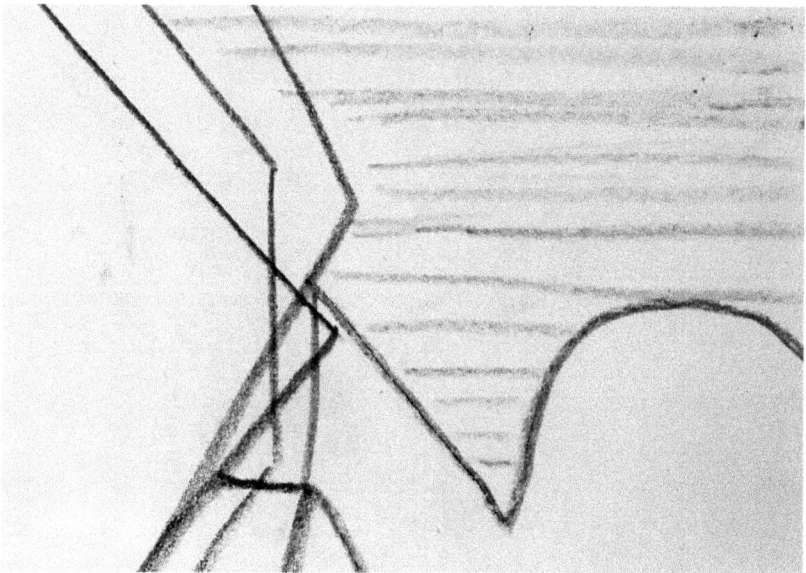

Figure 2 Drawing of energy lines from the scene in Figure 1.

As soon as I began, I started to feel the texture of the waxy crayons on paper and connected with the running lines. I just wanted to be in the lines. I became absorbed in the colours and lines, asking who wanted to run and where and how. As I ran with the lines, my body joined in. I could feel the meeting of energies from inside my body to the lines, to the flow, to the paper, to the colours and back again. It went on just like that, on and on, from one page to another. A dialogue running on. Then a break. A distinct shift in everything. I did not know what I was doing or why. I continued. Stilted. Something odd with the dashes and blocks. Then suddenly, from the right, the jagged edge, then diagonals, overlaying. New relationships. Inversions. Diagonal panels. A significant shift. What transpired was not so much the waves but the light - a new possibility. In this process, I am exploring, playing, experimenting, following and allowing whatever comes to come. I am not evaluating but merging and connecting with the energies as they present themselves and lending expression to them. This new reveal is kept open as a potential that may or may not be used consciously. I trust whatever is alive in me will re-emerge in some way.

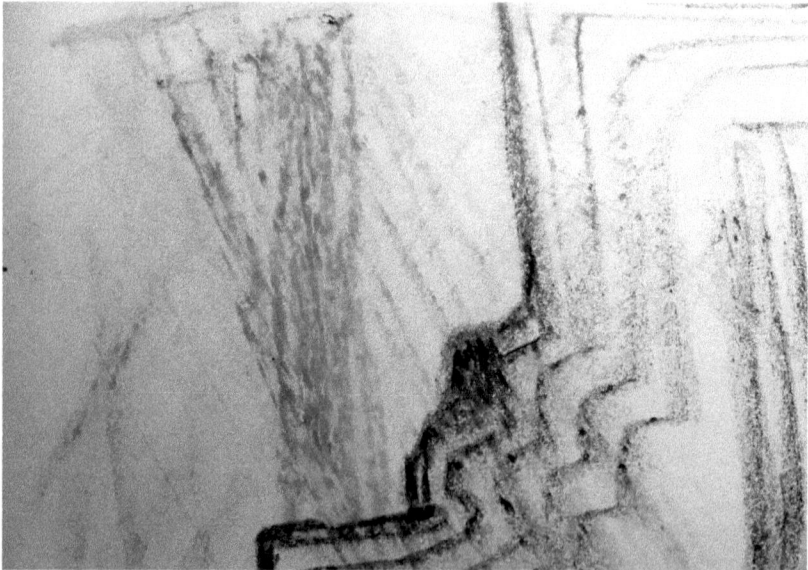

Figure 3 'Rays of Light', 18th November 2017, an iteration of Figure 2.

In the first week of December 2017 at a workshop, I continued with the exploration of lines and feelings of flow but also now, the energy contained and expressed by flow. I also wondered about working on larger surfaces akin to the canvas width I experienced in the art shop. A vast amount of material was generated over a 4-day period[50]. Here is a selection:

Figure 4 Line drawing of the feeling of 'fire'

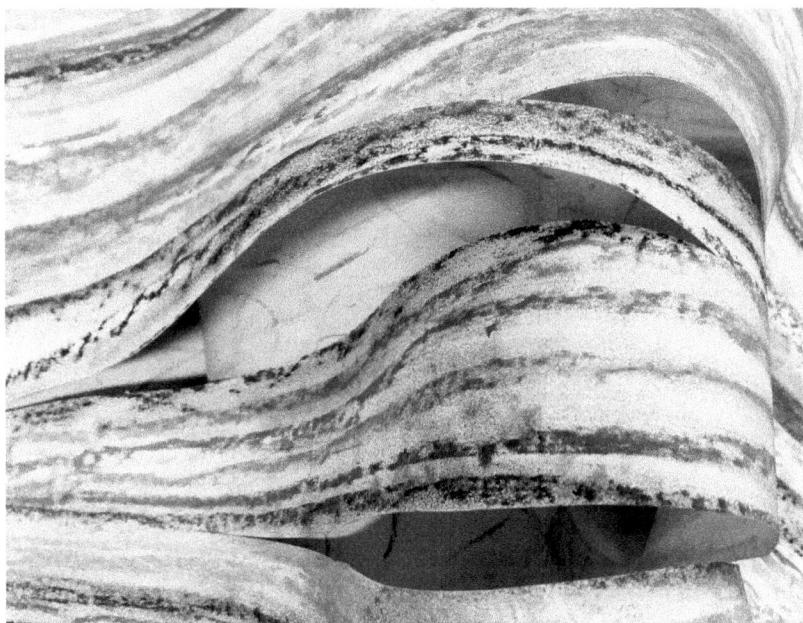

Figure 5 Whole body flow[51], charcoal drawing.

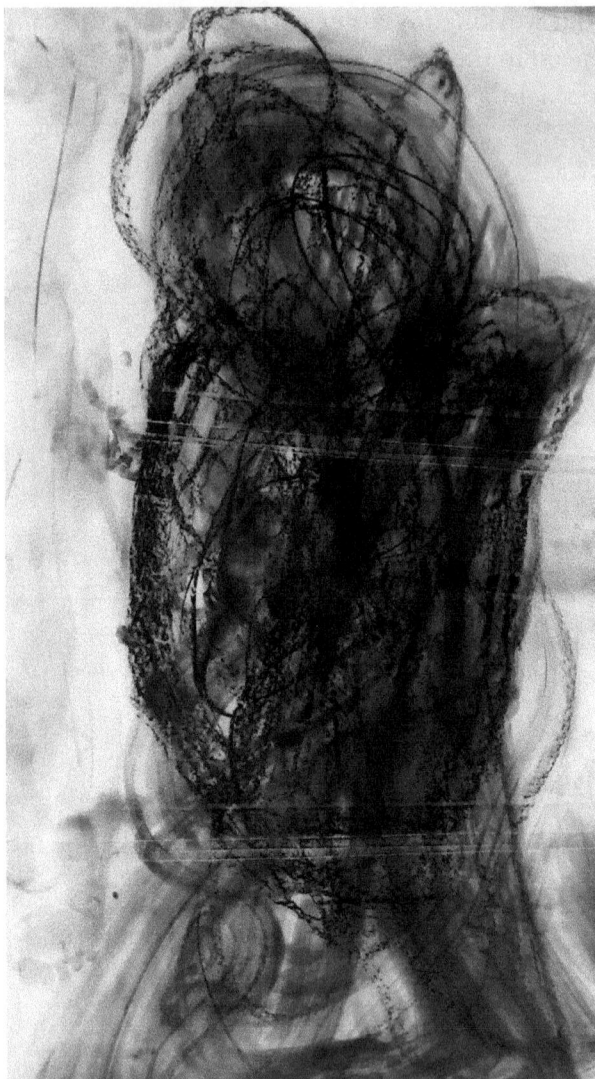

Figure 6 'Flow out', mixed media on paper.

I can see that aspects of Figure 1 were taken forward into 3-D in Figure 6 and, what is now appearing as a potential enquiry is something along the lines of barely seen presence, of the not obvious or waves within waves - possibly contained within the Tenerife scene but only now showing up. What was going on in creating the 3-D flow was a strong, even desperate, urge for me to include a different flow underneath the flow on top. And the need to include that piece, produced on day 1 of the workshop, was a feeling that it was both the source and the future that gave rise to the 'Flow out' in Figure 6. The journey to Figure 6 required continuous and unbroken connection to bodily feelings, for those feelings to find their own language.

Up to that moment, my personal experiences in Letting Come were similar to the first two facilitation examples given in this section in that in the space of Letting Come, there was an overall sense of free-flow without much effort in terms of 'what to do' or 'what's next'. We are not loaded up with expectations nor weighed down by the past. They were not loaded spaces, making it possible to not only treat the past as a useful reference point but also as a source of nourishment of our 'inner well' as described by Julia Cameron[52]. I think lightness and spaciousness are both conducive and essential ingredients.

Since writing about the examples above, my understanding of Letting Come has evolved as a result of returning to the large canvas. I started the 150cm wide large canvas in late September 2018. My initial approach to the canvas was one of indecision as I hesitated and held myself back from making marks from the past. I looked at many contemporary paintings and could not decide what was true for me. Even the background colour took a number of iterations. Each time the colours were applied, my reaction was preceded by 'too' – too bright, too dark, too dull, too vivid and so it went on. I was deeply dissatisfied. Then late into the night as I stared at what was probably the 'best' background I had painted for a long time, and I would have built on this background seven or eight years ago, it simply was not the painting that was being called forth this time. As I started to connect with what was wanting to come through in that moment, I found myself reaching for tubes of paint and, with my heart pounding, squeezed big blobs of paint directly onto canvas. I went with that energy and started to engage all of myself in following on from those initial gestures. Then the painting began to emerge. I was elated. The intention behind this canvas was to fill a large blank space on a wall in my living room. About two weeks into this process, I was unsure as to whether the painting was done. I contacted Lorna and this was her response:

'The feel of movement and animation/aliveness is palpable - to enhance this it could be helpful to make more contrasts within it so that the eye moves around more - if it is purely decorative like wall paper then this would not be a concern but if you are thinking expressive fine art then:

accentuate lighter and darker areas more in a non-regular way. Vary colours more – e.g. with any colour e.g. orange, maybe sometimes darker in some areas and lighter in other and vary sizes from one place to another - which you are doing already to some extent. More differences across and up and down the surface of the canvas. Regarding the background - you could try a more gradual colour transition from the centre area, from light to dark into the surrounding - so that sometimes it melts in more and sometimes stands out more - needs experimenting to see.... Exciting - send more pics if you do decide to take on any of the suggestions above - there is no right or wrong and the suggestions above may or may not work. Always aim for as much differentness as possible to keep the eye interested.'

I was very conflicted about 'wallpaper'. That word simultaneously felt right for the wall space and lesser than 'expressive fine art'. After a couple of days, the twin pull of not yet done and my desire to push myself to make something that was closer to 'expressive fine art' drove me to start putting some of Lorna's suggestions into action. It was a 'disaster'. Layer upon layer of 'disaster'. Let me stress here that it was not Lorna's suggestions but what I did with her comments that took me into the disaster zone. Frustration and impatience began to create very muddled colours. It was obvious to me it was not possible to go back to how it was. It was not possible to capture the spirit and energy that was alive in a given moment in time even if I could re-create the exact image. What was past was gone. For two weeks, I sat with choices of either completely painting over the entire canvas and starting from scratch or instead carrying on. Somehow, in the service of having a more intimate understanding of Letting Come, I decided to continue by engaging with what was there rather than what was not there. As I spent a few more days being with what I deeply disliked, gradually, colours were suggested to me from what was on the canvas. Moreover, in the disaster period when I was trying every possibility of working differently with paint, I noticed it was easier for me to express movement by working with thicker, less diluted paint. As I began to work in a way that was more closely related to what was emerging from the canvas and maintaining a direct expression from the gut, the more the painting began to come alive. Not only is the canvas not lost, it has a different quality than a month ago. What is profoundly different is the relationship I have with the developing work. This on-going process supports Beisser as per my previous quote in section 2, subheading, 'Staying With'. By adapting Beisser's description of how change occurs, my sense of Letting Come is:

When we fully engage our whole being in what is here now, what needs to happen next will be presented initially as a feeling. As we stay with and follow these feelings, they sort and shape themselves into future possibilities within the container of our enquiry until the possibility with the strongest resonance results in form.

My sense of allowing the future to presence itself in this way is a different process and energy from typical visioning sessions where a future state is created from a more deliberate selection of an end goal. What I am proposing here is rather than focusing on the end point, we keep the end outcome as open as possible and focus instead on allowing and following possibilities presented by the field. Choice-making in this context is a process of giving expression to a possibility that resonates most strongly within and we trust that if resolution is needed, resolution will find its own way when it is time to do so.

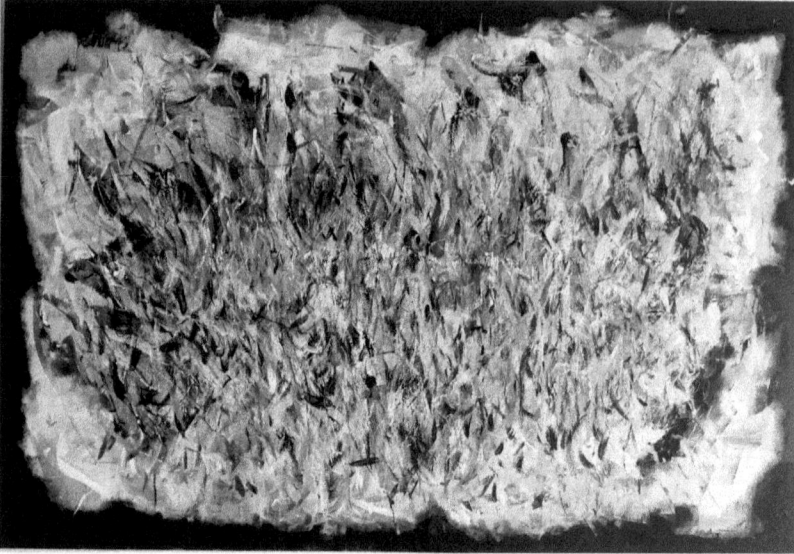

Figure 7 Finished large canvas, 150 cm x 100 cm, untitled, December 2018.

Conclusion from reflections on Letting Come process

It is customary for us to regard Letting Go and Letting Come as two sides of the same coin that is, in order for me to Let Come, I first have to Let Go. While this might be true some of the time, reflecting on practice suggests other possibilities.

One such possibility is Letting Come sometimes drives Letting Go. In this scenario, our primary focus is on where our energetic river is flowing. The more we allow ourselves to engage fully with what is new, the more clearly we will see what we need to let go. In two of the three examples described, engagement involved being immersed in and in sync with how the new way wants to unfold. When we do this, we are flowing with the energy contained within our new realities as they are presented to us and we are, even for a short period of time, living as fully as we can, in the new possibilities and seeing the world from that place. The more we can do this with freedom, the more we can explore and learn what the possibility feels like from the inside-out. There is a difference between talking *about* my vision of the future and talking *from* being in my vision. It is easier to know what furniture to bring with me from an old house to the new house when I stand in the new house! The significance of this insight is the possibility we approach U processes from the other direction, starting with Letting Come, and movement from the future creates a spiral with a clockwise vector.

Another possibility is to work with now and what new possibilities are emerging now without concerning ourselves with Letting Go of the past. This way of rolling with continuous emergence is potentially a radically different way of 'doing' a U process because not only is it not the same as "define future point A, come back to present point B then build an action plan to get from B to A", it is also not about letting go of aspects of my present, B, to clear space for something new. Rather, it is about being fully engaged with what is present, and as A solidifies from an amorphous feeling into something that resonates, we allow ourselves to enter as fully as we can into A. As I do so, other possibilities will continue to manifest and I allow myself to continue to create new possibilities AA, C, etc. The chances are, we would have already taken some aspects of what is useful from the past into new futures and if not, we can trust that whatever is no longer relevant will recede into the background. In this scenario, there is no U process, there is only presencing.

References

Argyris, C. and Schon, D. A. (1974). *Theory in Practice: Increasing Professional Effectiveness*. San Francisco: Jossey Bass Publishers.

Beisser, A. (undated) *The Paradoxical Theory of Change*. Retrieved 15th December 2017, from http://www.gestalt.org/arnie.htm (accessed 15th May 2020).

Clarkson, P. and MacKewn, J. (1993), Major Contributions to Theory in *Fritz Perls*. London: Sage Publications.

Chidiac, M.A, Denham-Vaughan, S. (2007). The process of presence. *British Gestalt Journal, 16(1)*, 9-19.

Damasio, A. (2000). *The Feeling of What Happens: Body, Emotions and the Making of Consciousness*. London: Vintage Books.

Denham-Vaughan, S. (2005). Will and grace: an integrative dialectic central to gestalt psychotherapy. *British Gestalt Journal, 14(1)*, 5-14.

Freeman, W. J. (2000). *How Brains Make Up Their Minds*. London: Orion Books.

Gendlin, E. T. (2003). Change in: *Focusing*. London: Rider.

Harrison, O. (1997). The four principles and the one law in: *Open Space Technology, A User's Guide* (2nd ed.). San Francisco: Berrett-Kochler Publishers Inc.

Hodges, C. (2003). Creative Processes in Gestalt Group Therapy in: M. Spagnuolo Lobb and N. Amendt-Lyon, eds. *Creative License- The Art of Gestalt Therapy*. Austria: Springer-Verleg Wien.

Kepner, J. I. (2003). The embodied field. *British Gestalt Journal, 12(1)*, 6-14.

Joyce, P. and Sills, C. (2001). Phenomenology and Field Theory and Awareness in *Skills in Gestalt Counselling & Psychotherapy*. London: Sage Publications.

Parlett, M. and Lee, R. G. (2005). Contemporary Gestalt Therapy: Field Theory in: Ansel L. Woldt and Sarah M. Toman, eds. *Gestalt Therapy History, Theory and Practice*. California: Sage Publications Inc.

Perls, F., Hefferline, R. and Goodman, P. (1951). The Structure of Growth in *Gestalt Therapy*. Maine: Gestalt Journal Press.

Roberts, A. (1990). The field talks back: an essay on constructivism and experiences. *British Gestalt Journal, 8(1)*, 35-46.

Scharmer, O. C. (2016) *Theory U: Leading from the Future as It Emerges* (2nd ed.). California: Berrett-Koehler Publishers Inc.

Senge, P., Scharmer, O., Jaworski, J. and Flower, B. S. (2005). *Presence: An Exploration of Profound Change in People, Organisations and Society*. London: Nicholas Brealey Publishing.

Stacey, R. D. (2003). Mind, Self and Society in: *Complexity and Group Processes- A Radically Social Understanding of Individuals*. East Sussex: Brunner-Routledge.

Westland, G. (2015). Being with The Self, Being with The Client in: *Verbal and Non-Verbal Communication in Psychotherapy*. London: W. W. Norton & Company.

Yontef, G. (1993). Gestalt Therapy: Clinical Phenomenology in: *Awareness Dialogue and Process*. Maine:Gestalt Journal Press Inc.

CHAPTER 11

The Long Arc of the Universe

Chris Taylor with contributions by Rhonda Fabian, Pat McCabe, Cynthia Jurs and Clio Pauly[53].

These stories, poems, photos and reflections have been mindfully assembled in an attempt to capture something of the process of Global Presencing. Our aim has been to give a flavour of what cannot be captured easily in words – that magical mess of emergence that happens when we find ourselves lost in the space between stories.

This is the place humankind finds itself at this time – when the old story no-longer excites or captivates us and yet we have only glimpses of what wants to take its place. To this extent we are entering an era of Global Presencing, when what's known become irrelevant and what's needed is just out of reach.

The contributions, both in words and pictures have for a large part been harvested from social media – from friends and fellow travellers. Words are credited but photos are often uncredited in this digital realm. In any case all photos have been modified and rendered in black and white by the author. Some of the poetry has been written collectively as part of workshops designed to envision The More Beautiful World. Knowing who is responsible for these words, other than the Collective Unconscious, is impossible and perhaps matters little.

So we invite you to step into the liminal space with us, to allow the words to carry you downstream to a place where you can hear the faintest murmur of the future that is calling you into presence. What part of the New Story will you pen?

Figure 1.0 The Long Arc – The Milky Way above the Arizona Desert

It may be that the long arc of the universe bends towards justice[54]. But this does not mean we can always see beyond the horizon. In the clatter and cacophony of news-wars, social media bombardments and battling opinions, it can be difficult to hear the low whisper of the future.

For sure the long arc is clear. From the primordial soup came simple atoms of hydrogen. From here evolved all the elements of the periodic table, planets, suns, asteroids. All humming to the song of the stars. Then life: microbes, dragonflies, angelfish, dolphins, cats, cows, and crows. Hundreds of thousands of species coming and going as the Earth breathes in and exhales across the ages.

The movement of the Universe is from simplicity to complexity. From homogeneity to diversity. From the first faltering building blocks of life to the splendour of a murmuration of starling conjuring sunset against the city skyline.

The evolutionary path is towards conscious self-awareness. A Universe becoming ever more aware of its own existence, its direction, its expansion, beauty and charm. A Universe settling into an understanding of right, abundance, compassion. A Universe entering into love and life.

But in the trenches, amid day-to-day challenges, betrayals and grief, things look far messier, far more nuanced.

Life is a series of moments. Moments of note that become

memories. The patterns that create structure, meaning, are not always visible at the time. They make sense at their deepest level only at the moment of death. Here everything falls into place, making sense, culminating.

The same might be said of the seismic changes shaking the modern world. The patterns and trends will become most apparent once the shift is complete. As we experience them, they can seem random, contradictory, just so much noise.

Which will ultimately be more significant: the moment we passed 400ppm of atmospheric carbon dioxide or the point where investment in clean energy outstripped investment in fossil fuels? Which will have greater impact on the run of history? The rise of authoritarian populism or the moment when a majority of the world's population identified itself first as a citizen of the world before being a citizen of any one nation?

We are bound by a single market, a single all-consuming consumer culture, an ever-stronger pull into ego mind-set. Will the pull of homogenisation snap us into the embrace of diversity? Will the frenetic noise of materialism awaken us to the still small voice that craves a life of meaning? Or is something more needed to entice us to embrace the global reimagining that stirs beneath the surface of our consciousness?

The truth is we're in a fix. And we haven't the faintest idea how to get ourselves out of it. In a cataclysmic excess of hubris, we have made a grab for control of the most fundamental processes of existence. We brag that we can master the laws of nature and rise above all we survey. And then, when we realise too late, that we cannot control what we have unleashed, we begin scrambling for survival, at once ashamed of our arrogance and simultaneously in denial that we are to blame.

And to say it again, at risk of labouring a point, we have no clue at all how to get out of this mess. If we did, we would have done it. And if we are already doing it and it is just those others who are not, then we still don't know. Because as sure as eggs is eggs, getting out of this will take everyone. Having created a global mega-system, it will take a global response to shift us to a new way of being.

And anyway, the idea that others are to blame, this sense of "us and them", separation from each other, from the rest of nature, from my own life, body, existence, is precisely what got us into this fix. How to get beyond that, globally, well that's precisely what we don't yet know.

What U Theory tells us about this, is that the deepest change emerges from the moment of stillness at the bottom of the curve. It arises when we have let go of everything we know and think we know. It emerges when we give up on tired, tried and tested solutions – knowing that they are solutions to old problems which we have long ago surpassed.

This realisation is not new. It is encoded deep within the human psyche. The I Ching of ancient China reminds us:

"Utter emptiness beckons fulfilment. When stillness is complete, action comes into motion."

An African adage has it like this:

"The Times are urgent. We must slow down."

The most fundamental change is counter-intuitive. Or perhaps it is counter-rational, deeply intuitive. It comes not from human will but from emergence; less from action than from allowance. We create the space where the future emerges into sight and listening to its call we follow it into the clearing.

If *Presencing* is defined as "seeing from the deepest source and becoming a vehicle for that source" (Senge, 2004) then *Global Presencing* is the process where humanity recreates the world by becoming its highest future self. In this process we reimagine human society at a global scale. Through processes of utter emptiness, we sense into our future potential and so create the more beautiful world our hearts know is possible (Eisenstein, 2013).

So where are these moments of emergence? Have they revealed their pattern yet? Is their shape visible or is it too early to tell?

What follows are a few instances – some large and significant, some local, mundane. All are potentially earth shattering. In their different ways, all are founded on Presencing, all feed into the field of emergence that will birth the next story in human evolution.

River in Time by Rhonda Fabian, USA

Figure 2.0. Rhonda Fabian (Facebook)

I am blessed to live in the woods, a beautiful place called Rose Valley, with a swift creek passing through all day and night long. Recently, as I sat on the bank aware of her unbroken song, yet empty of thought, I touched the icy water with my foot.

A spontaneous realization rose up in me. I was touching the entire river in that moment – from her origin as a tiny rivulet of rain high in the mountains, to her ultimate surrender to the sea – and every moment along her way. The river begins and ends in the same moment and transforms again to rain.

I realized that we are like the river. We already are what we seek to become. We have already awakened. We have already transformed. When we deeply touch the present moment, we can remember this. (Fabian, 2017)

Occupy the Future

2011 was the year of Occupy and the so-called Arab Spring. While the Presencing Institute held its first Global Forum to bring together change-makers from around the world, others took to streets and squares. Both were seeking to find out what was emerging in this time of turbulence.

Otto Scharmer opened the first Global Presencing Forum with these words:

One question that brings us together here now is what really is it that is going on? Because we are not coming together here out of context. We are part of a larger stream in history of many people before us.

It has to do with the rise of civil society. What does this mean for us – from the small beginnings we all have created in the different contexts we are in? (Presencing Institute, 2012)

What is it that really is going on? The same question was being asked and answered in hundreds of General Assemblies in parks across the world. What is going on and what can we do to birth it?

A new lens entered the public discourse. It was the lens of the 1%. It sought to convince us that humanity was united, had common interests, hopes, dreams. All except for a tiny minority - those who held on to power and wealth at the expense of the rest of us:

We condemn the current distribution of economic resources whereby only a tiny minority escape poverty and insecurity, and future generations are condemned to a poisoned legacy thanks to the

environmental crimes of the rich and powerful. "Democratic" po-
litical systems, where they exist, have been emptied of meaning,
put to the service of those few interested in increasing the power of
corporations and financial institutions.

The current crisis is not a natural accident; it was caused by the
greed of those who would bring the world down, with the help of an
economics that is no longer about management of the common good
but has become an ideology at the service of financial power.

We have awakened, and not just to complain! We aim to pin-
point the true causes of the crisis, and to propose alternatives.
(Occupy, 2012).

The whole point of these street movements of 2011 was that
they had no leaders. The crowd was in charge, stretching its muscles, hearing its own voice repeated in call and response because
megaphones had been banned. It was a time for the mass to
imagine horizontal rule, to debate and agree all things by
consensus.

Figure 3.0 Occupy Oakland protesters are arrested while in silent meditation.

Within this dogged devotion to anonymity there were moment
of renown. In one of these, Pancho Ramos Stierle reached cult

status in the Bay Area Occupy movement. Pancho, an undocumented Mexican activist, was arrested by Oakland Police while meditating. When spirituality is placed in service of system change it becomes a crime in the eyes of the status quo.

> *On Mondays we practice silence, and the police officer who arrested us thought that we were deaf because we were not speaking. So he got a notebook and a pen. It was very considerate of him, and I could feel his energy shift a little, and so when he gave me the notebook I wrote, "On Mondays, I practice silence, but I would like you to hear that I love you."*
>
> *When he read that, he had this big smile and looked me in the eye and he said, "Thank you. But, well, if you don't move, you're going to be arrested. Are you moving or not?"*
>
> *So I wrote back, "I am meditating." He said, "OK, arrest them one by one." (van Gelder, 2012).*

A student of non-violent direct action, Pancho sees the emerging social movements as a blend of spirituality and activism:

> *It is time for the spiritual people to get active and the activist people to get spiritual so that we can have total revolution of the human spirit. Because we have the idea that the self-indulgent people are just meditating—they are going to caves and meditation centers while all this madness is happening, or you have people at the meditation center that are asking how can you bring peace and calm and harmony to the world if you do not have that in your heart?*
>
> *I think that we need both now, and that we need to combine this inner revolution with the outer revolution to have the total revolution of the spirit.*
>
> *Then you can build the alternatives to a collapsing system built on structural violence.*
>
> *I believe that nine out of ten actions must be creating the community that we want to live in—we're talking about permaculture, independent media, restorative justice, gift economies, free currencies, and preventive medicine. By doing all that, we make ourselves stronger. (van Gelder 2012)*

290

Some say that Occupy failed, that the Arab Spring fell apart and allowed the military back into power. At one level this may be true. Zucotti Park was cleared of protesters. In the Middle East governments came and went, some states were recaptured by the military, others were left in chaos. The democratic high was followed by the inevitable come-down.

The argument goes that the protesters were naïve, had no clear platform, did not know how to take and wield power. One of the instigators of Occupy Wall Street, Micha White looks back on the experience from this point of view:

Occupy was holding assemblies in public squares to create a consensus-based democracy that we hoped would give us broad social legitimacy. The thinking was that, if every day people convened in these democratic assemblies, the police wouldn't be able to attack us because we would be the sovereign power.

Well, we realized that that's not true. Actually, sovereignty, in our societies, is only given to the people who either win elections or win wars. Winning wars isn't possible or desirable. Winning elections actually seems like something that can happen. (Griffiths, 2016)

At another level, this analysis misses the point. It takes us back into the existing paradigm of politics, where money and power rule. The idea behind these street movements was to prototype a new form of politics by creating space for emergence.

This is what made it a Presencing movement. By holding to the importance of process, by resisting the urge to find easy answers, Occupy was asking what the future was calling for. It was a glorious fleeting attempt to hold society at large in the liminal space at the base of the U.

Many of those directly involved saw the movement as valid in its own right. It was a glimpse of how the world could be organised, an experiment in mass democracy, mutual support, deeper understanding.

And some feel it has spawned a new, more spiritual form of change-movement:

This new spirituality is about doing something to help the world in a way that requires sacrifice rather than being spoon-fed easy answers. It is about discovering your true calling, your unique gifts and offering them... in service of compassion and justice. (Bucko, 2013)

Figure 4.0. Occupy Wall Street: Sit down, rise up.
(Karsten Braaten, Waging Non-Violence)

You may share this sense of emerging spirituality. You may not. That's not really the issue. What this trend points to is a rediscovery of simple wisdom – deep and old knowledge about how to live in harmony with those around us by simultaneously living at peace with oneself. Inner and outer balance. As Peter Senge noted at the first Global Presencing Forum:

So much of what's needed in the world right now is a kind of a relearning or a reawakening to elements of our traditional wisdom teachings. (Presencing Institute, 2012)

Becoming Indigenous

Figure 5.0 Buffalo have survived attempted extermination at the hands of European settlers (Laurenz Stoisser)

There is something about our moment on the arc of time that calls us to reconnect to our sense of oneness with the wonder of existence. It calls us to rediscover this felt-sense that indigenous peoples have kept alive for all of humanity despite our best efforts to wipe them off the face of the Earth.

It serves no-one to fetishize or appropriate the traditions of another's heritage. This is not about buying crystals, dream-catchers, sweat lodge experiences. It *is* about rediscovering a deeper connection to that part of the human soul that craves connection to mother earth, the star encrusted heavens, the consciousness behind the eye of an animal companion.

It is about becoming indigenous, having the time to listen to the cries, and signs and warnings of the world around. It is about spending time in deep contemplation and allowing the future to merge into our consciousness. It is about shifting the locus of action from action to allowance.

For those still in connection to their heritage, their ancient wisdom teachings, there is a thread to follow – however frail this has been worn by the ravages of colonialism and globalisation.

For others of us, this lineage has been all but completely severed. Uprooted from the land, driven into cities, wrenched from the skirts of the ancient wise women who kept our accumulated knowledge, we are at sea, rudderless. We may be victors in the scramble for material accumulation, but this comes at a cost to our souls.

It is hard to hear the future above the constant chatter of smartphones, Facebook feeds, twitter storms, 24hour news – fake or otherwise. It's hard to hear the future above our own dissatisfaction with current events: shouting at the news means we have scarce little bandwidth for a distant whisper. Ego is noisy when left to its own devices.

There is one sure way though. The pull of the land is strong. It sucks us from the city at the weekend. It calls throughout the year until we cannot resist in the vacations. We invite it in in easily manageable chunks – window boxes, pets, house plants. We venture out in equally undisruptive spells – park runs, beach walks, weekends in the garden.

There is peace in the outdoors. Health, healing, rejuvenation. Is it possible the land can teach us the secret of the future? Native American elder Kahontakwas Diane Longboat believes so:

> *We're told that Mother Earth is indigenizing all of us. That we are in a time and we are in a place where everything that we need to know about the future is going to come from the land. The land is going to tell us how to live, how to correct our behaviour, how to conserve and how to be good citizens in concert with Natural Law.*
>
> *The land is going to be reminding us of the rules of life because we as human beings have fallen out of balance with that. The land is going to shift our governance structures. It's going to shift our economy and it's going to shift the way we teach, the way we pursue our health, the way that we achieve mental health and wellbeing. The land is going to shift everything. The land is going to indigenize us. (Longboat, 2015)*

What might the land teach us if we were to listen to her for a moment? How to be at peace. How to wonder at the awe of a landscape. How to walk lightly leaving scarcely a trace of our passing foot. How to feed ourselves and her in the process. Limitless patience and forgiveness. To weather a storm and welcome the freshness that follows. To find food, water, shelter, medicine. To hold grief and release it into the night. All these things and more.

I can offer also an anecdote, from a time I was visiting the retirement estate of John Ruskin the Victorian art critic, visionary and nature advocate. It's a stunning estate on the hillside over-looking Coniston Water in England's Lake District. There is a calmness in the air, a deep green in the timeless hills.

Figure 6.0 Coniston Water in the English Lake District

Our guide, a crusty friend named Sally, dying of cancer and resembling Ruskin more the older she gets, walks us around the meadow on the lakeside. "Walk in silence. Notice with each step. Listen to the Land, what she wants, what she has to offer." As I turn back at the far end of the meadow, the reply comes clear as a bell: "Accomplish more by doing less."

Upon returning home I was reminded of a chapter in the *Tao Te Ching* written by the ancient Chinese philosopher Lao Tzu two and a half millennia ago:

Those who think to win the world
By doing something to it,
I see them come to grief.
For the world is a sacred object.
Nothing is to be done to it.
To do anything to it is to damage it.
To seize it is to lose it. (Lao, 1997)

The Hoop of Life by Pat McCabe (Woman Stands Shining)

Last week I was speaking at an event and I heard these words come out of my mouth: I am not compelled to speak as a woman, or as an indigenous person, a Diné tribal member. I am compelled at this time to speak on behalf of my species, as human being. I must answer for my kind now.

Figure 7.0 Woman Stands Shining: embodying the Hoop of Life

Some of you have heard me speak about the sacred hoop of life, that every life form has the honor of being given a place on this sacred hoop. Each family, plant, flying one, swimming one, creepy crawling one, four-legged one, two-legged one, must uphold its part of the hoop, or the integrity of the hoop begins to fail. We are a fiercely interdependent, inter-relational, "interbeing." Right now my kind, my species is not upholding its part of the hoop.

In "my section" of the hoop, there are really no distinctions of relevance: male, female, indigenous, "nonindigenous," rich, poor, intelligent, unintelligent, black, white, yellow, red, sane, insane, righteous, despotic, kind, cruel, spiritual, unspiritual. There is only the group known as "human being." Our effect on the hoop is the sum total of our actions as this group, all of us together. Our ability to maintain the integrity of the hoop is only as strong and effective as who we are as a collective. In this, we are bound together.

This realization has led to other surprising realizations. One that is arising right now is that never has it been so clear that my only option is to do all in my life to uphold the honor of being human being, to devote myself to remembering my perfect design for thriving life. This activity must consume all of my energy, Lifeforce, attention, willingness, ability. This means I must be willing to forgo other activities.

From this place, I understand that I cannot expect all injustices to be righted before I commit myself to Life. To wait until the injustices that I perceive touch me, my flavor of human being, to be corrected before I make this commitment to the honor of being human being, to Life, is beyond self-centered, beyond anthropocentric, it would be blasphemous to Life itself.

To engage in the infighting that is occurring within my species is fast becoming a deep insult on top of deep injury to all the other members of the sacred hoop of life. While I insist on justice from "The Other" within humanity, all of the other children of the Mother Earth are suffering, fully at my kind's hands. This is not honorable. There is no Honor, or not nearly enough Honor, being upheld in this activity at this time. Not relative to Thriving Life itself.

Perhaps this is extreme thinking. Perhaps for my kind, my species, to be able to right itself into paying attention to its commit-

*ment to Life, it needs to answer for the acts of atrocity it has com-
mitted one to another. But perhaps not.*

    *I feel that a part of upholding the honor of being Human
Being to me would be now to allow for the possibility that I may
have to forgo justice, as a woman, as an indigenous woman, as a
brown person, and as all of the categories I am perceived to be a
part of. I may have to forgo all the justice due all these categories,
if I am to answer the call of Life fully, with all of my heart. I am
examining myself and working to understand what it would take
for me to be able to let them go and prepare myself instead, to look
straight into the eyes of Life itself, and to hear what She wants of
me and for me. (McCabe, 2017)*

What is wanting to die in this world? What is wanting to be born?

It turns out that the completion of the Mayan Calendar did
not bring the end of the world in 2012. Mayan observers knew it
wouldn't – that their ancient knowledge had been misinterpreted
by some in the Western world.

It was never about the End of Days. It was always subtler than
this. Mayan shaman Ohky Simine Forest puts it like this:

*The majority of ancient prophecies around the world speak of the
shifting eras at the end of the twentieth century…All of them refer
to a major transition we are about to live, if we are not living it
already. (Forest, 2000)*

Opening the second World Presencing Forum in 2012, Otto
Scharmer described it a little more prosaically:

*We belong to a larger field of possibility, a movement of co-creat-
ing the social field and the key social institutions of society. These
are like seeds. So we want to role-model the future right here, right
now. (Presencing Institute, 2012)*

A hint at what global presencing might mean is contained in the title of this second World Forum: *What is Dying; What is Wanting to be Born?* This is a question to dwell on if ever there was one.

Ohky Forest has a take. Schooled as a shaman in her own Iroquois tradition, the Mayan tradition of her husband and the Mongolian shamanic tradition, she found striking similarities between the three cosmologies and their prophecies of a changing world.

The era that straddles the turning of the millennium has been a period of dreaming, envisioning. A period that marks a shift from the masculine era of materialism into a feminine period of community and deeper democracy. Truly a time of global presencing, when the world can reimagine itself from the stillness between stories. It started in the mid 1980s around the time of the fall of the Berlin Wall. It continues now as we dream in clusters, movements, waves of human consciousness, of a more beautiful world, manifesting what sits still and calm within our hearts.

2012 was also the year my eldest brother died. It would be usual to say he lost a four year battle with cancer. That was not quite my experience. Yes, he fought for life, to put his affairs in order before the cancer ate through his body one organ at a time. But in the end, in the final days he let go gracefully into the inevitable stream of death.

If I raked through the ashes of his death for clues about what wanted to die, it would be masculinity, or at least the caricature of masculinity we are asked to buy into. Strength, resolve, hard-work, powering through the stress, succeeding in a materialistic world. These were the things that killed him. The trappings of a millionaire lifestyle topped off with the Standard American Diet and a little too much smoking and drinking in his younger days – habits formed to protect a vulnerability that life knocked out of him.

Something tells me all this will need to die if we are to find a life at peace with ourselves and with the Earth that bears us. Some say we are midwifing the new era while we hospice the old. One or other of these tasks is challenging enough. Where are the skills and approaches to hold both roles? Simultaneously?

Two years after his death, my brother appeared to me in a dream with some advice. And because he was my older brother, and I looked up to him, I have followed it. He said, *"Close down the ordinary. Leave space and energy for the extraordinary"*.

Another World[55]

Another world does not exist
There is only this: past, present, future
not always in that order: inner, outer, unity.
Another world does not exist
There is only this: our sense of self-importance
our sense of self, as separate beings
giving way to collective being,
the wild intuitive voice within.
Another world does not exist.
There is only peace of mind:
understanding that thought creates feeling
feeling creates experience
experience creates understanding of each other.
Another world looks people in the eye
invoking faith in humanity
asking us to be all we can be.
Another world does not exist.
There is only this joy and beauty
that rushes toward me and through me
in this and any world.

600,000 Souls for Peace

Figure 8.0 Lighting a candle has long been a symbol of peace, remembrance, bringing the unseen to presence

Sharif Abdullah started out as a Black Panther, in the Sixties. These were days when the revolution prowled the streets, while its leaders were systematically hunted down, assassinated or imprisoned.

Now Sharif runs an international NGO called Commonway Institute, which is dedicated to *"the creation of a society that is in line with our deepest spiritual values – a global society that includes all peoples."* During the turning of the millennium, Commonway struck up a long-term partnership with an organisation in war-torn Sri Lanka called Sarvodaya. Here's how they describe what followed:

> *In August of 1999, the Sarvodaya organization started its Peace Initiative, calling for 100,000 people to join in a peace meditation. They got 200,000.*
>
> *Since 1996, Commonway has been assisting Sarvodaya with its Peace Initiative... The Commonway approach is based on the philosophy of inclusivity, a spiritual (but non-religious) knowing that all our lives are inextricably linked, that whatever is done to one is done to all, and that the search for peace has to be based in the notion that all parties to a conflict have to "win". (Commonway Institute)*

301

As the peace movement grew, Sarvodaya organised on-going meditations culminating in the largest the world had seen – over 600,000 people. Peace-makers from around the world were there, including veteran deep-ecologist Joanna Macy:

> *The trains began adding cars, the buses began driving for little or no fee, people started pouring in. What was so moving to me was that you couldn't tell whose side they were on... Physically they had the same brown skin and the same smooth dark hair, and they all wore white.*
>
> *I remember thinking "all praise be that I have lived to see this moment, that I can experience what it's like for people to come together out of something deeper than their hatred for one another, to come together in their hopes for peace."*
>
> *There's absolutely no way that I know that you can measure the effectiveness of that. But for those that were there you don't need any external metric...all you know is you've touched some core within yourself that also is the core in everyone else. You've entered a sacred temple that's in each human's heart. (Macy, 2017)*
>
> *Sharif agrees. In his book Creating a World that Works for All he writes:*
>
> *Do you feel the promise in these perilous times? Despite our many challenges, do these times feel hopeful to you in some way? Does it seem to you that something is ready to change? How are we going to capture the promise that lies within our present predicament?*
>
> *The hard fact is that getting to a world that works for all will take a more rigorous analysis and more sophisticated actions, both internal and external, than our current political, social, and even spiritual leaders are advocating. It will take fundamental change that must originate with you, as an emerging leader of the new millennium. If our current leadership were capable of it, they would have done it by now. (Abdullah, 1999)*

Sarvodaya is not alone. Since 2011 Mexico has hosted an annual gathering for peace and healing. This has grown from around 12,000 people to over 100,000[56]. David Nicol has studied these types of action and calls them "Subtle Activism" – concrete actions in the world based on the use of subtle energy, meditation and emergence:

> *To me, the power of subtle activism is simply this: There is nothing we cannot hold in our awareness together. There is no pain, no horror too intense for our collective spiritual presence to bear. Neither is there a level of joy or ecstasy too great for us to expand into with each other.*
>
> *We are an opening to the infinite, and through us can flow the unlimited powers of the cosmos. And, in being with the reality of our world situation in this way, we perform a service for the whole. Something in us and the world changes for the better. (Nicol)*

Nicol's own Gaiafield.net seeks to act as a portal to coordinate such actions, as does Unify.org which has coordinated meditations for global change involving over 100 million people during the past five years.

These mass-meditations are an attempt at Global Presencing. To use Joanna Macy's image, they are designed to connect the core of each to the core of everyone else. It is in this connection that emergence occurs, that the future reveals itself. This is The Field that holds eternal human wisdom, universal wisdom accessible to the human soul. It is The Field beyond all sense of intellect, ego, law, economy, politics. It is pure being and all that is shared by all life: consciousness, love, joy, pain, abundance, connection, grief, beauty. Somewhere amongst all of this is a future waiting to embrace our every hope and expectation.

But to sense into this Field requires a certain degree of openness. Open mind, open heart, open will. We have to be prepared to be shaped by it in unexpected, even uncomfortable ways. We have to first let go of everything we think might be the answer.

Across the world we are discovering and rediscovering methodologies to support this process of presencing. Many involve bringing in more intuition to allow us to sense into the unknown. Socio-drama, Social Presencing Theatre, Systemic Constellations all use our innate capacity to draw information from The Field, or as Jung called it The Collective Unconscious.

Guided visualisations are another tool of choice, turning up in the most unlikely places – academia, business, government. One such case was a small gathering in the historic Austrian city of Vienna in the summer of 2017. A group spanning business students, enterprise, NGOs met for a week in a room above a dappled courtyard restaurant. Their purpose was to envision the future of management education.

This group contained some of the very same people who were involved in the discussion that first invoked the phrase "Global Presencing" two years earlier in conversation with Martin Kalungu-Banda. Martin is a vibrant and engaging Zambian change-maker and facilitator at the Presencing Institute, whose eyes betray a longing for a more just and sustainable world.

For several days the group collaborated, planned and strategized. They did all the usual stakeholder analyses. They assessed strengths, weaknesses and the wider social context. Then they sank to the bottom of the U, the place where all the standard learning runs out. Here they visualised a future beyond the classroom. Through guided visualisation and a vivid process of systemic constellation, they called forth the future.

It was a future where the self-managing learner, emboldened by a new vision of society, left formal education behind and in the process dragged a flagging world economy into a new dawn. Beyond the dawn was a world where nature flourished again, the buffalo roamed the plains once more, and humanity had rediscovered its place within the whole.

Unfortunately, the formal record of this part of the event is lost. It is as if those taking part did not believe the vision they had conjured. All the other sessions were recorded for posterity. The future vision is the sole part of the week that is left uncaptured.

Perhaps we are not quite ready to fully embrace the future we crave. Perhaps there is still work to be done before we become the change we wish to see in the world.

It seems there is an iterative process between personal and global change. This to-ing and fro-ing creates a momentum which builds to becomes a wave. As Charles Eisenstein (2015) suggests, we do not make a movement. It makes us. If the revolution leaves us unchanged it has merely been a coup - we have fooled ourselves into accepting a new boss – the same as the old boss. Revolution without personal transformation is a mirage.

Rhon Fabian, who wrote the passage about sitting by the river, is digital editor of *Kosoms Journal* and a media educator. In collaboration with Dr Jennifer Horner, she has researched the Global Transformation Movement, a convergence of conscious efforts that is arising to shape and be shaped by our fast-changing world. She identifies five insights about this movement:

1. The Global Transformation Movement is self-organizing.
2. It manifests as a values-driven 'movement of movements'.
3. The Movement uses alternative forms of learning.
4. It emphasizes improvisation.
5. Global Transformation embraces a spiritual approach to change. (Fabian, 2014)

If these are not symptoms of a presencing movement I don't know what are.

The point being, we are in an era of Global Presencing. To a greater or lesser extent, the whole of humanity is in a space of not knowing. Tried and tested solutions no longer work. The desperate or powerful apply them with ever greater feverishness. The rest stand and watch bewildered or outraged. It is time to stop. It is time to allow the future to emerge. To find enough stillness to hear its whisper.

Another world is not only possible, she is on her way. On a quiet day, I can hear her breathing. (Roy 2003)

From Ego-system to Eco-system

The third Global Presencing Forum took place in 2014. Once again, Otto Scharmer framed the task facing us at this pivotal point:

To transform our current economic institutions takes a three-fold transformation: shifting the personal, the relational and the institutional awareness from ego to eco. (Presencing Institute, 2014).

This is a magic formula. A Golden Triangle: self, community, whole. I, We, All. Like all metaphors it is incomplete or inaccurate. It contains a false distinction. There is no I without relationship. I cannot maintain my mental or emotional health without others. I cannot maintain the health of my body or soul without the whole.

Nonetheless it draws our attention to these three core aspects of being a whole person, of living in peace, health and vitality. The pathway to personal health, community health, global health arises from the interplay of these three realms of existence.

Fine words. And how is it to be done? How do we shift from ego to eco when the entire weight of the world economic order is built on ego, self, power, wealth, control. And this in turn is built on destruction, consumption, never-ending feeding on the body of Mother Earth. How do you turn the world in a different direction?

Maybe this is where the difference is between those motivated by spirituality and those driven by activism. Maybe it is simply that some are starting with the personal and others with the institutional – and a whole host of counsellors, therapists and healers are working on the relational.

Does it really matter where we start? Might it not be that it's good to have people working in all three realms? Are we simply asking that we all give some awareness to the other two realms – the ones where we spend less time?

2014 is the year I met the four women who have contributed to this chapter. We all took part in a global gathering called The New Story Summit. Had I known about the third Global Presencing Summit maybe I'd have been there too. But I didn't so I went to The New Story Summit instead. I have an inkling we were engaged in a similar process, perhaps just coming at it from different angles.

Emergence eluded the New Story Summit – at least as I witnessed it. We did many other incredible things: healing, ceremony, deep learning. It was one of the most nourishing, transformative and collectively synchronising processes I have ever experienced. But sitting for more than a moment in real uncertainty proved too difficult. We stepped in and stepped back before we allowed the discomfort to turn to revelation.

Ego spoke about everything it already knew and we listened to that instead. We forgot that the discomfort of not knowing is the threshold to new learning. In the moment immediately before realisation is panic and a desire to walk away. This is ego preparing to give itself over to transcendence. This is where growth occurs.

8 Minutes of Silence

Three years later. Nineteen active, conscious individuals from all walks of life, all colours, all ages. Nineteen souls who have never met before.

They spend the first weekend of 2017 at a small, family-run retreat centre, to consider the state of the world and how to respond to the chaos and turmoil[57]. By the end of the first day they have said all there is to say, shared their vainest hopes and darkest fears. They fall silent. They sit together in spontaneous silence for eight minutes – until the gong sounds for dinner.

As their attention returns to the room, the convenor remarks on the conversation that birthed the term Global Presencing. What would it look like if the world stopped for a while to allow the future to emerge. What would a truly global process of reimagining civilisation feel like? Someone remarks "That was it. We just did it."

The following day they compose a collective poem crafted from scraps of words gifted by each person. Lines of truth and tenderness, stitched together:

> *I hear a call from beyond the soil*
> *in a language I don't understand.*
> *I hear a call to make a choice, make a change.*
> *In a world veiled in the smog of noise*
> *where man is drunk on power*
> *where we feel separate from each other*
> *from nature, from life itself.*
> *In a world of utmost beauty and unbearable terror*

a garden spinning in space
filled with infinite possibility
I hear a call
but I choose not to listen.
Life has shown me things I didn't want to see.
Life has shown me what it means to sit at the heart of a wound.
Do not dodge the rocky places or the shadows in the wood.
Learn to inhabit wild space – this is where the magic grows.
In a world of such anger, inequality and complexity
darkness and confusion
ignorance and illusion,
we know how to live the paradox
to lay down fear, cynicism and judgement.
We know how to live in ways that are spacious
Ways that seek silence
We know how to live ways that heal.
I will seek the silence
I will let time flow through me
I will trust I have all I need.

Questions, Only Questions

There is a tussle going on, a conversation rattling back and forth in the corridors of my mind. Corridors that remind me of school days, patrolled by Narks, dictated by bells and clocks.

My mind says this is all well and good. People sit for peace. 600,000 people sit for peace. Did it do any good? Didn't the war stop when the army had cornered and slaughtered every last one of the Tamil Tigers? While we sit in peaceful meditation aren't schoolgirls being kidnapped and raped? Isn't global warming spiralling out of control, unfettered?

My heart replies: have some faith. Isn't it beautiful enough in its own right? What if the world stopped for peace? What if the world woke up one morning to its own infinite possibility? We could change history that way. We would shift paradigms and systems, economies, politics. We could reinvent the lot in a blaze of creativity and reciprocity.

Mind ponders, trying not to race too far ahead. Yes, yes. I get it. But what would that look like? Are all these spontaneous sparks enough? Don't we need a strategy – history tells us the rich and powerful don't give up easily? Is this emergence enough? Wouldn't it at least need a coordinated process of presencing? Wouldn't we all need simultaneously to stop and allow the future to reveal herself? It's in the collective process that the magic happens. This is global revolution after all!

Body is impatient. It taps on the table, jiggles its crossed legs, taps its toes. Will you lot just hurry up! This is something I want to see before you return me to earth. Why are people so slow with the stuff that really matters – tied up in the trivialities of celebrity weddings, Facebook likes, mundane lives, "reality" TV. Let's get on with it. The world is burning after all!

Heart smiles a little. She has heard this all before. She loves the passion and will. She has infinite amounts of patience. Mind agrees with body. They are impatient for change. They can see the possibilities, if not the practicalities of "how". Looking around and back through time, they see too much suffering. They want to move on before their heart is broken, even if it means blundering ahead clumsily.

Spirit breathes deeply. Spirit lives for breath. The in. The out. The eternal pause between, where there is lightness, emptiness, space. Can you hear that?

What? they ask.

That pause. Can you feel the energy waiting in that pause? It's pregnant.

They smile together. They remember this feeling from the womb. They remember the rush, the calm, the disorientation, the commotion, the wild ride and sudden light.

You see, says spirit. This is the way it is. Has always been. Will always be. All is well.

They look into each other's eyes, deep into each other's eyes, and breathe.

What is the voice in the silence
The whisper in complete stillness?
Future waiting to be born?

Power of now?
The voice of the seventh generation
Tugging at conscience?
Your deepest desire
stealing away your heart?
What is the voice that reveals itself
Only when your own is still?
Wisdom of blood and bone?
Heartbeat of Earth stirring beneath your feet
Turning the soil to return to fertility?
Abundance awaiting the spring of ages?
Awaiting pollinators of new life?

A Wake-Up Call by Cynthia Jurs, New Mexico

She was wearing a heart monitor for a month during the time of the Great American Eclipse. So she was acutely aware of the heartbeat of the Earth. She was always aware of the Earth's pulse within her own but it was heightened now – her own heart was telling her something.

Figure 9.0 Cynthia Jurs, creator of the Earth Treasure Vase initiative

The moment of the eclipse was beautiful and profound, yet eerie. The light darkened into a greenish dusk, the birds and insects fell silent, hushed. A strange peace fell upon the land as a lunar darkness crossed over the glaring solar light. For a few moments, we earthlings experienced a shift in our consciousness – a moment led by the moon, cooling the flames of the sun. The temperature dropped 15 degrees. Her heart kept beating – or maybe it skipped a beat just then. During the standstill so many of us came to, a collective stopping like cancelled flights after 9/11, everything got quiet.

Then life went on. An astrologer told her that afterwards we might see some climate disruptions like earthquakes or floods. And with a fury they began. In Houston. In India and Nepal. In Bangladesh and Nigeria.

311

Unprecedented floods and hurricanes. Monsoon rains like never before. Her heart skipped another beat and the tears began to fall. Then the fires came into view. Raging all over the western states with temperatures well into the 100s in places that should not get above 70. Journalist Dahr Jamail reported 70 degrees in northernmost arctic Alaska where is should be 40 tops this time of year. Fires destroying the ancient sequoias. Destroying whole watersheds of mountain wilderness and ravaging metropolitan communities in the southlands. No one was safe.

And still the denial was everywhere. It's a scam, they said, a propaganda tool. Others insisting that Nature is turning against us in response to a system so corrupted by power and wealth that it is blindly destroying the little wild left. Life out of balance. And still we pretend we are untouchable. Her heart skipped another beat. Then it began to race. It was hard to breathe. The smoke in the air was suffocating. Another crack in the ice reverberated along the Earth's songlines.

The trees stood still while the winds of change blew through their branches and the animals fled to the edges of their world. Where do we go now? The Great Turning. What kind of collective awakening is this? She became aware finally, that she was witnessing Mother Earth's demise. She hated to admit it. Had held for so long to the belief that humans would wake up – that even a small number of us would manage to turn the situation around. But no, she still knew there was goodness to be found in the hearts of many and she would hold to that in her own faltering heart. The tears fell again.

But the devastation and destruction occurring now was going to take lifetimes, eons to recover from. And in that time span an artificial world could take root upon the natural one, the cycle of slavery repeating itself, along with civil wars in every direction. It was inevitable now. Her heart raced. She breathed to calm it. This helped. Perhaps the flooded petro-chemical plants in the port of Houston would be a warning to the military industrial complex and CEOs would reorient themselves.

She took another breath. The end of nature. We are witnessing this. And it's coming faster and more furiously than anyone expected. Let's not pretend. We are not immune. And yet we can create the conditions for peace to prevail. For wisdom to arise. Compassionate actions are occurring everywhere. This is the spirit we must feed, she insisted. I will do this until my dying breath. With every beat of my heart. Life on Earth is a beautiful thing. We did see this coming. Let's not pretend otherwise. Now, lets culti-

vate kindness. Nurture our love. Let's open our hearts even wider and breathe to calm the storms. Suffering is everywhere. I vow to end it. (Jurs, 2017)

Beyond Baby-Steps

If we look hard enough, we can see all around us the faltering baby steps of a new world walking blinking into the first rays of morning sun.

There are moments that act as a lightening rod for the more beautiful world. The falling of the Berlin Wall, the Unknown Professor standing with his shopping bags in front of the tanks in Tiananmen Square, Mohamed Bouazizi setting himself on fire and sparking the Arab Spring. They are moments within a tinderbox atmosphere where a single spark can ignite possibility.

Standing Rock became an almost magnetic attractor for these moments. One came when veterans from each of the US Armed Forces joined together to ask for forgiveness for the genocide against indigenous peoples[58]. In another, representatives of US Churches apologised for the Doctrine of Discovery which had provided religious cover for this genocide.[59] These are the moments that heal the divisions within humanity wrought by a system of greed, extraction and materialism.

How do we nurture more of this? More of these sublime moments. When the young woman protester brings the militarised cop to tears. When the skin-head poses for photos with the Black Lives Matters dad, so he can show his kids. When the holocaust survivor in her nineties forgives the Nazis because she does not want to take the hatred to her death.

How do we occupy this place in our hearts and bring it to our relationships and to our institutions? Can we find enough space, enough generosity to move from ego to eco at all three levels – I, We, The Whole? Surely it's not so hard. Surely it's an easier, kinder, more natural life. A slower, more connected, more indigenous life.

What would that feel like, if humanity stepped from ego to eco, if the world bent itself towards love, abundance, connection.

What an amazing place this would be to live. What if we dipped our toe into the long arc of change and felt its presence from source to ultimate surrender and all these moments in our lives in between. What if we remembered the future version of ourselves that we already are? It's not so far from here to there. These moments are all now.

The future is forgotten land
infinite potential,
longed-for memory
where sky meets earth in lingered kiss
and proud brown lioness beats out the path.
It confuses, with beauty, ecstatic pain
Entices, with excitement, adventure.
Language struggles to explain
why spirit craves nothing
soul seeks only acceptance, compassion, ease.
The long arc of horizon
bends towards night
tugging stars across the sky.
It nudges me to step from this path to the next –
from destruction, the violence of separation
into unity.
It calls me to banish this lie,
to recall that the essence of love is surrender.
Patience, it purrs -
Hope is the last to die.
Kindness the easiest gift.
On this slow and constant curve
there is no point of no return.
Just gradual incline, eons long
promising light, dawn, forgetting.
I do not trust my judgement any more
don't know how to seize this moment
cannot tell how much I believe
can't rely on the lens I use to gauge the turning.
Still I crave a whole sea that shifts the world apace.
Still I know there is nothing to be done
but wait for the seventh wave

of the seventh generation
Then celebrate the fragile brilliance of each human soul
cast up on the beach
edges smoothed by time and tide.

Lions by Clio Pauly, Namibia[60]

Figure 10.0 The Power of Africa, Lions Rising

Remember: we are many. Just because we are a cave full of slumbering lions does not mean we will never wake. We woke before and we shall wake again to defend what's sacred.

Even while we rest we do so in honour of Earth. We sleep-plant, sleep-reforest, sleep-recycle, sleep-heal ...

When all sleep-walking is done we shall dance wildly reclaiming, rejoicing, remembering, regenerating, revolting. Roaring rebels with a cause. That cause is Home. Our earth. (Pauly, 2017)

The Voice of a Virus

Now Corona Virus has opened another window on the world

of presencing. It has enforced a global moment of pause. In that pause we have witnessed fear and death and the pain of our most vulnerable kin spending their final moments without the presence of those they love. And we have seen how quickly nature repairs itself once the air is clear and the seas are not filled with cruise liners or container ships. We have seen animals return to empty city streets, heard birdsong louder than before, noticed the trees breathe a sigh of relief.

The Mamos, holy people of the Colombian Sierra Nevada directed us to the significance of this moment:

We were so powerful that in a blink of an eye we overheated the planet, thawed the poles, causing many brothers of flora and fauna to disappear. We polluted the breeze and the air. Very few have acted with a consciousness of transformation wanting to change the system. That chaos is what today governs us. Until now, we were playing with fire. We put ourselves off balance. And then, a virus, the smallest of the elementals, the most insignificant creature before the eyes of the younger brothers forced us to stop the pursuit of the race, without knowing after what we were running. That virus became a great teacher, an authentic messenger.[61]

Perhaps presencing then is the art of deciphering signs and symbols from the great unknown. Perhaps we find the future in the subtle messages of the natural world. As we come out of lockdown, what would we say we have really learnt from this experience? What did it teach us about the future we want and the past we long to leave behind? And what will we do now to lean into the future that whispers on the breeze of change?

References

Abdullah, S (1999), Creating a World That Works for All, Berrett-Koehler Publishers

Bucko, A & Fox, M (2013), Occupy Spirituality: A Radical Vision for a New Generation, Berkley, North Atlantic Books

Commonway Institute. Website retrieved from: http://www.commonway.org/sarvodaya -peace-action-plan

Eisenstein, C. (2013), The more beautiful world our hearts know is possible, Berkley, North Atlantic Books.

Fabian, R. (2014) Connecting for Change: Insights from an Emerging Global Transformation Movement. Magazine article retrieved from http://www.kosmosjournal.org/article/connecting-for-change-insights-from-an-emerging-global-transfor-mation-movement/

Fabian, R (2017), personal email correspondence

Forest, O.S. (2000), Dreaming the Council Ways, York Beach Maine, Samuel Weiser

Griffiths, R, (2016, March 18) Micah White: Occupy Wall Street was a constructive failure, The Globe and Mail. Retrieved from: https://www.theglobeandmail.com/opinion/munk-debates/micah-white-oc-cupy-wall-street-was-a-constructive-failure/article29294222/

Jurs, C. (2017) A Wake-Up Call, Facebook post retrieved from https://www.facebook.com/cynthia.jurs/posts/10155756791443466

Lao Tzu (1997), Tao Te Ching, A New English version by Ursula K Le Guin, Boston, Shambhala Publications.

Longboat, K.D. (2015) A Path to Sacred Healing: Answering Humanity's Great Call. Podcast retrieved from: http://indige-nouswisdomsummit.com/library/8681/7800

McCabe, P. (2017) The Hoop of Life. Facebook post retrieved from: https://www.facebook.com/pat.mccabe.5454/posts/1735746796455937

Macy, J (2017) Subtle Activism, the Great Turning, and the Work that Reconnects. Podcast retrieved from: http://positivesocialchange-summit.com/program/245

Nicol, D. Subtle activism: An idea whose time has come. Blog retrieved from: http://subtleactivism.net/subtle-activism-idea-whose-time-has-come/

Occupy, (2012, May 11) The Global May Manifesto of the International Occupy Assembly, Newspaper article retrieved from: https://www.theguardian.com/commentisfree/2012/may/11/occupy-globalmay-manifesto

Pauly, C. (2017) Lions. Facebook post retrieved from: https://www.facebook.com/clio.pauly/posts/10156188880473888?pnref=story

Presencing Institute (2011). Video file, retrieved from https://www.presencing.com/programs/global-forum-2011

Presencing Institute (2012). Video file, retrieved from https://www.presencing.com/global-forum-2012Presencing Institute (2014). Video file, retrieved from: https://www.presencing.com/programs/

global-forum-2014

Roy, A. (2003) War Talk. Speech to the World Social Forum retrieved from: http://www.outlookindia.com/website/story/ confronting-empire/218738

Senge, P., Scharmer, O, Jaworski, J & Flowers, B.S. (2004), Presence, New York, Doubleday.

Van Gelder, S (2012, February 23) Pancho Ramos Stierle: Nonviolence Is Radical. Magazine article retrieved from: http://www.yesmaga-zine.org/peace-justice/pancho-ramos-stierle-nonviolence-is-radical

CHAPTER 12

The dance between structure and skill:

Experiences from the LiFT project's experiments with the Collaboratory, an agile tool for applying Theory U in diverse contexts

Elke Fein

Introduction

"In our dreams, the collaboratory becomes the preferred meeting place for citizens to jointly question, discuss, and construct new ideas and approaches to resolving sustainability challenges on a local, regional, and global level" (Muff, 2014a, 12-13).

Otto Scharmer's Theory U (Scharmer, 2007) has been around for just over ten years now. Meanwhile, numerous integral and leadership coaches and practitioners have engaged in applications in various domains, from business to education to citizen involvement processes and beyond. Theory U based methods have proven to be extremely effective in bringing together diverse groups of stakeholders in view of developing joint actionable visions, helping them to translate these into project prototypes that can make a difference for society and the environment.

Among the pioneers of applying Theory U to complex societal challenges is the 50+20 working group of the World Council of Business Schools for Sustainable Business (Muff, 2013) who eventually gave birth to a method they called the "Collaboratory", based on the insights of Scharmer's theory. The Collaboratory has since then been applied and consolidated as a method through implementations in many differing settings across cultures and countries. One of the active experimenters with the method is the transnational EU funded strategic partnership "Leadership for Transition (LiFT)" who has meanwhile gained over five years of experience with Collaboratory workshops and is now offering facilitator trainings in order to disseminate its experience to interested individuals and the larger public.

This paper will explain what a Collaboratory is and spell out some methodological learnings by giving examples from LiFT's experience gathered over the last years. On this basis, it discusses a number of (pre)conditions and limitations for a Collaboratory to work, i.e. for the wisdom inherent in Theory U to unfold its full potential. By looking at the challenge to navigate the delicate balance between structure and necessary skills, it points at a few areas in which LiFT's action research helps to differentiate our understanding of Theory U in action.

Background and data base: The Collaboratory and the LiFT experience

> *"A collaboratory is a facilitated space open to everybody, and in particular to concerned stakeholders, to meet on an equal basis to co-create new solutions for societal, environmental or economic issues by drawing on the emergent future. It is a place where people can think, work, and learn together to invent their common futures, an inclusive learning environment where the formal separation of knowledge production and knowledge transfer dissolves."* (Muff, 2014a, 12-13)

The emergence of the Collaboratory

The Collaboratory as described in this article[62] has emerged in 2010 in the context of the 50+20 initiative of the World Council of Business Schools for Sustainable Business (WCBSSB) and has been further developed since then. The WFBSSB covered 13.000 Business schools worldwide at that time[63] and was looking for ways to recalibrate business education for the coming years.[64] Given that many of the partner schools were located in the developing world, it soon became clear to all involved partners that the task was no less than to globally work towards "a world worth living in" by finding new ways of living together in our societies (Muff, 2013). Based on this shared understanding, the initiative committed to developing a "radically new vision for management education in the hope of inspiring business schools to embrace their societal responsibilities and to develop responsible leaders" who display "the courage and the solidity to shape the transformation we need" (Muff, 2014, 9 and Muff, 2013). Sure enough, this was going to require a transformation that would shift business "from maximizing short term profit to serving the common good" (ibid.), thereby questioning the then dominant concept of what business schools were all about.

The Collaboratory was born in the process of defining and developing the group's joint vision and mission, during which they went through phases of brainstorming, intensive discussions, radical criticisms, taking everything apart, before turning to visioning, harvesting their joint vision and building projects based on it. While many participants experienced these phases as a sometimes chaotic and confusing process at the time[65], readers familiar with Theory U will immediately see that the steps the group went through basically corresponded to the typical phases and elements of a U process. And since the outcome was more than convincing, these elements got prototyped into a collaborative format named the "Collaboratory".

Why was the format called the Collaboratory and not simply "Theory U approach" or "U process"? One distinction to have in mind is that between Theory U as a *theory*, and the Collaboratory as a *method* or, more precisely, a meta-method that is *based on* Theory U as one of its core inspiration, among others. Theory U is the theory that Scharmer has built around his ten-year-long research into differing fields of awareness and communication in groups and their relation to the outputs that tend to be possible (or not) when a group operates in one of these specific fields. The theory explains how collective awareness and a certain quality of outcomes tend to be interrelated. As a theory, it does not, however, offer more practical tools and instructions about how to create specific fields, let alone with different audiences, and how to move from one field to the next, in other words, how to actually implement a process through the U. So is the Collaboratory a U process then? Yes and no. The simple answer would be: ideally yes. But reality usually goes beyond simple ideal-types. If we understand a U process as a facilitated process that leads a group, first, down through all four fields of the left side of the U and then back up through the subsequent three fields on the right side of the U, then the more complex and differentiated answer would be: More often than not, a Collaboratory might not be a "full" U process in this strict sense of the term, for the simple reason that not all settings allow for this ideal-typical structure to be implemented. What's more, we have found that to apply such a "clean" version of the U process 1:1 is often not even desirable, due to all sorts of needs, constraints and challenges that specific audiences and settings pose to process design. So, whereas the term "U process" is understood here as a rather ideal-typical construct, which of course informs Collaboratory design as a kind of "template principles" at any moment, an actual Collaboratory is likely never the same as any other. It is always already the result of a "reflective digestion" of the core ideas and principles underlying theory and process templates on the one hand and their confrontation with the "needs of the now" in a given context of application.

Also, note that there is more theory behind the Collaboratory than just Theory U. Other sources of inspiration are, for example, circular and whole person learning, Appreciative Inquiry, scenario planning, Design Shop or open space work. For more info see parts 1 and 2 in (Muff, 2014).

Given its first successful application in the WCBSSB context, the Collaboratory appeared as a good approach for conducting similar stakeholder involvement processes around the globe, as a format providing a clear enough structure and which was at the same time flexible enough to be adapted to different contexts and conditions. Business School Lausanne (BSL) and their partners have since then gained extensive experience with the Collaboratory in various settings and locations. A first book compiling some of it came out in 2014 (Muff, 2014). A second one is currently in print as a product of BSL's partnership in the LiFT project (Muff, 2018). Both serve as references to this paper, besides the LiFT experience itself.

The Collaboratory meets LiFT

"Each Collaboratory is different!" (Burck et al, 2014)

The "Leadership for Transition (LiFT)" project came into being as five organizations[66], engaged in the fields of either leadership, education and/or societal transition, gathered in 2013 in a Grundtvig Learning Partnership convened by the author around the goal of exchanging best practices for facilitating transformative change in Europe. BSL being a partner in the project, its dean, Katrin Muff suggested we try out the format of the Collaboratory as a tool for implementing LiFT's core intention, namely to bring together innovative researchers, practitioners and citizens engaged in the fields of leadership, education and societal transition to promote more integrative, more effective and thus more sustainable ways of living in Europe and beyond. The Collaboratory seemed to be a perfect tool for applying the project rationale, holding that in times of multidimensional crisis, leadership increasingly needs to empower individuals and society at large to take over responsibility for working towards the common good.

LiFT set out to experiment with the format, and started hosting public workshops in each partner country. Usually the local LiFT partner would provide the venue, chose a burning topic as a focus that was relevant to their organization or environment and invite a basic network of stakeholders and participants to the event. While the first LiFT workshop (held in Trondheim, Norway in spring 2014[67]) was still mainly a learning place for us to get to know Katrin's format and approach, the project team became more creative soon after that. Workshops began to differ from the standard ideal type adapted from the "clean" U process and to creatively adopt the latter to all sorts of contextual settings. In fact, LiFT provided an ample playing field for testing out the format with varying group sizes, stakeholder constellations, available time spans, topics etc. This was all the more the case when LiFT received a new and more extensive round of funding as a Strategic Partnership for another three years (2015-18).

In its second funding phase, two additional partners[68] came in, and the goals – and stakes – were higher than before. LiFT now turned into an action research project. Building on its previous experience, it adopted a research strategy aiming at a more systematic analysis of what happens at a Collaboratory by focusing on the factors that either make it a success or prevent it from succeeding. It looked at the dynamic interrelations between two complex variables: first, the diverging contexts of each workshop and second, the facilitation design that has been chosen to best address the specific context. This research strategy was based on the insight that the success of a Collaboratory seemed to largely depend on the skill with which the design elements, tools and methods chosen for each phase of the U process were a good enough fit to meet the specific needs and challenges we were confronted with in the respective context.

Over the course of five years, nine public Collaboratory workshops were hosted by the LiFT partnership in different locations in Norway, Sweden, Germany, Luxembourg, Austria and Switzerland, and several more in other locations beyond the project itself. Most of them have been thoroughly documented, evaluated and reflected in view of the overall course of the process, pitfalls, options, alternatives and methodological learnings. As an outcome of harvesting this experience, the project has published a number of intellectual outputs, designed to disseminate LiFT's experience to a wider audience of practitioners.[69] They include a book on the foundations and resources of integral leadership

(Fein, 2018a), a Collaboratory methodology book (Fein, 2018b), a case book with detailed descriptions and evaluations of each individual LiFT workshop (Kunze & Fein, 2018), a book summarizing Collaboratory "midwife" Katrin Muff's learnings about how the Collaboratory can facilitate societal transformation (Muff, 2018), and a train-the-trainer course (Fein & Molz, 2018).

This chapter is the condensed result of our analysis of an extensive set of field notes and interview material[70] gathered during the action research project, as well as on the previous experience documented in Muff 2014. It summarizes some of the key insights and findings regarding LiFT's main research question, namely when and how the Collaboratory can best be used in differing contexts. Based on this, it offers some meta-level insights on how Theory U can inform processes supporting large, diverse stakeholder groups working towards innovative solutions to joint problems by going beyond conventional discussion modes. So how is the Collaboratory drawing on Theory U?

The Collaboratory and Theory U

> *"We believe that, if we properly assemble the players into a system, orient them toward a purpose, engage them in the right interactions, ask them the right questions, and allow them so self-organize, the system will reach a moment of truth. In the words of Nobel Prize winning chemist Ilya Prigogine, the system is 'shifting into a higher order' – a true quantum leap – such that a new order emerges from the chaos of the old and produces the needed solution."* (Burck et al., 2014, 53)

The Collaboratory draws on Theory U in at least four respects: intention, focus, process and approach, even though not every Collaboratory will implement a full, "clean" U process (see paragraph above).

Transformative purpose and intention

First, the core intention and motivation behind a Collaboratory process is a transformative one, in other words, it aims at inviting and bringing about deep changes of how participants perceive and act upon their respective problem or challenge. This is due to Einstein's insight that the methods and modes of thinking that have brought about a problem are usually inadequate to find lasting solutions to it. Scharmer elaborates on this, holding that "new solutions require new spaces for thought", and that "as long as we take a problem-based approach, we limit our creative power to the same thinking we had when we created the "problem" (Scharmer, 2014, 101). The Collaboratory experience supports the claim that the further down you go the U, on the continuum from superficial to deep inquiry, the more innovative, powerful and effective the solutions will be.

The story of the emergence of the Collaboratory is a symptomatic example of the transformative "magic" of drawing on the wisdom of collective intelligence that is at the core of the Collaboratory method itself. As explained earlier, the Collaboratory format emerged almost accidentally from the global Business Schools' community's efforts to come up with a joint, actionable vision around educating globally responsible leaders. For this, so the group acknowledged, it needed a fundamental shift in leaders' understanding of their own role, a shift from research and teaching about how to maximize profit towards how business could best serve the people, the planet and the common good. So the shared intention to create a new kind of business school of the future implied and demanded the willingness to let go of familiar models, ideas and identities, and to go through a process of facing uncertainty while taking the old model(s) apart for something qualitatively new to emerge.

Focus on consciousness and the collective fields of awareness

Based on this transformative purpose and intention, second,

"a core aspect that makes the Collaboratory different from any other co-creative approach is its deliberate and courageous concentration on the *group consciousness* and the visionary power that lies therein" (Scharmer, 2014, 101, my highlight). Working with this realm of group consciousness essentially means to actively perceive, sense into and ultimately create and transform the "field qualities" that Scharmer identified and described as the invisible resource that determines the quality of interpersonal communication and its results (see section on skills below). Building upon Scharmer's core insight that the quality of the outcomes first and foremost depends on the "field of awareness" created by leadership through certain qualities or modes of communication and presence, the whole method is designed to create structures and tools to allow for specific fields of awareness to emerge as needed. Moreover, the Collaboratory is about purposefully navigating participants through increasingly dense fields of awareness to eventually tap into the realm of collective intelligence.

Following the steps and process-design suggested by Theory U:

In order to do this, the Collaboratory actively draws on the four fields of awareness described in Scharmer's model, using the four different listening modes corresponding to them: downloading, factual, emphatic and generative listening, which are later followed by a more action-oriented, co-creative part. As mentioned before, the first and foremost goal of a Collaboratory is to take participants beyond what might be their usual mode of addressing the problem in question, into deeper fields of awareness, enabling new ways of perceiving the problem. Therefore, its setup and structure are ideally designed to enable – and actively invite that shift to happen. More precisely, its set up gradually takes the group through all four fields of awareness, from mode 1 to mode 4 (Presencing) in a relatively short period of time. In order to be successful, this shifting of awareness must happen in a way that is appropriate to the respective group and their respective point of departure and/or experience. In other words, it must be facilitated in a way that is responsive to the needs and reactions of the group (see section on skills below).

In the second (or rather third[71]) part of the process, it then re-designs the space several more times to take participants from harvesting and crystallizing visions into prototyping and co-creating novel solutions as suggested by Theory U, again, depending on the available time and setting. So, in this sense, the Collaboratory translates the wisdom of Theory U into actionable steps and elements of a comprehensive process that, as an ideal type, is designed to allow the collective intelligence of the larger fields that the respective group is part of to unfold its full potential.

Pragmatic and outcome oriented approach

Finally, the Collaboratory is inspired by Theory U's hands-on, pragmatic and outcome-oriented approach. Coming from the realm of business, its pretense is clearly to produce meaningful results, not just to offer fancy spaces for lively discussion or cozy dialog. Moreover, the Collaboratory tries to build the knowledge inherent in Theory U into a process that ultimately serves the goal of enabling next stage solutions to emerge. So, going through the four modes of awareness and of (ideally) diving deeply into mode 4 is not so much an aim in itself – even though helping a system to see itself is certainly of great value for all involved stakeholders. Rather, inviting participants into the presencing mode, and thus drawing on insights generated by collective intelligence is ultimately put in service of the goal of developing novel, transformative solutions.

To sum up, drawing on the core insights and wisdom of Theory U turns the Collaboratory into a compact, often condensed, consolidated and at the same time very flexible and agile tool for framing and scaffolding stakeholder involvement processes to address problems of common concern in an outcome-oriented way. – And so much for the most important bit of "theory" behind the Collaboratory.[72] The following paragraphs now look at the more practical side of using the format and discuss what can be learnt from LiFT's experience.

The dance between structure and skill: Experiences and learnings from LiFT

As indicated above, the EU funded strategic partnership "Leadership for Transition (LiFT)" has been experimenting with the Collaboratory format for over five years now. It has hosted more than a dozen Collaboratories in six European countries and beyond, and has accompanied them by action research. This has provided us with substantial, qualitative insights regarding our understanding of Theory U in action.

In a nutshell, we can say that the standards and measures of success of a Collaboratory are similar to those implicit in Theory U itself. The two most important and strongly interrelated indicators are, first, the depth and transformative quality of the process of inquiry, and second, the kind and quality of its outcomes (including their long term effect and impact). Moreover, the combination of both is decisive for a successful Collaboratory. But how can depth and impactful results be brought about? What are the preconditions and ingredients of a good Collaboratory process? The following section takes a closer look at what seems to be at the heart of our learnings about how to design and facilitate good Collaboratories as gained during the LiFT journey.

While we could easily formulate several specific learnings about how a Collaboratory design can and should be put together, how it can be tailored and flexibly adopted to specific hosting contexts, the deeper learning behind this is connected to the challenge to balance the dimensions of structure and skill. What do I mean by this? Theory U describes the field qualities of awareness, which generate different qualities of communication, collaboration and (co-) creation. The process built upon this knowledge and which implements theory U provides a structure that scaffolds the emergence of specific field qualities in specific moments. Certain ways of structuring the process help to create certain field qualities and contents in various phases of the process. So, a U-process is a kind of meta-structure consisting of a whole series of changing scaffolding structures during the journey through the U. Only together, they provide the guard rails or "safety fence" for the process to gradually take a given group down the U and thus enable transformative learning. At the same time, structure alone is probably insufficient to successfully lead a group of stakeholders through the U if the respective phases are not facilitated in appropriate ways. While the structure might still achieve considerable results as compared to more conventional formats, just by taking participants beyond their usual modes of thinking and communicating, the degree of experience and skill of facilitators can add greatly to desirable outcomes.

We have found that structure and skill are the two complex variables, the combination of which appears to be "secret" behind Collaboratory success. The next sections provide some more detailed insights into both dimensions and their complex interrelations. Moreover, it will soon become clear that a strict separation between structure and skill is difficult due to these interrelations.[73]

The value and impact of structure: cookbook and ingredients for a good Collaboratory

"Being prepared extremely well is a pre-condition for being flexible. A Collaboratory is a careful collective improvisation rather than a strict procedure. Being spontaneous and having fun is very important for a creative atmosphere." (Muff & Dyllick, 2014, 135)

While increasing the chances of a good meal, a good cook book and recipe are no guarantees for the former if the cook is inexperienced or misreads certain instructions. This metaphor applies even more since the elements of the Collaboratory recipe outlined below are complex sets of activities in themselves and require a certain degree of skill and understanding in the first place. However, we can translate the LiFT experience into a couple of "ingredients" that are likely to help users to structure a successful event. Since most of the structuring work happens before the actual event, the focus will be on the preparation phase.

Defining and designing the context

First, note that the Collaboratory – as most other methods – is a powerful tool only if used in the right context. For it to be a suitable method, users should either have the following elements in place or work towards creating them:

A joint challenge or problem and a central guiding question around this, focusing on how the challenge can be addressed or how the problem can be solved

The Collaboratory is designed to support diverse stakeholder groups to address complex issues of joint concern in a deep, visionary and outcome-oriented way. Therefore, if the issue at hand is not framed adequately and does not have enough traction for a broad enough network of stakeholders to feel a sense of concern or even urgency in view of co-developing actual solutions to the underlying problem or challenge, it might not be the right method. If the interest is mainly to inquire more deeply into a topic or share perspectives between a range of participants to better understand each other and the complexity of the problem, without the need and urge to actually do something about it, other approaches might be a better choice. In contrast, if you have a suitable challenge at hand, make sure you can formulate it as a question, ideally one which invites joint action, such as "How can we.... (achieve xyz)", for example "how can we make tap water the favorite drink in Switzerland?"[74]

A local stakeholder (usually the local host) who 'owns' the problem or issue

It is critically important that the local host or topic owner has a sufficiently strong, vested interest in the chosen challenge being addressed in a more efficient way, or even have it solved. Otherwise there is likely not enough focus and commitment to engage in a substantial collaborative process over a certain period. A host committed to productively solving or at least constructively addressing the issue at hand is also an important precondition for bringing together a sufficiently large and diverse network of motivated stakeholders, who are usually invited by the local host (Fein, 2018b, Kunze & Fein, 2018).

A diverse network of stakeholders (social actors who play a role in relation to the challenge/problem and) are willing to be part of the collaborative process

Regarding the range of stakeholders to be invited, diversity is crucial in terms of viewpoints/perspectives, needs, experiences, assumptions etc. Preparation should make sure from the very beginning that all actors who have a stake in and/or a say with regard to the respective problem or topic (be it as producers, originators, affected, concerned or profiteers) are included, regardless of their political affiliations or orientations. Other criteria for selecting stakeholders are their special independent expertise about the issue or their ability to mobilize resources that are relevant for making progress on potential solutions. Otherwise one might end up with a typical idealist orientation of how "they" i.e. those in power, should take action. The above outlined set of stakeholders can either be invited as participants and/or, in addition, in the role of "experts" opening the explorative inquiry of the topic in a more prominent way. The more tension there is between stakeholders around a given topic, the more productive a Collaboratory *can* be – and the more important it is to give controversial perspectives a voice very early in the process.

The above listed aspects are essential structural preconditions for a Collaboratory to be a suitable method. Once they are in place, make sure you schedule sufficient time for the following preparatory steps, because finding the right structure for a specific context needs some explorative efforts.

Preparation is everything – building the team and co-creating the setting and stage

Since each context is different, every Collaboratory is different too. The challenge is to find the right responses and design elements to match the given context. This has multiple aspects. An important part of preparing the setup is to build up a team that includes not only the local host and the facilitators, but ideally also representatives of the most relevant stakeholder groups. This allows for creating alignment between all parties that are going to be part of the event and to make sure that expectations and responsibilities are shared from the beginning. The following aspects need to be considered by the preparation team:

Physical and temporal setting

The setting should provide the necessary time and space for a Collaboratory to unfold in the given context – which can mean different things in different contexts.

We have found that the minimum amount of time should be one day (depending on the issue and concrete circumstances). Two days are better, unless the event is taking place locally, i.e. with participants having possibilities to come together and follow up with each other easily after the first or main event. We have also found that if Collaboratories are part of other, larger events, even if with similar thematic agendas, the latter tend to dictate various context factors (such as available time slots, breaks or rooms), and to create distraction by the other surrounding issues and activities. All of this makes it more difficult to fully focus on the core issue.

The size, character and energetic qualities of the venue also play a central role in view of the success of a Collaboratory workshop. Larger physical spaces are preferable to small ones in order to have more options available when it comes to designing the process and making adaptations during it. Daylight and a view onto nature are preferable to closed rooms and artificial light. Warm colors and natural materials might add to a welcoming atmosphere. If the venue is not optimal in any of these regards, consider how the overall hosting atmosphere could be improved purposefully.

Facilitation team

This section being about structure, the choice of facilitators is a decision that can and should be made at least partly by certain "hard" criteria in advance. Put simply, the preparation team needs to make sure that facilitators' experience matches the complexity of the challenge. So what should Collaboratory organizers look for in a facilitator? At this point, experience and skill clearly help to make good choices as do trust and a healthy intuition – which illustrates to what degree good structuring work is always already the product of a certain degree of skill. So, as to the more formal selection criteria, facilitators should of course have some knowledge about and experience with the method and should not have any personal stake in the topic themselves. What this means in more detail will be explained in the section below on "skills".

In a nutshell, facilitators should display a set of skills that allow them to embody an attitude of detachment and of letting go of any substantial personal goals with regard to the outcome of the process, in order to be able to serve the latter as such. This appears as a prerequisite for facilitation to adequately respond to whatever happens in the course of the process, rather than getting triggered emotionally or intellectually by it. The facilitator(s)' responses should be driven by the overall intention of the event, rather than by their own. This capacity enables facilitation to navigate uncertainty and to deal with unexpected situations in adequate ways, ideally from a silent inner place, an embodied capacity to listen, observe and sense without judgement. As Otto Scharmer puts it: "Leadership in its essence is the capacity to shift the inner place from which we operate." (Scharmer & Kaeufer, 2013, 248)

Building alignment around the purpose and approach of the event

Finally, as a foundation of building any powerful and appropriate scaffolding structure, the preparation team needs to define and structure its own functioning. Assumptions and expectations about various aspects of an event, including its purpose and the approach to be taken are often implicit and not necessarily shared between all partners and stakeholders in the team. It is therefore a crucial and constant challenge to work towards aligning these between all involved parties in the course of the preparation phase. This helps to create a clearer focus and momentum, which can then also be spread by the stakeholders across their networks. At this stage, it is also important to get a sense and feel for the background of the group one will be working with, especially with regard to the degree of previous experience they might have with similar collaborative methods. Will they likely join the collaborative flow easily, or are they exposed to this kind of approach for the first time and might thus need additional, specific framing in order to be able to fully show up to and be part of the process? The Collaboratory requires a certain openness of the participants to engage in a deeper level of collaborative inquiry than what they might be used to in their everyday life. Alignment work therefore helps to make sure that the event can build on a sufficient degree of shared understanding of the method.

Designing facilitation, tools and alternative options

"By designing a journey that takes the participants into the realm of play, you loosen the current reality's hold on them and enhance their ability to entertain a future, quite different reality." (Burck et al., 2014, 57)

This is the main arena where structuring takes place. By framing the conversation between stakeholders in ways that help to bring about, sustain and transition to certain qualities of awareness, a good design takes participants through the phases of the U process. Here is a short sketch of how this happens during a Collaboratory.

In the first part you want to make sure to create a warm, welcoming atmosphere even before the event starts. This can be done through gestures of personally welcoming participants, offering tea and coffee and the like. The next important part is the opening of the workshop where an introduction and framing of the process should be offered that sets the tone to the overall event. It should also provide sufficient orientation through and overview of the process for participants to develop the necessary curiosity and trust to follow any instructions and guidance that facilitation will offer. As part of the opening, we generally use some kind of icebreaker exercise to allow people to get to know and connect with each other on a more personal level, before diving into more topic-focused work. After that follow the *Downloading and Dialog* phases. Depending on the context and kind of group, these should be framed in ways that allow for including a sufficiently broad range of stakeholder perspectives into the conversation and to invite participants to engage with views differing from their own in respectful and constructive ways. In a first step, this is done in a more factual way; in a second step, participants are invited to enter deeper and more personal dialogs, usually in smaller groups. The duration and tools chosen for these phases can vary substantially across contexts.

After the topic has been explored in sufficient breadth and depth, the group is ready to enter the *Presencing* phase, in other words, to let go of any ideas they previously held or currently hold about the topic and make space for new ideas and perspectives to emerge from the realm of collective intelligence. This bottom-of-the-U phase being the most important phase of the process, it needs to be well adapted to the respective group's ability to open up to the field of not-knowing, letting go of control etc. If a group is unfamiliar with meditation practices, for example, a simple time travel exercise, backcasting or future laboratory might be more suitable in this phase than a visioning exercise with closed eyes. Note that not every group might be open or able to go as far down into the U (see Fein, 2018c), nor does time always allow to do the necessary preparatory work (sufficiently extensive downloading and sufficiently intensive dialog) to prepare the group for having an adequate presencing phase. For these cases, appropriate alternatives or adaptations should be considered in advance (see section on skills below).

After the presencing, the design should provide a space for *harvesting* the collective vision, i.e. inviting participants to look for overlap and synergies between the visionary ideas they might each have accessed during the presencing. In the last part of the Collaboratory which can consist of several distinct phases, participants are given the opportunity to develop actionable steps that can help to bring (parts of) their vision into being. They are invited to join forces and team up around practical projects and define next steps to enact and implement them. Open Space is a classic method supporting such a phase. When it comes to wrapping up and closing the Collaboratory, facilitation should make sure that all projects that have been developed can present their "next steps" and appoint a person who can be contacted for following up with the project. Finally, a short closing ceremony acknowledges and celebrates the work that has been done during the journey and hands whatever results participants have come up with back over to the host of the event for further processing.

This basic structure is generally a very powerful way to scaffold participants' entering into specific fields of awareness and to transition between these as the process moves on to the next phase. The change of set-ups, group sizes and focus from phase to phase tends to already prepare most of the space and quality of awareness that is needed in a specific phase to achieve the corresponding quality of conversation. At the same time, the elements of the chosen structure can only be as powerful as, on the one hand, they "fit" participants' capacity and openness to engage with them. On the other hand, therefore, facilitators' skill to navigate tensions between the prepared structure and the actual needs of the people in the room can be an essential "add-on" for the structure to truly unfold its own power. For instance, they might have to play with different methodological tools and alternative options in order to respond to challenges coming up during the process (see section on skills below). For in most cases, it will be difficult to get a sufficiently reliable grasp of participants' needs and capacities – and thus about what "just the right stretch" will be for them before the actual start of the event.

Logistics of hosting

Finally, an important component of structure that Collaboratory hosts and designers can put into place to support a successful process is the material and logistic dimension of hosting. This includes all aspects of "good organization" of both space (the venue) and time, for example providing adequate catering, decorations supporting the overall intention of the event, tools and materials such as marketing materials, flipcharts, visual and sound technology, sticky notes, pens, and the like. To have things like this in place or easily accessible, as well as to have someone in charge of them frees up a lot of mental energy during the process and can help the facilitators to keep their focus on managing the dynamics of the group. It also includes what has become known as the "art of hosting" collaborative events, i.e. the many facets of making participants feel welcome and to invite their openness, contribution and creativity.

It has already become clear up to this point that structure and process design closely interact with certain skills that enable the preparation team to adapt the former to the specific needs and challenges of the given context. The dimension of skill becomes even more important when it comes to the dynamics of facilitation during the event itself as the collaborative process unfolds. The next section takes a closer look at what skillful facilitation means in this context and what kinds of skills can help facilitators to adequately respond to the challenges they are likely to be confronted with during a Collaboratory.

Useful skills for facilitating good Collaboratories

"As leaders, we create space through the quality of our presence, consciousness, and actions." Jonathan Reams (2012, 108)

The "ingredients" outlined in the previous section for building up the scaffolding structure supporting facilitators to take workshop participants on the journey through the U process came across in a "how to" cook book and recipe style. In contrast, the dimension of useful skills is less straightforward to describe – and to acquire. As opposed to recipes in cook-books that can at least theoretically be applied by anyone reading the book – and that require a lesser degree of experience –, developing specific facilitation skills is generally also a matter of personal growth. Often, it is connected to an initial, conscious intention, a commitment to learn and a set of practices the person needs to engage in over a longer period. So with this dimension, we are touching the more implicit and subtle factors of success that are relevant in combination with the structural ones. While we can give a general description of certain skills, thereby giving some orientation and incentive, it is hard to outline the right "amount" or degree to which a facilitator should possess each of them. Among the skills and qualities we have found to be relevant in a successful Collaboratory facilitator are the following:

Experience with the method and beyond

Any facilitator will confirm that leading a group through a process of inquiry and joint decision-making is a complex task that requires not only thorough preparation but also a certain degree of practical knowledge gained in real life application contexts. While the standard structure of a U process and the possible Collaboratory formats based on it are important background knowledge, hardly any real life event exactly follows that structure. Since every event is different, being able to draw on experiences about which tools and strategies had what effect on the participants and process in a given context is an important asset. This is true for both the design and preparation phase and whenever unexpected challenges need to be dealt with during the event itself. Therefore, being able to make "good mistakes" and to reflect these in suitable, protected spaces with peers is a good way to sharpen one's awareness for typical pitfalls and challenges in the facilitation of group processes. LiFT has provided this kind of reflective space before, during and after each event as part of the action research project. While we have made the essentials of the experience gained from this accessible to practitioners through our books and facilitator training course (Fein, 2018a, 2018b, Kunze & Fein, 2018, Fein & Molz, 2018, Muff, 2018; see the Resources & Materials tab on the LiFT project website), theoretical knowledge can arguably not completely replace personal exposure and experience.

State of awareness and presence of the facilitator(s)

"The team's operating model must have flexibility and robust capacity for improvisation to meet the needs of the now." (Burck et al., 2014, 57)

The single most important skill in any situation or phase of the Collaboratory – besides being well prepared and aware of contextual challenges – is probably the interior condition of the facilitator(s). Scharmer himself has quoted O'Brian's insight numerous times that "the success of any intervention depends on the *interior condition* of the intervener" (italics in the original. Scharmer, 2007, p. 7). This corresponds to his overall observation that the quality of the field of awareness in a group or organization impacts the quality of their conversations and the outcomes they produce in result. If we look at this interior condition more closely, it is mostly about two, partly interrelated things: first, the degree and quality of presence the facilitator is displaying (an inner *state*), and second, their personal cognitive development (their access to structural *stages* of complexity). This section will look at the first aspect, the last section looks at the second one.

While the quality of presence of a facilitator can partly be connected to the degree of experience they have (in the sense that less experience might lead to a lower level of calmness and relaxation about the task of facilitation and vice versa), it is above all an expression of the facilitator's overall ability to direct, focus and flexibly shift their conscious attention both inside and outside, centering and decentering it as necessary. LiFT coordinator Jonathan Reams often uses the metaphor of "reading the room" for describing this activity of centering, presencing and of sensing into the "needs of the now" of a given group:

> *I think there are multiple levels or layers of this. In one sense, it is as simple as paying attention to body language, faces, tone of voices etc. Of course that requires free attention that is not wrapped up in cognitive task demands or emotional or ego hooks that divert attention inward.*
>
> *Another form of this is listening to the content of what people in the room are saying as an indication of the structure of their thinking, giving clues, as well to what might be implicit for them that is encountering different or diverse tacitness in other perspectives, for example in the design of process and its facilitation. Listening for what is between the lines, or assumptions in a perspective that can give you relevant information about what's going on in a room.*[75]

Another layer that Reams mentions is connected more to the subtle dimension of it. In his piece about the "heart and soul of leadership"[76], Reams identifies "consciousness as the relationship between soul and embodiment, embodiment referring to mind, emotions and physical body" (Reams, 2010, 11). He refers to findings by the Institute of HeartMath, according to which

> *"'the heart generates by far the most powerful and most extensive rhythmic electromagnetic field produced in the body' (McCraty et al., 2009, p. 55). McCraty et al's research shows that the heart has sixty times greater electrical voltage amplitude and 5000 times stronger magnetic field than those produced by the brain. This electromagnetic field 'can be measured several feet away from the body with sensitive magnetometers', thus providing 'a plausible mechanism for how we can 'feel' or sense another person's presence and even their emotional state, independent of body language and other signals' (p. 55). From this it appears that our heart states will not only have a significant impact on the body*

and brain, but also generate a field that can be detected by other people." (Reams, 2012, 106-7)

This means that skilled facilitators are capable to shift their focus from the mind to the heart and thus, to sense the electromagnetic fields produced in a given group on the heart level by using the modes of knowing and sensing of their "heart brain". So, Reams adds, "being able to tune into that and 'sense' the energy that people in a room are embodying would be a foundational layer of reading the room" (Reams, see Fn. 13). What's more, on this basis, skilled facilitators can also actively create specific fields of awareness "through their *quality of presence*" (Reams & Caspari, 2012). The challenge in a U process being to tap into the realm of emptiness and not-knowing at the bottom of the U in order to open up towards future possibilities, this means that „sensing the future is possible" (Reams, 2012, 107). And the facilitator's quality of presence helps others to connect and sense into these deeper fields of possibilities as well.

By directing our focus in this skillful way and by "cultivating access to pre- sensing what wants to emerge from the future, (...) we give life to what we chose to give attention to" (Reams, 2012, 107). This implies that we have a considerable power of (co-) creation if we learn how to focus conscious awareness and presence. The skilled facilitator thereby creates the soil for future possibilities to take root, a process and quality that "can be sensed energetically by those around us" (Reams, 2010, 16) and by which the latter are invited and supported to join and thereby amplify that field. Admittedly, "with this (also) comes the responsibility to be conscious of how we choose to direct our attention" (Reams, 2012, 107). So at this point, skill can complement structure and even outperform it.

In practical terms, the more a facilitator has developed this personal skill and quality of presence, the deeper and more successful they will be in "tuning in" to the field of awareness that is generated by and among the participants – and thus to respond to the latter in a way that best helps them to connect to and co-create from their future possibilities.

Understandably, this activity and "skill" of the heart goes far beyond technical knowledge. It can nevertheless be developed and cultivated through practice. In order to learn similar awareness skills one needs to engage in some kind of continuous practice of centering and/or meditation over a longer period of time, independent of the (more technical) Collaboratory work.

Teaming up for facilitation

"When it comes to changing the world, less is not more. One person alone cannot understand the changing landscape in all its complexity or achieve the leverage necessary to effect change. Neither can a small group." Burck et al. (2014, 52)

Since the skills described above are both important and rather rare in individuals, it is generally a good idea to co-facilitate Collaboratories as a team. In that case, the skills of several team members can add up and complement each other. Our experience is that – especially if Collaboratories last one day or more – it is recommendable to split up the facilitation role and spread it between several shoulders. The ideal constellation we found was two teams of two who can shift turns and mutually support each other. This is helpful especially in view of the challenge of generating the appropriate field of awareness to support the kind of conversation that is desired in a specific phase. If more people consciously work together to co-create a specific field quality, the latter tends to become stronger and clearer. At the same time, this releases the burden of the lead facilitator(s) who can thus focus more on their immediate interventions.

Working in well-aligned teams is therefore of great value also in view of creating momentum for the complex collaborative process as a whole which (including the preparation phase) likely stretches over several months. And with the latter, some of the work of creating an adequate field and soil can in fact be shifted to a space before the actual event. Moreover, a team that works together on building an appropriate level of presence, decentering and alignment in itself has a better capacity to capture the field of stakeholder perspectives right, which is important to have in the process, and thus, to prepare the space and ground with all involved parties in an optimal way.

The facilitator's inner, personal development

"If our interior condition impacts the success of our interventions, then the view we act from is the highest leverage point we have."
(Reams, 2007, 257)

The second most important aspect regarding the inner condition as a personal skill of the facilitator(s) and their impact on the process as a whole is their personal consciousness development in various dimensions, including their action logics and the vertical complexity of their reasoning structures. Multiple models describe and explain levels of personal development in terms of an increasing complexity and differentiation with which individuals perceive and are able to act upon their outer reality as they mature (Cook-Greuter, 1999; Graves, 1974; Kegan, 1982 and 1994; Loevinger, 1976; Torbert & Associates, 2004; Wilber, 2000). This is of particular importance in leadership when it comes to working with diverse groups on complex challenges in view of developing mutually beneficial solutions. As a leader's maturity increases, they will take a broader, more and more systemic (even meta-systematic) perspective. This enables them to perceive and respond to higher levels of dynamic complexity in both outer and inner systems, i.e. their own and their participants' states of consciousness and structures of thinking, from an appropriate inner level and place.

Describing the field of structural adult development in a more exhaustive way goes far beyond the limits of this article and is done in some more detail in Fein, Deeg & Reams (2016) and in LiFT's Foundations and Resources book (Fein, 2018a). At this point, I will limit myself to mentioning how some of the many skills that usually go along with higher levels of consciousness development are important in different phases of preparing and designing a Collaboratory. As consciousness develops, individuals increase their level of perspective awareness both inside and outside of themselves.

This includes sub-skills such as perspective taking, perspective seeking and perspective coordination, all of which are helpful especially during the preparation phase of a Collaboratory where stakeholder perspectives need to be actively included and aligned. The same is true for the sub-skill of context awareness and collaborative capacity. Finally, the latter is closely related to the person's degree and capacity of self-transcendence (see above).

As development increases, individuals will have a more decentered perspective and are more likely to work from a place of transcending their own views and perceptions. This is important not only for cooperating with and aligning the team of stakeholders during the preparation phase, but also for the facilitator not having their own stake in the process or its outcome. As indicated earlier, the latter is important for facilitators to be able to serve the process as a whole. Note that subtle qualities like self-transcendence cannot necessarily be guaranteed by a simple formal separation of roles. Even if there is a separation between the hosting and the facilitation roles, as it was almost always the case in the LiFT project, the facilitator can still have a "stake" in the process in the sense that he or she is aiming or hoping for a certain kind or quality of outcome (for example as a confirmation of their "success" or professionalism). They could also have some kind of attachment to a general aim of somehow "changing the world for the better" through the process they are facilitating. Even though similar hopes are understandable, they can also be a pitfall and, as Reams holds, "impair the interior condition of the intervener and lessen the effectiveness of any interventions" (Reams, 2007, 258).

While there is not yet sufficient empirical research and evidence to back up this relationship, our comparative experience from LiFT clearly supports the assumption that non-attachment to the outcome of the process is a useful skill and prerequisite for successful Collaboratory facilitation. As the degree of self-transcendence and non-attachment (which ultimately are two sides of the same coin) are both related to the level of vertical complexity of a person's development of cognition, we can say that this "meta-level skill" to some extent facilitates many of the other (including the more practical) dimensions of Collaboratory success.

Summary, discussion and concluding remarks

This paper has presented examples from LiFT's methodological experience with the Collaboratory format and explored some of the insights gained in the course of this journey, which help to differentiate and deepen our understanding of Theory U in action.

First of all, practitioners of Theory U and users of the Collaboratory need to acknowledge that not every context and not every problem lends itself to a similar process. A number of criteria have to be met in order for a U process-based Collaboratory to be a suitable method. Once that decision has been taken, the main factors that contribute to Collaboratory success are the quality of depth of the conversation and the quality of impact of its outcomes. To bring both about is a delicate, sensitive and complex challenge demanding a certain combination of knowledge, experience and skill on the part of the organizers and facilitators.

In our experience, the key to Collaboratory success is the right interplay or "dance" between a powerful structure and its skillful facilitation. While the whole process is set up to provide an optimal space and structure for transformative deliberation and collaboration to happen, the way of creating and constantly re-creating this space as interactive dynamics unfold is as much an art than a method or applied science. Therefore, our Collaboratory "cook-book" is about arranging helpful context conditions and working on one's own skills and inner attitudes as much as it is about hands-on, single-step instructions.

To start with, the process of preparing, designing and structuring the Collaboratory already provides numerous possibilities for framing and setting up the process on good rails. This begins with the very preparation phase where making a good choice of and creating a good alignment between the core stakeholders builds up the foundations for a productive process. As outlined earlier, the process of structuring itself requires certain skills and sensitivities in the design and preparation team.

The main part of the structuring work then concerns the design of the changing set-ups and tools to be used in different phases of the process itself. If designed carefully, the structure of the Collaboratory can in fact do a lot of the work of taking participants on a journey through the U – by supporting the shifting of perspectives, modes of communication and perception from more factual towards deeper, more personal and ultimately self-transcending fields of awareness in the first part, and by re-shifting them back up towards more active, co-creative modes in the second. Yet, how much of the work is done by the structure is hard to specify in a general way.

For once the process is running, facilitation skills determine the degree of depth that can be achieved with a given structure in a given group and a given situation. So while being the foundation for a good Collaboratory process, a good structure and design might not be sufficient in themselves. While they can certainly open the doors for different kinds of experiences by creating suitable spaces that go beyond most participants' everyday communication habits, it needs deliberate and constant focus on the energetic dimension of the group consciousness, i.e. on the qualities described by Theory U, to allow the Collaboratory's full potential to unfold. The latter is very much connected to the skill of "reading the room" as LiFT coordinator Jonathan Reams has called it, meaning the facilitator(s) capacity to put themselves into an inner state of intense presence that allows to sense and perceive the subtle flows of awareness, focus and energy as they occur in every moment in a group of people interacting with each other and with the facilitator(s). So while a good design and structure can scaffold a process, the impact and momentum which this structure can unfold depends on or is at least "facilitated by the level of cognition and or state experience and presence of a facilitator" (Reams, 2010). Therefore, both structure and skill must be seen as complementary in contributing to successful collaborative processes, i.e. processes that lead to innovative solutions based on a conscious activity of pre-sencing or sensing into the future.

At this point, we cannot yet make more detailed claims about the exact qualities and capacities that are necessary in the domain of skills. Nor can we specify what exact level of higher order cognitive capacities is necessary for hosting and conducting a collaborative process successfully as a holding space, which invites a certain kind of state experiences. Exploring this interdependence more thoroughly will start to happen during future LiFT facilitator trainings. For the time being, therefore, we suggest the more general wisdom that successful collaborative processes are best conducted as a well-reflected collaborative (team) effort, joining the forces and skills of the core team members. Then processes such as the Collaboratory can at the same time be powerful embodiments of the U process and go beyond Theory U itself.

References

Burck, B., Rüger, S., Frick, P., Williamson, A., Serikoff, G. (2014). Facilitating a collaborative space. In Muff (2014).

Cook-Greuter, S. (1999). *Postautonomous ego development: A study of its nature and measurement*. Boston, MA: Integral Publishers.

Fein, E. (2018a). *Foundations and Resources of Integral Leadership*. Online Resource.

Fein, E. (2018b). *LiFT Methods Book: Designing and facilitating Collaboratories*. Online Resource.

Fein, E. (2018c). LiFT Collaboratory in Rastatt, 2016, In I. Kunze & E. Fein, *LiFT Case Book. Hosting Collaboratories: Insights and learnings from different cases*, pp. 44-60. Online Resource.

Fein, E., Molz, M. (2018). Designing and facilitating a Collaboratory – LiFT Course Curriculum. Online Resource.

Fein, E., Deeg, J., & Reams, J. (2016). From Ego to Eco – Theoretical challenges and practical implications of a 'next generation' approach to Responsible Leadership as a collaborative endeavor. In G. Aras & C. Ingley, +. Farnham, UK: Ashgate, 199-224. Graves, C. (1974, April). Human nature prepares for a momentous leap. *Futurist*, 8 (2), 72-87.

Kegan, R. (1994). *In over our heads. The mental demands of modern life*. Cambridge, MA: Harvard University Press.

Kegan, R. (1982). *The evolving self. Problem and process in human development*. Cambridge, MA: Harvard University Press.

Kunze, I., Fein, E. (eds.) (2018). *LiFT Case Book. Hosting Collaboratories: Insights and learnings from different cases*. Online Resource.

Loevinger, J. (1976). *Ego development: Concepts and theories*. San Francisco: Jossey-Bass.

McCraty, R., Atkinson, M., Tomasino, B. & Bradley, R. (2009). The coherent heart: Heart-brain interactions, psychophysiological coherence, and the emergence of system wideorder. *Integral Review*, 5 (2), 4-107.

Muff, K. (2018). *Five superpowers for co-creators. How change makers and business can achieve the Sustainable Development Goals (experiences from the field)*. Abingdon, UK: Routledge and Online Resource.

Muff, K. (2014) (ed.). *The Collaboratory. A co-creative stakeholder engagement process for solving complex problems*. Sheffield: Greenleaf.

Muff, K. (2014a). Defining the collaboratory. In Muff (ed.), *The Collaboratory. A co-creative stakeholder engagement process for solving complex problems* (p. 11-15). Sheffield: Greenleaf.

Muff, K. (2014b). Designing a collaboratory: a narrative roadmap. In Muff (ed.), *The Collaboratory. A co-creative stakeholder engagement process for solving complex problems* (p. 229-245). Sheffield: Greenleaf.

Muff, K. (2013). TED talk, online: https://www.youtube.com/watch?v=jvipxPqS_38.

Muff, K., Dyllick, T. (2014). Students leading collaboratories: University of St. Gallen. In Muff (ed.), *The Collaboratory. A co-creative stakeholder engagement process for solving complex problems* (p. 134-149). Sheffield: Greenleaf.

Reams, J. (2012). Integral Leadership. Opening Space by Leading through the Heart. In Pearson (ed.), *The Transforming Leader. New Approaches to Leadership for the Twenty-First Century* (p.102-109). San Francisco: Berrett-Koehler.

Reams, J. (2010). *The Heart and Soul of Leadership: A Transpersonally Oriented Examination of How Quality of Presence Impacts Leadership.* Paper presented at the Integral Theory Conference (unpublished).

Reams, J. (2007). Illuminating the blind spot: An overview and response to Theory U. *Integral Review* (5), 240-259.

Reams, J., & Caspari, A. (2012). Integral leadership: generating space for emergence through their quality of presence through quality of presence. In *Wirtschaftspsychologie*, n°3, 34-45.

Roy, B. (2006). A Process Model of Integral Theory. *Integral Review*, n°3, 118-167.

Scharmer, O. (2014). Stepping into the emerging future: principles of Theory U. In Muff (ed.), *The Collaboratory. A co-creative stakeholder engagement process for solving complex problems* (p. 101-101). Sheffield: Greenleaf.

Scharmer, O. (2007). *Theory U: leading from the emerging future*. San Francisco: Berrett-Koehler

Scharmer, O., & Kaeufer, K. (2013). *Theory U: Leading from the Future as it Emerges. From Ego-System to Eco-System Economies. Applying Theory U to Transforming Business, Society and Self*. San Francisco: Berrett-Koehler.

Torbert, W. & Associates. (2004). *Action inquiry. The secret of timely and transforming action*. San Francisco: Berrett-Koehler.

Weinmann, K. (2018). Tips: hosting and facilitation – is there a difference? Blogpost, January 18, 2018, online at: http://www.thecircle-way.net/articles/2017/12/31/tips-hosting and-facilitation-is-there-a-difference.

Wilber, K. (2000). *Integral psychology. Consciousness, spirit, psychology, therapy*. Boston: Shambhala Publications Inc.

Wulf, W. (1989, March). The national collaboratory. In *Towards a national collaboratory*. Unpublished report of a National Science Foundation invitational workshop, Rockefeller University, New York.

CHAPTER 13

Social Presencing Theater: Practical Application in Organizations

Michelle N. Moore

Social Presencing Theater: Practical Applications in Organizations

Social presencing theater (SPT) is a sensing and embodiment practice whereby members of a group embody (i.e. give a concrete form to; represent or exemplify within the physical human body) something they are trying to create, change or innovate. A group does this by allowing shapes or gestures to arise in their bodies that represent or model a system or challenge they are currently in (Scharmer, Kaeufer, 2013). "SPT is a method that blends mindfulness, social science theater, and constellation work. The focus of SPT is on making visible the deep structures of the social field - and how they can evolve." (Scharmer, 2018, p. 92)

Each of the three terms in the name are crucial to the practice and are delineated as follows: Social means that the practice is done as a group activity. Participants allow movement to arise in the body, together, to form social sculptures. Presencing is a hybrid of presence, the state of being in the present moment, and sensing, feeling the future possibility (Scharmer, Kaeufer, 2013). Theater in this context means making something of importance in a system visible, where it was not seen before. It does not in any way refer to acting, performance nor improvisation because practitioners allow the body's wisdom to form the shape rather than the mind telling the body what to do.

SPT may also be referred to as a body-based, experiential learning toolkit, consisting of eight exercises, which contributes to organizational learning. "It is a method for helping organizations and larger social systems get in touch with the knowledge they already have about the deep interpersonal structures that inhibit real changes from happening," stated Otto Scharmer in Strategy & Business magazine (Kleiner 2017).

Social Presencing Theater was developed at the Presencing Institute, Sloan School of Management, Massachusetts Institute of Technology. It was co-created by Arawana Hayashi and Otto Scharmer. SPT is a type of social technology which is part of Theory U, "a framework for learning, leading, innovating and profound systemic renewal". (Scharmer, Kaeufer, 2013, p.18)

The building blocks of SPT include embodiment (defined above), an awareness of what are called the "three bodies," and mindfulness. The three bodies are the Earth body (the planet we stand on), our own physical body, and the visible social body (the group, team, organization, system). There is also an invisible social field. Scharmer writes, "I define social field as the quality of relationships that give rise to patterns of thinking, conversing, and organizing, which in turn produce practical results." (Scharmer, 2018, p. 14) Further, an awareness of the body as a 360-degree sensor combined with an awareness of the surrounding space is key.

Mindfulness, "the awareness that arises by paying attention on purpose, in the present moment, and non-judgmentally" (Kabat-Zinn, 2013, p. xxxv), was made famous by Jon Kabat-Zinn for stress and pain management. Mindfulness is evolving in the organizational realm as well. As detailed in David Gelles' 2015 book, *Mindful Work: How Meditation is Changing Business from the*

Inside Out, mindfulness is now used as a practice in companies for improved focus, compassion, social responsibility and leadership.

Mindfulness practice involves getting out of the head and into the body by anchoring attention in the breath or sensations in the physical body. This may also be referred to as mindfulness of body. It is an individual practice though people often practice together. In contrast, SPT is a collective practice. Teams practice inquiry into the wisdom of the social body (i.e. the group, team, organization or system). As Otto and Arawana describe in their instructional videos (Hayashi, Presencing Institute, 2018), "SPT is a tool to notice, recognize, feel, see the true potential goodness in the situation or challenge in a team, organization, or system. SPT functions on a deeper level of awareness. SPT does for the collective what mindfulness does for an individual." (Hayashi, 2017)

Why Social Presencing Theater?

Too much thinking, talking, and messaging is the norm. In the Western world, linear, analytical thinking dominates. Bill George, Harvard Senior Fellow, emphasized this during an interview in the documentary film Innsaei, The Power of Intuition,

"In the last 20-25 years of my life we have seen the dominance of rational thought. It's dominated a lot of our academic institutions, the media, and its taken away from the capacity to advance intuitive skills. Now for the first time we are starting to realize that problems are not getting any better. We have to step back and take a whole new approach to these problems. One of the challenges we have recently had in business is by going to the fully rational side and by focusing everything on near term measurement, analytical tools, we have ground out or expunged creativity from our companies and 100 billions dollars are being wasted" (George, 2016).

SPT offers access to creativity via primary knowing as defined by cognitive psychologist Eleanor Rosch who introduced the articulation of two types of knowledge or knowing, one analytic, the other primary.

"The problem is that most of us have spent our lives immersed in analytic knowing, with its dualistic separation of subject and object. There's nothing wrong with analytic knowing. It's useful and appropriate for many activities.....but if it's our only way of knowing, we'll tend to apply it in all situations." (Senge, 2004, p. 99) "Primary knowing characterizes a sensing and presencing type of cognition in which one is said to know by means of inter-connected wholes (rather than isolated contingent parts) and timeless, direct presentation (rather than through stored re-pre-sentations). Such knowing is open rather than determinate." (Scharmer, 2009, p.167) Through SPT, organizations are enabled to tap into the collective wisdom of their teams. Wisdom here refers to "primary knowing" discussed above.

Further, SPT offers an approach opposite to the typical sur-face level approach to change. Often, a problem is recognized in the mind and a voice of judgement, fear or cynicism arises, criti-cizing another team member or dismissing the issue as impossi-ble. The highest potential in a situation is not able to reveal itself in this case. SPT goes below the surface to unearth highest poten-tial. SPT results in new information used to guide teams in deci-sions and actions (Hayashi, 2017).

SPT Principles

Based on experiences and training in SPT, combined with the wider body of Theory U practices, below are some of the main principles applied during SPT exercises.

First, a leader leader must be aware of the vulnerability inher-ent in the SPT practice. The leader creates and holds a safe space for the team to engage through the body. No one embodies their own role during group social sculptures. This removes existing organizational hierarchy during the practice. Participants are encouraged to keep an open mind, open heart and open will during all exercises. At the same time, participants welcome uncertainty and curiosity and bring intention and attention to the practice. Thus, they can let go of reaction while welcoming an attending to source, i.e. sensing the self and others. The result is that more time is spent on letting the future emerge than downloading past patterns.

Theory U refers to three voices which can inhibit participants' ability to see the highest potential of the challenge they are working with. Therefore, participants suspend the Voice of Judgement (VoJ), Voice of Cynicism (VoC) and the Voice of Fear (VoF).

Participants bring mindful attention to the three bodies, maintaining a focus on physical sensation in the body to enable agenda-less, unplanned movement to arise from the body, i.e. a "true move". A "true move" emerges from the thinking body rather than from the thinking mind.

Finally, the social sculptures include not only system stakeholder roles such as government, customer, employee, etc. but also the Earth, highest potential and most vulnerable stakeholder. These three stakeholders represent Scharmer's three divides which are ecological, social and spiritual, and refer to the disconnect between self and nature, the disconnect between self and other and the disconnect between self and self (Scharmer, 2018, p. 4-5). Including such a holistic set of stakeholders helps organizations be inclusive and empathic while allowing the highest potential of the challenge they are working with to emerge.

SPT Exercises

The following eight exercises[77] comprise the main SPT toolkit as of May 2018. Variations of these exercises exist and a core SPT team at the Presencing Institute is prototyping new exercises and tools. Given the COVID pandemic, SPT has been adapted for the virtual environment as well.

While each exercise is useful for gaining new insights, they do not all serve the same purpose. The first four exercises are primarily preparatory, and generally practiced without specific organizational input. These include 20 Minute Dance, Duet, Village and Field Dance.

The last four are applied, as they are framed with individual or organizational context and can be used to guide decisions and actions. Applied exercises include Stuck, 4D Mapping, Case Clinic and Seed Dance. The four preparatory exercises enable the practice of more complex exercises, emphasize major SPT principles, and allow a group to arrive in their bodies. Mindfulness meditation is often used at the beginning of an SPT session. This practice is not further elaborated on in this chapter. The four applied exercises are presented in the second half of this chapter through real examples.

SPT exercises are practiced in rooms with floors clean enough to lie down on and large enough to accommodate all participants lying down. Any chairs in the room should have no wheels and remain at the outside edge of the space. A participant may use a chair if there is discomfort in sitting on the floor or lying down. Participants wear comfortable clothes enabling ease of movement. Each person has a journal.

Preparatory SPT Exercises

The four preparatory exercises are described below. An experienced SPT facilitator can guide groups through these exercises. Experienced groups can also facilitate themselves.

20 Minute Dance. This is a silent mindful movement and sensing exercise, practiced together, for ten, fifteen or twenty minutes. Participants pay attention to physical sensations in the body and avoid language and goals. Eyes can be closed or open, gaze down. Participants alternate between stillness and movement in three positions - lying down, sitting, and finally standing. Time is divided about equally between the three positions. Participants attend to sensations in the body, allowing thoughts of past or future to float by without judgement. (Hayashi, Presencing Institute, 2018)

Duet. The Duet is a silent mindful movement and sensing exercise, practiced in pairs, for five to seven minutes. Participants feel and sense the social field and trust the process of allowing something to emerge. Duet teaches empathic listening with the whole body, whereby participants engage in a co-created conversation in a new way, without words or goals. Participants cultivate authentic openness through their own vulnerability of "not knowing" what movement is coming next.

In the Duet, pairs alternate between still gestures and movement, using a "MA" (time-space interval between gestures) to emphasize the shared space. After both the 20 minute dance and the Duet, participants reflect by journaling in silence and/or speaking in pairs using the first person voice to complete the following verbal statements 1) "I noticed about myself......" 2) "I learned about myself........." 3) "I saw patterns of......" 4) I noticed about the MA that...." 5) "The essence of the duet is...." (Hayashi, Presencing Institute, 2018)

Village. Village is a silent mindful movement and sensing exercise, practiced in groups of 5 people or more, (ideal with larger groups of 15, 20, 30+ people), for 10-20 minutes. Participants practice using the body as a 360° sensor to expand awareness to the social body. They begin to notice the individual body as an integral part of the collective and develop an ability to redirect attention outwards, with the wellbeing of others in mind. Participants also notice inclusion, exclusion and relationships with others. They co-create a village. They cultivate curiosity and a sense of comfort with uncertainty. They notice and release three voices of fear, judgement and cynicism.

During Village, participants pay attention to three things: 1) the level of the body, 2) the spatial proximity of their own body to other bodies and 3) direction faced. They hold their attention on the whole space, using peripheral vision. (Hayashi, Presencing Institute 2018).

Field Dance. The Field Dance is a silent mindful movement and sensing exercise involving a presenter and an audience, practiced in groups of about fifteen people. Timing is one hour and fifteen minutes.

Participants explore what it means to attend to and be present with a social field, i.e. the audience, allowing the expression of the field to become visible and motivate the presenter to make a "true move". Participants practice letting go of performance, separateness from the audience. They focus on paying attention to the whole.

Participants sit in a semi-circle facing a stage area. Everyone assumes the role of audience and presenter during the exercise.

Each person, one by one, walks in front of the audience as a presenter and faces the audience upon reaching the center, then turns away and walks to the other side of the stage. (Hayashi, Presencing Institute, 2018)

Applied SPT Exercises

The following four exercises are useful for practical application in an organizational context for insight and innovation. The case examples provided in this chapter demonstrate this. For the group exercises described below, a facilitator guides the group through the exercises and facilitates the spoken reflections.

Stuck. Stuck is a silent mindful embodiment and sensing exercise, practiced individually and in groups, which takes participants from a current reality to an emerging future in the physical individual or social body. The entire Theory U process is experienced. Length of time varies greatly. Stuck is the core SPT exercise. 4D Mapping, Case Clinic and Seed Dance are variations of Stuck.

A Stuck is something a group or individual is trying to create, change or innovate which is not moving forward. Stuck is not a problem and "you are not your stuck". Stuck is not sustainable in any system. It will eventually emerge to a future state. It is part of the creative process and can be a gold mine of information. Every individual and every group has many stucks.

The key practice in Stuck is that participants suspend habitual problem-solving. Instead, they sense deeply into current reality using the body's intelligence. They focus on physical, felt sensations rather than emotions or analysis.

There are two ways to practice Stuck, applying an individual or personal stuck or engaging group members amplify and inform the individual Stuck by forming a group Stuck.

Individual Stuck. In the Individual Stuck, groups of 3-5 people form seated circles. Each participant writes down a Stuck from their own work or career. Participants reflect on the current state felt sense of the Stuck in their body. The stuck feeling comes into the body as a physical shape or gesture, forming sculpture 1, the current state (SC1). One by one, each person in the group makes their Stuck shape concrete and visible in the space of the group.

After each group member has shown their SC1 shape to the group, each person shares an experience about another person's Stuck with the group, without analysis.

Next, each person repeats their SC1, without the spoken reflection afterwards. Then they exaggerate the shape or lean into it. After pausing, the participant waits for their body to decide when and how the shape moves. The shape keeps moving until it decides to stop, arriving in sculpture 2, the emerging future state of the Stuck (SC2). There are three parts to every Stuck, i.e. SC1, the transition from SC1 to SC2 and SC2. After everyone has completed their SC2, the spoken reflection from above is repeated. The three experiences of SC1, the transition, and/or SC2 are shared.

Group Stuck. Now the group practices in the social body. Six to eight people form seated circles and sit for two minutes to sense the social body of the group. There are two options for a Group Stuck. In option A, one person volunteers to embody their individual SC1 again. Option B applies if the group is a real team, working together on common goals. The group writes down a shared Group Stuck on a flip chart and hangs it on the wall nearby. One person volunteers to embody their felt sense of the shared Group Stuck.

Next, applicable to A or B above, the volunteer instructs half of the other group members to be the sticking forces of their Stuck, to emphasize, exaggerate that Stuck. The social body in SC1 exaggerates the Group Stuck, together, allowing the social body to decide when the shape moves. When the shape stops moving, the group sculpture has arrived in SC2. This is the emerging future state of the Stuck. (Hayashi, Presencing Institute, 2018)

4D Mapping. This a mindful group embodiment and sensing exercise, using the social body to "map" or "make visible" the current reality and highest aspiration (potential future state) of a social system. Examples include school system, health care system, government, cell phone market, fashion industry, etc. Group size is ideally 16 or more. Time is 1-2 hours. 4D refers to the three dimensions of the human body plus the emerging future as the fourth dimension.

Participants can quickly generate new insights about the system. They may see something significant which was not visible in the system before, including leadership blind spots. These insights inform decisions and actions. Participants see their own creative process and practice releasing old patterns, mind-sets or frames of reference. Practitioners suspend the problem-solving habit to gain access to primary knowing and tap into collective wisdom. Teams gain the benefits of broader perspectives and the ability to build trust in the social body's knowing.

In advance of the exercise, a team member describes the situation to the SPT facilitator, including the eight to ten stakeholder roles in the 4D Map. The roles of Earth, Highest Potential (of the system) and representation from the most vulnerable, marginalized group in the system (for example, children) are always included.

Before the group begins the exercise, the team member describes the situation. Other team members volunteer to embody a stakeholder role. The remaining participants are mindful observers (space-holders). Observers sit in a circle, leaving enough space for the stakeholders to move around easily inside the circle.

The group participates in the entire Theory U process during this exercise, beginning with co-initiation, co-sensing, co-presencing and then crystallizing.

As a reflection, players and observers engage in generative dialogue around the seen and feltexperience of the movements in SC1, the Transition, SC2. They share their experiences related to sense of space, time, self and other. Participants answer the questions, "What top 3 features of the map changed?", "What next steps will you take as a result of this experience?" "What ideas for prototypes emerged?" (Hayashi, Presencing Institute, 2018)

Case Clinic. This is a mindful group embodiment and sensing exercise, using the social body to generate insight on a leadership challenge or a question. Peers or team members are coaches to assist a case giver in a non-hierarchical manner. Three to six people can participate. Time is typically 1-1.5 hours. In this exercise, participants develop new approaches in response to the leadership challenge or question, accessing the wisdom of the group to help respond to an immediate challenge.

(Hayashi, Presencing Institute, 2018)

Seed Dance. This is a mindful group embodiment and sensing exercise, using the social body to bring a person's future vision into practice through creative expression, resulting in concrete next steps. The group size is four to five people. Timing is one and a half to three hours.

Often ideas of what we want to create in the world are muddled by hidden agendas, notions of success, etc., disabling our ability to answer to the question, "What is my real work?" Seed Dance enables a practical answer.

(Hayashi, Presencing Institute, 2018)

Cases

The following ten cases capture a wide range of possibilities for application of SPT in organizations working on real challenges:

1. Optimizing Grants Management, Nathan Cummings Foundation, New York;
2. Improving Board Engagement, Peel Art Gallery, Museum & Archives, Ontario, Canada;
3. Visioning for High Potential Education, Teach for Armenia, Yerevan, Armenia;
4. Visioning Total Compensation & Impact, GrantBook Inc., Toronto, Canada;
5. Developing Potential for Refugees, Immigrants & Citizens, Umbria Region, Italy;
6. Enabling Better Dialogue on Nuclear Power in Japan, Tokyo, Japan;
7. Strategic Technology Team Prototyping, Lima, Peru;
8. Team Optimization for AIDS Advocacy, North America, Africa, Asia;
9. Exploring Democracy in Tremp, Catalonia, Spain;
10. Enabling the Future of the Granada Project, Granada, Spain.

Optimizing Grants Management, Nathan Cummings Foundation, New York

Case background. The Nathan Cummings Foundation (NCF) is a family foundation, rooted in the Jewish tradition, working to create a more just, vibrant, sustainable and democratic society. They are pursuing justice for people and the planet and supporting social movements and catalytic solutions to climate change and inequality. NCF encourages visionary thinking and bold action.

In October 2017, the foundation was about to embark on a new Grants Management System (GMS) selection and implementation. To facilitate team alignment on the future state of grants management, part of the ten-member project team spent a half-day applying embodiment practices to inform their project from a different perspective.

The challenge. A highly motivated GMS project team, keen to optimize technology, processes, and their ability to collaborate, was nevertheless feeling frustrated. They were overwhelmed from lack of time, and stressed. A lot of process change was implemented in a relatively short period of time. New staff joined during the previous year. Internal communication and coordination was a challenge. There was a desire to include a broader team to shape the future-state.

The social sculptures. During a half-day workshop, participants warmed-up with meditation, 20-Minute Dance and practiced Individual Stuck, Group Stuck, and 4D Mapping. NCF defined their Group Stuck in advance of the workshop as follows. "NCF has been trying to change and innovate the grants management process for several years...but has been unable, collectively, to move toward a future state vision for grants management."

The challenge for the 4D Map was defined as, "NCF's work enables grantees to achieve incremental, point in time impact... but long term impact goals, i.e. long term systems change, is not enabled." The stakeholders in the 4D Map included: NCF leadership team and board, similar foundations, grantees, corporate sector, NCF grants/programs department, government.

Main insights. The NCF participants shared feedback after practicing SPT for the first time via a post-workshop survey. Some of the main insights are summarized below.

71.4% responded 4 or 5 (out of 5) that: "The quality of my attention was higher than usual. I was fully present with the group and in the moment." "My intention for the day was set and top of mind for most of the session." "When body and mind are synchronized, we have access to additional information."

Participants noted how they felt at the end of the session: "Energized and motivated" (71.4%), "More connected to the group" (71.4%), "Tired or neutral" (28.6%).

Some participants noted what surprised them during the workshop: "How much movement spoke to a different part of my experience," "the level of mutual respect and equality in the room," "it brought out some unexpected tensions," "the emotional response I had to others' movements," "the empathy I experienced during the session," "the lack of connection I felt between our overall mission, work and purpose of the activities."

Some participants had "aha" moments during or after the session: "There was an increased sense of empathy and shared responsibility with the team." "It was obvious how incredibly stressed out everyone was." "We need more time for play." "Physical expression can lead to greater understanding."

The Individual Stuck left most participants unsure about new realizations or how to overcome their Stuck. The Group Stuck in contrast, resulted in 100% of participants realizing something about the group, their role or themselves they did not know before.

New actions. Participants expressed the following changes in behaviour since the session: Paying attention to others differently (28.6%), noticing how you are in your body (14.3%), paying attention to the feeling of the body on the ground (28.6%), paying attention to the body as a 360° sensing organ (0%), no change in behaviour (28.6%). 85.7% participants recommended SPT as a useful tool and/or would want to practice SPT again.

Learnings. It was key to have the CEO of the foundation in the room. However, other leadership team members did not participate. In future, I would encourage a more equal mix of leadership and staff.

This is a vulnerable practice. Thus, more attention could be drawn to this fact, combined with highlighting that the benefits of being vulnerable include accessing creativity and innovation, reducing loneliness, improving accountability and provoking compassion.

Janet Disla, Senior Grants Manager, Nathancummings.org, provided organizational input. Michelle N. Moore, Advanced SPT Practitioner, Managing Director, Grantbook Inc., facilitated the session.

Improving Board Engagement, Peel Art Gallery, Museum & Archives, Ontario, Canada

Case background. Peel Art Gallery, Museum and Archives (PAMA) is a government organization serving the Peel Region with exhibitions, programs, events and school resources. To facilitate PAMA staff and board alignment, six board members and nine staff spent a half-day practicing embodiment exercises. The main goals of the session were to form stronger connections between board and staff and to better understand how the Board can support PAMA's objectives.

The challenge. The staff and board did not know each other very well. There was no history of strong collaboration to co-create impact for the region. Objectives had typically been set separately without a strong, common vision.

The social sculptures. During a half-day workshop, participants warmed-up with meditation and practiced Village, Individual & Group Stuck, and 4D Mapping. PAMA defined their Group Stuck in advance of the workshop as, "PAMA staff and board have been trying to create greater community involvement through special projects...... which do not seem to produce significant impact". The challenge for the 4D Map was, "Membership has stayed constant at less than three hundred over the past ten years, regardless of exhibitions, programs, or the facility's expansion." Stakeholder roles included: PAMA member (family), PAMA member (individual), single adult citizen, youth citizen, Peel teacher, Peel corporation, board, staff, reciprocal membership, organization, Peel regional government (senior leadership, elected municipal official).

Main insights. The PAMA participants shared feedback after practicing SPT for the first time via a post-workshop survey. Some of the main insights are summarized below.

85.7% responded 4 or 5 (out of 5) that, "The quality of my attention was higher than usual." "I was fully present with the group and in the moment." "My intention for the day was set and top of mind for most of the session."

90% agreed, "When body and mind are synchronized, we have access to additional information."

At the end of the session participants felt energized, motivated or more connected to the group (85.7%), tired or neutral (28.6%).

Some participants noted what surprised them during the workshop: "My body tuned in and responded." "Senses and emotions surfaced." "Often I try to envision Stuck as a physical form." "Group dynamics and who participated or didn't was noticeable." People seemed to get into it."

Some participants noted "aha" moments during or after the session. "It is important for all voices to be heard, this changed people's way of thinking." "Accuracy of body sculptures in response to the issue we were examining and, perhaps what surprised me is how much was accomplished at the end of 3 hour session. I would compare it to about 10 hours of a problem solving/typical strategy building sessions..." "Removing personal walls can empower." "Each person is important regardless of role, with similar ideas about what is possible, who our audiences are, and where more effort is needed." "Perspectives of what the Board does, and how, and of its members' motivations, vary widely."

The Individual Stuck helped 62% understand, see or realize something about themselves they did not know before. The Group Stuck in contrast, resulted in 100% of participants realizing something about the group, their role, the system or themselves they did not know before.

New actions. Board and Staff to continue co-creation of an action plan to expand a program. They are developing a prototype for the Creative Expressions program to bring arts education to citizens of the Peel region of have suffered brain injuries or have other challenges such as autism. The group is looking at opportunities to increase individual membership, engage youth as a source of energy and movement, align art & innovation for change, get Peel corporations involved, and hear what the Peel government does and align their actions with that.

Participants expressed the following changes in behavior since the session: Paying attention to others differently (28.6%), noticing how you are in your body (14.3%), paying attention to the feeling of the body on the ground (0%), paying attention to the body as a 360° sensing organ (57.1%), no change in behavior (0%). 100% participants recommended SPT as a useful tool and/ or would want to practice SPT again.

Learnings. In the 4D mapping exercise, it must be emphasized that observers are as important as players, in particular because only they have a more holistic view of the sculptures. The instructions to "hold a safe space", observe with "attention and intention" can be further highlighted by suggesting that arms and legs are uncrossed with feet flat on the floor.

Marty Brent, Manager, PAMA, provided organizational input. Michelle N. Moore, Advanced SPT Practitioner, Founder, mindequity.ca, facilitated the session.

Visioning for High Potential Education, Teach for Armenia, Yerevan, Armenia

Case background. Teach for Armenia (TFA), teachforarmenia.org, harnesses the energy, enthusiasm, and drive of exceptional university graduates to infuse great teachers into Armenia's most disadvantaged schools and to cultivate lifelong champions for educational excellence. In July 2017, the TFA was preparing for impact growth and team expansion. To facilitate team alignment on the future state, the 6-member leadership team spent a day applying mindfulness and embodiment practices to gain new insights and to create space for a high potential future to emerge.

The challenge. A highly motivated team, keen on making high quality education available to all Armenian children, was feeling frustrated, overwhelmed from lack of time, and stressed. Internal communication and coordination was a challenge. A strong sense of possibility for the great impact the team could achieve was often absent. The Voice of Fear was noticeable in the common, shared thought pattern, "This can't work in Armenia."

Embodiment practices. The team practiced mindfulness meditation and the 20-Minute Dance to arrive in the body, in the present moment and to engage with intention and attention as a team. Each leader reflected on their personal goals in TFA over the past year and embodied an Individual Stuck.

Figure 1.0 Armenian Education – Group Stuck Future State

They leaned into their current state Stucks and allowed the future to emerge in the body. Reflections were shared in small groups.

TFA worked with a shared Group Stuck around their vision, "...an Armenia where all children, regardless of their socioeconomic circumstances, have the opportunity to unlock their full potential through an excellent education". Outside forces including difficult government collaboration and funder demands were holding that vision back.

Main insights. TFA participants shared feedback after using SPT for the first time via a post-workshop survey. Some of the main insights are summarized below.

100% responded 4 or 5 (out of 5) that, "The quality of my attention was higher than usual, I was fully present with the group and in the moment" and "When body and mind are synchronized, we have access to additional information."

84% responded 4 or 5 that "My intention for the day was set and top of mind for most of the session."

At the end of the session, participants felt "energized and motivated" (83.3 %), "more connected to the group" (66.7%), "tired and ready to sleep" (33.3%), "confused and disconnected" (16.7%)

Some participants noted what surprised them during the workshop: "How easy it went." "How the energy in the room changed, and how open we all were to a such a method of team building, as it is not common in Armenia." "How our bodies reacted to the division in the room." "How natural social presencing came to me and most of our team."

Some participants noted "aha" moments during or after the session: "I continuously refer back to that day and remind myself of the healthy mindsets that I learned. Several aha moments, but mostly about bringing my whole self to work, or better yet making sure that I am actually bringing my whole self to work."

"The day was productive in terms of revisiting TFA's mission and vision. Exploring generative mindset."

"I am struggling to get out of my comfort zone and to excel outside of my domain. I am learning new work habits and methods. I am readapting my approach to team work and am taking the time to try various strategies/tools for incorporating all voices into the work."

"I realized that although our team feels tensions (both overall and between one another for various reasons), when the going gets tough we are there for each other."

Regarding Individual Stuck, 66.7% understood, saw, or realized something about themselves they did not know before. The Group Stuck in contrast, resulted in 100% of participants realizing something about the team, their role or themselves they did not know before.

New actions. Participants expressed the following changes in behaviour since the session: taking time for reflection (50%), taking conscious breaks from any screens (16.7%), taking time for self-care (16.7%), paying attention to the feeling of the body on the ground (16.7%), paying attention to the body as a 360° sensing organ (0%). 100% participants recommended SPT as a useful tool and/or would want to practice SPT again.

Learnings. In the Armenian context, there is a tendency to focus more on a challenge then on the highest future potential. Thus, more insights may have been gained if Seed Dance, with its future focus, instead of Group Stuck, had be applied. Further, the team was not encouraged to note down new ideas for prototypes emerging which in hindsight, was a missed opportunity to enable specific outcomes from the workshop to continue immediately afterwards.

Michelle N. Moore, Advanced SPT Practitioner, Founder, mindequity.ca, facilitated the session. Larisa Hovannisian, founder and CEO, teachforarmenia.org, provided organizational input.

Visioning Total Compensation & Impact, GrantBook Inc., Toronto, Canada

Case background. GrantBook Inc. is a Benefit Corporation providing philanthropic and digital consulting to grantmakers and impact investors to help them reach their highest potential. In August 2017, GrantBook held a team retreat. To facilitate team alignment on the future state vision, the thirteen member team spent one day applying embodiment practices (Individual & Group Stuck, 4D Mapping) to gain new insights from a different perspective.

The challenge. The six year old social purpose team did not want to grow just for growth's sake. Rather, they collectively desired healthy, sustainable growth that would enable innovation and improved compensation along with work life balance and a pricing strategy which would not alienate their nonprofit sector clients. Further, they were struggling with a Big Hairy Audacious Goal (BHAG) to "Improve the flow of $100 billion in capital to drive catalytic social change", an impact statement that is very hard to measure.

The social sculptures. GB defined their team Stucks in advance of the retreat as follows. Group Stuck: "Important levers for growth (in addition to enabling improved total compensation) are increased chargeable utilization & higher billable rates. However, utilization remains at about 50% and the hourly rate is only slowly creeping up to $195." System Stuck: "We are this social purpose business but we can't even tell you what concrete impact we have had." The stakeholders in the ecosystem included: GrantBook Organization, Grantee, Beneficiary, Philanthropic Foundation, Technology, Citizen, GB Employee.

Figure 2.0 Compensation and Impact. Future State 4D Map.

Main insights. The following comments were provided by participants in relation to growth : "When there is tension in current state it can't maintain itself and it will fall down on its own", "The transition between SC1 and SC2 is as important as how SC1 forms and how SC2 ends up," "Simplicity is desirable, it's good, don't shy away from simplicity,"

Participants articulated emerging future qualities revealed from the Stucks including: "Personal initiative is required", "There is no need to find relief alone....get support from the whole," "Don't focus so much just on the relief but on the future state", "Inclusive, simplicity is good," "Acknowledge fear of change, practice release mechanisms," "Acknowledge the possibility that increased chargeability & rates can occur with ease," "Reimagine how we plan & spend time (chargeable vs. non-chargeable)," "We can be energy efficient, there is energy elsewhere to enable everything," "Consider that symmetry may be impossible to sustain; release can open up space, freeing energy; maybe there's a sense of comfort with dissymmetry if it provides a supportive solution."

Prototype ideas. The following ideas for prototypes to support growth were noted: 1) personal: articulate personal action needed to achieve future, inclusive state, recognizing own personal willingness to be included, 2) design utilization transition phase: maintain sense of unity in transition & moving to future; design non-chargeable structure (for example 10% time on innovation, 10% time on vacation/sick, 10% learning etc.), 3) include key design elements for growth: design higher utilization pressure release mechanism, a support structure, including individual skills, temperaments, stakeholder insights; 4) design for ease in GB's evolution: look at growth in terms of growth rate (# of staff added per year) rather than target # of staff; 5) brainstorm and document pros and cons behind the various compensation scenarios so we have a collective understanding of the impact. Include the more emotional/perception reactions to the scenarios; 6) explore the alternative to purchasing extended benefits, i.e. having an internally managed fund that GB contributes to monthly, and staff can apply to get reimbursement for health expenses; include concerns about admin burden and individual privacy; 7) test out a more granular approach to hours tracking to try to cover some of the "miscellaneous time" that is spent on a mix of projects and currently isn't getting tracked; 8) experiment with different billing rates for different client types; 9) template process to direct organizations to get funding.

"The exercise allows us to formulate future states more easily than having endless verbal meetings about it," noted James Law, Partner Relationship Development, GrantBook Inc.

Main insights. The team also had insights and questions related to the BHAG which included, "Mind map the system we operate in to better understand it and the role we can play - because it's all so big, what we are passionate about and what we can excel at; include government as a player, for example", and "GB is so focused on foundations but maybe that's not the best thing for GB to support; should beneficiaries be more included?"

Prototype ideas. New prototype ideas to support the BHAG emerged: 1) re-design the BHAG around the relationships & connectedness in the system, with citizen and beneficiary in mind, in terms of overcoming the foundation's own divided self (disconnection with self and other); 2) GrantBook employees can foster new behaviour such as deeper relationships with the grantee, act as bridge between foundation and grantee; 3) create new messaging for conversations, blogs, proposals to let foundations know that they are fully supported and give them permission not to be in total control; 4) obtain foundation stories on the impact of GB work; 5) develop a post project review survey for client feedback.

"Participating in the SPT activities revealed new answers to our organization's long standing existential questions. Adding the body as a source of insight alongside right & left brain faculties is invaluable," noted Peter Deitz, Co-Founder, GrantBook Inc.

Learnings. I was a senior leader in this social field and stepped out of that role to be the facilitator, playing a neutral, third party role. It is likely better practice not to facilitate our own teams. Based on this experience, I am aware that I did not have any opportunity show the same vulnerability the team members showed in their sculptures because I did not participate in the sculptures themselves. This resulted in me cutting myself off from the experience and somehow becoming an outsider.

Peter Deitz, Co-Founder, GrantBook Inc., enabled and held space in the session. Michelle N. Moore, Advanced SPT Practitioner, Managing Director, Grantbook Inc, facilitated the session.

Developing Potential for Refugees, Immigrants & Citizens, Umbria Region, Italy

Case background. The Italian immigration system in the Umbria region has been challenged by the large influx of migrants requesting refugee status since the Arab Spring in 2011. The Dublin Convention, enforced since 1997, obliges migrants to stay in the country where they arrive even if their desired destination is further north.

In December 2017, SPT practitioners in New York created 4D Maps of the Italian immigration system in order to enable the case giver, a consultant working to create constructive dialogue, to discover untapped opportunities and help the system to see itself.

The challenge.For the past 3 years, migrants arriving by boat have been held in so-called "emergency" detention centers called Centri di Accoglienza Straordinaria (CAS). The are run by the Italian Interior Ministry local branch through coops, associations and hotels. Migrants are often held for up to 2 years, receiving some language and professional training. 70% of refugee status requests are rejected. Thus, migrants usually disappear to escape deportation orders. They become illegal and often resort to prostitution, join one of four Italian mafias or are exploited as extremely poorly paid farm laborers in the south.

The Italian state does not know how to help migrants, nor Italian citizens, realize their full potential. Italians receive little attention or care as individuals, much less career guidance. Thus, the immigrant is the worst example of how people are treated by Italian institutions. This treatment is not substantially different from the state approach towards Italian citizens themselves.

The social sculpture. The twelve Italian immigration system stakeholder roles embodied for the 4D Maps were: European Union (EU); CAS; the Umbria branch of the Interior Ministry (Prefettura); Federal Immigration Office; the municipal Sistema di Protezione per Richiedenti Asilo e Rifugiati (SPRAR); Umbrian residents; legal immigrants; illegal immigrants; home country; third party facilitators; Earth, and Highest Potential, define for the exercise as "Government considers each citizen and immigrant a resource for Italy".

373

Twenty observers formed a circle. Twelve volunteers embodied a stakeholder role, entered into the circle (the system) and voiced their felt sense of the current state (SC1). Stakeholders clarified SC1 (formed inside of the circle held by the observers) and remained present until movement arose in each body towards a future state (SC2). After about seven minutes the social sculpture arrived in SC2. The stakeholders remained in SC2 and voiced their felt sense of the emerging future state.

Figure 3.0 Italian Immigration. Current State 4D Map.

Main insights. The following insights emerged during the 4D Map.

Human focus is needed. The potential for addressing the challenge lies with permitting the people involved within the process to see the problem in systemic terms and to understand how they can contribute to the solutions. This requires changing a mindset from the provincial to the universal and addressing the needs of administrators to create humane solutions and for immigrants to be enterprising within a state of law.

The home country has a role. Its fear of government institutions (EU, Interior Ministry) can shift towards collaboration with immigrants, Highest Potential and Earth, including the EU and the Municipality in the dialogue. The role of CAS is less essential.

There appears to be a new triangle of opportunity between the Umbrian resident, illegal immigrant and the facilitators. During the 4D map, Umbrian residents declared both their love of the land and their experience of hunger. They moved towards the illegal immigrants as did the facilitators, who see this movement as the greatest potential for impactful dialogue. Umbrian resident inclusion is key for change, given their own current economic struggles.

Highest Potential is very close to Earth, along with the illegal immigrant, in tandem with Umbrian residents whose care for Earth is heightened due to the recent experience of devastating earthquakes. Highest Potential also sees borders going away with legal immigrants and Umbrians collaborating. Illegal immigrants care most about the relationship with their home country, legal immigrants and, perhaps surprisingly, local Umbrian residents.

The case giver stated, "I was surprised by the reaction of the residents to the problem and by how the Municipalities immediately responded with a movement towards immigrants. I had not envisaged the strength of the relationship between immigrants (legal and illegal) with their home country. It was this last role which moved most between sculpture one and sculpture two and when they touched, there was an electric spark between them. The EU collapsed while seeking to move towards Earth.

This approach has allowed me to have another view of the problem and to evaluate if it would be possible to do a mapping with the real stakeholders. This approach does not signal a single truth but permits one to envisage solutions not imagined before. It also allows participants to share experience and a common language to discuss the issues."

New actions planned. The facilitator is motivated to take the following new actions: 1) Use Umbria as a pilot region, given the cultural sense of solidarity and ecumenicism of the area. The city of Assisi is key in this. 2) Find out how Umbrians really feel about accepting refugee claimants and potential new immigrants. Then include Umbrian residents in the dialogue to convince other municipalities to participate in absorbing refugee claimants equally across the region. 3) When engaging in dialogue with immigrants, integrate the connection to their Home Country. 4) Form partnerships with local government including the Prefettura, Immigration Office- Questura and the Health office as well as the managers of CAS and SPRAR. 5) Recommend (to National Association of Italian Municipalities) knowledge transfer from SPRAR to CAS.

Susan George, Advanced SPT Practitioner, President of the Association for Public Participation, Italy, provided input and was interviewed for this case.

Enabling Better Dialogue on Nuclear Power in Japan

Case background. In the aftermath of the March 2011 Fukushima accident, the nuclear power system, represented by political and economic forces, continues to be strong. In December 2017, SPT practitioners in New York formed 4D Maps of this system to enable the case giver, a Japanese citizen working to create constructive dialogue on nuclear power through the "Dialogue Project", to see new opportunities.

The challenge. Authentic open dialogue is difficult. Loud, pro-nuke stakeholders drown out less powerful, soft voices and marginalized citizens, i.e. Fukushima residents and children. A Japanese cultural norm prevents voicing of opinions.

Figure 4.0 Japanese Nuclear Power Dialogue. Future State 4D Map.

The social sculpture. The stakeholder roles embodied for the 4D Maps were: power company, government, corporations, pro-nuke scientists, anti-nuke scientists, Japanese citizens, Dialogue Project team, Fukushima residents, Fukushima children, activists, the Earth. Highest Potential was defined as, "Japanese citizens speak up to voice their opinion on nuclear power are heard and enabled to co-create the country's future based on real consensus." Corporations moved first in the future state sculpture (SC2) and emerged as being in service to the community. Activists widened their attention. Children stayed with Fukushima residents. The power company moved towards Earth and Fukushima residents became a bridge between the Dialogue Project team and the community. Earth remained at a very low level. Children moved towards Earth.

In SC1, the system did not have a particular shape, i.e. most stakeholders were spread out, not connected physically or visually. In SC2, the system became circular, looking inward towards each other. Even the government was part of the circle.

Main insights. The potential of the power company as a force of positive change was revealed. The case giver was able to see her own blind spot, a bias against the good will of the power company. The inward facing circle gave the case giver hope. "SC2 showed me I can have unconditional confidence in the basic health of the system, in the tendency of the system to move towards health. This gives me the feeling I am on the right track, i.e. to one by one get all the stakeholders talking to me and my group and then eventually all together."

New actions planned. As a result of the social sculpture, the Dialogue Project plans to evolve its relationship building to include many more stakeholders, in particular with the power company. The intent is to convene a multi-stakeholder dialogue event in a private, safe space to enable sharing of feelings and building of trust. Then a more open, public, fully inclusive multi-stakeholder dialogue can occur.

Kanae Kuwahara, Advanced SPT Practitioner, Dialogue Project Founder and Faculty, Japan Process Work Center, provided input and was interviewed for this case.

Strategic Technology Team Prototyping, European Chemical Company, Lima, Peru

Case Background. The Latin American regional information technology (IT) team of a European-based global chemical company, a diverse twelve-person group from eight countries, mostly engineers with ten to twenty years of company experience, wanted a different annual meeting. They desired a safe space for generative thinking around new approaches for building a strategic relationship between IT and the business. Also, they intended to design a path for elevating their participation in global innovation projects. The team envisioned a more relaxed meeting which combined team building, fun while achieving meeting goals.

The challenge. IT was viewed as a transactional support function (i.e. not strategic). Lean country IT teams worked alone responding to country business needs with a minimal contribution to company innovation. The Latin American IT team needed to up-skill and become current on global issues emerging in order to be respected and become part of the company's global innovation ecosystem.

Social sculpture prototyping. To prepare the group for prototyping using the social body, more than a day prior was spent introducing various mindfulness and movement exercises. The setting was a waterfront hotel with access to nature, the beach, barefoot walking, opportunity for reflection and journaling. Theory U principles of open mind, open heart, open will, along with suspension of the voices of judgement, cynicism, and fear were introduced as key leadership capacities needed for innovation. The group practiced 20 Minute Dance and Individual Stuck. A Village was co-created, walking on the beach and ending in the water. These preparations provided basic experiential learning needed for creating a prototype using embodied practices. Participants recognized that a change in both the self and the team was required.

A customized version of Seed Dance was used to create a an IT function that is close to the business, collectively and individually. The team built the prototype using tents, string, balloons, balls, sticks, tubes of plastic and their own bodies. They created a large platform, representing IT, in the sand, with a part in the water (representing business).

The team needed to stay close to the water but separated from it, and pay attention to the question emerging, "If this is right, how can we be in the water without getting wet, i.e. how can we relate to the business without being slaves or supporters, be in relationship and seen as strategic."

Main insights. Some personal, team and practice insights were revealed during the exercises. Participants realized, "It is important to reconnect with self, taking time to reflect and feel ourselves in a strategic IT role, keeping awareness of what is emerging and what we need to let go of." They said, "We can function in a new way and be a big asset when integrated with the business. We can look outside of our team in a different way, initiating the conversation on new roles with connection to the business."

The team also recognized that mindful embodiment work is a practice. They want to sustain these new ways of working in the team, being more connected with the individual body, with nature (Earth body), and the social body....so that this is not forgotten.

Benefits. The team articulated the following general benefits of the experiential meeting: "We can shift from guilty people not responding fast enough, to being strategic, and in collaboration with the business." "We are letting go of the fear (internal personal barriers) of participating actively in global IT projects. We continue to practice letting go of fear." "The continuation of automatic and habitual thinking was stopped." "More talking would not have enabled trying new, riskier, approaches." "The approach enabled great openness and we are surprised how easy it is to be so open, so fluid, the body enabled the ease in this." "We felt an easiness to connect with how we felt with our emotions, the environment, making a shift in our role."

New actions planned. Each of the IT Team leaders plans to schedule a conversation with the business, to present themselves in a new way and listen in new ways, committed to try different ways of being with the business. The Latin Regional Team committed to being strategic, i.e. more innovative, with increased visits to the European headquarters. They will seek more operational permission to do things, launch process and policy change to have more power, better response times, and alignment with the business.

Ernesto Yañez, Advanced SPT Practitioner, Docent and Consultant, Universidad Del Pacifico and Universidad de Ciencias Aplicadas, and Inés Gabaldón, Senior Associate at Partners in Performance, Lima Peru facilitated the exercises and were interviewed for this case.

Team Optimization for AIDS Advocacy, North America, Africa, Asia

Case background. A Global AIDS Advocacy nonprofit with staff in North America, Asia, Africa had their 2017 annual strategic meeting in the U.S. with ten attendees. The team meets only once a year in person. The team wanted to remove barriers to optimal team functioning. Many had a long history with the nonprofit. There were wide differences in age between old and new team members.

The challenge. As AIDS activists, imminent death of the population they support, is always present. Thus, there exists a general hesitancy to spend time on interpersonal behaviour or internal team dynamics.

The team had difficulty verbalizing internal problems, especially when these were specific to one person. Time zone diversity made communication logistically complex. Many team members expressed difficulty connecting with the leader. Effective communication was a general challenge. Silence was the rule and issues were often neither voiced nor resolved. Disconnects with outside stakeholders also existed, often due to age differences.

The Individual Stuck. The group embodied mindfulness practice to identify stuck places in themselves as well as places of wellbeing. They understood that Stuck was not a problem. Rather it was part of the normal creative process. They began to accept that Stucks are natural in individuals and organizations and that there could be useful information in a Stuck.

Individual Stucks were practiced in order to collectively cultivate increased system health, team functioning and healthy high performance. Major patterns emerged like Stucks pulled in different directions. Limbs were extended with an unstable base in SC1 which moved to supportive body shapes in SC2. Other Stucks exhibited top-down pressure, i.e. heavy pressure on top of head, sinking under the weight of something from above, head down, chest collapsed, on center, little periphery in the shape. In SC2 the shapes moved towards the floor and then some shifted up.

Main insights. Participants noted several insights which emerged during the embodiment exercises.

Support staff is being pressured from the top down and needs more support from the top. The support staff Stuck shape revealed an imbalance in the base which needs further exploration. They sensed an opportunity to end organizational denial.

Mindfulness practices enabled the team to connect with each other in person more deeply as well as be vulnerable with each other. It is safer to show Stuck than to talk.

Participants expressed having less shame about their struggles combined with relief that all team members are challenged.

Actions planned. The team intends to practice mindfulness in order to surface new ideas, to create a space to innovate or do new things. For example, in meetings, they will incorporate a one minute pause to breathe more freely before the meeting. They wish to make small changes to promote team wellbeing. Finally, there is interest to meet again to unpack their Stucks, exploring insight on what opportunities surface organizationally.

Kate Johnson, SPT Teacher, Consultant, Coach, Writer, facilitated the exercises and was interviewed for this case.

Eroles Project, Exploring Democracy in Tremp, Catalonia, Spain

Case background. The Eroles Project, erolesproject.org, works to create conditions for personal and political change towards a sustainable and equitable world. During the summer of 2017, two-week residencies were run in Tremp, a small village in Catalonia, in the Pyrenees Mountains. The 2017 theme was Democracy with one residency exploring "Deepening Citizenship" and the other "Emerging Politics". Village was used to practice a new level of awareness and attentiveness in a public space, i.e. the main square of the village of Tremp.

The challenge of deepening citizenship. The first residency included political activists, academics, writers and arts graduates from various European countries, ranging in age from 20-65. The challenge was to re-imagine activism through the body and create a village for deepening the sense of citizenship.

Social sculpture preparation. To prepare the group for sensing the social field of a real village, mindfulness and body awareness was emphasized, coming from a philosophy that being connected in our bodies enables better awareness of what is happening in the world. The idea of the body having thousands of antennae extended outwards 360° helped participants understand the connection wider than themselves. In our society, there is often the tendency to block the extension of ourselves out into a space. Exploring bodies in relationship to each other takes the theoretical exploration of what it means to be citizens to the experiential level.

To further prepare for Village, participants walked about Tremp for half an hour in order to feel what it is like to move around as a citizen of Tremp. Each person walked alone, in silence, and practiced using their antennae. They took their physical body into Tremp and allowed the body to notice what it was naturally attracted to. Many were on edge because they didn't know cultural norms, understand what's allowed.

In the central square the group debriefed and shared major insights from the walk including: "When we normally walk about, there is an absence of genuine observation, we always have an agenda." "This agenda-less way of being enabled a freedom to just be, see, feel, and felt very liberating." "We felt like strangers and this gave us permission to explore without usual guardedness or set of cultural restrictions we would have in our hometown."

The deepening citizenship social sculpture. A 20-minute Village was created in the Tremp public square. It is a pedestrian only zone, a vast, and ugly space, with big metal, contemporary structures. The group was already connected to some of the theory about limiting language in public after reading Hannah Arendt, "Words can be relied on only if one is sure that their function is to reveal and not to conceal." Some people were nervous andor eager to begin, wanting to know what happens when Tremp citizens react. The instruction was to "play with it".

During Village, running and other patterns emerging were very defined through the space. Shapes and rhythms formed. Patterns repeated. One participant, a woman in her 60's, who had been very reserved, was incredibly liberated and playful. It was surprising when she lay down in the middle of the square, walked on benches, and was generally playful. This gave others the sense of permission to "go for it", letting inhibition go. Her approach to lying down early on in the middle of the square caused the group to shift towards play. At the 10-minute point, the facilitator made a funny sound which added even more humor to the process.

A Tremp woman with a buggy, walking with older kids, started running through the square behind the participants. Then the group imitated her. From then on there was more interest from other Tremp citizens. For example, two participants were lying on the square and an elderly woman walked past and instructed them to stay in the shade, concerned they would overheat from the beating sun.

Main insights from activists. The activists in the group commented that they organize protests primarily to be seen. In political direct actionthe aim is to be as visible to the press in order to gain as much attention as possible to the cause. They don't pay attention to the social field. They focus only on the concrete intended outcomes of their own political or social agenda. There was an insight about widening the narrow activist agenda to include the social field, not just as spectators but also as influencers and participants. Then generative value-added outcomes could arise.

When activist movements are built, many participants take huge personal risks and feel unsupported. Further, there often is a separation between types of movements (human rights vs. climate change vs. local activism). These activists have separate meetings, agendas and ways of deciding what to focus on.

The Village exercise revealed the opportunity to understand activism as a whole (social field), with all members taking positive steps forward. The activist village can expand and all activists can support each other as a whole in an interconnected dynamic. This can enable really stepping into the unknown with open mind, open heart and open will, suspending the voice of judgement.

Finally, the experience in the Village of taking the lead or stepping forward showed the ability to be part of an ecosystem in which activists stay connected whether they are physically connected or not.

General insights. Many general insights were revealed in participant comments: "Village increases our ability to pay attention" "There was a sense of how social movements grow and die, what the small micro ripple effects are that start a movement". "There was a strong sense of supporting someone who took a lead in new physical movement." "The ripple effect which occurred after someone started a new and radical move was a reflection on sensing the outsider vs. the insider, the sense of inclusion vs. exclusion, and enabling outsiders become part of the flow." "There was a sense of experience of plurality, of the ability to hold in the same moment what my inner landscape is doing and to have awareness and respond to what is happening outside myself. "I had the ability to understand some dense theoretical ideas through the practice and Village offered the space to go from theory into practice. "Creating Village is like creating a live work of art."

New actions. Participants were motivated to train themselves more, via practices like Village, in order to hold the plurality along with what is going on inside each person. There is an opportunity to explore (embodiment practices.)

The challenge of emerging politics. The second residency included participants involved in local or national politics, most from the United Kingdom, ranging in age from 30-40, Emerging Politics . There were many facilitators. The group was less diverse than the first. The atmosphere was tense as the 2017 Barcelona terror attacks had occurred the week before. There was police presence on the way to the town (but none in the Tremp square). Thus, the energy of the group was more hesitant. Some felt a real a block about being in a public space. Nevertheless, all participated. One person in particular was uncomfortable, feeling scared the whole time, pushing himself to the edge of his risk tolerance.

Social sculpture preparation. Similar preparation was provided as described in the Village above. However, this time many participants wanted much more of an explanation on the reasons for doing Village. Some objections included, "If it was a performance, I would understand it." "I don't want to take this into my work." There was a great sense of fear of being seen as "strange". The facilitator was challenged to make the case that when experiential learning is over explained in advance it can result in a loss of experiential depth. She encouraged the group to focus on the felt sense of Village, including the uncertainty inherent in it. "This is a chance for us to reduce our constant use of language and to bring our awareness to the complexity of how we interact with others, structures and space."

Participants went on a walk to understand the politics of Tremp by sensing the social field, in particular, noticing which physical structures, like benches, facilitate the activity, are inviting vs. not inviting. The group was invited to sense structures created by the municipality vs. by the people. They explored question: How long do you have to know a space to contribute or enact in it?

The emerging politics social sculpture. The 20-minute Village exercise was limited to the Tremp main square again. A few Tremp citizens stood and watched. Some participants thought this was great, that outsiders wanted to watch. Others felt they were making people angry through this activity.

Main insights. A feeling of self-consciousness for some dissipated during the exercise and for others tensions increased. One person said, "The energy of fear encourages us to transform the energy into something useful." The facilitator received confirmation that giving clear and minimal instruction while holding a safe space is critical to avoiding a cerebral exercise which would diminish the experience.

New actions planned. One Italian participant expressed motivation to facilitate a Village in The Apennines, impacted by the earthquake. The Village exercise could enable a sensing of devastated spaces to better understand the relationship with the ruined space and with each other in that space, and the potential new ways of interacting. Two participants from London, both coaches, saw opportunity in exploring the political body. "How we move and how we embody experience has an impact on who we are politically. If people in power have trauma or hold trauma, and are not able to connect with themselves, they may externalize that in their relationship. This can be observed and help us empathize and engage differently, rather than just being reactive."

Ruth Cross, Advanced SPT Practitioner, Co-founder, erolesproject.org facilitated the exercises and was interviewed for this case.

Enabling the Future of the Granada Project, Spain

Case background. The Granada Project emerged from the 2016 Eroles residency, "A camp as if people matter". This residency focused on migration and self-realization to co-create a permaculture via creative forms of expression, led by migrants and refugees. Since August 2016, ten part-time members shifted the Granada project from migrant camp to long term migrant integration. As a result, the Spanish non-profit, La Bolina Association, was registered in July 2017. Las Bolina enables integration and regeneration of land, cooperative creation, and sustainable agro-ecology. La Bolina is a feisty local plant with bright yellow flowers. It represents the resilience of the project migrants and refugees.

The challenge. In July 2017, the core team was indecisive about where to physically locate the project permanently. There was much frustration and uncertainty regarding the tension between fundraising or finding a location. Also, while the team is great at outside field research, meetings with mayor, rural development agencies, they were struggling with integration of that information. There was information overload and no processing of the data. Too many linear meetings were not resulting in progress. Finally, a common vision had not been co-created.

The social sculpture. In a village near Granada, outdoors on a terrace overlooking the mountains, the customized version of Seed Dance consisted of six stakeholders: Earth, migrants, funders, the project itself, partners, and Highest Potential, i.e. the best possible global impact the project could have. First, each person one by one embodied the project itself. That person chose where to place the stakeholders in SC1 and then the shaped moved to SC2. Thus, six different future states emerged. There was one minute of silence in between each person. After six shapes were formed, the team journaled for ten minutes in silence. Then, they divided the terrace into Yes and NO sections. Questions were answered by people placing themselves on the yes/no spectrum with their bodies.

Main insights. The Seed Dance showed a new, great way to make decisions. Energetically everything flowed. There was integration, sustainability, regeneration in the social sculpture. This can be a positive example of a land based sustainable cooperative enterprise with migrants and refugees. The enterprise can make money from the sale of products (fresh produce and later olive oil, almond butter, jam) sold in markets, hotels, local restaurants, and through vegetable box schemes. The team can regenerate land in villages close to villages from its degraded state caused by mono-cultures and sea plasti.

Key results. The key vision to be based rurally, in Saleres, Granada Province, 30 minutes south of Granada was a breakthrough of the Seed Dance as the core team had really different location preferences, as did the migrants. Now twelve core team members are renting one big house and the project has been given several pieces of land by the municipality for free.

The Seed Dance was pivotal in enabling team members from more than eleven countries to deliver training twice a week on permaculture and agriculture. Participants are coming from all over the world.

A more stable structure was created, so refugees would understand what to do when they joined the project. How to access the project was simplified and short information days for migrants and refugees are regularly held.

New actions planned. The following action plan was established: 1) create a business plan, 2) talk about the project in a simple way so it's understandable, 3) first and foremost, obtain more project funding, 4) connect more partners, 5) develop the network to recruit more migrants and refugees and listen to their needs, 6) use embodiment exercises again for visioning in the core team in January 2018.

Ruth Cross, Advanced SPT Practitioner, Co-founder, Granada Project, facilitated the exercises and was interviewed for this case.

Cross Case Analysis

The ten examples of practical applications in organizations using SPT are diverse. Geographically, there were four North American cases, four European, one South American and one Asian case. Eighty percent of cases were given by non-profit organizations. Twenty percent wee for profit companies. The challenges chosen for application of SPT were overwhelmingly societal in nature.

When cross analyzing the four cases (Nathan Cummings, PAMA, Teach for Armenia, GrantBook) in which participants filled out survey questionnaires, the following highlights are useful:

- About 75% of participants had more intention and attention during the workshop than in usual meetings or other workshops. They
- About 75% agreed that when body and mind are synchronized, more information is available.
- Most felt connected and energized through SPT practices.
- The Group Stuck exercise revealed insights about the team or challenge not seen before, in 100% of survey respondents.
- In contrast, the Individual Stuck exercise revealed new insights in only about 63% of survey respondents.
- Only about 30% of respondents increased their noticing of others in a social field or of themselves, their own bodies, in the two months following the workshop.
- Less than 30% of survey respondents became aware of their own body as a 360 degree sensing organ after the workshop.
- 85% of respondents thought it would be useful to practice SPT exercises again in the future.
- Comments about feelings and experience in the SPT workshop were provided in the survey as well. These revealed several words repeated by multiple respondents including: empathy, equality, emotional, openness, physical body being tuned in, the speed at which insights were reached.

When cross analyzing the remaining six cases , the following trends arose :

- Many of the insights revealed opportunities pay attention to new stakeholders, possibly previously ignored, i.e. in general widening the scope of inclusion.

- Connection to self as part of the whole was noticed, including the importance of paying attention to the self in the context of the larger ecosystem.
- Deep connections with team members were possible and surprising with a realization that silence, wholeness and body connection facilitates this.

Common trends related to new actions in the remaining six cases included:

- New ideas for pilots and prototypes were planned.
- There was great interest in changing the design of stakeholder dialogues, i.e. shifting and / or expanding the diversity of participants.
- In three cases (Global AIDs NGO, Eroles Project, Granada Project), participants committed to changing their personal habits, i.e. add mindfulness and well-being practices in their lives. These same three agreed amongst themselves to practice SPT exercises again regularly.

Conclusion

The cases in this chapter represent single events lasting from three hours to more than one day. There were two additional cases which applied SPT exercises multiple times over the course of more than one year and are ongoing. However, due to the sensitive nature of these cases, the organizations involved did not aprove case publication, one involving transformation of a school system and the other, international NGOs working against human trafficking. The vulnerability arising in SPT work may continue to pose a challenge in documenting, photographing or filming organizations in the practice.

Because SPT is not yet widespread, it is difficult today to document any longer term outcomes. As SPT practitioners, it is understood that SPT is a practice, much like meditation or physical exercise, which must be applied on a regular basis in order for results to appear. Thus, the next challenge is to encourage a more regular, repeated utilization of SPT in organizations. Just as mindfulness is now embedded in numerous corporations and schools, so SPT could become an integral practice in learning and innovative organizations. Opportunities are great for using the social body as a source of ideas, innovation and transformative systems change.

References

George, W. (2016). *Innsaei - The Power of Intuition*, Zeitgeist Films, interview, https://zeitgeistfilms.com/film/innsaeithepowerofintuition.

Hayashi, A. (2017). U Lab course, *Leading From the Emerging Future*, SPT video, Part 2, edX, https://www.edx.org/course/u-lab-leading-emerging-future-mitx-15-671-1x-0.

Hayashi, A. (2017). U Lab course, *Leading From the Emerging Future*, SPT intro video, edX, https://www.edx.org/course/u-lab-leading-emerging-future-mitx-15-671-1x-0.

Hayashi, A. (2018). Resources page. https://arawanahayashi.com/watch.

Kabat-Zinn, J. (2013). *Full Catastrophe Living*, New York, Bantam Books.

Kleiner, A. (2017). What the Body Tells us about Leadership. *strategy + business magazine*, Issue 88.

Presencing Institute (2018). Tools page. https://www.presencing.org/#/resource/tools.

Scharmer, O., (2009), *Theory U*, San Francisco, Berrett-Koehler Publishers, Inc.

Scharmer, O., Kaeufer, K. (2013). *Leading from the Emerging Future*, Oakland, Berrett-Koehler Publishers, Inc.

Scharmer, O. (2018). *The Essentials of Theory U. Core Principles and Applications*, Oakland, Berrett-Koehler Publishers, Inc.

Senge, P., Scharmer, O., Jaworski J., Flowers, B. (2004), *Presence*, New York, Crown Business.

Sources of Case Material

The content for these cases was drawn from author facilitation, observation and interviews with other SPT facilitators. For all cases, the key individual involved in the case approved the content for submission.

The author facilitated the examples in New York, Canada and Armenia, obtaining feedback from participants via spoken debriefs and post workshop surveys. The following persons provided organizational input and approved the case content: Janet Disla, Senior Grants Manager, Nathan Cummings Foundation; Marty Brent, Manager, Peel Art Gallery, Museum & Archives; Larisa Hovannisian, founder and CEO, Teach for Armenia; Deitz, Co-Founder, GrantBook Inc.

Through live observation, the author documented the Italian and Japanese cases. In follow-up, the case givers were interviewed to confirm their insights: Susan George, President of the Association for Public Participation, Kanae Kuwahara, Dialogue Project Founder and Faculty, Japan Process Work Center.

For the cases in Peru, Spain and North America, the following Advanced SPT practitioners were interviewed: Ernesto Yañez, Docent and Consultant, Universidad Del Pacifico and Universidad de Ciencias Aplicadas, and Inés Gabaldón, Senior Associate at Partners in Performance; Kate Johnson, SPT Teaching Faculty; Ruth Cross, Co-founder, Eroles and Granada Projects, Catalonia, Spain.

Sources of SPT Information

The information provided is primarily based on the author's personal experience including: practicing the exercises as shown in the SPT modules in the u.lab (2015-2017), Practicing directly with Arawana Hayashi in Boston November 2016 and as a member of the Advanced Social Presencing Theater Cohort #4, Presencing Institute, Massachusetts Institute of Technology (2017-2018); facilitation in various environments including: pilot workshops (2) with Toronto business persons (summer 2016), a u.lab SPT-focused hub (2017), a Toronto SPT practice group (2017-2018), SPT Workshops in four organizations: Teach for Armenia, Peel Art Museum & Archives, Nathan Cummings Foundation, GrantBook Inc. (2017) and amazing.community (2018).

Author Note:

A warm thank you to Arawana Hayashi, Presencing Institute, for her teachings. I am greatly appreciative to Janet Disla, Senior Grants Manager, Nathan Cummings Foundation, Marty Brent, Manager, Peel Art Museum and Archives, Ontario; Larisa Hovannisian, founder and CEO, Teach for Armenia, Yerevan; and Peter Deitz, Co-Founder, GrantBook Inc., Toronto, who had the open mind, open heart and open will to welcome Social Presencing into their organizations.

Thank you to my colleagues in Advanced Social Presencing Theater Cohort #4, Presencing Institute, who took the time to be interviewed and share their cases: Susan George, Kanae Kuwahara, Ernesto Yañez, Kate Johnson, Ruth Cross, Joan O'Donnell, Liz Alperin Solms and Manish Srivastava.

I also wish to thank my father, Dr. Lee E. Moore, Dr. of Neurophysiology, Université Paris Descartes, and my sister, Andrea Moore, PhD, Musicology, Smith College for their constructive and invaluable comments on this chapter.

CHAPTER 14

Applying Theory U through SHAPE to Develop Student's Individual Entrepreneurial Orientation in a University Eco-System

Thea van der Westhuizen

Introduction

The focus in the first half of this chapter is a single, brief, but a very powerful moment in an 11-week Theory U-inspired initiative for aspiring young entrepreneurs at the University of KwaZulu-Natal in Durban (UKZN), South Africa. Presencing occurred during Meet Your Business Friend Day, where student entrepreneurs co-initiated, co-sensed, co-inspired, co-created and setting the tone co-evolve with possible Business Friends, in the spark of forming an eco-system of deep support. Student entrepreneurs interacted during Meet Your Business Friend Day with peers, private sector entrepreneurs, mentors from the local municipality, mentors from the local chamber of commerce and mentors from the provincial Local Economic Development Unit. The aim of bringing them together was to co-initiate a potential future eco-system for students, through co-sensing and co-inspiring, to enable them to be more entrepreneurial. At the time of the event, such an actual eco-system of Business Friends and the interrelationships between role-players didn't exist. After this powerful moment, students were requested to write reflections on their experiences building up to this day and during this day. As they've been *en route* through the U-journey, their reflections at this stage were ripe for analysis. Utilizing participant's account in a survey and reflective writing, I will be exploring the thematic relationships between Theory U levels and IEO dimensions.

SHAPE (Shifting Hope, Activating Potential Entrepreneurship) is a social technology that draws its participants from students with entrepreneurial aspirations who are registered for undergraduate and postgraduate degrees in business studies at UKZN. SHAPE, at the time of writing, has run successfully for four years. In this chapter, we provide an account theoretical overview groundwork, planning, and implementation for a one-day event called "Meet Your Business Friend Day." With 60 student participants and 20 mentors, this meeting took place in October 2014 as part of the inaugural cycle of the SHAPE social technology. SHAPE, in turn, was, and continues to be, part of a larger systemic action learning and action research project in which the cycles and phases of the project build on the cycles of Theory U. This project also specifically considers whether a positive correlation exists between aspects of Theory U and dimensions of a participant's individual entrepreneurial orientation, namely risk-taking, innovation and proactivity.

Seen systemically, each individual constitutes a micro-system closely linked to various processes at differing levels of systemic development. The 2015 Global Entrepreneurship Monitor notes that a person's heartset and mindset, and his or her entrepreneurial profile, attitudes, activities and aspirations, are directly linked to national and indeed global socio-economic development (Herrington & Kew, 2016). If entrepreneurialism is to spur socio-economic development, one possible starting point could be to develop those internal domains of aspirant individuals – the individual micro-system – by tapping into resources that are reachable at other systemic levels (Van der Westhiuzen, 2016). These resources can include intermediaries from: a) universities, b) municipality business support units, c) communities, d) private sector practitioners who support youth entrepreneurs, e) para-statals and agencies set out to develop commerce or f) a Local Economic Development Unit embedded within a government entity (van der Westhuizen, 2016).

Connection with Theory U

Theory U identifies four fundamental meta-processes of the systemic levels, which we speculate, develop different dimensions of one's IEO. Systemic levels include micro-field processes (individual thinking and orientation), meso-field processes (group conversing), macro-field processes (institutional structuring), and "mundo-field" processes (global eco-system coordination) (Scharmer & Kaufer, 2013). For Scharmer (2008) and Hannon, Gillinson and Shanks (2013), the development of the micro field starts at a deep level of an individual's connection to knowledge, then reacts to internal and external domains, generating new thought and opportunities, and creating new possibilities to tackle challenges. The Theory U trajectory resonates with an entrepreneurship training shift from classroom teaching to action learning – static and content-oriented teaching no longer matching the needs of change-driven economies (Bodhanya, 2014; Goodman, 2014; Oyugi, 2014).

This chapter explores the systemic levels that influence the development of IEO propensities present in the SHAPE social technology , outlines how it evolved theoretically, and draws on Theory U during the illustrative moment of 'Meet Your Business Friend Day.' Our study demonstrates that applying Theory U as a social technology, theoretical framework and research methodology, can play a significant role in boosting youth entrepreneurship in South Africa and lead to the significant and radically-positive transformation of young people's aspirations.

Theoretical framework

The elements of IEO and Theory U relate to one another in the entrepreneurial process in the following ways (Van der Westhuizen, 2016):

IEO risk and Theory U co-initiation:

Risk-taking propensity is a behavioral dimension of IEO which may drive the pursuit of opportunities. Broadly, IEO leads the way for innovative action on the part of an individual, and reactiveness is associated with an individual's response to competitors or external stimuli (Lumpkin & Dess, 1996; Ramkissor & Cassim, 2013). Co-initiation of IEO occurs on an intrapersonal level and an interpersonal level (Gardner, 2003). Individuals find resources within themselves that inspire them to initiate the entrepreneurial process, and they also engage with others in various environments and in the public domain to explore entrepreneurial options and possibilities.

IEO risk and Theory U co-sensing:

The co-sensing stage is paramount because entrepreneurs can break through old patterns by stepping into different but relevant experiences (van der Westhuizen, 2016). The co-sensing stage helps the would-be entrepreneur to build relationships with key stakeholders, acquiring a widened perspective of the environment as an undivided reality where fragmented social realities are deconstructed, and collective growth is encouraged (Pillay, 2016). According to Scharmer and Kaufer (2013), individuals observe and are influenced by actions and interactions in various systems around them, and there are four levels of system that influence IEO: a) the *micro system,* synonymous with an individual's mindset; b) the *meso-system,* or direct environment where the individual is co-sensing the entrepreneurial process; c) the *macro-system,* including local economic development field in which the individual is located; and d) the *mundo-system,* the bigger economic picture on a national and global scale (Jackson, 2003; Scharmer & Kaufer, 2013).

IEO innovation and Theory U co-inspiring.

One definition of entrepreneurial innovation cited by Lumpkin and Dess (2001) is a "willingness to support creativity and experimentation in introducing new products/services, and novelty, technological leadership and research and development in developing new processes. In an earlier paper (Lumpkin & Dess, 1996:), the same authors note that, as an IEO propensity, "innovation is an important means of pursuing opportunities."

Intrapersonal and interpersonal integration potentially makes individuals more receptive to a source of inspiration (Scharmer & Kaufer, 2013), and more likely to reach an 'aha' moment of insight (Jung-Beeman et al., 2004; Weinberg, 2014).

In the Theory U process, co-inspiring is synonymous with pre-sensing (Scharmer & Kaufer, 2013). With this alternative term, the emphasis is on the birth of a creative and novel idea, or an 'aha' moment that can lead to innovation. The link between successful innovations in entrepreneurship and the interrelationship between Theory U co-inspiring and IEO innovation is therefore crucial not only to boost entrepreneurship but also to transform entrepreneurial thinking amongst individuals.

IEO proactivity and Theory U co-creating.

For Callaghan (2009:), "proactiveness is related to initiative and first-mover advantages" through the pursuit of new opportunities and acting in anticipation of future problems. For Lumpkin and Dess (1996:), the importance of proactiveness is its "forward-looking perspective" for entrepreneurial activity and innovation. Fiebig (2015) describes proactiveness as a behavioural trait where individuals constantly seek opportunities and have a forward-looking perspective.

When IEO leads to entrepreneurial intention, the individuals concerned are engaging in the process of co-creation. This process can occur on an intrapersonal level, where the individual moves towards entrepreneurial activity. Interpersonal co-creations occur, where the individual moves towards more formal business friendships or entrepreneurial activities. Scharmer and Kaufer (2013) indicate that these co-creations often lead to prototyping, where one creates ideas, innovatively develops them and tests them in the market. Prototyping of entrepreneurial intention may thus result in entrepreneurial activity. Prototyping that stems from entrepreneurial intention thus may result in entrepreneurial activity (Weinberg, 2014).

IEO proactivity and Theory U co-evolving.

After developing a prototype, individuals might move into entrepreneurial activity either alone or through partnerships. According to Scharmer and Kaufer (2013), the extent of entrepreneurial activity marks the outflow intensity of the U process.

The literature suggests that a possible way to boost youth entrepreneurship in South Africa is to develop levels of IEO. The processes outlined in Theory U offer a potential pathway for individuals to move from a reactive response field to a generative response field, with the potential enhancement of IEO.

Empirical investigation: correlation between IEO and Theory U factors

As part of a pilot for the SHAPE social technology , we investigated the potential correlation of IEO and Theory U factors using a structured questionnaire with 27 question items. Examples of question items that are associated with IEO and U factors are: "*I can handle risky situations with confidence*"; "*I am creative and new business ideas comes easily to me*"; and "*I am comfortable moving into new situations*". The questionnaire was administered to 380 second-year students at UKZN. The data we collected gave us a baseline for the SHAPE development. Differences in IEO and Theory U factor scores were examined between male and female participants. Since none of the scores were normal, a non-parametric test supports that, overall, IEO and Theory U scores of male and female participants were similar. Both genders indicated similarities in moving from a reactive to a generative response field. We found that no significant differences exist in scores on IEP and Theory U dimensions for participants of different ages.

However, there was a statistically significant correlation

(p<0.01) between IEO scores and Theory U scores. Theory U suggests that there should be a positive correlation between co-inspiring and co-initiating or co-sensing.

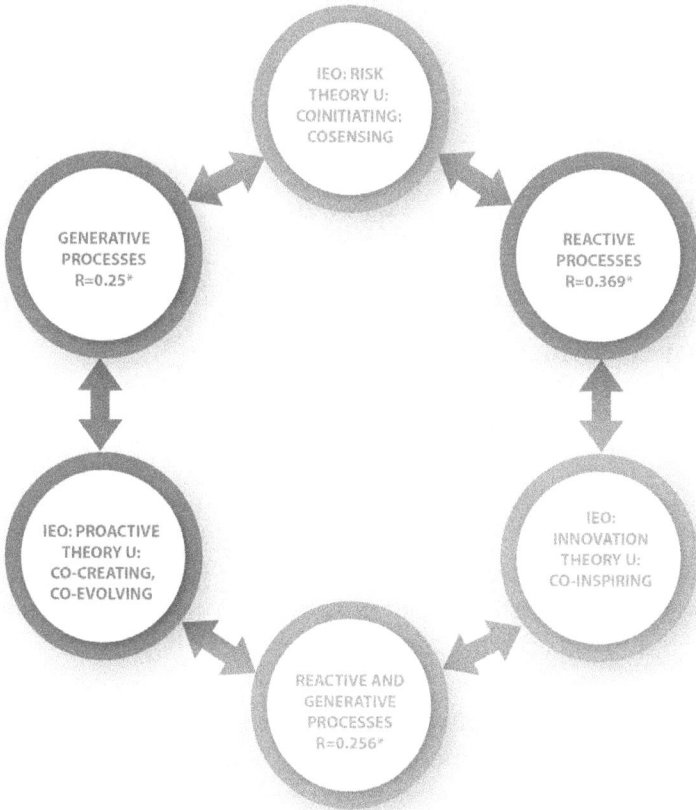

Figure 1: Correlations between IEO Propensities and Theory U (Source: van der Westhuizen, 2016)

In addition, co-inspiring should be correlated positively with co-creating and co-evolving. Our results showed that risk factors, which are part of Theory U's reactive processes of co-initiating and co-sensing, were significantly related to innovation as a co-inspiring factor in Theory U, confirming Theory U's interrelationships (van der Westhuizen, 2017). We also found that co-inspiring was significantly related to co-creating or co-evolving, likewise confirming Theory U's interrelationshipsInterrelationships and correlations between Theory U and IEO factors (Figure 1) were used to plot the sequence of events and activities for Meet Your Business Friend Day.

Background to practice

We give an account here of the systemic action learning and action research that preceded Meet Your Business Friend Day which enabled it to become an event for enhancement of co-inspiring/presencing.

Enhance co-inspiring/presencing

Building on the notion of action learning and action research as outlined by Revans (2011), Schweikert, Meissen and Wolf (2013) propose a *systemic* extension of this approach, which they describe as an interactive process between local stakeholders and the researcher that enable individuals involved to bring diverse knowledge and a dialogical process to a problem or challenge [and] that allows the researcher to observe and act upon dynamics at the systemic level. The SHAPE social technology involves systemic interactivity between student entrepreneurs, their intermediaries from the business world, and the practitioner-researcher to (jointly) investigate and find solutions to challenges that young entrepreneurs inevitably encounter. van der Westhuizen (2016) identified systemic intermediaries to support student entrepreneurs. However, within the process of intermediaries supporting student entrepreneurs, several barriers prevented successful and sustainable interaction. These stem mostly form personal barriers that student entrepreneurs have with their interrelationships to intermediaries. IEO as a personality trait can therefore be seen as either a barrier of an enabler to entrepreneurial action. Developed levels of IEO from student entrepreneurs might lead to improved relationships and collaboration with various systemic roleplayers and eventually result into socio-economic development, as a result of entrepreneurial momentum gained throughout systemic levels.

Meet Your Business Friend Day

Meet Your Business Friend Day was a concluding workshop for SHAPE participants, representing Phase 8, of the overall SHAPE social technology . Figure 2 shows a full outline of the phases and timelines in the SHAPE cycles, as guided by overarching stages in the Theory U cycle. In this case, Theory U was used as both a framework for the project social technology and as a research methodology.

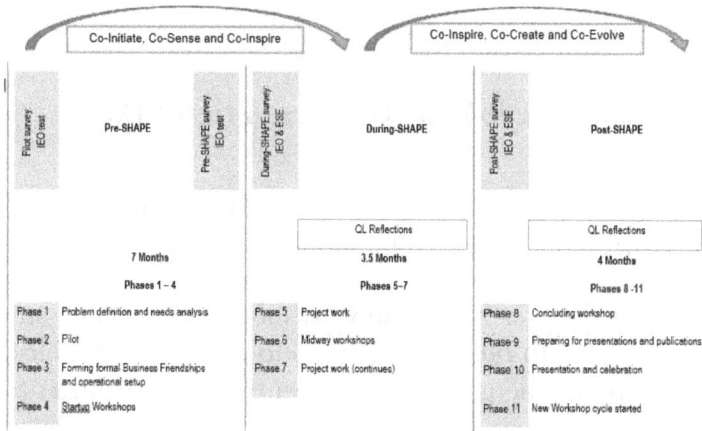

Figure 2 : Phases and Timelines in the SHAPE Social Technology / Research Methodology (Source: van der Westhuizen, 2016)

In the Meet Your Business Friend Day event, student entrepreneurs engaged with business professionals to explore possibilities for further entrepreneurial action through mutual co-inspiration, co-creation, and co-evolution in "Business Friendships" potentially formed between them. The event was also facilitated by intermediaries for the student entrepreneurs previously engaged for the project (municipality mentors, government mentors, Local Economic Development tutors; UKZN practitioner-researcher), who helped to bring in the experienced entrepreneurs and business professionals. At this point in the program, students arrived at a full experience of the U process, encountering what Scharmer calls "Economies of Creation" (Page reference?). In 'Meet Your Business Friend Day' the spiral cycles of the SHAPE systemic action learning and action research methodology materialized as looped experiences and actions: firstly, through the student entrepreneurs' inner experiences, secondly through relationships experienced with their peers, and thirdly through relfection upon the supporting structure involving the university, municipality mentors, Chamber of Commerce mentors, and tutors from the UKZN Local Economic Development unit.

Logistics for "Meet Your Business Friend Day"

Meet Your Business Friend Day activities: beginning action learning and action research methods

The overall objective of the workshop was to match student entrepreneurs with business mentors to stimulate possible partnerships between them. Each student entrepreneur had a nascent business idea – a basic and novel idea for creating a new venture to be shared with a business mentor who would be a sounding board, helping them with advice, counsel, and networking opportunities to shape the raw and underdeveloped ideas into a viable business opportunity.

The planned sequence of sessions was designed to match each young entrepreneur with a business mentor not necessarily on the strength and detail of the business idea but on the 'chemistry' and resonance between the two parties. This objective was based on the Theory U principle of having an Open Heart, where participants in a systemic action learning and action research project develop capabilities to listen emphatically to one another and try to see the world, and their entrepreneurial passions, through the eyes of somebody else (Schweikert et al., 2013). This called for a workshop design that would allow participants to explore their characteristics and attributes more holistically, going beyond just conceptual and intellectual issues.

Session 2, 'Building the Network,' was designed as a self‐ reflexive exercise for holistic exploration by each participant of the various facets of their identity and construction of self, taking account of the following dimensions:

- emotional
- mind / cognitive
- harmony / musical / balance
- active / kinesthetic
- spiritual / religious
- other information / general

These helped participants explore and illustrate important facets of their identity and arrive at a concise self-description; they were each given an identity board and asked to allocate 18 points among these six dimensions.

Using the identity boards, 'speed-dating' then took place with two concentric circles facing each other; young entrepreneurs in the inner circle and business mentors in the outer circle. Three minutes were given to share identity boards and to engage in discussions, after which the outer circle rotated by one space and the process repeated itself until all those in the inner circle had shared identity boards with all those in the outer circle.

The next step was for participants to self-organize in a way that matched business mentors (business friends) with young entrepreneurs. With the number of student entrepreneurs exceeding the number of business mentors, this meant that each business mentor was allocated a group of student entrepreneurs. Once this allocation was completed, participants began sharing business concepts.

For Session 3, 'Beach Activity', participants were divided into ten groups, each including business mentors and young entre-preneurs, competing in team-building activities on the beach (or sometimes in the water) designed in various ways to elicit and model fact-finding, business intelligence, decision-making, skills assessment, information sharing, resource allocation, motivation, skill, stamina, and leadership.

Session 4 was devoted to developing a business canvass model for each of the business ideas. Business mentors assisted their young entrepreneurs with 'teasing out' their business concepts in more detail, focusing explicitly on key attributes of their business concept as set out in a template covering eight broad categories:

- resources
- funding
- costs
- revenues
- value chain activities
- competencies
- value proposition
- team members

In addition, the business teams considered issues of competitiveness and engaged in a creative activity to design an appropriate tag line.

The business canvass used at this point was a more elaborate form of the basic business model canvass that had been used during contact sessions in the preceding phase (Phase 7) of SHAPE. It was accordingly familiar to the student entrepreneurs but new to the business friends.

In Session 5 the beach-clubhouse venue was turned into an Arabian-style 'Souk' marketplace. Each of the business teams was allocated space and an assortment of materials (play dough, foil, crayons, old magazines, empty toilet rolls, etc.) to exhibit and demonstrate their business concept at a stand in the Souk. The objective was to develop a prototype or some other kind of presentation of the core business concept that gave 'visitors' a convincing impression of the value of the proposition. The exhibit could be a physical replica of a product or a symbolic and metaphorical depiction of the underlying business concept. Once the exhibits were constructed, some teams remained behind as exhibitors and others became visitors to the Souk. This continued through a few cycles until all participants had been both an exhibitor and a 'visitor' to view and engage with the other exhibits. This was followed by a debriefing to extract the lessons and make connections between the activities and the way they related to the overall purpose of the workshop.

Connection on an emotional level was a continuous thread linking all sessions, with the initial emphasis on entrepreneurial 'heartset' rather than mindset, followed by shared reflections on personal identity, then team beach activities, putting both student entrepreneurs and their potential business friends in a more receptive frame of mind for co-creating and co-evolving possible entrepreneurial activity.

The workshop ended with a feedback activity, coordinated by the lead researcher, in which all participants made music for themselves with tapping and drumming to accompany words and singing. This served as an object lesson showing how it was possible for all to arrive at a point of coherence and synchronization.

Figure 3: The Clubhouse Venue (Source: Van der Westhuizen, 2016)

Figure 4: Discovering Team Member Skills (Source: van der Westhuizen, 2016)

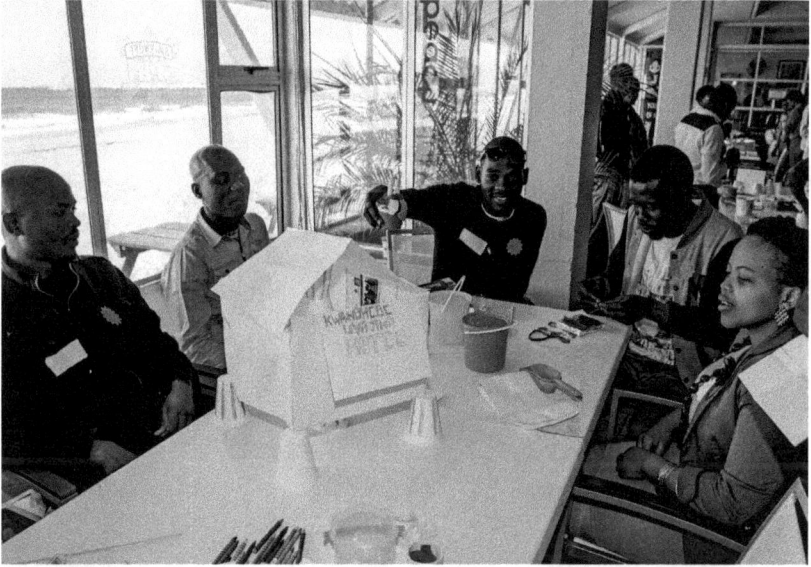

Figure 5 : Prototyping and Co-Creating a New Business Concept (van der Westhuizen, 2016)

Figure 6: Speed Dating: Identifying Entrepreneurial Heartset before Building Entrepreneurial Mindset (Source van der Westhuizen, 2016)

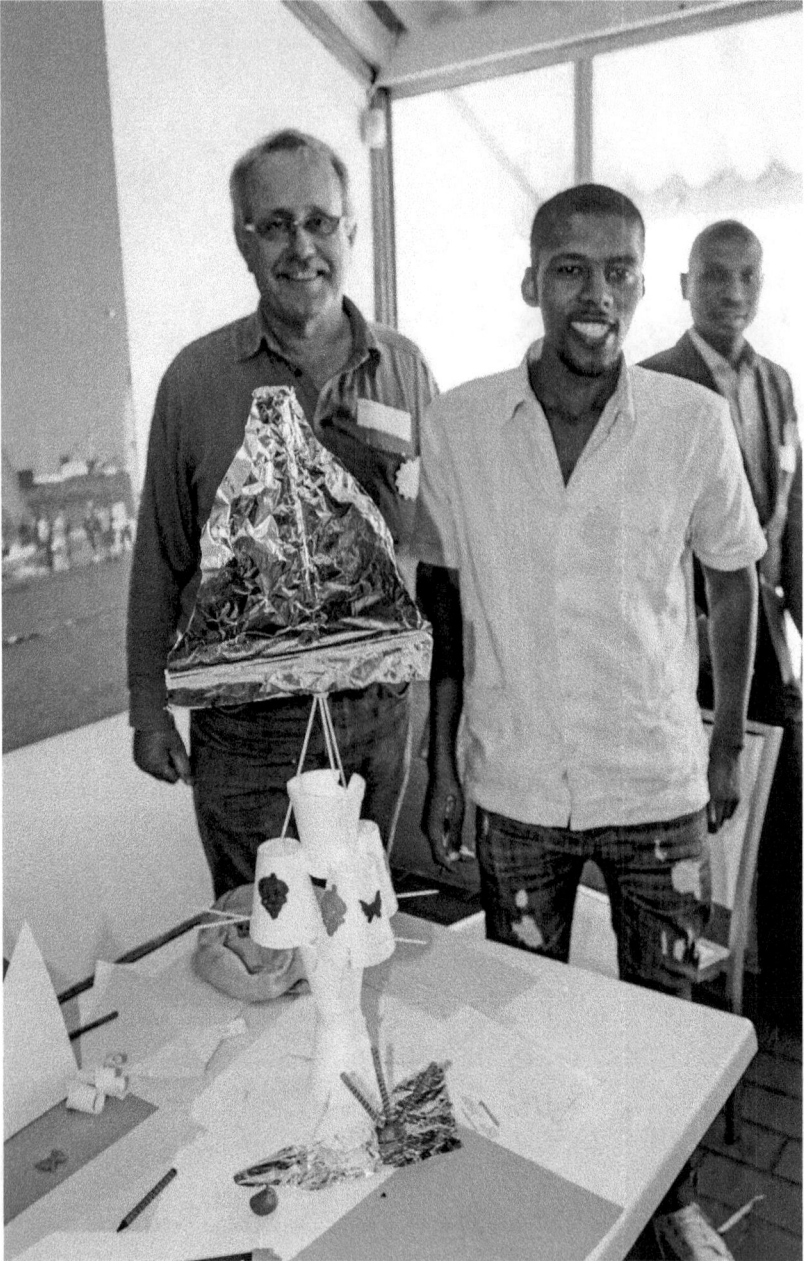

Figure 7 : Student Entrepreneurs and Business Friends ready to Co-Create and Co-Evolve (Source: van der Westhuizen, 2016)

Figure 8: Working on the Business Canvass (Source: van der Westhuizen, 2016)

In a follow-up analysis of the workshop event, the following categories emerged:

- Student entrepreneurs who wished to co-create and co-evolve solo with their business ideas;
- Business professionals who wished to co-create and co-evolve solo with their business ideas;
- Student entrepreneurs who wished to co-create and co-evolve together with other student entrepreneurs with their business ideas;
- Student entrepreneurs who wished to co-create and co-evolve together with other student entrepreneurs and business professionals with their business ideas; and
- Business professionals who wished to co-create and co-evolve together with other business professionals.

Qualitative Methodology

Participants (sample size N = 60) were volunteering second-year B.Comm undergraduates at the University of KwaZulu-Natal . Students were asked to write reflections which were
published on the project website. A qualitative thematic analysis
of data was used where themes were allowed to emerge from the
data. From the inductive coding process, themes and nodes
emerged from the text and were identified, along with simultaneous sub-themes and sub-nodes. Word frequencies, word tag
clouds and word trees were identified in the During-SHAPE and
Post-SHAPE stage from participants' reflections to support the
thematic analysis.

All indicated that they would like further support from systemic structures that were in place to assist the student entrepreneurs such as the University, the Municipality, the Chamber of
Commerce and the Local Economic Development Unit. They
also indicated that they would welcome further business development support from financial institutions such as banks.

A number of subsequent student comments on what they had
gained from Meet Your Business Friend Day and from the SHAPE
social technology overall, reflected the aptness of the Theory U
social technology underlying the concept of Business Friendship
and the broad design of SHAPE.

The Business Friendships not only made possible actualization of the student entrepreneur's aspirations for a higher state
of Self and Work, but also created opportunities for expressing
these aspirations. One comment made clear the need of co-devel-
opment with others to realize inner aspirations:

> Having my own business was definitely on the top of my
> list of goals but I just didn't know how to get there, who
> were the right people I had to talk to, and how to go about
> getting everything that I needed.

SHAPE used Theory U as a) research methodology, b) an
applied social technology and c) a theoretical framework. The
role that relationships and Business Friendships play in develop-

ing IEO for the student entrepreneur are evident in the following:
Another comment captured the broad advantage for IEO of a Business Friendship:

> Relationships, networking, and just generally interacting with multiple stakeholders serve multiple purposes.

As another student remarked,

> When you are young, the concept of networking is very alien and you don't know how to go about raising capital. SHAPE decides to close that gap, so exciting!

The first Business Friendship or partnership identified by the students was indeed SHAPE itself, which students saw as a means to reach their previously internal aspirations:

> Partnerships with team leaders and facilitators serve the purpose of allowing us to think beyond our own realm of thought -- and start thinking about other sources of information necessary for further growth.

The next set of Business Friendships or partnerships they identified were with their peers. For the first time, they had met and interacted with like-minded individuals:

> Relationships with classmates and other people on the program serves to encourage them, and help to think and discuss matters on deeper levels.

Meet Your Business Friend Day highlighted the benefit offered by external stakeholders creating important opportunities in the external environment, where students gave expression to their ideas and ultimately achieved both personal and societal-level goals.

Partnering with [representatives of] UKZN/Municipalities

etc. – make opportunities for practicing and implementing ideas a reality.

Two common themes emerged in the discourse around Business Friendships: interaction with: like-minded individuals, and interaction with people seen as key roleplayers in helping the young entrepreneur achieve goals and come to terms with Self and Work aspirations.

The first theme – the ability to interact with like-minded individuals – demonstrates that the ability to have an Open Heart often develops simultaneously and not as a separate or fragmented process, since it is important to listen emphatically to other individuals and to be receptive to their ideas in order to adjust their own mental models to identify and connect with those of others (Southern, 2013). This evidently happened with the SEs, as is also shown in the following quote:

> It has been such an eye-opening experience when I got the chance to interact with peers who also share the same thoughts about what society needs and what we as individuals need.

The second theme is identifying people to assist in realizing aspirations for Self and Work to create more business opportunities, thereby demonstrating the development of entrepreneurial mindset about opportunity identification (Cox et al., 2002) and proactivity (Callaghan, 2009). This was also evident in the reflections from SEs:

> I believe [that] for my business to grow I will need to have people to advise me. I feel honored to get into SHAPE because we will get to meet other successful entrepreneurs who might be interested to join forces in the field I'm interested to get [in]to.

The next quote refers to the second type of Business Friendship (partnership) – ability to partner with like-minded individuals, or peers, allowing for a deeper discussion and understanding of common matters of interest. Reflections correspond with the argument put forward by Hannon et al., (2013) that deep-learning practices such as the U process can enable individuals to develop collectively a Bigger Picture in their pursuit of socio-economic development:

In addition, another student entrepreneur notes that their common ground relates back to having common interests, ideas and goals:

> knowing that there are young people that are as ambitious and dedicated to fulfilling their dreams of being successful entrepreneurs.

Being able to talk to like-minded peers about matters of shared concern suggests there is something common to this group of people – something that will need to be explored first: inherent differences between applicants and non-applicants for SHAPE, or conversely, inherently similarities between all applicants.

Responses such as these indicated that three aspects of Theory U were taking place:

- Student participants recognized like-mindedness with other SHAPE applicants.
- Student participants shared a common sense of like-heartedness.
- Student participants saw SHAPE as a means to link like-minded and like-hearted people for goal actualization.

As one student put it, if a little ungrammatically:

> SHAPE *came in a right time to right people.*

However, the enhanced socio-economic developmental attitudes, aspirations and activity bring forward challenges and obstacles as the journey to potential entrepreneurial action continues (Xavier, Kelley, Kew, Herrington. & Vorderwülbecke, 2013), and these are discussed in the remainder of this chapter.

Applying Theory U to develop individual entrepreneurial orientation

The objectives of this research included investigating how using the Theory U conceptual framework as a social technology develops the risk-taking, innovation and proactivity propensities of IEO.

IEO risk-taking propensity

The aspirant student entrepreneurs were now looking at the potential risks involved in becoming an actual entrepreneur. They had no previous experience with entrepreneurship before participating in SHAPE, so taking risks as an entrepreneur now took on a new reality for them. The risk-taking propensity of IEO is also related to the construct of opportunity identification (Callaghan, 2009). The students began to grasp that there are real risks involved in realizing their identified opportunities:

> Yes, I feel afraid to take risk but I always try to take risks because for me taking risks can reveal my abilities which I did not know about [them] before and I believe winning is[a] close friend of failing that [is] what make[s] me take risk[s] [to gain] new opportunities.
>
> That you can go from having all the money in the world to being bankrupt, and in debt. That risks are part of business should be seen as motivation to defy the odds.
>
> Taking risks [is] are part of the characteristics of an entrepreneur.
>
> Yes, I don't like taking risks. However, I do understand that the life of an entrepreneur is largely based on risk-taking.

Taking risks is a big part of being a young entrepreneur. One cannot embark on starting a business without taking any risks. From financing the business, to marketing and even deciding what kind of business to start up, every single decision is risky.

I am aware of the many risks involved in business now, and I feel that one has to be teachable and use opportunities available to try and overcome all the risks involved.

Thus, although some students commented that they did not like taking risks, they also realized that deciding to take some entrepreneurial risks is crucial if one wants to start a new business. Lumpkin and Dess (1996) consider that lack of experience in taking real entrepreneurial risks and in performing entrepreneurially under risky situations, as faced by these students, contributes significantly to how problem-solving is conceptually framed. This implies that the students now need to apply their newly framed entrepreneurial mental models to address challenges at hand in taking entrepreneurial action.

The reflections cited below suggest that by taking risks and embracing opportunities available to them, the students will unlock their aspirations for Self and Work that are vital if they hope to sustain their businesses. Hays (2013) notes that developing a higher sense of Being through questioning the Self and Work is quite difficult, as it was for the students because in a sense, risk forces you to get to know yourself better:

Yes, I feel afraid to take risk but I always try to take risks because for me taking risks can reveal my abilities which I did not know about [them] before.

The risk-taking propensity was also perceived as necessary in order to advance personally and professionally:

Yes. I believe risks occurs when you do not know what you are doing and unless you are willing to go the extra mile and find out, risks will always affect your thinking. And with that said, I believe taking risks is part of what it takes

417

to get ahead and that is what I plan on doing. I realized that without taking risks, you like doing nothing to move forward. You'll never know about something unless you try, investigate or pursue it.

And ultimately to reach the best possible future they envision for themselves,

> ... there is much risk in the entrepreneurial environment, but you have to be able to take risk, because risk is one of the aspects of entrepreneurs. You have to take risks in life to achieve a certain goal. Yes, I feel like being successful requires you to take risks. You cannot win a war with your gun on safety.

Risks are seen as an inevitable consequence of starting up a business (Lumpkin & Dess, 1996). The strategies of SHAPE enabled them to observe other entrepreneurs in real-life situations and also to interact with these entrepreneurs. Every respondent reflected on risks and the role of risk in developing their entrepreneurial abilities.

> I feel as I can take these risks because the businessmen have taken this risk.

In becoming young entrepreneurs, they perceive themselves as more resilient, able to pick themselves up after failure, and to realize opportunities that arise as a consequence.

> It is much easier to take risk as a young entrepreneur than when you [are] old and have a lot of responsibilities. So, if the[re] was a right time to take risks, I'd say that time is now.

Therefore, they see that being a young entrepreneur in South Africa sets them apart from older generations, confirming a similar observation made by Mitchell and Harris (2012). In a way, they, as youngsters, have more of an Open Will than older entrepreneurs do, possibly because opportunity costs for young entrepreneurs are relatively low (Hulsink & Koek, 2014).

Risk is seen as something that can be understood and managed if 'calculated' (Poole, 2014):

I as a young entrepreneur need to be able to calculate the risks at hand and [to] evaluate which is better for my business and myself.

Risk, when it is 'calculated' seems to become less likely to disable the young entrepreneurs' ability to pick themselves up in the event of failure. Here a risk is calculated, based on:

- Anticipating risks and their consequences involves the ability to predict and to take the appropriate action to prevent or to minimize its eventuality;
- A cost-benefit ratio that requires awareness of the consequences of risk; weighing up the benefits associated with the risks; and
- An internal locus of control that is the extent to which the individual sees the risk as manageable.

Anticipating risks and their consequences

The ability to anticipate risks is linked closely to the proactivity propensity in IEO (Lumpkin & Dess, 1996) and it is also an essential factor in willingness to take risks, which implies that the aspiring young entrepreneurs were able to identify possible risks and to do something about them in an attempt to control the risk.

Student entrepreneurs reflected on their vision for themselves as young entrepreneurs in the emerging future. What was the future then, is the current now, (Korthaugen, Hoekstra & Meijer, 2013), and a new future had started to emerge in which they saw themselves now faced with needing to take potential risks to make their vision a reality.

I learned that being proactive helps you with avoiding

problems in your business. You can expect them and start planning early how to solve them or [to] avoid them. I learned a lot about being in business and handling the pressure of it.

It is important as an entrepreneur to see things before they can or will actually happen and try to alleviate problems from happening or growing even bigger than what they are.

I [have] come a long way. Risk is a very broad word. I realized that taking risks needs a lot of thinking and having to be aware of the consequences of your risky decisions.

From these reflections, it seems as if the aspiring young entrepreneurs learned from their interaction and experiences with other entrepreneurs – an opportunity that the SHAPE social technology made possible for them. It also seems as if they began to think about possible solutions to the potential risks that they might encounter, as well as the potential costs and benefits to them.

Cost–benefit ratio

The aspiring young entrepreneurs, in starting to anticipate entrepreneurial risks, also started to calculate the social and economic cost-benefit ratio – which again required them to look critically at their financial, social and environmental wealth (Zahra, Newey & Li, 2014). The aspiring young entrepreneurs seem to have developed an awareness of the consequences of taking risks as an entrepreneur:

I realized that you have to take calculated risks. Not every risk is worth taking. You have to look at your opportunity cost. Taking risks is a big deal and is something that has to [be] thought [about] carefully and weighed against all benefits. Risks can turn out unsuccessful or successful but the aim is to get what you want done, so it is worth it to take a risk and have alternative plans in-case [this] doesn't work out. The life of an entrepreneur is largely based on risk taking; therefore I am willing to do so but making every necessary provision for alternative outcomes. Yes, I am more aware of taking risks. Initially I thought I was fine with taking risks but when taking such huge risks there's always that possibility that the risk will not pay off.

These reflections suggest how students were acquiring the ability, or strengthening their ability to weigh the potential benefits and losses associated with entrepreneurial risk – benefits and losses that Zahra et al., (2014) distinguish as a) financial, b) social and c) environmental. In Theory U terms, this is critical thinking and introspective learning, which the aspiring young entrepreneurs develop in the course of their transformative journey in the U-Curve (Korthaugen et al., 2013).

Internal locus of control

Internal locus of control relates to the extent to which the aspiring young entrepreneurs see the risk as manageable, and relates closely to their levels of Entrepreneurial Self-Efficacy and Individual Entrepreneurial Orientation (Dunwoody & Griffin, 2014). The aspiring young entrepreneurs began to think about how they would handle potential entrepreneurial risks:

It is better to take a calculated risk, one that I know I can manage as an individual. There are a lot of risks that occur in the process but the ability to manage and tolerate those risks is important. Yes, I am aware[of] the risk of having a fail[ed] business. What if your business idea doesn't work out and what if it does work out and doesn't make any profit? I am aware of all these risks and I feel like [that] I still need to assess myself if I can [be able to] handle them. Personally, I think that taking a risk is dangerous but it is better to take a calculated risk, one that I know I can manage as an individual or one that I know will not affect other people.

The aspiring young entrepreneurs reflected that they might be able to mitigate the 'riskiness' of risk by taking things whence they came. This shows an element of the self-tolerance factor in Entrepreneurial Self-Efficacy (Dunwoody & Griffin, 2014), which will be discussed as a further theme in this chapter. In a way, tolerance mitigates the extent of the risk, and risk can also be mitigated by taking advantage of appropriate opportunities and being proactive. Through reflection on how they saw themselves managing risks as an aspiring young entrepreneur, they also developed a problem-solving capacity concerning the entrepreneurial risks that might arise.

This questioning of problem solving and anticipation of entrepreneurial risks might, therefore, lead them to generate new knowledge and thus come up with some form of individual innovation – thereby undergoing transformation, which implies a change in developmental maturity (Fitch & O'Fallon, 2013).

IEO Innovation propensity

In moving to become actual entrepreneurs, the students were still developing their business concepts. There was no evidence of reflections about product innovation in the Post-SHAPE stage, but intrinsic individual transformation and innovation were strongly evident in the During-SHAPE stage – which implied a change in developmental maturity (Fitch & O'Fallon, 2013). A possible explanation for this is that students had already moved beyond the co-inspiring or presencing phase of the U-Curve as they now began to co-create and co-evolve as aspirant young entrepreneurs.

IEO Proactivity propensity

Intrinsic to innovation is an element of proactivity in that the individual acts on an idea or pushes further when an opportunity arises. This relates back to the empirical findings that an individual who is proactive acts from both the reactive and the generative response fields. Dealing with the problem reflexively requires both innovation and being proactive.

> It is crucial to be innovative as an entrepreneur because the obstacles that come up sometimes requires there to be change.

Also, individuals need to be well aware of the opportunities available to them to ensure that they are proactive:

> Being proactive as a young entrepreneur requires a lot of time and commitment. It requires you to be well versed about the opportunities available around you.

For the aspiring young entrepreneurs to be proactive they need to have knowledge and information available to them. Without the support of intermediaries, or educational information, the ambitious young entrepreneurs feel unable to see their way to implementing and anticipating and acquiring the necessary tolerance in business activity.

> Yes, as a new entrepreneur almost every move is a risk, as you would be new and would be literally blindly feeling your way through business.

Again the role of the 'other' becomes explicit in knowledge generation, management, and self-awareness and confidence. When sufficient entrepreneurial skills are developed, and information is available and has been absorbed, the aspiring young entrepreneur is in a better position to anticipate and calculate risks and to take the necessary steps to mitigate them and improve the chances of success:

> Yes, I feel risk-taking is a good thing because it's always 50/50 either you pass or fail, but you can ensure that you go into a risk with enough information that might aid in getting a business success rather than a failure.

In the beginning my biggest challenge was doubt and not having that much belief in my ability to be a successful entrepreneur. one of the bigger challenges is not having information or enough of it.

Information is of such importance to the aspiring young entrepreneurs that they feel unable to take risks until they are sufficiently informed:

I think I will not be able to take risk[s] at the moment, at least I will learn more about business before I start my own.

Anticipating risks implies proactivity:

Being proactive as an entrepreneur is about taking charge and knowing that if things do go wrong along the way that you will take full responsibility and move on from there.

Being proactive allows the aspiring young entrepreneur to anticipate risks, and as previously discussed, when a risk can be anticipated, its effect can be mitigated, increasing the aspiring young entrepreneur's capacity for tolerance:

I learn[ed] that [to] be proactive enable[s] entrepreneur[s] to anticipate challenges that she/he did not know about before and also [to] bring about confidence in entrepreneurship.

Again, the link between proactivity, innovation, and tolerance is made, and often in relation to risk.

Enablers of actualizing entrepreneurial vision: Open Mind, Heart and Will

Open Mind

Open Mind refers to an individual's capacity to suspend old patterns of thought and listen to what others are saying. In this case, 'others' alludes to previous discussions on relations with other people, including peers and intermediaries, giving support to the aspiring young entrepreneurs. Through these interactions, they listen to the 'other' and internalize what has been said to bring about changes within themselves. Guttenstein, Lindsay and Baron (2013) believe that these collective processes enable individuals to cross thresholds together, therefore to change collectively in developmental maturity.

Here, the participants acknowledge how SHAPE and the intermediaries they have been exposed to, assisted in their individual development and further assisted them to have an open mind:

I have been exposed to many different people from different walks of life who have planted ideas in my mind which has made me think more intensively.

It is evident here that through interactions with others the participants acknowledge differences in perspectives and different ways of thinking, and instead of shutting them out they allow their minds to be opened to new ways of thinking and doing things.

This is the first programme,[sic] I have actually been part of. Through this programme[sic] I have actually realized that I am a dedicated person, I given 100% to whatever I sign up for This has been myself finding myself through being part of the programme.[sic

This new way of thinking and doing things is further evident in the next statement:

> I learned about how to listen attentively and [about] breathing exercises

By allowing themselves space within which to reflect on what others, with different opinions, have imparted to them, they begin to interrogate their own self-concept and belief, and introspectively gain a better understanding of who they are. Peschl and Fundneider (2013) suggest that primary or deep knowledge, which is related to the notion of wisdom, might the result of an observation process that is conducted with a highly open mind. Therefore, one might say that transformation, or a change in developmental maturity occurred (Fitch & O'Fallon, 2013).

As they come to know and develop themselves better and their self-concept [grows], so too their way of thinking around business changes.

> I learned that it is important to invest in a business idea that is your niche. It surprised me [at] how many times my business idea changed because of the lessons I was taught.

This change in developmental maturity, which enables the student entrepreneur to move from an old self to a new Self might be an indication of movement through the U-Curve from a reactive to a generative response field (Gunnlaugson & Walker, 2013). Therefore, the reactive propensity of IEO Risk, the generative propensity of IEO Innovation and the reactive/generative propensity of IEO Proactivity (opportunity identification) has developed (Van der Westhuizen, 2017).

Open Heart

Having an Open Heart refers to an individual's capacity to empathize or to see a situation through the eyes of somebody else. Unlike the Pre-SHAPE and During-SHAPE phases, where expression of empathy was chiefly aimed at bringing about positive change in society as a whole (feelings of ubuntu78), there now seems to have been an acknowledgement of the role of self in relation to the whole. In other words, when the participants first embarked on SHAPE, they were only aware of change that needed to take place on a systemic level to bring about socio-economic improvement. Thus they were aware of transformation that needs to happen in communities where they live, or in South Africa as a whole. However, the blind spot seems to have been an inward journey towards their own Entrepreneurial Self-Efficacy and IEO abilities and capabilities to bring about entrepreneurial action needed for systemic change. In other words, they failed to acknowledge their own innovative entrepreneurial action that leads to the change they want to see within the external whole. This echoes Pillay's (2014) comment that correlates with the view that as the entrepreneurial mindset develops there is more cognizance of internal orientation in relation to the external whole. This acknowledgement of both individualistic and collective ways of thinking and acting is indicative of a developing entrepreneurial mind (Richardson & Hynes, 2008; Kickul et al., 2009).

Seeing situations afresh through the eyes of a newly developed Self is indicated in the following quote:

> I learned doing things that will make you happy at the end. I learned that I should do things that are from the bottom of my heart. first thing[s] first is to find yourself and what you like. I learned to be innovative and creative. It has been amazing

This might imply that the students had a change in developmental maturity in the way they see entrepreneurship and making money. They suggest they are beginning to realize the importance of 'learning a living' rather than 'earning a living' (Hannon et al., 2013) where living creatively and positively means that you are living for more than just financial gain

Open Will

Having an Open Will (the ability to let go and let come), the young entrepreneurs come to realize how little they previously knew; therefore, change has occurred in their developmental maturity. Moving from a reactive response field, where individuals let go of past preconceptions and personal experiences, a certain internal realization needs first to take place – this is also referred to as 'Presencing', 'co-inspiring' or 'connecting to the Source' (Scharmer, 2009). This Presencing moment results in a generative response field, where an individual enables the emerging future. Thus an individual's Open Mind and Open Heart enables the Open Will to let go of past ways of thinking and doing, resulting in receptiveness to letting into their entrepreneurial mindset new ways of feeling, thinking and acting (Fitch & O'Fallon, 2013).

Evidence of first letting go to allow for letting come:

> As optimistic as you should be as an entrepreneur, the first step always takes blind faith and the belief that what you doing is right. I've learned to be free, more open minded especially of my surroundings and not (to) be negligent.

Letting come often created meaningful interactions with others whereby new things were learned:

> I have learned so many things including to have a good relationship with mates, working together with groups, we combined many different new ideas with others and listen to other ideas.

By letting go, participants could allow assimilation of new perspectives, and these new perspectives ultimately allowed the new Self to emerge.

> Coming up with new ideas has grown me physically and mentally, being innovative gives you more opportunities/ alternatives to succeed in building your future or career.

And in letting go, participants created the space to allow learning new experiences, and this emergent knowledge allowed them to also learn new things about themselves:

> I have learned about myself the following: Self-Confidence, Communication Skills and Being around Peers with Business Minds.

In the context of this research, the 'somebody else' can be interpreted as the participant in relation to other individuals, and also as the participant as transformative human being.

> I have learned a lot from SHAPE, including how important perseverance is, what it takes to be successful and I also learned that everything that you want to pursue do it with your love, heart and be passionate about it. I also learned you shouldn't rush at things just give [it] time and relax.

These reflections on Open Will might indicate that transformative learning took place – since the student now sees both themselves and the Whole (the systems or the world they live in) differently (Korthaugen et al., 2013). It also might imply that they developed the ability to deconstruct their own mental models (their preconceived realities) and open up to new knowledge and new realities, not only about entrepreneurship but about themselves as well (Schweikert et al., 2013). Therefore, a transformation of the entrepreneurial mindset occurred – contributing positively to sparking socio-economic development in South Africa, starting on a micro scale where a change in developmental maturity occurred in entrepreneurial hearts and entrepreneurial minds of this youthful group.

Systems Perspective

Seen systemically, each individual constitutes a micro-system closely linked to various processes at differing levels of systemic development. The 2015 Global Entrepreneurship Monitor notes that a person's heartset and mindset, and his or her entrepreneurial profile, attitudes, activities and aspirations, are directly linked to national and indeed global socio-economic development (Herrington & Kew, 2016). If entrepreneurialism is to spur socio-economic development, one possible starting point could be to develop those internal domains of aspirant individuals – the individual micro-system – by tapping into resources that are reachable at other systemic levels (Van der Westhiuzen, 2016). These resources can include intermediaries from: a) universities, b) municipality business support units, c) communities, d) private sector practitioners who support youth entrepreneurs, e) parastatals and agencies set out to develop commerce or f) a Local Economic Development Unit embedded within a government entity (van der Westhuizen, 2016).

Conclusion

Taking the happenings of 'Meet Your Business Friend Day' a few years into the future as in November 2017, we surveyed the 2014-2015 cycle participants to investigate how they progressed in their lives as young entrepreneurs and potential graduates. The results showed that nearly all of them were strongly committed to continuing their education and to improving their academic qualifications: 49 percent were now in their honors year at university and 36 percent were doing post graduate courses such as a Master's degree. What's more, of those still at university, 36 percent were in part time employment, well above the national employment rate for this age group, and an incredible 59 percent were engaged part-time with an entrepreneurial activity.

Also, the SHAPE cycle of 2014–2015 was repeated in 2017 with amendments made from past lessons learned from both action learning and action research perspectives. During the 2017 cycle, 200 participants completer the 'renewed' version of Meet Your Business Friend Day' and the cycle resulted in 73 new business concepts that were prototyped and are ready for the next incubation phase. The research reported on in this chapter showed that cultivation of the Individual Entrepreneurial Orientation in terms of Theory U can indeed enhance the level of entrepreneurship among students in South Africa with positive consequences for youth entrepreneurship in general. Specific connections between Theory U and Individual Entrepreneurial Orientation were identified. These connections were between risk-taking in IEO and the co-initiating/co-sensing factors of Theory U, between innovation in IEO and the co-inspiring factor of Theory U), and between proactiveness in IEO and the co-creating/co-evolving factors of Theory U. It can be concluded that through observing and investigating over a period of time, the application of Theory U and Individual Entrepreneurial Orientation can be used to boost youth entrepreneurship.

Acknowledgements

This chapter, in part, is derived from the PhD thesis, supervised by Professor Kriben Pillay:

Van der Westhiuzen, (2016). *Developing individual entrepreneurial orientation: A systemic approach through the lens of Theory U.* (Unpublished PhD thesis). Durban: University of KwaZulu-Natal. South Africa.

Professor Kriben Pillay for mentoring the author in writing this chapter.

This work is based on the research supported in part by the National Research Foundation of South Africa (Grant Numbers: 122002).

Photo credits: Jon Ivins.

References

Bodhanya, S. (2014). *The nexus model for local economic development. Problems and Perspectives in Management, 12* (3), 7-15.

Callaghan, C. W. (2009). *Entrepreneurial orientation and entrepreneurial performance of central Johannesburg informal sector street traders.* (Unpublished M Comm Thesis). University of the Witwatersrand, South Africa.

Dunwoody, S. & Griffin, R. J. (2014). Risk information seeking and processing model. In H. Cho, T. Reimer, & K. McComas,. (Eds.) *The SAGE Handbook of Risk Communication.* Thousand Oaks, CA: Sage.

Fitch, G. & O'Fallon, T. (2013). Theory U applied in transformation development. In Gunnlaugson, C.Baron, & M.Cayer, (Eds.) *Perspectives on Theory U : Insights from the Field.* Hershey, PA, : Business Science Reference. USA.

Franke, N., & Lüthje, C. (2004). Entrepreneurial intentions of business students—A benchmarking study. *International Journal of Innovation and Technology Management, 1*(03), 269-288

Gardner, H. (2003, April). *Multiple intelligences after twenty years.* Paper presented at American Educational Research Association, Chicago, Illinois, USA.

Goodman, M. (2014. 25-28, March). *South African Presencing Foundation Course* [Workshop]. Cape Town, South Africa.

Goss, D. 2005. *Schumpeter's legacy? Interactions and emotions in the society of entrepreneurship.* Entrepreneurship Theory & Practice, Vol. 29, No. 2. pp. 205-218.

Gunnlaugson, O. & Walker, W. (2013). Deep Presencing leadership coaching: Building capacity for sensing, enhancing, and embodying emerging selves and futures in the face of organizational crisis. In O. Gunnlaugson, C. Baron, & M. Cayer, (Eds.) *Perspectives on Theory U : Insights from the Field.* Hershey, PA, USA: Business Science Reference.

Guttenstein, S., Lindsay, J. & Baron, C. (2013). Aligning with the emergent future. In O. Gunnlaugson, C. Baron, & M. Cayer,(Eds.) *Perspectives on Theory U : Insights from the Field.* Hershey, PA, USA: Business Science Reference.

Hannon, V., Gillinson, S., & Shanks, L. (2013). *Learning a living: Radical innovation in education for work.* Dohar: Bloomsbury.

Hays, J. (2013). Theory U and team performance: Presence, participation and productivity. In O. Gunnlaugson, C. Baron. & M. Cayer

(Eds.) *Perspectives on Theory U : Insights from the Field*. Hershey, PA, USA: Business Science Reference.

Herrington, M. & Kew, P. (2016). *Global Entrepreneurship Monitor: South African Report 2016. Is Sa Heading for an Economic Meltdown?*. Development Unit for New Enterprise, UCT, Cape Town

Hulsink, W. & Koek, D. (2014). The young, the fast and the furious: A study about the triggers and impediments of youth entrepreneurship. *International Journal of Entrepreneurship and Innovation Management, 18* (2-3), 182-209.

Jackson, M. C. (2003). *Systems thinking: Creative holism for managers.* Chichester, UK: Wiley.

Jung-Beeman, M., Bowden, E. M., Haberman, J., Frymiare, J. L., Arambel-Liu, S., Greenblatt, R., Reber, P. J. & Kounios, J. (2004). Neural activity when people solve verbal problems with insight. *PLoS biology, 2* (4), 500-510.

Kickul, J. & D'Intino, R. S. (2005). Measure for measure: Modeling entrepreneurial self-efficacy onto instrumental tasks within the new venture creation process. *New England Journal of Entrepreneurship, 8* (2), 6.

Kolb, A. Y. & Kolb, D. A. (2005). Learning styles and learning spaces: Enhancing experiential learning in higher education. *Academy of Management Learning & Education, 4* (2), 193-212.

Korthaugen, F. A. J., Hoekstra, a. & Meijer, P. C. (2013). Promoting presence in professional practice: A core reflection approach for moving through the U. In O. Gunnlaugson, C. Baron, C. & M. Cayer, (Eds.) *Perspectives on Theory U : Insights from the Field.* Hershey, PA, USA: Business Science Reference.

Lumpkin, G. T. & Dess, G. G. (1996). Clarifying the entrepreneurial orientation construct and linking it to performance. *Academy of Management Review, 21* (1), 135-172.

Mitchell, T. & Harris, K. (2012). *Resilience: A risk management approach.* Retrieved from http://www.odi.org/ publications/6271-resilience-risk-management-climate-change.

Oyugi, J. (2014). Effectiveness of the methods of teaching entrepreneurship courses to developing self-Efficacy and intention among university students in Uganda. *International Journal of Social Sciences and Entrepreneurship, 1* (11), 491-513.

Peschl, M. F. & Fundneider, T. (2013). Theory U and emergent innovation: Presencing as a method of bringing forth profoundly new knowledge and realities. In O. Gunnlaugson, C. Baron, C. & M. Cayer (Eds.) *Perspectives on Theory U : Insights from the Field.*

Hershey, PA, USA: Business Science Reference.

Pillay, K. (2014). Learning, the whole and Theory U: Reflections on creating a space for deep learning. *Problems and Perspectives in Management, 12* (4), 340-346.

Pillay, K. (2016) Learning and the illusion of solid and separate things: Troublesome knowledge and the curriculum. *Disrupting Higher Education: Undoing Cognitive Damage*, Samuel, MA, Dhunpath, R, Amin, N (eds). Rotterdam: Sense Publishers, pp.81-92.

Poole, L. (2014). *A calculated risk: How donors should engage with risk financing and transfer mechanisms.* n.p.: OECD Publishing.

Ramkissor, M. & Cassim, S. (2013). The entrepreneurial orientation and intention of UKZN MBA students.(Unpublished MComm thesis). Durban: University of KwaZulu-Natal. South Africa.

Revans, R. (2011). *ABC of action learning.* Burlington, VT: Gower Publishing, Ltd. USA.

Richardson, I. & Hynes, B. (2008). Entrepreneurship education: Towards an industry sector approach. *Education & Training, 50* (3), 188-198.

Scharmer, C. O. (2008). Uncovering the blind spot of leadership. *Leader to Leader,* (47), 52-59.

Scharmer, C. O. (2009). *Theory U: Learning from the future as it emerges.* San Francisco CA: Berrett-Koehler Publishers. USA.

Scharmer, C. O. & Kaufer, K. (2013). *Leading from the emerging future: From ego-system to eco-system economies.* San Francisco CA: Berrett-Koehler Publishers. USA.

Schweikert, S., Meissen, J. O. & Wolf, P. (2013). Applying Theory U: The case of the Creative Living Lab. In O. Gunnlaugson, C. Baron, & H. Cayer, (Eds.) *Perspectives on Theory U : Insights from the Field.* Hershey, PA, USA: Business Science Reference.

Southern, N. (2013). Presencing as being in care: Extending Theory U in a relational framework. In O. Gunnlaugson, C. Baron, & M. Cayer (Eds.) *Perspectives on Theory U : Insights from the Field.* Hershey, PA, USA: Business Science Reference.

Van der Westhiuzen, (2016). *Developing individual entrepreneurial orientation: A systemic approach through the lens of Theory U.* (Unpublished PhD thesis). Durban: University of KwaZulu-Natal. South Africa.

Van der Westhiuzen, T. (2017). Theory U and individual entrepreneurial orientation in developing youth entrepreneurship in South Africa. *Journal of Contemporary Management, 14*(1),.531-553.

Weinberg, I. (2014). The complete triangles model. *Pninet*. Retrieved from http://www.pninet.com/articles/Memory.pdf.

Xavier, S., Kelley, D., Kew, J., Herrington, M. & Vorderwülbecke, A. (2013). *Global Entrepreneurship Monitor (GEM) 2012*. Global Report. *GERA/GEM*.

Zahra, S. A., Newey, L. R. & Li, Y. (2014) On the frontiers: The implications of social entrepreneurship for international entrepreneurship. *Entrepreneurship Theory and Practice, 38* (1), 137-158.

CHAPTER 15

Using Theory U tools and principles to plan, organize and manage a Sporting Event in a Sustainable Way.

Cristiana Buscarini, Sara Franzini Gabrielli and Fabio Cerroni

Introduction

At the beginning of the new millennium, the United Nations' Members States adopted Millennium Development Goals (MDGs) and in 2015 they adopted Agenda 2030 for Sustainable Development. This clearly illustrates the unsustainability of the current socio-economic model. Agenda 2030 provides 17 Sustainable Development Goals (SDGs), an integrated set of goals, comprehensive in scope, directed to all countries and aimed at mobilizing all stakeholders (United Nations, 2015).

Many sporting bodies have committed to implement sustainable strategies; for example, The IOC (International Olympic Committee) demonstrated this by placing Environment as one of the three pillars of Olympic Movement alongside Sport and Culture.

There are two main documents to support this; Agenda 21,

which encourages all players of the Olympic Movement to play an active role in the sustainable development of our planet (IOC, 1999) and Agenda 2020, the IOC's strategic roadmap through which the IOC hopes to implement sustainability in all the aspects of the Olympic Games (IOC, 2014).

A few years earlier, the United Nations adopted Agenda 2030 and the International Organization for Standardization prepared "ISO / DIS 20121: 2012 Event sustainability management systems - requirements with guidance for use, published on June 15, 2012". This defines the requirements of an event sustainability management system, aiming to minimize the impact of an event on the community and on the environment in which it takes place. These guidelines foster the implementation of appropriate criteria for all three dimensions of sustainability and the adoption of methodologies that allow the systematic analysis of the contexts in which events are organised, taking into consideration expectations and relevant issues for all stakeholders and minimizing related risks.

Theory U and ISO20121: theoretical background

In this chapter, we aim to improve the culture of sustainability in Sport Systems by focusing on the organization of events, following ISO 20121 guidelines and through the principles and tools proposed by Theory U. The framework and the methodology of this Theory were developed in the last decade by a group of academics and action researchers at MIT led by Otto Scharmer (P. M. Senge, O. Scharmer et al, 2005; O. Scharmer, 2009, 2016; O. Scharmer, K. Kaufer, 2013).

Theory U is proposed as a methodology to foster the application of ISO 20121. It encourages an integrated approach that embraces the following three aspects:

1. A theoretical framework that helps to uncover and understand the root systemic causes that bring an organization to react with patterns and behaviors which generate the observed problems ("symptoms") and unintended consequences.

2. A methodology with tools and practices designed to facilitate profound innovation and transformation projects in a multi-stakeholder context.

3. An inner-leadership component (Presencing), aimed at developing the capacity of individuals and the group of stakeholders to re-connect to a more authentic self and "sensing and actualizing one's highest future possibility—acting from the presence of what wants to emerge."

The governing assumption of Theory U is that "the quality of results in any kind of socio-economic system is a function of the awareness that people in the system are operating from."

This methodology fosters internal cohesion and strengthens relationships within an organization and across different stakeholders. Additionally, and most importantly, it identifies "listening" as the single "most valuable" asset to take advantage of. Therefore, it can be applied both as a tool to develop internal aggregation for the organization, as well as to cultivate stakeholders' engagement, promoted by a shared awareness of the interdependencies of their actions on the whole system.

In the language of Theory U, this corresponds to the development of the capacities of

- the "open mind" (suspending judgment and access to the power of curiosity),
- the "open heart" (suspending cynicism and access to the power of empathy),
- the "open will" (the capacity of letting go of the fear of change to allow the current situation to evolve towards a more sustainable and inclusive future).

These capacities allow the group of stakeholders to co-develop and implement, through experimenting and rapid-cycle prototyping, new solutions to address the current challenge.

We decided to apply Theory U to support the implementation of sustainability guidelines throughout the whole process of event planning and management (ideation, planning, implementation, and legacy) as it promotes an "eco-centric" perspective on the overall process. Although there are other methodologies and organizational approaches available, we believe Theory U could be highly effective because it leads to an integral vision of the human person and of existence, strongly connected and interdependent with the other members of the community.

Many studies focus on the critical aspects of "traditional change programs", highlighting the need to rethink the "human being" and the vision of organizations to transform traditional planned change programs into generative approaches of both competences and processes. We see the necessity to involve people in the definition of change processes and to improve the quality of interactions (Passmore in Reason P., Bradbury H., 2001) and specifically the quality of dialogue (Argyris C., 2010; Beer M., 2011). Furthermore, Bradbury H., Mirvis P., Nielsen E., Passmore W., (2008) suggest that many organizations concerned with sustainability have not created the conditions for a sustainable culture. Changing behavior is not easy, launching initiatives and maintaining momentum is a huge challenge.

At the beginning of the Century, some authors analyzed the effectiveness of change methodologies showing that widely used interventions have led to poor results or have come to a complete stop (Boonstra JJ., 2004, Novara F., 2003, Del Val M.P., Fuentes C.M., 2003). This depends on a reductive vision, where the individual and the organization are considered as two independent realities. Organizational behavioral interventions and Human Resources are focused on the individual, considering the organization as an independent context (Hosking D.M.,, Morley I.E.,1991). Also, organizational theories do not consider the peculiarities of human nature within the working environment, making rationalistic reductions. In both cases, this harms motivation which becomes a major obstacle to the expected change (Rizziato E.,2020; Rizziato E., Nemmo E., 2018).

We now need to reconnect people with their social identity, contribute to the community and promote a new operational method based on stakeholder engagement and generative listening.

Theory U can be useful in applying ISO 20121 (Buscarini C, Franzini Gabrielli, S., 2019). The Standard provides a template for event organizers and their suppliers to develop a more sustainable management system co-created with stakeholders. The approach recommends engaging stakeholders in defining first the relationship between their expectations within the context of the event. The Standard requests that event organizers consider all the stakeholders; everybody who has a specific interest in the event, such as the participants and visitors, lenders, workers, suppliers, communities (local or professional), associations and future generations. The third feature of the rule is the recommendation to analyze the whole life cycle of the event, at all stages and for the entire supply chain. For each phase, it is necessary to analyze:

- the design (maximum design and detail design),
- the implementation (preparation, conduction, and verification),
- the closure and return checks (legacy and reporting).

Finally, two technical aspects must be considered: first, ISO is a contractual standard[79] and secondly, its scope is extremely wide. These two aspects make it a "universal" standard. ISO 20121 provides benefits to everyone involved in the event, organizers, workforce, restaurateurs, builders, transporters, participants, community and many more. It promotes organizational growth in terms of efficiency, efficacy, competence, and awareness. It increases the risk management capability of the organization, encouraging organizers to delve deeply into the issues and work on compliance, management, and the evaluation of critical aspects of the locations more consciously. These issues can occur anywhere for example in security at assembly and disassembly, when requesting permissions and warranties from suppliers, when training volunteers, in agreements with the municipalities hosting the events, etc. The Standard also provides an in-depth mapping process for the stakeholders to allow event organizers to manage critical areas pre-emptively, and them to involve other actors. Other important benefits of implementing ISO 20121 are: the improvement of the quality of event management, the ability to stand out from competitors credibly and transparently, the opportunity to spread the culture of sustainability to stakeholders, to enhance the image of organizers and those who are involved in the event.

ISO 20121 uses the "Plan-Do-Check-Act" scheme and includes some of the features of ISO 26000 Guidance on Social Responsibility. The Sustainable Event Management System was first applied at the 2012 London Olympics. It is considered rather comprehensive, as it takes into consideration three dimensions that the event organizers must consider: environmental, social, and economic. Firstly, the economic aspect is value creation. Secondly, the social aspect is inclusion and respect for shared values. Lastly, the environmental impact or the footprint of the event is reduced by optimum management and the implementation of best practices.

ISO 20121 is not intended for certification for regulatory or contractual purposes but provides a process to manage a sustainable organizational system.

In this context the bibliography focused on the organization of sporting events is not wide, due to a lack of sustainable managerial culture. We refer to the authors that have studied the application of ISO 20121 standards (Bakos A.R., 2017; Pasholikov M., Bavina P., 2013; Walker A.S., 2012). Also, we can consider some authors that have focused on the theme of sustainable events and the impact of mega -events (Jones M., 2018; Boggia A., 2018;Musgrave J., Henderson S., 2015; Boscolo S., Decarli P., et al., 2015, Lienhard P., Preuss H. 2014).

Applying Theory U in sporting events: methodology and findings

At the beginning of 2016, we investigated the level of knowledge of ISO 20121 through a questionnaire to verify the Italian Sports Federations' understanding and compliance with the standard (Buscarini C., Franzini Gabrielli S., 2019). As the respondents did not apply the ISO 20121, we decided to demonstrate the benefits of the standard by applying it retrospectively. International BNL of Italy for Tennis, Seven Hills Trophy, Energy for Swim (Swimming); the Italian Road Racing Championship in

Imola; the Italian Round of the World SBK Championship in Imola; the Italian Vintage Endurance Championship in Vallelunga; the 17th FINA World Championship[80] in Budapest and XXX Summer Universiade (Naples 2019) have been our testbed to promote the sustainability culture of sports events through ISO 20121, with the support of the Theory U's tools.

We applied Theory U in the way it is taught by Otto Scharmer, to demonstrate how this new way of thinking can create an evolving reality in a synergy between the organization and its stakeholders.

Theory U is based on letting go of assumptions and prejudices, and opening up to a transcendent dimension, to operate with the highest level of awareness (to become aware of the situations and effects of own's actions) and conscience[81] (to know and be aware of what is right and what is wrong, in the triple evaluation of oneself, the other and the general situation). The result of this method was a new path for a responsible, ethical, and sustainable development.

The Theory U tools applied in the sporting events mentioned above are as follows:

- Sensing Journey
- Stakeholder interview
- Shadowing or Shadow Walking.

Sensing Journey

Sensing Journey is a tool that allows participants to break through patterns of seeing and listening by stepping into a different, but relevant perspective. This experience and can help in relationship building with key stakeholders (Scharmer, O. 2009).

We used Sensing Journey during an international sporting event to observe the organization and its targets, the points of strength or weakness and to analyze which changes to utilize to improve sustainability. For example, we could address the concern surrounding single-use plastic. At most events, plastic bottles are not recycled but treated as general waste. We hope that international laws will start doing something tangible regarding this issue, considering the facts arising from recent studies that found plastic traces in human bodies (Smith M. *et al.* **2018**).

This research was completed thanks to the consent of the CONI Services Ltd[82] and some of the most important Italian Sports Federations.

Within each event, attention was paid to the main stakeholders (staff, athletes, those responsible for different sectors, volunteers, etc,) to empathetically learn and see these new and different sports worlds through their eyes. The benefit of the neutral point of view of an outsider allowed us to highlight the positive contribution of interpersonal dynamics. The Theory U tool encourages us to invest in relationships helping to reduce the stiffness and resistance to change that can obstruct new ideas and opportunities.

Sensing Journey introduces a more efficient and responsible organizational process, not only for social dynamics but also to reduce environmental impacts (e.g. pollution problems and footprint). Sensing Journey pulls participants out of their daily routine and allows them to experience the organization, challenges and system through the eyes of different stakeholders.

Sensing Journey helps to find answers to questions from a different perspective. It allows participants to move into unfamiliar environments, immerse themselves in different contexts and step into relevant experiences. Sensing Journey could also help in building relationships with key stakeholders and gaining an overall system perspective. This tool increases the awareness of different aspects of a system and its relationships; it enhances awareness of different perspectives of stakeholders and participants in the system, connections between stakeholders and participants. In Appendix A you can find an example of Sensing Journey that we conducted in the field.

Stakeholder interview

Theory U considers interviews with all the relevant stakeholders as a useful tool to explore their expectations towards the event, the level of satisfaction about the results from their previous experiences and to collect feedback on how to improve it. It can be used as a method to collect feedback during all the events. It enables event organizers to develop a general map of the expectations and needs of their stakeholders.

By applying deep listening and empathy in these interviews, organizers can understand the stakeholders' point of view and acknowledge how their actions can have a positive impact. All the relevant stakeholders could be profiled and meet before the event. Interviewers selected from the sport event organisations' staff, could be invited to ask personal questions to understand what stakeholders want. Senior executives could hold brainstorming sessions with the entire organization to identify all the relevant stakeholders and set aside time to connect with them.

We used this tool as a method to collect feedback during all the events mentioned above, and this enabled us to produce a generalized map of the expectations and needs of the stakeholders across events. We collected as much feedback as possible, formulating different questionnaires handed out at different times of the event (before, during and after). These questionnaires provided important information to improve the number of participants (also in terms of tickets sold) and customer loyalty. Also, it was important to understand the needs of volunteers and staff to give them the most suitable position. It may help with motivation and the expression of potential skills as well.

The organizers of sporting events became closer to stakeholders and could establish a relationship based on trust and transparency through the interview process. It was possible to take on new and interesting ideas about how to organize events in the most sustainable way possible.

For our field research, we took into consideration the following stakeholders: Staff (Volunteers and Organizers), Spectators, Athletes and Teams, Suppliers and Sponsors.

In each case, we analyzed how each stakeholder felt, considered, and listened in his needs. Thanks to this tool and the stakeholders' suggestions and feelings collected through the deep listening process, the organization could give the event a wider appeal, especially regarding sustainable themes and projects.

In Appendix B you can find the structure of the interview we used during the Stakeholder Interview field research

Shadowing or Shadow Walking

Shadowing is a tool of Theory U that involves "following as a shadow" the person who plays a certain role or performs a specific task within an organization. The person who wants to learn any kind of role will follow, like a shadow, someone that owns the know-how, learning from this observation. This practice can allow people who follow their reference subjects as "shadows" to:

- observe and learn from experts, professionals,
- enter the work experience of a specific subject,
- connect to someone who is facing similar challenges (Scharmer, O., 2009)[83.]

The objective of this practice is to observe and make notes on the work and attitude modalities of the subject being followed and, in doing so, acquire a new perspective on that work.

It also allows the participant to carry out a task in real-time with an expert, a leader working with him/her in the field. In this way, new ideas could be developed to improve and implement that role and their respective tasks and to have more clarity on the skills required, the challenges to be faced and the objectives to be set

Shadowing works best when people do not know each other and operate in unfamiliar areas. The goal is to observe and immerse oneself in the chosen context (Scharmer, O., 2009). Shadowing is not a practice that follows pre-structured procedures but allows things to happen and goes with the flow.

During our field research, the practice was useful to explain roles and tasks to new members of the organization, volunteers, and managers. Each subject could be entrusted to a specific area manager, enabling them to get to the heart of the position, acquire the necessary skills and learn how to carry out the work in the most efficient way.

We used Shadowing during the organization of 17th FINA World Championships (Budapest 2017) and in XXX Summer Universiade, Napoli 2019[84.]

People in charge of different organizational areas and assigned to specific tasks (mainly the Sustainability Manager and Operational Managers) were followed. This facilitated the understanding of the work, the obstacles and the possible pitfalls involved. It has proved to be a useful tool due to the short length of time required to learn a certain task, cover a role, and take on some responsibility.

People that put this methodology into practice in the organization of sporting events, found more ease in understanding the work and skills needed to achieve the goal. We noticed that people learned skills related to the task more quickly and in more depth. People that were following sustainability managers were able to understand the process of the organization proposed by ISO 20121 more easily.

In Appendix C and D you can find two examples of Shadowing that we used during this field research.

Conclusions and future research

The aim of this study was to verify if Theory U' principles and tools can be used to implement the process' sustainability of sporting events organisation. The results of field research carried out in the context of some international sporting events support our initial hypotheses: Theory U principles can be useful to focus on self-assessment, assessment of others, task learning and to facilitate or tackle challenging situations, during the organization of sustainable sporting events following the ISO 20121 standard.

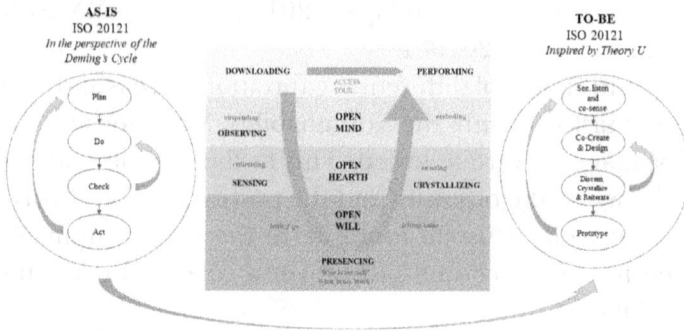

Figure 1: A new approach in the PDCA process using Theory U tools and principles.

As we can see in the figure above, the integral approach of Theory U can be useful to change the operational processes that have been used until now (AS-IS) leading to a new way to manage sporting events in a sustainable way applying the ISO 20121 guidelines (TO-BE).

The Laboratory of Economics and Management[85] of the University of Rome "Foro Italico" wants to support the sports federations and clubs, at a national and international level, in the organization of events in a sustainable way, with the Theory U tools and principles as a possible way to implement the standard ISO 20121. This research intends to put down roots to foster the development of a new research strand and to contribute to boosting sustainability in the world of sport, in particular, in this case, focusing on the organizational process of sports events, encouraging the spread of a sustainability culture and changing behaviors within the organizations.

Theory U can, therefore, be applied either in every single phase of the organization process (i.e. a U-process within each phase of the Plan-Do-Check-Act cycle) or as a guideline for the entire process:

- Plan - becomes See, Listen & Co-Sense;
- Do - becomes Co-Create & Design;

- Check - becomes Discern, Crystallize & Reiterate;
- Act - becomes Prototype.

We experimented with the methodology and tools of Theory U and found them extremely valid to facilitate the dissemination and adoption of sustainable principles in each phase of the organizational process provided by ISO 20121 framework.

We think that at the core of the new sustainability paradigm there is an awareness that organizations must learn to actively connect and listen to the different stakeholders linked with the organization to understand their expectations, motivate and engage them in the process of co-creation of a common objective.

We are enthusiastically open to international collaborations aimed at developing this project even further and applying this approach to more cases. Thanks to this research and the opportunities that we had in the field to learn the "state of the art" processes of the organization of sporting events, it has been possible to observe various aspects of this sector and we believe that there is a powerful argument to reinforce the principles and the values of sustainability.

We are all reminded that the IOC calls for sustainability, and it is time to accelerate this cultural change.

References

Argyris, C. (2010). Organizational traps: Leadership, culture, organizational design (Vol. 15, p. 2019). Oxford: Oxford University Press.

Bakos, A. R., O'Brien, D., & Gowthorp, L. Planning For Sustainability: A Case Study Of The Implementation Strategy Of ISO 20121 For The 2018 Commonwealth Games, Conference proceedings at the 25^ EASM Conference, 2017.

Beer, M. (2011). Developing an effective organization: Intervention method, empirical evidence, and theory. In Research in organizational change and development. Emerald Group Publishing Limited.

Boggia, A., Massei, G., Paolotti, L., Rocchi, L., & Schiavi, F. (2018). A model for measuring the environmental sustainability of events.

Journal of environmental management, 206, 836-845.

Boonstra, J. J. (Ed.). (2004). Dynamics of organizational change and learning (p. 512). J. Wiley & Sons Incorporated

Boscolo, S., Decarli, P., & Jaksche, J. (2015). Management della sostenibilità degli eventi sportivi: l'esperienza del Giro Lago di Resia. Eurac, Istituto per il Management Pubblico.

Bradbury, H., Mirvis, P., Neilsen, E., & Pasmore, W. (2008). Action research at work: Creating the future following the path from Lewin. The SAGE handbook of action research: Participative inquiry and practice, 2, 77-92.

Buscarini, C., Franzini Gabrielli S., (2019). ISO 20121 and Theory U: A new way to manage sporting events. In Global Sport Business (pp. 298-310). Routledge.

Buscarini C., Manni F., Marano M. (2006). La responsabilità sociale e il bilancio sociale delle organizzazioni dello sport. *Milano: Franco Angeli.*Buscarini C., Mura R. (2011). Nuovi sviluppi in tema di rendicontazione sociale nelle Federazioni Sportive Nazionali (FSN). *Azienda Pubblica 4.2011, 406.*

Buscarini C., Mura R. (2013). *Routledge handbook of sport and corporate social responsibility.* Abingdon: Routledge. *Chapter 20.* Italian sport federations: communicating CSR through the social report.

Collins A., Flynn A. (2008). Measuring the Environmental Sustainability of a Major Sporting Event: A Case Study of the FA Cup Final, Tourism Economics.

Collins, A., Jones, C., & Munday, M. (2009). Assessing the environmental impacts of mega sporting events: Two options? Tourism management, 30(6), 828-837.

Cornelissen S., Bob U., Swart K. (2009). Towards redefining the concept of legacy in relation to sport mega-events: Insights from the 2010 FIFA World Cup, Journal of Sport & Tourism.

Del Val, M. P., & Fuentes, C. M. (2003). Resistance to change: a literature review and empirical study. Management decision.

Djaballah, M., Hautbois, C., & Desbordes, M. (2015). Non-mega sporting events' social impacts: a sensemaking approach of local governments' perceptions and strategies. European Sport Management Quarterly, 15(1), 48-76.

European Commission (2007). White Paper on Sport.

European Council (1992). European Charter for Sports.

Gallagher A., Pike K. (2011). Sustainable management for maritime events and festivals, Journal of Coastal Research.

Godfrey P.C. (2009). Corporate social responsibility in sport: An overview and key issues. *Journal of Sport Management*, *23*(3), 698-716.Grichting A. (2013). Scales of flows: Qatar and the urban legacies of mega events. Archnet-International Journal of Architectural Research.

Henderson S. (2011). The development of competitive advantage through sustainable event management, Worldwide Hospitality and Tourism Themes.

Hosking, D. M., & Morley, I. E. (1991). A social psychology of organizing: people, processes and contexts. Harvester Wheatsheaf.

International Olympic Committee (1999). Olympic Movement's Agenda 21.

International Olympic Committee (2014). Olympic Agenda 2020.

ISO 20121, Sustainable events: Event Sustainability Management Systems.

Jones M., (2018). Sustainable Event Management, a practical guide, Third Ed., Earthscan from Routledge.

Koosha M., Yoosefy B., Khabiri M. (2017). Understanding major sport events leveraging as social development: Future prospect of Iran, *Choregia: Sport Management International Journal*.

Laing J., Frost W. (2010). How green was my festival: Exploring challenges and opportunities associated with staging green events, International Journal of Hospitality Management.

Lesjø, J. H., & Gulbrandsen, E. A. (2018). The Olympics: institutionalization and standardization of sustainability. In B. P. McCullough & T. B. Kellison (Eds.), Routledge Handbook of Sport and the Environment (pp. 137-148): Routledge.

Lienhard P., Preuss H. (2014). Legacy, Sustainability and CSR at Mega Sports Events: An Analysis of the UEFA EURO 2008 in Switzerland, Springer Gabler.

Mallen C., Bradish C., MacLean J. (2008). Are we teaching corporate citizens? Examining corporate social responsibility and sport management pedagogy. *International Journal of Sport Management and Marketing*, *4*(2/3), 204-224.

Marano M. (2001). Implementing management control and performance measurement systems in large non-profit sport organizations. *Proceedings of the 9th Congress of the European Association for sport Management*.

Musgrave J., Henderson S. (2015). Changing audience behaviour. A pathway to sustainable event management, The Routledge Handbook of Tourism and Sustainability. Routledge.

Novara, F. (2003). Si può guarire l'organizzazione. Esperienze professionali, pro-poste metodologiche e teoriche.

Pasholikov M., Bavina P., (2013). Standard ISO 20121--Factor of Competitiveness Russian Organizer of Business Events, Croatian Quality Managers Society, Zagreb.

Reason, P., & Bradbury, H. (Eds.). (2001). Handbook of action research: Participative inquiry and practice. Sage.

Rizziato, E. (2020). Verso un umanesimo della vita organizzativa: Generare sviluppo nella complessità con la leadership orizzontale. FrancoAngeli.

Rizziato, E., & Nemmo, E. (2018). Competenze di sviluppo sistemico evolutivo per la leadership e le organizzazioni orizzontali. Working Paper IRCrES, 4(13).

Scharmer, O. (2009). Theory-U: Leading from the Emerging future. The social Technology of Presencing. Oakland, CA: Berrett-Koehler Publishers.

Scharmer O. (2016). Theory U: Leading from the Future as it Emerges 2nd Edition, McGraw-Hill Education, 2016.

Scharmer O., Katrin Kaufer (2013). Leading from the Emerging Future: From Ego-System to Eco-System Economics, Berrett-Koehler Publishers, 2013.

Schulenkorf N. (2016). The Contributions of Special Events to Sport-for-Development Programs, University of Technology Sydney.

Scrucca, F., Severi, C., Galvan, N., & Brunori, A. (2016). A new method to assess the sustainability performance of events: Application to the 2014 World Orienteering Championship.Environmental Impact Assessment Review, 56, 1-11.

Senge P.M., Sharmer O. Jaworski, J., Flowers, B. S., (2005), Presence: An exploration of profound change in people, organizations, and society. Crown BusinessSmith A. (2009). Theorising the Relationship between Major Sport Events and Social Sustainability, Journal of Sport & Tourism.

Smith, M., Love, D. C., Rochman, C. M., & Neff, R. A. (2018). Microplastics in seafood and the implications for human health. Current environmental health reports, 5(3), 375-386.

Tinnish, S.M., Mangal, S.M. (2012). Sustainable event marketing in the MICE industry: A theoretical framework, Journal of Convention & Event Tourism.

United Nations Conference on Environment & Development (1992). Agenda 21.

United Nations (2015). Transforming our world: the 2030 Agenda for

Sustainable Development. Division for Sustainable Development Goals: New York, NY, USA.

Various authors (2013). Routledge handbook of sport and corporate social responsibility, Routledge.

Walker A.S. (2012). Process vs. Performance Standards for Sustainable Meeting and Event

Management, Osgoode CLPE Research Paper No. 17/2012.

APPENDIX A:

HOW WE APPLIED THE SENSING JOURNEYS DURING THE 53rd SEVEN HILLS THROPHY

We conducted a Sensing Journey during the Seven Hills Trophy, (Swimming event), held in Rome on the 24th, 25th and 26th June 2016 to analyze which changes could be brought in to reach sustainable solutions. Thanks to Sensing Journey, at the end of the event, we obtained a clear picture of what tends to go right and wrong, what could be improved and what should be changed from a sustainable perspective.

Step 1

What does Theory U say: Identify Learning Journeys: find places, individuals, organizations that provide you and the group with a new perspective.

What we did: As the objective of the research was to assess the sustainability of sporting events, we selected one of the most important international meetings in the swimming discipline that takes place in Rome: Seven Hills Trophy. It takes place in the "Foro Italico" swimming pool every year in June. Our core team[86] made up of future sport managers, were put into contact with both the organizers of the event (CONI Sevices Spa) and the Italian Swimming Federation.

Step 2

What does Theory U say: Prepare as a group by discussing the following;

1. What is the context of the experience?
2. Who are the key players that we will talk to?
3. What questions do we want to explore?
4. What assumptions do I bring with me? What do I expect?
5. Share your most eye-opening sensing experience to date

Start by developing a short questionnaire (7-10 questions) to guide your enquiry process. Continue updating your questionnaire as the process unfolds.

Prepare the host: share the purpose and intent of the visit. Communicate that it would be most helpful for the group to gain some insight into their "normal" daily operations, rather than a staged presentation. Try to avoid "show and tell" situations.

What we did: Our core team of 4 people discussed the questions above and realised that the sporting context is very different from all the other existing contexts as its key players are also the athletes and the spectators, the staff and the volunteers. There is a wide range of players that can influence the event. We built some questionnaires to investigate each key player and his/her satisfaction, improvements, and advice. This was all completed with a focus on sustainability, sustainable actions and perceptions. We expected to have, at the end of the event, a clear picture of what goes right and what goes wrong, of what could be improved and what must be changed.

We sent the questionnaires to the Seven Hills Trophy's organizers as to keep them informed.

Step 3

What does Theory U say: Travel in small groups to the host's location;

Whilst at the site: Trust your intuition and ask authentic questions raised by the conversation. Asking simple and authentic questions is an important leverage point in shifting or refocusing the attention to some of the deeper systemic forces at play.

Use deep listening as a tool to hold the space of conversation. When your interviewee has finished responding to one of your questions, do not jump in automatically with the next question. Wait to see what is emerging from the now.

Example questions for sensing journeys:

1. What personal experience or journey brought you into your current role?
2. What issues or challenges have you been confronted with on a day to day basis?
3. Why do these challenges exist?
4. What challenges exist in the larger system?
5. What are the blockages?
6. What are your most important sources of success and change?
7. What would a better system look like for you?
8. What initiative, if implemented, would have the greatest impact for you? For the system as a whole?
9. If you could change just a few elements of the system, what would you change?
10. Who else do we need to talk to?

What we did: during the event, we divided into different roles. Each one of us had one or more categories of stakeholder to be interviewed and one or more areas to be observed (for example, HR, waste management, transport, logistics etc.). In this way, we tried to collect as much data and information as possible to have a substantial amount of useful information for research purposes. Each interview and observation were made following the principles and guidelines of Theory-U.

Step 4

What does Theory U say: After the visit, reflect and debrief: to capture and leverage the findings of your enquiry process, conduct a disciplined debriefing process right after each visit. Do not switch on cell phones until the debriefing is complete.

Here are a few sample questions for the debriefing:

1. What was most surprising or unexpected?
2. What touched me? What connected with me personally?
3. If the social field (or the living system) of the visited organization or community were a living being, what would it look and feel like?
4. If that being could talk: what would it say (to us)?
5. If that being could develop—what would it want to morph into next?
6. What is the generative source that allows this social field to develop and thrive?
7. What limiting factors prevent this field/system from developing further?
8. Moving in and out of this field, what did you notice about yourself?
9. What ideas does this experience spark for possible prototyping initiatives that you may want to take on?

What we did: we recorded everything that was said and made a note of our first impressions. At the end of the day we listened, both together and alone, to the highlights and the most important things were recorded in a notebook. Thanks to this, we could see the differences between the areas and the people, the things that we should observe better and ask about the next day. Not only so that the event should continuously improve, but also our work, our research, and our way to carry out the research.

Step 5 and 6

What does Theory U say: Close the feedback loop with your hosts: Send an email (or other follow-up note) expressing a key insight you took away from the meeting (one or two sentences) and stating your appreciation for their time.

Debrief as a whole group: After a one-day learning journey, this debriefing would take place at the next meeting with the whole group. In the case of a multiple day learning journey, you can plan to meet between the individual days, if logistics allow.

Structure of the whole group debrief meeting:

1. Get everyone on the same page by sharing concrete information about the Journeys: Where did you go, who did you talk to, what did you do?
2. Talk about your findings and generate new ideas.

What we did: At the end of the work, after having elaborated and analyzed the data, we prepared a report of the event and provided it to both the University professor and the event's managers. Each member of the team had a personal copy of the report and at the end of the event, we gathered to see the next steps to be done for future research.

APPENDIX B:
HOW WE APPLIED THE STAKEHOLDER INTERVIEWS DURING SPORTING EVENTS

In this appendix, we provide an example interview that was used for spectators during the following events: International BNL of Italy for Tennis, Seven Hills Trophy, Energy for Swim for Swimming; the Italian Road Racing Championship in Imola; the Italian Round of the World SBK Championship in Imola; the Italian Vintage Endurance Championship in Vallelunga.

This method enabled us to produce a general map of stakeholders' expectations and needs.

It is important to highlight that there is no closed or fixed list of questions. Therefore, the interview can be modified for each case.

Laboratory of Economics and Management

Stakeholder Interviews

This questionnaire was used exclusively for university research proposed by the Lab of Economics and Management coordinated by Prof. Cristiana Buscarini (University of Rome

"Foro Italico") to receive feedback from the main stakeholders of sporting events. In particular, the last three questions were designed to investigate the knowledge, awareness, and sensibility of sustainability during the organizational process of events.

1. What do you think of the event? What do you like? What do you think should remain the same? What would you improve (and how?)?
2. What are your expectations for the event?
3. What are your expectations of the organization and therefore the organizers of the event?
4. Is this an event you have already participated in? If yes, what are the biggest differences compared to previous years? What improvements have been made?
5. Are you passionate about this sport?
6. What do you think is the most important thing for a spectator attending an event like this?
7. Do you know what Sustainability is? Do you think it is important that an event like this is organised according to the principles of environmental, economic, and social sustainability?
8. What do you think is the best way to disseminate the values of sustainability within the sports world and events?
9. Do you have any tips to improve the events' sustainability (e.g. waste management, transport etc)?

APPENDIX C:

HOW WE APPLIED THE SHADOWING DURING THE 17th FINA WORLD CHAMPIONSHIPS

We performed the "Shadowing" process during the 17th FINA World Championship, held in Budapest (Hungary) in July 2017. This tool enabled us to understand the work and skills needed to achieve the goal more easily.

Step 1

What does Theory U say: Define the objective of the process and identify an appropriate target person to shadow. The target person and the context should be both interesting and unfamiliar.

What we did: 17th FINA World Championship. During this competition, I provided support to the Media Area, near to the photographers and helped to educate people working near the pool deck to recycle rubbish effectively. This was also useful because the unsightly rubbish cannot appear on TV. Having completed a period of general training, the area manager provided me with further training on specific tasks.

Step 2 and 3

What does Theory U say:

- Make an appointment with the person you wish to shadow.
- Let them know that you are interested in just following their daily practice and routines and that there is no need for any special program or treatment. There is no need for them to set aside extra time for you except at the end of the day for the closing/debriefing interview (30 minutes – 1 hour). This could also be done during lunch or dinner.
- Let the person you wish to shadow know what you are particularly interested in learning about. They can then select the best day for your shadowing experience.
- Confidentiality: clarify that anything you observe or hear will be handled confidentially.
- Prepare for the shadowing exercise by taking 10-20 minutes to:
- Focus on the purpose of the shadowing: what do you want to learn?
- Imagine the best possible outcome of the day for you and for the person you are shadowing.
- Imagine the future that you want to create and think about how shadowing might be a small first step in that direction.

Once you arrive in the office of the person you are shadowing, be transparent and establish trust about the purpose and the process of the shadowing exercise.

Establish a personal connection early on; use observations in your interviewee's office or return to themes that came up during the first moments of the conversation to establish a personal connection.

Let the person you are shadowing know that whatever you learn during the day is for your personal use only and will not be shared with others.

During the shadowing exercise listen with an open heart and mind, take notes, and follow the principles of Theory U

What we did: After observing the movements and understanding the behavior of the person who was specifically focused on the photographer's area, I tried to perform that task myself. I followed his daily practice and routines both in stressful times and relaxed ones. I asked some questions to establish both the movements, the things to say or not say and places where to direct people to throw rubbish. I wanted to learn how to deal with photographers, with athletes and also with other volunteers as my task was both to accompany the athletes from the victory ceremony to the photographer's area for photographs and also to manage access to the various poolside areas of both press officers, photographers and volunteers. During the time that I followed the person I was shadowing, I listened with an open heart and mind, took notes, and followed the principles that I had learned on the Theory U course.

Step 4

What does Theory U say: Debriefing Interview. At the end of the day or during lunch, conduct a brief interview with the person you shadowed. Bring up any questions that the observations throughout the day sparked in your mind. Here are a few questions that you might consider.

Sample questions for de-briefing:

1. What journey brought you to your current position?
2. What good and bad examples of leadership have you experienced?
3. What key challenges are you currently dealing with?
4. What is your work as a leader? What would your organization be missing without you? What value do you add?
5. When you started in this position, what did you have to let go of (unlearn), and what new competencies did you have to develop?

6. What barriers exist in the current system that prevents your team/organization from realizing its full potential?
7. What personal practices do you use to achieve your best?

After all the interviews have been completed, review the interview data, and summarize results.

What we did: I asked some further questions of the person I was shadowing to help me understand both the movements and the things to say or do not say and regarding sustainable actions. I was extremely interested in his professional background and how he came to be working in this field. I would also like to organize sporting events sustainably.

Step 5

What does Theory U say: "Debrief" and crystallize straight away; capture observations and insights in your journal; do not make phone calls or have conversations between your shadowing experience and recording your thoughts and impressions; use a structured debriefing process as suggested below, if possible.

1. What are your 2-3 key observations from today?
2. What are their implications for your work?
3. What were 2–3 important leadership challenges the person you were shadowing facing today?
4. What was an intervention performed by the person you were shadowing made that changed the course of that challenge?
5. Reflect on any interventions that have failed.
6. Were there moments you felt uncomfortable with how things went? Why?
7. Were there moments you felt inspired during the day? Why?
8. What other things did you notice?
9. Other observations or key take-aways?

What we did: during the exercise, I made notes on my experience and impressions. At the end of the day, I listened to the highlights and the most important things I summarised in a notebook.

Step 6

What does Theory U say: Send a thank-you note. Close the feedback loop by sending the person you were shadowing a brief email or voice mail to say thank you for the day (within 24 hours). You can also use it to say something about the most important insight you gleaned from the day or the closing interview.

What we did: at the end of each day, I thanked the person I was shadowing for the opportunity and the organizational and managerial skills that he was passing on to me.

APPENDIX D:

HOW WE APPLIED THE SHADOWING DURING THE XXX SUMMER UNIVERSIADE

We performed Shadowing during the XXX Summer Universiade, held in Naples (Italy) in July 2019. The use of the tool at this event, as for the previous one (appendix c), enabled us to understand the work and skills needed to achieve the goal effectively.

Step 1

What does Theory U say: Define the objective of the process and identify an appropriate target person to shadow. The target person and the context should be both interesting and unfamiliar.

What we did: XXX Summer Universiade, Napoli 2019. During this competition, I had to perform a lead function in the Arrivals and Departures Area, both at the airport and the train station. As I was the only manager of that area, I had some assistant managers, coordinators and volunteers helping me.

Regarding my staff[87], after having completed a period of general training (very short in April 2019), I assigned each one of them to a different manager; to volunteers, I assigned a specific coordinator, to coordinators I assigned a specific assistant manager. Therefore, this was a double process occurring at two different times because coordinators began working after assistant managers and volunteers after coordinators.

Step 2 and 3

What does Theory U say:

- Make an appointment with the person you wish to shadow.
- Let the person you wish to shadow know that you are interested in just following her daily practice and routines and that there is no need for any special program or treatment.
- There is no need for her to set aside extra time for you except at the end of the day for the closing/debriefing interview (30 minutes – 1 hour). This could also be done during lunch or dinner.
- Let the person you wish to shadow know what you are particularly interested in learning about. The person you wish to shadow can select the best day for your shadowing experience.
- Confidentiality: clarify that anything you observe or hear will be handled confidentially.

On the morning of the shadowing day, prepare and take 10-20 minutes before the exercise to:

- Focus on the purpose of the shadowing: what do you want to learn?
- Imagine the best possible outcome of the day for you and the person you are shadowing.
- Connect to the future that you want to create—and think about how your shadowing might be a small first step in that direction.

Once you arrive in the office of the person you are shadowing, create transparency and trust about the purpose and the process of the shadowing exercise; establish a personal connection early on; use observations in your interviewee's office or return to themes that came up during the first moments of the conversation to establish a personal connection. Let the person you are shadowing know that whatever you learn during the day is for your personal use only and will not be shared with others. During the shadowing exercise listen with your mind and heart wide open, take notes, and follow the principles below.

What we did: I observed the movements, words used, people involved, documents mentioned as they performed the tasks. They followed daily routines both in the office and in the venue.

I also organised some "venue exercises" trying to recreate the same scenario as experienced during the event. This allowed them to learn by doing and to delve deeper into the task. They asked a lot of questions on several different topics.

Inside our venue, we had a waste manager, an energy manager, and a transport manager. I explained to them the concept of sustainability is in general with a few examples related to the specifics tasks I had observed. I also reminded them to listen with their hearts open and to take notes.

Step 4

What does Theory U say: Debriefing Interview. At the end of the day or during lunch, conduct a brief interview with the person you shadowed. Bring up any questions that the observations throughout the day sparked in your mind. Here are a few questions that you might consider.

Sample questions for de-briefing:

1. What journey brought you to your current position?
2. What good and bad examples of leadership have you experienced?
3. What key challenges are you currently dealing with?
4. What is your work as a leader? What would your organization be missing without you? What value do you add?
5. When you started in this position, what did you have to let

go of (unlearn), and what new competencies did you have to develop?

6. What barriers exist in the current system that prevents your team/organization from realizing its full potential?
7. What personal practices do you use to achieve your best?

After all the interviews have been completed, review the interview data, and summarize results.

What we did: at the end of each "exercise" I asked them what they learnt during the day and assisted them to crystallize their findings.

Step 5

What does Theory U say: "Debrief" and crystallize straight away; capture observations and insights in your journal; do not make phone calls or have conversations between your shadowing experience and recording your thoughts and impressions; use a structured debriefing process as suggested below, if possible.

1. What are your 2-3 key observations from today?
2. What are their implications for your work?
3. What were 2–3 important leadership challenges the person you were shadowing facing today?
4. What was an intervention performed by the person you were shadowing made that changed the course of that challenge?
5. Reflect on any interventions that have failed.
6. Were there moments you felt uncomfortable with how things went? Why?
7. Were there moments you felt inspired during the day? Why?
8. What other things did you notice?
9. Other observations or key take-aways?

What we did: during the exercise, I recommended that they tried to note down their conversations and their impressions. At the end of the day, we went over the highlights and noted the key findings.

Step 6

What does Theory U say: Send a thank-you note. Close the feedback loop by sending the person you were shadowing a brief email or voice mail to say thank you for the day (within 24 hours). You can also use it to say something about the most important insight you gleaned from the day or the closing interview.

What we did: at the end of each day we all thanked each other because together we developed new ideas, new ways to solve issues and grow together.

Biographies

Amy Barnes is a creative facilitator who applies her knowledge and skills in different domains: corporate consulting, executive coaching, leadership development, complementary therapy and art making. Common themes across all domains are change, transformation, healing and growth. Where she is most effective is in working with 'real people dealing with real issues in real-time'. Her experiential way of working with clients is shaped by her in-depth training in Gestalt psychotherapy studies and by her qualifications in bodywork and energy-based therapies. To complete the yin yang of the whole picture, she holds an MBA (Distinction) from Warwick Business School, facilitated numerous change initiatives as internal and external consultant, and co-created and co-led a successful start-up consultancy in Poland providing leadership development and OD consulting to some of the largest CEE and global corporations.

Nicolò Francesco Bernardi, PhD, is a professional coach and facilitator for individuals and organizations. He enthusiastically offers a holistic approach that combines neuroscience, mind-body health, participatory management of organizational change and systems thinking. His work focuses on emotional resilience, leadership development and mental health in the workplace. Personal website: www.nicolofrancescobernardi.com

Cristiana Buscarini is an associate professor at the University of Rome "Foro Italico", she is currently the scientific director of the Laboratory of Economics and Management. She is a reference for the Italian Academy of Business Economics. She has published volumes and articles on entrepreneurship related to corporate social responsibility, in particular sustainability in companies operating in the sports sector. Cristiana.buscarini@gmail.com ORCID Account: orcid.org/0000-0002-4361-418X

William Brendel is an Assistant Professor of Organization Development and Change at Penn State University and is the CEO of the Transformative Learning Institute. William has over 20 years of experience as an organization development consultant, researcher, author and trainer. His publications on mindful leadership and organizational change span academic journals and popular press. His consultation and workshops have led to measurable transformations in organizational culture and performance across the U.S., China, India and Africa. William has previously held academic positions at Texas A&M, Temple University, and the University of St Thomas, where he has taught graduate courses in Organization Development, Leadership Development, Change Management, Talent Management, Group Dynamics, and Transformative Learning. William received his Doctorate in Adult Learning and Leadership, and Master's degree in Organizational Psychology at Columbia University in New York.

Vivianna Rodriguez Carreon is associate lecturer and honorary researcher in the Department of Peace and Conflict Studies at the University of Sydney, Australia. Her research interests are in human agency and human experience through the lenses of phenomenology, consciousness and capabilities with a focus on education, well-being and community engagement. Her manuscript on the dynamics of human agency in post-war is in process for publication. She is part of the u.lab research community and the Societal Transformation Lab at the Presencing Institute, member of the Human Development and Capability Approach, IEP (Institute for Economics and Peace) Peace Ambassador, and new investigator to the 2020 MLSRI (Mind and Life Summer Research Institute). Her engagement with u.lab started with running a virtual hub called the Intercultural Cosmovision Lab project, which emerged from her research to "create and enable community with openness and understanding."

Beatriz Carrillo is senior lecturer in the Department of Sociology and Social Policy at the University of Sydney (Australia). Her broad research interest is in social development and social change in contemporary China, with a focus on social inclusion/exclusion, welfare policy, social determinants of health, and philanthropy. She is author of *Small Town China: Rural Labour and Social Exclusion* (Routledge 2011), and co-editor of the *Handbook of Welfare in China* (Edward Elgar 2017), *China's Changing Welfare Mix: Local Perspectives* (Routledge 2011) and of *China's Peasants and Workers: Changing Class Identities* (Edward Elgar 2012). Between 2016-2018, while working as an associate professor at Xi'an Jiaotong-Liverpool University (XJTLU) in Suzhou (China) she began her engagement with u.lab and Theory U, hosting a Social Innovation Hub at that university. Since then she has continued to engage with the literature on Theory U, transformative and embodied learning, and their links to social change.

Fabio Cerroni is a PhD student at the Department of Communication and Social Research, Sapienza University of Rome. He cooperates in research with the Laboratory of Economics and Management of the University of Rome "Foro Italico". Expert in sustainability and sustainability reporting, since 2015 he collaborates with the Italian Swimming Federation for the drafting of the sustainability report. fabio.cerroni@hotmail.it ORCID Account: orcid.org/0000-0001-7835-9011

Kirsty Deacon is a Post-Doctoral Fellow at the University of Strathclyde, building on and developing work from her What Works Scotland funded PhD research on young people's experiences of a parent and/or sibling's imprisonment. She has over fifteen years' experience of working or researching within the criminal justice system in Scotland, and her wider research interests include children and young people, families, and imprisonment.

Elke Fein is a social and political scientist and lecturer at the

University of Freiburg (Germany). She holds degrees in political science and East European studies and a PhD in political sociology, focusing on the systemic transition processes in post-Soviet Russia. She has worked as a researcher in various academic fields and contexts, including in Russian studies, history, leadership and organization studies. Her passion is to explore the relationship between adult development and socio-political analysis. Elke is also co-founder and managing director of the Institute for Integral Studies (IFIS), where she has initiated the EU-funded Strategic Partnership Leadership for Transition (LiFT). In its third iteration – as LiFT Politics – she is coordinating the project's exploration of integrally informed innovations in the realm of politics.

Sara Franzini Gabrielli graduated in economics and international marketing, master's degree in sports management, and a degree in a highly specialized Olympic management course. A working experience with a focus on Sustainability, Media, and Operations. Researcher at the Laboratory of Economics and Management of the University of Rome "Foro Italico". Passionate about sports and a professional swimmer for seventeen years. Specialized in sustainability especially in managing sports events in a sustainable way. Advisor in many major sporting events and both national and international federations to develop sustainable strategies. s.franzini93@gmail.com ORCID Account: orcid.org/0000-0002-5944-9131

Olen Gunnlaugson serves as an Associate Professor in Leadership and Organizational Development at Université Laval (Canada) where he offers MBA courses in leadership, management skills and group communications. With an eclectic research background in leadership growth, development and consciousness-based approaches to transformation, as well as contemplative and generative practices of communication, he received his Ph.D. at the University of British Columbia and did his Post-Doctorate at Simon Fraser University, Vancouver. To date, his work has been published in 13 books as well as 35 articles and chapters in leading academic journals and books. He has presented and keynoted at numerous international conferences, received five prestigious faculty level awards for excellence in teaching from universities in Canada and the USA and taught several thousand emerging leaders, managers and executives at leading schools in Canada, USA, Austria, Sweden and South Korea. Over the past several years, he has been researching and developing Dynamic Presencing. As the focus of his recent book, Dynamic Presencing is an in-depth process for helping leaders, coaches, creatives and change agents develop our current practice of presencing into a deeply immersive and transformative way of orienting one's work and life. Email: Olen.Gunnlaugson@fsa.ulaval.ca

Arawana Hayashi works as a choreographer, performer, and educator is deeply sourced in improvisation and collaboration. She is currently on the faculty of the Presencing Institute and heads the creation of Social Presencing Theater (SPT), an aware-ness-based embodiment practice that supports change in individuals, teams, and larger social systems. Arawana offers training programs in Social Presencing Theater worldwide. She is on the faculty of the Society for Organizational Learning's Executive Champions Workshop, and has taught at the Naropa University ALIA Authentic Leadership program in the US and the Sustainable Co-Creation program of SYNerGAIA in Denmark. She is a meditation teacher in Shambhala, a global community that joins meditation with the creation of a good society. She is the author of the forthcoming book, Social Presencing Theater: The Art of Making a True Move.

Rachel Hentsch is an architect-turned-digital-entrepreneur from a multi-cultural background. As Head of Communications at the Presencing Institute, she blends her writing and graphic skills with a deep commitment to understanding and illuminating the multiple dimensions of leading social change. Rachel is passionate about empowering individuals, teams, communities and organisations to unleash their highest level of contribution, to create the best possible individual and collective future. She designs programs that help people to discover, explore and develop their creative and entrepreneurial mindset and attitude. Rachel is fascinated by communities and has been researching and prototyping ways to keep global community members connected meaningfully. She was co-host of the Rome u.lab hub in 2017. Rachel speaks five languages and holds a BA in Architecture from the University of Cambridge, a BA in Architecture & Building Technology from the University La Sapienza, and is an MIT-Certified Teacher in New Ventures Leadership.

Michelle N. Moore, B.A., M.B.A., is the Founder of MindE-Quity Corporation advising clients on humane technology development and transformation for social impact. Michelle applies Theory U practices and principles in her work with a focus on enabling the collective body-mind connection for creativity, insight and innovation in learning organizations. She currently serves on the boards of GrantBook Inc., Amazing Community and chairs the board of the Peel Art Museum and Archives. Her 25 year career as a management, transformation & innovation consultant spans work in USA, Germany, Russia and Canada. From 1995 - 2009 she was based in Eastern Europe and served as an equity partner with both Ernst & Young and Pricewaterhouse-Coopers (PwC). During that time, Michelle launched and built two technology practices and helped former Soviet enterprises transition to a market economy. In Canada, Michelle served in leadership roles with PwC, World View Adoption Association, Stage-Gate International, and GrantBook Inc.

Keira Oliver is the research and learning lead for Collective Leadership for Scotland and has led on the Scottish Government support of u.lab, a change leadership programme since 2015. She is a facilitator and Principal Social Researcher within the Scottish Government, previously working in areas of public sector reform, children and young people and organisational development.

Charles Scott teaches at Simon Fraser University in the Faculty of Education as an Adjunct Professor and at City University in Canada in the School of Education as an Associate Professor. At SFU, he is a co-coordinator of a Master's program in Contemplative Inquiry and Approaches in Education, and the co-editor, along with Olen Gunnlaugson, Heesoon Bai and Ed Sarath of a series of books published by SUNY Press on contemplative inquiry in postsecondary education. He is also author or co-author of a number of articles on spirituality and contemplative inquiry in education. He teaches courses at SFU and CityU at both undergraduate and graduate levels in contemplative inquiry; reflective practice; curriculum, pedagogy, and assessment; educational program design; critical thinking, and research methods in education.

Chris Taylor is a facilitator, community organiser and activist. He has been involved in movements for global change since the late 70s. Chris lives on a communal organic farm where he is learning the intricacies of regenerative living. He is a member of Extinction Rebellion's Guardianship Circle and author of The Tao of Revolution (Stairwell books, 2019).

Luca Versteegen is a Doctoral Student at the Department of Political Science, University of Gothenburg. He holds a Bachelor's degree in Psychology (B.Sc.) from the University of Hamburg and a Research Master's degree in Social and Behavioral Sciences (M.Sc.) from Tilburg University. His research explores conditions in which people feel to be included and meaningful in society and how this informs the way they engage in politics and societal challenges. He currently focuses on experiences driving right-populist voting intentions.

Ursula Versteegen is an action researcher and process consultant. She is a co-founder and research fellow of the Presencing Institute, a co-founder of the Institute of Mindful Agriculture and a team member of the Eurasia Learning Institute for Happiness and Well-Being. Ursula's action research work brings together awareness-based research and practice in the fields of transformational social change and innovation in corporate, education, special education, organic farming and NGOs. Her special interest is the art of social process design and leadership and how to cultivate fertile "social soil" in all kinds of organizations and communities. She holds a MA in Public Health from Harvard School of Public Health and a PhD in Psychology from the University of Freiburg, Germany.

Thea Van der Westhuizen is a multi award-winning academic professional, serving as the chair for the Entrepreneurship Development in Higher Education (EDHE) community of practice to develop entrepreneurship in academia through teaching, learning and research. Founder of SHAPE (Shifting Hope, Activating Potential Entrepreneurship) which received an international award in 2018 at The Innovative Youth Incubator Awards (held in Washington DC, United States): Winner, "Excellence in reaching out to the community" and Best Youth Development Organisation in KZN. She is the International Director of Paddle for the Planet: official flagship project of the International Olympics Committee (2018). Dr van der Westhuizen has over 15 years of international work experience in the corporate and academic sectors. High profile collaborations with ambassadors, municipality managers, Sheikhs as well as CEOs of multi-national companies all form part of her portfolio. Her professional experiences stretch over a period of 20 years, starting off as a young entrepreneur who initiated, developed and owner-managed two businesses: Tesen Tourism Planning and The Garden Route Tourism Academy – both located in the Garden Route of South Africa. Orcid Account: https://orcid.org/0000-0001-8795-4023

Anne Winther lives and works in rural Scotland as a transdisciplinary researcher and activist. Her PhD investigating the sustainability of rural communities in Scotland was at the University of Stirling. She is a member of the international u.lab research network and is a Director of the Centre for Human Ecology.

Endnotes

1   (From a presentation titled "Wisdom Together" at the Conscious Leadership Conference, Oslo, Norway, October 20–21, 2017.)

2   u.lab Hub Roma & u.lab Hubs Italy. (2017) Youtube channel. Retrieved from https://www.youtube.com/channel/UCbvJpH-TC-YMG36pmiX5EUw/videos

3   Presencing Institute website, Resources. Retrieved from https://www.presencing.org/#/resource/tools

4   Hentsch, R. (2018). Survey of Italian Hub Hosts from Brianza, Firenze, Livorno, Milano, Trieste, Rome and virtual. Retrieved from https://drive.google.com/file/d/1fo0zsyrWqUh2osc1I4UKMn-9poEw_SxP0/view?usp=sharing

5   Arts, J. & Fransen, S. (2017). *Hub Host Guide*. Retrieved from https://juliearts.gitbooks.io/hubhostguide/content/welcome.html

6   (Ibid.) section: Schedule Hub Host Support u.lab 2018

7   Presencing Institute website, Resources. Retrieved from https://www.presencing.org/#/resource/tools

8   (Ibid.1) p.2

9   Hentsch, R. (2018). Survey of Italian Hub Hosts from Brianza, Firenze, Livorno, Milano, Trieste, Rome and virtual, p.4

10   (Ibid.) p.5

11   Scharmer, C.O. (2018). *The Essentials of Theory U - Core Principles and Applications*. Oakland: Berrett:Koehler Publishers, Inc.

12   https://www.presencing.org/resource/tools

13   See https://elihw.org, for more information on the institute.

14   See https://www.hs-osnabrueck.de/de/studium/studienangebot/weiterbildung/seminare-und-lehrgaenge/gross-national-happiness/,

for more information on the program.

15   Scharmer, C. O. (2007, p. 183). *Theory U: Leading from the future as it emerges*. SoL Press, Cambridge, MA.

16   Bohm, D. (1980). Wholeness and the implicate order. London; Routledge

17   Beaumont, H. (1998). The Field of Soul. British Gestalt Journal, 7:2, 77-87

18   Jacobs, L. (2003). Practices of Care and Inclusion. British Gestalt Journal, 12:2, 88-96.

19   Gilbert, M. and Evans, K. (2000). *Psychotherapy Supervision*. Buckingham: Open University Press.

20   Lloyd DM (2009) The space between us: A neurophilosophical framework for the investigation of human interpersonal space. Neurosci Biobehav R 33: 297–304.

21   Wright, N. (2012) *Gestalt Meets Cognitive Behavioural Coaching*, Training Journal, Fenman. January, pp. 64-69.

22   Buber, M. (1958) I and Thou. (trans Smith, R.G.). Scribner. New York

23   Bache, C. (2008). *The living Classroom: Teaching and collective consciousness*. Albany, N.Y.: State University of New York Press.

24   Nonaka, I. and N. Konno (1998), *The Concept of "Ba": Building a Foundation for Knowledge Creation*. In: California Management Review. Spring 1998, Vol 40, No. 3, 40-54.

25   Bohm, D. (1996). *On dialogue*. London; New York: Routledge.

26   Buber, M. (1958). *I and thou* (2nd ed. Walter Kaufmann, Trans.). New York: CharlesScribner's Sons

27   Gunnlaugson, O., Brabant, M. (2016). *Cohering the Integral We-Space: Developing Theory and Practice for Engaging Collective Emergence and Wisdom in Groups and Teams*. Integral Publishing House: San Francisco

28   From *The Hidden Heart of the Cosmos*, Marynoll, New York. Orbis Books, 1996

29   Sheldrake, Rupert. (2009). *Morphic Resonance: The Nature of Formative Causation*. Park Street Press.

30   Laszlo, Ervin, (2007). *Science and the Akashic Field: An Integral Theory of Everything*. Inner Traditions.

31   Kleiner, A. (2017). *What the body tells us about leadership*. Strategy & Business. Autumn 2017, Issue 88.

32   Nhat T. H. (2000). *The Path of Emancipation*. Parallax Press Berkley California.

33   Nichol, D. (2016). *Subtle Activism: The Inner dimension of Social and*

Planetary Transformation. Suny Press: New York

34   Macy, Joanna (2003). *World as Lover, World as Self: Courage for Global Justice.* Parallax Press.

35   Arawana Hayashi led the 'SPT basic course' in Oxford, March 2017.

36   The way I am using the terms is the more generic and flexible way facilitators of group and individual developmental work tend to adopt. There is an interesting discussion thread which high-lights the lack of reference point in our use of these terms in facilitation circles. http://artofhosting.ning.com/forum/topics/the-art-of-holding-space. It is different from the way the terms 'container' and 'holding' were used by Donald Winnicott and referred to in some therapeutic modalities though at times, depending on the work in process, the concept of mothering, containment, holding, nurturing can be experienced by partici-pant and/ or facilitator.

37   This chapter was first written before COVID-19. By the time this chapter was in final edit, we are still in COVID-19 national 'lock-down' in the UK. In a COVID-19 context, touch has indeed become a high-risk activity. By the time this chapter is published, we are likely to be in a post-COVID world. It will be interesting to see if and how our relationship with touch will change.

38   For more information on contact improvisation try https://contactquarterly.com/contact-improvisation/about/ where there is a write up on the background and application of contact improvisation.

39   Biodynamic Body Psychotherapy was developed by Gerda Boyesen. In the UK, practitioners can be certified in Biodynamic Massage Therapy as a standalone discipline or they can include Biodynamic Massage Therapy as part of their Body Psychotherapeutic practice. One of the aims of Biodynamic Body Pscyhotherapy is to facilitate the client to get in touch with their 'primary personality' which has echoes of Fritz Perl's 'organismic functioning.'

40   Julia Cameron's short video 'Artist Date' is on her website http://juliacameronlive.com/ where she speaks about creative work being a continuous process of 'drawing from an inner well' within and the importance of taking time to refill the well.

41   Doctors prescribing patients spend time in nature in conjunction with other treatments to reduce blood pressure and anxiety as well as boosting happiness was reported in mainstream media in 2017

and 2018.

42   See Argyris, C. and Schon, D. A. (1974), Theory in Practice: Increasing Professional Effectiveness. San Francisco: Jossey Bass Publishers. Chapter 4 for 'Model I' especially Table 1 for the main issues in relation to this way of interacting. Then Chapter 5 for a description of Model II and Table 2 for the differences when practicing this double loop way of interacting.

43   The use of improvisation in my work was inspired by attendance at several comedy improvisation workshops facilitated by Sprout Ideas and Jerry Thompson respectively. Drama akin to psychodrama was used with external consultants during 2002-2003 while facilitating culture change as an in-company Organisation Effectiveness Partner. Subsequent exposure to use of experiments drawn from psychodrama and family constellation methods were through Gestalt Psychotherapy training at the Gestalt Centre in London. In SPT, Arawana also briefly made references to constellation work and stated that SPT and constellation/ systemic constellation are different approaches. For original theory and methodology please refer to J. L. Moreno for Psychodrama and Bert Hellinger and Sophie Hellinger for Constellations work.

44   I attended workshops by Charlie Morrissey during 2006- 2007. For more information on Charlie and contact improvisation http:// www.charliemorrissey.com/teaching/.

45   Julia Cameron op.cit., notion of 'play' at 1:47 and notion of refilling the well from 1:57 to the end of the video.

46   Arnold Beisser and his Paradoxical Theory of Change is one of the most quoted theories in Gestalt. It has been incorporated into Gestalt as an intrinsic aspect of Gestalt Theory. This quote was accessed on 15.5.20 via http://www.gestalt.org/arnie.htm and not dated.

47   In Otto Scharmer's 2016 book 'empathy' was described as something that contributed to a conversational field that was capable of allowing for depth and creative emergences.

48   This was a technique learned in improv worshops as described in endnote iv.

49   Lorna Carmen McNeill facilitated using a unique approach to 'unlocking creativity' at the Art Academy in London by inviting us to focus on connecting, connections, feelings and feeling. The space she created was exploration and phenomenologically led rather than form-specific. Techniques and medium become

resources to enrich and enhance experiences. Her workshops in general are very much 'inside out' and do not sit neatly within institutional 'art' though they are obviously concerned with art and rooted in art.

50   4-day workshop facilitated by Lorna Carmen McNeill called 'Movement and Flow Unboxed'. The workshop was stimulated by sensory connections to Deep Time and elements of fire, water, wind and earth.

51   The process I used to engage my whole body to find expression through being at one and in contact was inspired by the works of Heather Hansen.

52   Julia Cameron, op.cit.

53   This is a specially edited and adapted summary of the book *The Tao of Revolution, 2020, Stairwell Books*. Much of the content of this chapter is taken from social media. The four credited pieces have been checked and revised by their authors. Photos have also been lifted from social media, so original photographers are not known. They have anyway been modified, cropped, adjusted and rendered to black and white by the curator. Poetry is generally collectively written: individuals in a group write their own lines, these are then crafted into a single poem by the curator.

54   For an account of the origins of this phrase, made famous by Martin Luther King Jr. go to: https://quoteinvestigator.com/2012/11/15/arc-of-universe/

55   Collective Poem created by a group exploring The More Beautiful World They Envisage.

56   http://www.rootlight.com/library/globalgathering.htm

57   A video portrayal of this event and its poem can be found on youtube: https://www.youtube.com/watch?v=98zoI2eS6J4&t=3s

58   This can be watched on Youtube: https://www.youtube.com/watch?v=OjotlPIlRqw

59   Available on Youtube: https://www.youtube.com/watch?v=q1x6zuYp0g0&t=3s

60   Facebook post

61   https://www.thegreatbalance.org/2020/03/27/dont-say-they-didnt-tell-us/

62   In the past, the term has also been used in other ways, for instance in the area of IT, as a "center without walls, in which the nation's researchers can perform their research without regard to physical location, interacting with colleagues, accessing instrumentation, sharing data and computational resources, [and] accessing

information in digital libraries" (Wulf, 1989), or as "an exclusive online community whose members share their experiences, thoughts and opinions in research studies" (see http://www. the-collaboratory.com/).

63   Meanwhile, their 50+20 initiative has been taken on by the Globally Responsible Leadership Initiative http://grli.org/.

64   For a TED talk given by Katrin Muff, co-founder of the initiative, in 2013 about this process see https://www.youtube.com/ watch?v=jvipxPqS_38.

65   Katrin recalls: "It was a total mess, everybody criticizing every-thing, and the whole thing was almost falling apart. Then someone had a great idea: Why don't we all sit down and write down the vision in our own words? When harvesting the visions everyone read out (…), we realized they were all pretty much the same, just using other words. We had been sitting on the solution for three months." (Muff, TED talk, 2013)

66   Institute for integral Studies (IFIS, Germany), Norwegian University of Science and Technology (NTNU), Business School Lausanne (BSL, Switzerland), Center for integral Leadership (ZIF, Vienna/Austria) and Initiativ Samutveckling (iS! Sweden).

67   For a thick description of this see Muff 2014b.

68   LiFT 2 is made up of seven partners from six European coun-tries. Besides the previous five, the Alliance for the Future (A4F, Luxembourg) and the University of Natural Resources and Life Sciences (BOKU, Vienna) joined the team.

69   For more information see the project website at www.leader-ship-for-transition.eu.

70   Reflective interviews have been conducted with about 50 partici-pants of our events, as well as with five of the main team members.

71   …depending how one counts. The first part takes the group down to the U, where ideally a phase of presencing should happen (main part 2, even though it is usually considerably shorter than parts 1 and 3). Then the way back out of the U and into activity would be the third main part.

72   There is actually more theory behind the Collaboratory than just Theory U. Other sources of inspiration are, for example, circular and whole person learning, Appreciative Inquiry, scenario plan-ning, Design Shop or open space work. For more info see parts 1 and 2 in Muff 2014.

73   Besides these two dimensions, Katherine Weinmann (2018, The Circle Way) points at the tension between facilitation and hosting

– or between outer (traditional) and inner facilitation (hosting) with the latter focusing on a "practice of presence to attending to what is really emerging, and being willing to change the design to best serve the group". I am grateful to Katrin Muff for directing me to Weinmann's recent blogpost.

74   This was the guiding question of a series of Collaboratories held in St. Gallen in 2013, see Muff & Dyllick, 2014.

75   Personal communication, January 8, 2018.

76   Paper presented at the Integral Theory Conference in 2010.

77   For videos, please see https://www.presencing.org/#/aboutus/spt.

78   *Ubuntu*: 'shared humanity'; An Nguni language term from South Africa indicative of human interdependence.

79   A contractual standard is a technical specification, a rule that can only be referred to by reference to the number, can be used in public regulations and provisions (for example, for patronage), can be certified and verified by an independent third party.

80   In this appendix you will find sentences in which we use "I", this refers to one of the two authors, the one that completed this experience in this case was Sara.

81   "Natural law is, definitively, the only valid bulwark against the arbitrary power or the deception of ideological manipulation. The knowledge of this law inscribed on the heart of man increases with the progress of the moral conscience. The first duty for all, and particularly for those with public responsibility, must therefore be to promote the maturation of the moral conscience. This is the fundamental progress without which all other progress proves non-authentic. The law inscribed in our nature is the true guarantee offered to everyone in order to be able to live in freedom and to be respected in their own dignity.", Address of his holiness Benedict XVI, to the participants, in the international congress on natural moral law 12/02/2007.

82   Coni Services Ltd was a company totally financed by the Italian state that, until 2019, supported the CONI in carrying out its activities. With the 2019 budget law has been transformed in Sport e Salute S.p.A.

83   See also https://www.presencing.org/resource/tools/shadowing-desc.

84   In this appendix you will find sentences in which we use "I", this refers to one of the two authors, the one that completed this experience in this case was Sara.

85   The Laboratory of Economics and Management (LEM) of the

University of Rome "Foro Italico", currently coordinated by professor Cristiana Buscarini, study the issues of sustainability in sport the field since 2006, focusing in particular on the NSF (National Sports Federations). In the first phase of its activity, studies were carried out aimed at formulating the guidelines for the preparation of the social report in the FSN (Buscarini C., 2006; Buscarini C., Mura R. 2011; Buscarini C., Mura R. 2013). From 2011 to 2015, a study was carried out which allowed the construction of a sustainability positioning model, according to the guidelines of the ISO 26000 standard, through which any organization can detect, describe and measure its own degree of sustainability (Buscarini C., Masia R. 2016). Since 2012, after the London Olympics, the laboratory has also focused on sporting events and their organization, according to principles of sustainability (Buscarini C., Franzini G. S., 2017).

86 At this event we completed sensing journeys with a group of 4 people (University student and future sport Managers). Below you will find sentences in which we use "We", this referred to a Team of four people in which we also operated (Cristiana and Sara).

87 Staff was composed by assistant managers, coordinators, and volunteers.

www.ingramcontent.com/pod-product-compliance
Lightning Source LLC
Chambersburg PA
CBHW070347200326

41518CB00012B/2161